Producing Palestine

SOAS Palestine Studies

This book series aims at promoting innovative research in the study of Palestine, Palestinians and the Israel-Palestine conflict as a crucial component of Middle Eastern and world politics. The first ever Western academic series entirely dedicated to this topic, *SOAS Palestine Studies* draws from a variety of disciplinary fields, including history, politics, media, visual arts, social anthropology, and development studies. The series is published under the academic direction of the Centre for Palestine Studies (CPS) at the London Middle East Institute (LMEI) of SOAS, University of London.

Series Editor:

Dina Matar, Chair, SOAS Centre for Palestine Studies and Professor in Political Communication, SOAS, University of London, UK and Adam Hanieh, Professor of Political Economy and Global Development, Institute of Arab and Islamic Studies (IAIS), University of Exeter, UK; Joint Chair in Area Studies (Middle East) at IAIS (Exeter, UK) and IIAS (Tsinghua, China)

Board Advisor:

Hassan Hakimian, Director of the London Middle East Institute at SOAS

Current and Forthcoming Titles:

Palestine Ltd.: Neoliberalism and Nationalism in the Occupied Territory, Toufic Haddad

Palestinian Literature in Exile: Gender, Aesthetics and Resistance in the Short Story, Joseph R. Farag

Palestinian Citizens of Israel: Power, Resistance and the Struggle for Space, Sharri Plonski

Representing Palestine Media and Journalism in Australia since World War I, Peter Manning

Folktales of Palestine: Cultural Identity, Memory and the Politics of Storytelling, Farah Aboubakr

Dialogue in Palestine: The People-to-People Diplomacy Programme and the Israeli-Palestinian Conflict, Nadia Naser-Najjab
Palestinian Youth Activism in the Internet Age: Social Media and Networks after the Arab Spring, Albana Dwonch
The Palestinian National Movement in Lebanon: A Political History of the 'Ayn al-Hilwe Camp, Erling Lorentzen Sogge
The Foreign Policy of Hamas: Ideology, Decision Making and Political Supremacy, Leila Seurat
Global Media Coverage of the Palestinian-Israeli Conflict: Reporting the Sheikh Jarrah Evictions, Noureddine Miladi

Producing Palestine

The Creative Production of Palestine through Contemporary Media

Edited by Helga Tawil-Souri and Dina Matar

I.B.TAURIS
LONDON · NEW YORK · OXFORD · NEW DELHI · SYDNEY

I.B. TAURIS
Bloomsbury Publishing Plc
50 Bedford Square, London, WC1B 3DP, UK
1385 Broadway, New York, NY 10018, USA
29 Earlsfort Terrace, Dublin 2, Ireland

BLOOMSBURY, I.B. TAURIS and the I.B. Tauris logo are
trademarks of Bloomsbury Publishing Plc

First published in Great Britain 2024

Copyright © Helga Tawil-Souri and Dina Matar, 2024

Helga Tawil-Souri and Dina Matar and Contributors have asserted their rights under the Copyright, Designs and Patents Act, 1988, to be identified as Author of this work.

Cover design: Adriana Brioso
Cover image: Palestinian during a demonstration at the Israel-Gaza border fence in Khan Yunis, Gaza, 2021. (©SOPA Images Limited/Alamy Live News)

All rights reserved. No part of this publication may be reproduced or transmitted in any form or by any means, electronic or mechanical, including photocopying, recording, or any information storage or retrieval system, without prior permission in writing from the publishers.

Bloomsbury Publishing Plc does not have any control over, or responsibility for, any third-party websites referred to or in this book. All internet addresses given in this book were correct at the time of going to press. The author and publisher regret any inconvenience caused if addresses have changed or sites have ceased to exist, but can accept no responsibility for any such changes.

A catalogue record for this book is available from the British Library.

Library of Congress Cataloging-in-Publication Data
Names: Matar, Dina, editor. | Tawil-Souri, Helga, editor.
Title: Producing Palestine : the creative production of Palestine through contemporary media / edited by Dina Matar, Helga Tawil-Souri.
Description: London ; New York : I.B. Tauris, 2024. | Series: SOAS Palestine studies | Includes bibliographical references and index. |
Summary: "Palestine has often been defined and constructed in the global imaginary through conflict, resistance, oppression and violence. It's representation is so overridden with conflicting claims and associations that it remains inaccessible, even to Palestinians. Producing Palestine addresses the creative labour of producing Palestine, particularly in technological and media spaces that are defined by their porousness and by their intermediality - crossing genres of popular culture and disciplinary boundaries. It offers eighteen 'episodes' which collectively conceptualize, engage in, and invite readers to participate in the production of Palestine and its theorization. These episodes cover a wide array of spaces of production such as poster art, TikTok, virtual technologies, digital mapping, drone footage, online cooking shows, documentaries, music videos and many more. Producing Palestine contends that representations of Palestine carry a multitude of meanings, that Palestine is continually produced and reproduced, dynamically generating new knowledge production across media, languages, temporalities, geographies and disciplines"– Provided by publisher.
Identifiers: LCCN 2024009526 (print) | LCCN 2024009527 (ebook) |
ISBN 9780755654260 (hardback) | ISBN 9780755654253 (paperback) |
ISBN 9780755654277 (epub) | ISBN 9780755654284 (ebook)
Subjects: LCSH: Palestinian Arabs in mass media. | Digital media–Palestine. | Mass media–Palestine. | Palestine–In mass media.
Classification: LCC P94.5.P35 P76 2024 (print) | LCC P94.5.P35 (ebook) | DDC 305.89/274–dc23/eng/20240304
LC record available at https://lccn.loc.gov/2024009526
LC ebook record available at https://lccn.loc.gov/2024009527

ISBN:	HB:	978-0-7556-5426-0
	PB:	978-0-7556-5425-3
	ePDF:	978-0-7556-5428-4
	eBook:	978-0-7556-5427-7

Typeset by Integra Software Services Pvt. Ltd.
Printed and bound in Great Britain

To find out more about our authors and books visit www.bloomsbury.com and sign up for our newsletters.

Contents

List of Figures	viii
List of Contributors	xi

Introduction: Producing Palestine: Representational
(Im)possibilities *Helga Tawil-Souri and Dina Matar*   1

1. A Place Called Return *Rayya El Zein*   13
2. Imagining Return: Countless Palestinian Futures *Danah Abdulla and Sarona Abuaker*   27
3. Re-centering Palestine and Palestinians in Poster Art *Dina Matar*   39
4. Becoming *Al-Mulatham/a:* Fedayee Art, Abu Oubaida, and Palestinian TikTok *Nayrouz Abu Hatoum and Hadeel Assali*   51
5. Vertical Visions of the Nakba: Toward a Topography of Layers *Viviane Saglier*   63
6. Virtual Returns: Rehearsing and Remediating Return in Palestinian Video Practices *Kareem Estefan*   79
7. Reincarnated: Common Sense and the Poetics of Elsewhere *Aamer Ibraheem*   95
8. Fugitive Crossings: On the Condition of Being Palestinian *Kiven Strohm and Nadeem Karkabi*   107
9. Marking Bodies: A Catalogue of Keffiyehs *Sary Zananiri*   119
10. "We're Still Alive, so Remove Us from Memory": Asynchronicity and the Museum in Resistance *Lara Khaldi*   147
11. Forging Revolutionary Objects *Stephen Sheehi*   155
12. Cooking Online with Chef Fadi *Anne Meneley*   169
13. Producing Palestine as Layers of Historical Evidence with Interactive Documentaries *Dale Hudson*   181
14. Palestine and the Question of Queer Arab Becoming *Sophie Chamas*   199
15. Refractions *Helga Tawil-Souri*   211
16. Terra ex Machina *Hagit Keysar and Ariel Caine*   224

Epilogue	243
Bibliography	248
Index	265

Figures

1.1	Yafo Creative House. Photograph courtesy by Amnon Ron	16
1.2	The Israel Falafel. Photograph by the author, July 4, 2014	17
1.3	Estate at Wadi Hunayn. Photograph from Palestine Remembered	20
1.4	Close-up from the photograph of the Estate at Wadi Hunayn from Palestine Remembered	21
1.5	Estate at Wadi Hunayn. Photograph by the author, 2014	24
2.1	Countless Palestinian Futures game. Image by Danah Abdulla	29
2.2	Countless Palestinian Futures game. Image by Danah Abdulla	29
2.3	Countless Palestinian Futures game. Image by Danah Abdulla	32
3.1	All for the Resistance. Ismail Shammout	42
3.2	Nous Vaincrons (We Will Win), by Ismail Shammout	42
3.3	Palestine Uprising Hues: We Will Return, 2023, Sama Geith, Courtesy of the artist	47
3.4	Palestine Uprising Hues, Her Total Liberation Has Begun, 2023. Sama Geith, Courtesy of the artist	47
4.1	Screenshot of Abu Oubaida's "Tweets" on the Qassam Brigades' website	52
4.2	Poster from Cuba, 1975. YaHala Studio Archive	54
4.3	Monther Jawabreh. *As Once Was Known*. Acrylic on canvas, 2012. Courtesy of the artist	55
4.4	Laila Shawa. *Fashionista Terrorista II*, 2011. Courtesy of the artist and October Gallery, London	55
4.5	Abu Oubaida giving a speech in Gaza	56
5.1	Dima Srouji, *Sebastia* (2020). The Bible is laid over the map of Israeli-controlled Area C where the Roman forum is located. *Sebastia* by Dima Srouji commissioned by Het Nieuwe Instituut and e-Flux	65
5.2	Dima Srouji, *Sebastia* (2020). The footage of Lankester Harding's 1930 excavation (smaller layer) reveals the exploitation and dispossession of Palestinians that made colonial museums' wealth possible (green layer underneath). Courtesy of Dima Srouji	67
5.3	Dima Srouji, *Sebastia* (2020). Moshe Dayan's two passions: archeology, and the art of war. Courtesy of the artist	68

5.4	Palestine Remembered. The satellite view of al Dawayima. Courtesy of Palestine Remembered	70
5.5	Trailer for the iNakba app in 2014. Courtesy of Zochrot	71
5.6	The model of Emwas in Dima Abu Ghoush's *Emwas* (2016). Courtesy of the artist	74
6.1	Still from Razan AlSalah, *Canada Park* (2020). Courtesy of Razan AlSalah	86
6.2	Still from Razan AlSalah, Your Father Was Born 100 Years Old, and So Was the Nakba (2017). Courtesy of Razan AlSalah	87
6.3	Still from Basel Abbas and Ruanne Abou-Rahme, *At Those Terrifying Frontiers Where the Existence and Disappearance of People Fade Into Each Other*, 2019, Video/Sound Installation view at Fisher Center, Bard. Photography by Maria Baranova. Courtesy of the artists	90
6.4	Basel Abbas and Ruanne Abou-Rahme, film still from *At those Terrifying Frontiers Where the Existence and Disappearance of People Fade into Each Other*, 2019,Video/Sound Installation view at Fisher Center, Bard. Courtesy of the artists	90
9.1	Keffiyeh of "A Nazarene." Drawn from a touristic photograph made for the souvenir market *c.*1900–20	122
9.2	T.E. Lawrence's Keffiyeh. Lawrence in Palestine, 1918	124
9.3	A Bedouin Keffiyeh. Nabi Rubeen 1922	126
9.4	Costume Keffiyeh: Simon the Cyrene. Hollywood film, 1927	128
9.5	Costume Keffiyehs: The Three Wise Men. From a Passion Play held at the Jerusalem YMCA 1934–9	130
9.6	Costume Keffiyeh: Moses. Hollywood cinema 1956	132
9.7	Costume Keffiyeh: Disguise. Hollywood Cinema, 1960	134
9.8	Costume Keffiyeh: Jesus. Hollywood cinema, 1965	136
9.9	Arafat's Keffiyeh. Organization of African Unity conference, 1975	138
9.10	Solidarity Keffiyeh. Image of Cuban solidarity with Palestine, 1980	140
9.11	Costume Keffiyeh: Terrorist. Hollywood cinema, 1994	142
11.1	Night of the Gliders. Courtesy of Hafez Omar	162
13.1	A map available through iNakba visualizes Palestinian dispossession. Courtesy of Zochrot	186
13.2	A screen from the iNakba app that projects the historic Palestinian village of al-Walaja on top of the present-day Jewish settlement Aminadav, similar to the one of the kibbutz where Zayta once existed. Courtesy of Zochrot	188

13.3	Screen grab of Nando Schtakleff's home movies repurposed as part of *Jerusalem, We Are Here*. Courtesy of Dorit Naaman	192
13.4	A choice of interactive virtual tours within the documentary. Courtesy of Dorit Naaman	192
14.1	Still from "*Cavalry.*" A young Palestinian girl confronts an Israeli soldier standing atop a tank. Courtesy of Mashrou' Leila	202
15.1	Ahed Tamimi, age eleven, pointing her fist at an Israeli soldier. Abbas Momani, AFP, November 2, 2012. https://www.alamy.com/stock-photo-nov-2-2012-ramallah-west-bank-palestinian-territory-palestinian-girls-51324683.html?imageid=7B5C08EA-25E8-4162-9F43-10A503444896&p=151045&pn=8&searchId=71a3e8161da8e66ada2972230559f821&searchtype=0	212
15.2	Ahed Tamimi, left, age fourteen, biting a masked Israeli soldier who is restraining her twelve-year-old brother. Her mother, Nariman, is on the far right, one of her aunts in the middle. Abbas Momani, AFP, August 28, 2014. https://www.gettyimages.com/detail/news-photo/palestinian-girl-and-women-figth-to-free-a-palestinian-boy-news-photo/485541916?	212
15.3	Prints of Ahed and others from the Tamimi family used by activists protesting in London calling for the release by Israeli authorities of Ahed Tamimi, December 2017	213
15.4	Screenshot of an Instagram page that shows Ahed Tamimi standing in front of the mural of herself on the Wall holding up a sign thanking Jorit, the artist who created the mural. @remikanazi, August 20, 2018	215
15.5	Postcards and magnets made of Jorit's graffiti of Ahed. In one of these you can see Jorit on a ladder in the process of painting. https://www.alamy.com/fridge-magnets-of-16-year-old-palestinian-ached-tamimi-who-gained-world-fame-by-slapping-an-israeli-soldier-and-was-sentenced-to-eight-month-in-jail-in-her-home-in-the-village-nabi-saleh-on-the-west-bank-february-7-2019-foto-eva-tedesjo-dn-tt-kod-3504-image441586955.html?imageid=6E016063-EFFA-40F0-ADC7-2F4540F46C4E&p=1746242&pn=1&searchId=07b34a70b5cf77ee95d568be49f30c26&searchtype=0	217
15.6	Jorit's completed graffito. Jorit Agoch, CCO 1.0. https://openverse.org/image/b2531e1e-5df3-494f-bcac-41786c10a821?q=ahed%20tamimi	219
16	All images by Hagit Keysar and Ariel Caine The images 16.3, 16.4 and 16.5 are by Barak Brinker, Hagit Keysar and Ariel Caine	222–241
E.1	Palestinian Slingshot, Courtesy of Ahmad N. Shaqour	244

Contributors

Aamer Ibraheem is a doctoral candidate in anthropology at Columbia University and recipient of a dissertation fieldwork grant from the Social Science Research Council (SSRC), the Wenner-Gren Foundation, and the Palestinian American Research Center (PARC). His research focuses on reincarnation theology and political time in the contemporary Middle East, and his ethnography is located in the occupied Golan Heights. Besides his academic work, Ibraheem is interested in translation, and he is the cofounder and editor-in-chief of the "Voice of Insaniyyat" podcast, hosting conversations on Anthropology and Palestine.

Anne Meneley graduated with a PhD in anthropology from New York University. She is now a professor of anthropology at Trent University in Canada. Her book on women's competitive hospitality in Yemen, *Tournaments of Value: Sociability and Hierarchy in a Yemeni Town*, was released in its 20th Anniversary Edition in 2016. Her recent work deals with the production, circulation, and consumption of olive oil in Italy and Palestine. She has published in various journals including *American Anthropologist*, *Annual Review of Anthropology*, *Cultural Anthropology*, *Environment and Planning E: Nature and Space*, *Ethnos*, *Food, Culture & Society*, *Food and Foodways*, *Gastronomica*, *History and Anthropology*, *Jerusalem Quarterly*, and *Social Analysis*. Her current work is on the anthropology of consumerism, walking (quantified and nature walking), human-nonhuman interactions in plant materialities, and food politics.

Ariel Caine is a Jerusalem-born London-based artist and researcher, currently a postdoctoral fellow at the ICI (Berlin). His practice centers on counter-dominant and collaborative capacities of spatial optical media, modeling and survey technologies, examining their political operation within the production of cultural memories and national narratives. He received his PhD (2019) from the Centre for Research Architecture, Goldsmiths University of London, where between 2016 and 2021 he was a project coordinator and researcher at the Forensic Architecture Agency. Ariel's works have been exhibited widely, in museums and galleries such as Tate Britain (Turner Prize nomination with Forensic Architecture), Kunsthal Charlottenburg, MACBA (Barcelona), and CCA (Tel-Aviv). His writing appears in publications such as *Journal of Visual Cultures*, *Jerusalem Quarterly*, *Photo Researcher*, and *KALEIDOSCOPE*. In 2023, alongside Kineret Lourie, Ariel cofounded CHEMIST, a South-London artist-run gallery space.

Danah Abdulla is a designer, educator and researcher interested in new narratives and practices in design that push the disciplinary boundaries and definitions of the subject. She is a Reader in Anti/Post/Decolonial Histories, Theories, Praxes at the

Decolonising the Arts Institute at the University of the Arts London. Danah is the author of *Designerly Ways of Knowing: A Working Inventory of Things a Designer Should Know* (Onomatopee, 2022), a founding member of the Decolonising Design platform, and founded *Kalimat Magazine* (2010–2016), an independent, non-profit publication about Arab thought and culture www.dabdulla.com.

Dale Hudson is an associate professor at New York University Abu Dhabi. His recent publications include a special double issue of the *Middle East Journal of Culture and Communication* on "Film and Visual Media in the Gulf" (2021) and *Reorienting the Middle East: Film and Digital Media Where the Persian Gulf, Arabian Sea, and Indian Ocean Meet* (2023), both coedited with Alia Yunis. His work on Palestine and Southwest Asia appears in *Afterimage, Arabian Humanities, Jadaliyya, Journal of Palestine Studies, Social Research*, and *Studies in South Asian Film and Media*. He also coordinates Films from the Gulf for the MESA (Middle East Studies Association) Film Festival and serves on the board of the Association of Gulf and Arabian Peninsula Studies (AGAPS).

Dina Matar is a professor at the School of Oriental and African Studies (SOAS), University of London, where she is currently the director of the Centre for Global Media and Communication and director of the Centre for Gender Studies, in the School of Law. She is also the Chair of the Centre of Palestine Studies. Dina works on narrative politics, media and conflict, political communication, cultural politics, memory, oral history, and Islamist movements in the Arab World and its diaspora. Her recent work focuses on narrative politics and cultural and media histories in Palestine. Dina is the co-founder and co-editor of the *Middle East Journal of Culture and Communication*, the first transcultural and cross-disciplinary space for critical engagement with communication, culture, and politics of the contemporary Middle East. Her publications include *What It Means to Be Palestinian* (2010) and *The Hizbullah Phenomenon* (with Lina Khatib and Atef AlShaer, 2014). She has recently co-edited *Narrating Conflict in the Middle East: Discourse, Image and Communication Practices in Lebanon and Palestine* (with Zahera Harb, 2013); *Gaza as Metaphor* (with Helga Tawil-Souri, 2016).

Hadeel Assali is a postdoctoral fellow in the Center for Science and Society and a lecturer in the Department of Earth and Environmental Sciences at Columbia University. She recently completed her PhD in anthropology, where her research focused on the colonial legacies of the discipline of geology and how these legacies came up against local forms of knowledge of the land in southern Palestine, especially in Gaza. She is a former chemical engineer with nearly ten years of experience with a major oil corporation, which is where many of her inquiries on geology began. She is also a filmmaker and has written on visual cultures in Palestine as well as on personal family stories of dispossession.

Hagit Keysar lives and works in Israel/Palestine. Her research is practice-based and brings together visual work, critical theory, and activism. In her PhD thesis she critically examined the political potential of civic/community science and open-source technologies for articulating politics and reclaiming rights in settler-colonial context. She is currently exploring and teaching critical, feminist data practices for open, collaborative, and situated research and activism.

Helga Tawil-Souri is an associate professor in the Department of Media, Culture, and Communication and the Department of Middle Eastern and Islamic Studies at NYU. Helga's work deals with spatiality, technology, and politics in the Middle East, with a particular focus on contemporary life in Palestine-Israel. Helga has published on topics including Arab media; Palestinian cinema, television, video games, and popular culture; telecommunications and internet infrastructure and development in the Palestinian Territories; and cultural/territorial politics, checkpoints, identification cards, and surveillance in Palestine-Israel. She is the co-editor, with Dina Matar, of *Gaza as Metaphor* (2016) and currently serves on the editorial board of *Social Text and Public Culture*.

Kareem Estefan is an assistant professor of film and screen studies at the University of Cambridge. His research centers on questions of witnessing and worldbuilding in Palestinian visual culture, and more broadly explores activist engagements with colonialism in contemporary art and film. Kareem's writing has recently appeared in *Feminist Media Histories*, *Journal of Palestine Studies*, *Journal of Visual Culture*, *Third Text*, and *World Records*. He is the co-editor of *Assuming Boycott: Resistance, Agency, and Cultural Production* (2017), an anthology of essays on BDS, cultural boycotts, and transnational solidarities.

Kiven Strohm is an assistant professor in anthropology at the National University of Singapore. His research and writing are focused on the intersections of contemporary visual art and material politics. Over the past decade he has been exploring how artworks emerge from and organize political life for Palestinians within a settler colonial situation and is presently completing a book manuscript on this research titled *Experiments in Living: Art and Politics in Occupied Palestine*.

Lara Khaldi is a curator based in Jerusalem and Amsterdam. She is currently a member of the artistic team of documenta fifteen and was head of the Media Studies Program at Alquds Bard College, Jerusalem. In her research and curatorial projects, she addresses the recent emergence of museums in the occupied Palestinian territories in relation to the performance of a state. Among others she has curated Shifting Ground (2017), Sharjah Biennial 13 project in Ramallah, and Walter Benjamin in Palestine (2015), Birzeit University, and International Academy of Art, Palestine.

Nadeem Karkabi is an associate professor in the Department of Anthropology at the University of Haifa. His research on the Palestinian alternative music scene examined the relations between pleasure and politics, cosmopolitanism, middle-class urbanity, playful subjectivities, and perceptions of self-liberation. Currently, he is working on intersecting aspects of language, ethnicity, religion, and nationalism in the performance of popular music in Arabic among Mizrahi-Jews in Israel.

Nayrouz Abu Hatoum is an assistant professor in the Department of Sociology and Anthropology at Concordia University, Montreal. Her research explores visual politics in Palestine and focuses on alternative imaginations, people's place-making, and dwelling practices in contexts of settler-colonialism. Currently, she is working on her book project that examines the art of visual politics and its role in expanding Palestinian imagination.

Rayya El Zein is an interdisciplinary writer, researcher, and thinker. She has worked as a teacher, editor, and project manager among anthropologists, technologists, musicians, journalists, and performance artists. Her writing has recently appeared in the *Journal of Palestine Studies* and the *Middle East Journal of Culture & Communication*. She is currently the forum editor at *Lateral*, the journal of the Cultural Studies Association, and she tweets from @rayelz.

Sary Zananiri is an artist and cultural historian who is interested in how visual culture sheds light on the transformations of identity categories such as gender, nationalist and religious identification, communalism, and class, particularly in the modern Middle East. He was a Postdoctoral Fellow at Leiden University, a Visiting Scholar at Dar al Kalima in Bethlehem, an Honorary Fellow of the Australian Archaeological Institute at Athens and a consultant with the Saudi Arabian Heritage Commission. He has co-edited multiple volumes on Palestinian culture during the British Mandate period and exhibits widely in the Arab World, Europe and Australia.

Sophie Chamas is a lecturer of gender studies at SOAS, University of London. Their research sits at the intersection of feminist and queer political theory, Middle East studies, political economy, and cultural studies. Their work is focused on the study of the life, death, and afterlife of the radical political imagination in the Middle East and its diaspora via a critical engagement with contemporary activist discourses and ideologies.

Stephen Sheehi (he/him) is the Sultan Qaboos professor of Middle East studies in Asian and Middle East Studies Program, Modern Languages and Literatures Department, and Asian and Pacific Islander Studies Program at William & Mary. He is also the founding director of the Decolonizing Humanities Project. A scholar of modern Arab culture, photography, and politics, Islamophobia and racism in North America, and decolonial studies, Sheehi is the author of numerous articles, book chapters, and books, the most recent of which are *Psychoanalysis Under Occupation: Practicing Resistance in Palestine* (with Lara Sheehi, 2022), *Camera Palaestina: Photography and Displaced Histories of Palestine* (with Salim Tamari and Issam Nassar, 2022), and the co-edited special issue on "Settler-Colonialism as State-Crime: Abolitionist Perspectives" in *State Crime Journal* with Nadera Shalhoub-Kevorkian (2022).

Viviane Saglier is a lecturer/assistant professor of film studies at the University of St. Andrews. She is currently working on two book projects: the first one analyzes the tensions between cinema infrastructures, human rights economies, and histories of liberation in Palestine; the second one traces feminist histories of decolonization and solidarity across the Arab world. She also curates programs of Arab cinema and political documentaries as well as video exhibitions.

Introduction: Producing Palestine: Representational (Im)possibilities

Helga Tawil-Souri and Dina Matar

In the global imaginary Palestine has often been defined by and constructed as conflict, resistance, oppression, and violence. Palestine is so overridden with claims, associations, and conflicting representations, continuously "framed, hedged about, shaped, controlled, and surveilled from every possible perspective," that, in WJT Mitchell's words, "it is a wonder that the earth's crust does not buckle under their weight."[1] Yet Palestine, to Palestinians especially, also remains inaccessible: an ongoing settler-colonial experiment that is exclusionary and violent in its destruction and attempted erasure, a scattering of fragmented and diminishing lands locked up behind walls on the other side of which are disappearing traces of erased villages, an expanding and distant diaspora forbidden from return or even a visit, a political project and cultural identity that are continually contested and whose past existence and narratives are contested too.

Because of the multitude of claims and counterclaims, representations and misrepresentations, Palestinian cultural expression and production is frequently attempting to "correct" or readjust these representational politics, while also contending with continued and changing forms of representations, repression, silencing, and erasure. Moreover, the relationship of Palestinians to Palestine is often defined by inaccessibility, immobility, and insecurity, and thus, again, Palestinian cultural production contends not only with how to disrupt the current order of things but with how to access, how to preserve the disappearing and ephemeral, how to survive and make meaning out of and despite continuous political impasses, how to conjure a future that is generative and inclusive rather than forlorn and exclusionary. As such, grasping Palestine, accessing Palestine, depicting Palestine, as well as even "correcting" the image of Palestine, in short, *producing Palestine*, is a multilayered activity, mobilized by various actors taking myriad different routes (not all of which are tangible), relying on both "old" and "new" technologies, stimulating and in some cases also simulating new visualizations, realizing Palestine while also contending with its possible and impossible horizons.

How do we interrogate the generative features of these spaces and practices without unduly celebrating their potential for agency, resistance, creation, and affirmation while not discarding that potential from the outset? How can we think about the production of Palestine as an episteme, a practice of knowledge production, without making this production an exceptional, or indeed overridden, practice? How can *producing* Palestine be generative to understanding the potential dimensions of the digital age?

Why *Producing* Palestine

"Producing" Palestine, we suggest, refers to a series of overlapping active processes: the experimentation and experience that take place through cultural, mediatic, and technological modes of action; through analysis, juxtaposition, and challenging of these creations by an array of "producers"; and through interpretation of all of these by "readers," which in turn (re)invigorate new creative expressions. Creative production is undertaken at multiple points, by multiple actors, successively and simultaneously considering, generating, and reinscribing what is and what remains possible. Producing Palestine, thus, means to actively partake in transcendent activities across media, across languages, across temporalities, across geographies, and most certainly across disciplines.

Producing Palestine refers not simply to a monitoring or documenting project, or only a theoretical or speculative undertaking; it is an enlivened and enlivening praxis that engages "producers" and "readers" (as kinds of producers themselves) of different kinds. Our orientation around production is based on the recognition that all social formations are heterogeneous arrangements and relations—of material and immaterial forces, of matter, images, desires, languages, technologies, among other processes—that resonate together. This productive labor is complex, time-consuming, individual and collaborative, conceptual, interpretive, relational, perhaps ultimately also ontological. This kind of labor also occurs in continuous relation to how Palestine has been and continues to be presented, represented, misrepresented—"contained" if you will—from both within and without.

"Production" necessarily opens us to considering the complexity of the social, of recognizing that there is no single hegemony that is to be filled with different content, but rather, that "Palestine" is about the possibilities that emerge through social arrangements of varying scales that operate in the production of life. In other words, Palestine is produced because Palestine has been, is, and becomes the possibilities brought about by creative productive labor, labor that is often initiated by contending with different kinds of past and present inaccessibilities, dispossessions, as well as with ambition for a (decolonial) and emancipatory future.

To produce is to reconfigure a place, whether in its material infrastructure, its political possibilities, or its aesthetic or technological forms. Production is, by definition, aspirational, experimental, fecund. Thus, when we say *producing* Palestine, we mean that Palestine is forged through such continual, iterative practices, through a whole series of connections between people, discourses, objects that are actively involved in producing a "territory."

Producing Palestine entails a familiarity with Palestine that is marooned and lured by its territorial element at the same time as it exceeds its borders. It embodies one of our world's current political paradoxes: the recognition that conceiving of a national collective according to territory is problematic, that nationalism is exclusionary and often violently so, that diaspora and exile are an increasingly common condition which can afford certain uneasy freedoms, yet still finding it necessary to implicate the territorial aspect, to locate the "where," to apprehend what is going on "here" (or what went on in the past, or what could in the future, but always "here"). Whether as prisoners in place, outcasts in a country where we still live in our ancestral homes, refugees in our own and others' back yards, as diasporians or exiles, everywhere we are, we connect to some definition of territory, some kind of "Palestine." Consequently, as Edward Said once hinted at, space—as in the struggle over geography, over reconfiguring a place—is the ontological material in which we—all Palestinians—find ourselves.[2] Space is the material which producers find themselves working with.

We consider the production of Palestine as an effort to resituate and reconfigure Palestine, not as a pre-determined bounded entity but as an entity that by necessity is always in conversation with its imagined spatiality and temporality. As both an active process and a concept, *producing* Palestine denotes de-colonial imagination, building and rethinking intended to challenge, imagine, reinvent, and disrupt narratives of what Palestine and Palestinianness mean—narratives that have remained fixed in an imagined utopian nationalist past and that have often prescribed Palestinianness as a singular identity with fixed origins, roots, and routes, which we, in this book, collectively challenge. And yet producing Palestine does not deny Palestine as a territory and imagined spatiality but approaches it as a practice and process that affirms, and insists on its existence and its real and imagined significance, to Palestinians, as well to others. It offers a compass through which to ask how ordinary people, as knowing subjects, are continuously engaged in creating, revealing, challenging, and subverting structures and systems of knowledge, systems so powerful that they construct and are responsible for fashioning the modern idea of Palestine.

"Producing Palestine" as a process allows us to theorize the dynamics between media and politics beyond dominant approaches that remain bounded by Eurocentric privileging of media as an anchor in social practices[3] that have emerged within the closed worlds of media organizations and structures. Such a proposition demands a critical engagement with continuous meaning-making and productive labor of and by ordinary people within and beyond formal structures or institutions. It also demands interrogation of the overused concept of representation as reductive, particularly when talking about colonized Palestine, because of its genesis in Western epistemologies and its unfolding within specific contexts of histories and institutions of empire. Producing Palestine underlines the act of production by Palestinians transformed—and able to transform themselves—through their knowing practices[4] and structures of feeling.[5] For it is through practices that the intersections of knowledge, embodied action, and social life come alive. Producing is thus a moment of vitality, of turning into something living, a moment of (political) becoming, an act that becomes part of a common moment and participates in the articulation of the collective's potential.

Producing Palestine: A Global Concern

Imagining and producing Palestine is more than just a Palestinian, or "local," problem. It is a global concern impacting and impacted by other global concerns—colonialism, Black lives, indigenous movements, racism, gender issues, as well as global crises.

As Rashid Khalidi writes, "half a century ago, simply putting Palestine back on the map, and asserting that the study of Palestine and the Palestinians was a legitimate endeavor, represented an arduous and frustrating task in Western academia, media, and political circles, let alone popular culture."[6] Khaled Furani and Dan Rabinowtiz[7] declared as much about the "arrival" of Palestine, that is, the admissibility of Palestine, in academia as a legitimate and recognizable domain of intellectual inquiry, and, we'd add, intellectual *production*.

A number of conjunctures have occurred in the past decades that have made this possible: the awareness of Palestine's central position in relation to questions such as race, gender, queerness, (settler) colonialism, and postcolonialism;[8] the euphoria and failures of the "peace" and subsequent state-building processes; the rupture of Israel's exceptionalist discourses (such as in the opening debates about Zionism and settler colonialism, to name but two); the recognition of Palestinians' worldliness—as Ann Stoler put it, "[m]obile, diverse, multilingual, critical, and grounded in dissensus, this is a people with connectives that cut across many places and populations in the world."[9] And, equally important is the plethora of "new" media and communication technologies, the ease of producing and sharing media texts, and quotidian practices and aesthetics across the transnational Palestinian cultural world.

Today, the globality of Palestine is thus also due, no doubt, to overwhelming media attention to the Palestine "problem." *Producing Palestine* comes at a moment for Palestinians, who, arguably for the first time since the loss of their homeland in 1948, are setting the terms for their narrative themselves and directly challenging dominant Zionist discourse which has—for decades—dehumanized them into non-actors, or worse yet, non-humans. This is an ongoing battle: the material and discursive re-eruption of war, destruction, erasure, and silencing in October 2023 have made these tensions even more apparent, and to an even wider "audience." And yet, despite the "moral indolence" of mainstream media, and "despite the sinister baiting of Palestinians and pro-Palestine protesters, it is probably fair to say that there have been more Palestinian voices on television, radio and in print than before."[10]

Producing Palestine is also producing media. Media can enhance public support; it can equally render issues distant through mediated spectacles, thus making the Palestinian "problem" easily co-optable—and misunderstood or misrepresented—by others. The tension between support and opposition has become even more pronounced with the expansion of digital platforms, offering more and more spaces to make Palestine visible, but also *in*visible, creating a media landscape of contradictory visibilities. This tension, of course, cannot be discussed as a media problem alone, or, in other words, through a rush to overtheorize media technologies without attending to the political, social, and historical, or by omitting to account for the continued Nakbaization—that the 1948 *Nakba* (catastrophe) was not simply a one-time event but is ongoing, as the continuous violence waged on Palestinians in Gaza, Jerusalem, and beyond make abundantly clear.

Palestine remains an existential concern, in the sense that Israeli colonial and discriminatory practices, including overt military, physical, and symbolic violence against Palestinians, have accentuated the liminal nature of Palestinian existence within and beyond borders. Palestinian narratives continue to be constrained by attempts to stifle interest in or advocacy for Palestine, in academia and elsewhere, increasingly made by the spurious claim that such outlooks are tainted with anti-Semitism. This libelous accusation—a constant in the relentless campaign to suppress sympathetic or even objective discourse on Palestine in the academy, on campus, and in the media, as well as in politics and other public spaces—has been ramped up in recent years to unprecedented levels. As such, the global concern of Palestine is also a reaction to the systematic—albeit changing forms of—exclusion of Palestine from consideration in so much of progressive and radical discourse. It is within these contexts that Palestine has taken on a new urgency. The response to the brutal destruction of Gaza in 2023 has also made apparent the extent to which global solidarity with Palestine is a manifestation of material and symbolic rebellion against the current world order.

In Media Res

Everyday media interactions in the contemporary moment are neither linear nor occur in clearly defined spaces: they are not separated by medium, not categorized by mode or sense-stimulation, not necessarily organized according to a bounded geography, language, or even color or font. Media don't simply saturate our lives; we *live* in media. Media "affordances" (the relationship between our abilities and the features of the system) are different than they were a few decades ago. Media interactions have become much easier for producers and readers to understand, partake in, create and recreate, tweak, edit, share and continuously build on. Our media interactions and media themselves are increasingly in media res—always already in the middle of things, where every situation is an extension of previous ones and developed in later ones. This is not to say that we do not—and therefore cannot theorize—create, use, or share media for different purposes, with different outcomes, and in different ways.

Media can function as venues and means for historical context and memory. When the arsenal of political and military strategies used by the Israeli state has meant the literal erasure of Palestinian presence on the land, media depicting the making of local dishes, the ability to digitally map and layer, and (re)connect through reincarnation, illuminate that displacement, and reveal a past life that continues its existence in another form, becomes relevant. Media thus testify to Palestinian attachment to spatiality, severed as it is by occupation and exile, attesting to a continued presence, keeping the claims of Palestinian belonging alive, and visible. Media demonstrate and are part of the quotidian resilience of a systemically oppressed community who prevails despite destruction, displacement, and disenfranchisement.

We produce media often because of their potential to function as centralizing spaces that act as and *are* nodes of our sociality and promote human interaction. We create card games, paint murals, share photographs, or make videos to bring us together. These do not merely depict or represent forms of resistance or activism (or any other politics) by themselves but are inextricably bound in political discourses. They demand, sometimes even command, space in discourses whose limits are no longer solely determined by institutional gatekeepers such as museums, national news stations, or multinational corporations. Rather, like memes gone viral, they can emerge as their own political and visual language, that is, to some degree, beyond the realm of mediation, enacting their own generative politics. They carve out the space to construct (new) publics and means of conversations in and through networks that are transnational or global that do not necessarily succumb to—or are solely constructed by—the institutional or geopolitical.

Media production of Palestine has become and is more quotidian: easy, daily, accessible for more people to participate in, to create and co-create, to interpret and make meaning of, to riff on and be playful, to disassemble and reassemble. Less and less is held, determined, or controlled by institutional forms. Politics then happens not only in formal spaces but in cooking, furtive crossings, singing, graffitying, digital mapping, donning a keffiyeh. Politics happens in unexpected places and through unremarked practices. Politics is everywhere.

Media are subjunctive: they provide presence and legibility, both of which hinge on being there, being recognized, being "seen" by others, enacting the demands of collective life. A website, an Instagram post, a documentary film, and an app are spaces where and through which Palestinians practice those rights. These perform a broader, transnational, mobile, global visuality that is central to self-expression and recognition. The operations facilitated by ("new") media are not only imminent to the rupture of hegemony but are also constitutive of (political) life itself.

In being subjunctive, media also make visible what is imagined or wished possible, providing spaces for articulation, experimentation, speculation, immanence. Spoons, drones, maps, posters, virtual reality become artifacts, tools, technologies, sites, infrastructures, and relations through which Palestinians engage in acts of world-building. The potentialities of the medium shape the perceptual and relational nature of experience, of a particular mode of subjectivity and the kinds of actions that are embedded in it. They display, reconstitute, and re-engender distinct subjectivities.

Virtual representations of the Palestinian space have long acted as tools to communicate certain political claims and to produce geopolitical territorial arrangements. Representations of Palestinians have also been part of the decolonial and revolutionary struggles for liberation. What is different today is the coming together of these elements. Films, websites, digital archiving tools, maps, photographs, and tweets, among others, are not just evocative but result in an expansion of what Palestine is. Tawil-Souri has argued that it might be more appropriate to think of an all-encompassing variety of re-territorializations within, among, between, and through different time-places; to not keep rendering Palestine, the experience of displacement, uprootedness, loss of land, as pathological, and instead, to highlight the power of discourses and practices in creating both movement and stasis, to embrace the negotiation of (often contradictory) spaces they engender as part and parcel of Palestinianness.[11]

Over the past few decades, the "power" of media, and our theorization thereof, has been enlarged or expanded, not because of informational or computational quotients and measures but by the ways through which they reshape visibility, spatiality, subjectivity, and agency. Palestine, then, is interpreted not only to be as strictly a story of the territory lost to Israel but as an engagement with the production of media. In the latter, space is necessarily open. Palestine becomes a process that emerges through that practice and its constant "reterritorialization." In other words, films, websites, digital archives, mapping apps, posters, graffiti circulating on social media, photographs, and recipes, among other examples brought together in this book, are not simply detached and marginal cultural or virtual expressions but part of the reconfigurations of (political) power.

Cases

Producing Palestine attends to the creative labor of producing Palestine, particularly in technological and mediatic spaces that are defined by their porousness and intermediality—crossing genres of popular culture and disciplinary boundaries—as well as by their fluidity and mobility. Each contribution is an original piece, written, drawn, traced, collaged, juxtaposed, layered, unflattened, or otherwise. Each is conceived as an individual installment *and* part of a collective whose overarching goal is to conceptualize, engage in, and invite readers to participate in the production of Palestine and its theorization.

The book offers a series of "cases" (rather than "chapters") in which the vision and the reality of Palestine are addressed as co-creative and productive: attempting to craft a future within which the past is echoed, whether unequivocally or abstractly; contending with how present limitations and impasses constrain, but also provoke, creative expressions, mediatic spaces, technological infrastructures; and providing alternative perspectives reclaimed through different relations and processes. The cases are themselves organic, deliberate, and contingent on one another; they are forms of creative labor that attempt to blur the distinction between a (media) producer, artist, reader, interpreter, scholar. Individually and collectively, they reflect on, demonstrate, partake in, and generate multiple expressions and imaginaries of producing Palestine.

Each case contends with images, technologies, territories, or concepts that are being dynamically generated into new knowledge production. Each carries a multitude of meanings. These cases, we suggest, are informed and indeed animated by a process of searching and looking for a center, despite the very fact that de-centering Palestine— that is, dislocating Palestine and releasing it from territorial and representational boundaries—is also at the heart of this book. We have purposefully not categorized the cases under overarching sections because we hope that as you, dear "reader," go through the images and prose, you will appreciate the disjuncture and interconnectedness of each case and the symbolism each contains, on your own terms.

Rayya El Zein's "A Place Called Return" draws on her experiences visiting Yaffa and Wadi Hunayn to explore the imagination, affects, and politics of return. Pulling from a semi-private archive of interactions with family and friends in the United States and Lebanon on different social media platforms while in Palestine, she unfolds an awareness of class and Palestine that oscillates between the promise of realizing a return and the realization of the impossibility of that promise. Reaching for an imagination of return outfitted to a political horizon that explicitly engages difference in Palestine and in the diaspora, she gestures toward new visions of Palestine and return while playfully teasing the technologies informing her passage.

In their case "Imagining Return: Countless Palestinian Futures," Danah Abdulla and Sarona Abuaker discuss the process of co-creating a card game called *Countless Palestinian Futures*, which attempts to unpack what return would materially look like and which emphasizes the role of imagination therein. Detailing the public events during which the game was played, they review the multiple understandings and ideas brought by participants through the questions that were played, how both the players and the game-creators were challenged to orient their ideas toward the future and contend with the question of what and who are we—as Palestinians—after the struggle, after return.

Dina Matar's "Re-centering Palestine and Palestinians in Poster Art" considers revolutionary-era and present-day Palestinian poster art as an affective space through which Palestine is reappeared and re-centered in aesthetic and political interventions that reappropriate material and immaterial symbols to intervene in the relationship between Palestinians, as the ruled, and Israel, as the ruler. Matar suggests that these posters, enabled by the convergence of expression, production, and revolution in particular sociopolitical contexts and temporalities, articulate Palestinians' changing experiences and social presence in the world while also actively producing Palestine.

Nayrouz Abu Hatoum and Hadeel Assali's "Becoming al-Mulatham/a: Fedayee Art, Abu Obaida, and Palestinian Tik Tok" addresses how social media platforms such as TikTok can be used as sites for archival practices and forms of documenting and presenting political expression and resistance. Their case focuses on different iterations and imaginations of the masked figure of *al-mulatham/a* as expression and symbol of underground resistance, an image that has neither been commodified nor entirely neoliberalized, but one that endures because it is constantly reclaimed by ordinary Palestinians.

By focusing on an experimental film and mobile apps that all use new mapping technologies, Viviane Saglier's "Vertical Visions of the Nakba: Toward a Topography of Layers" disentangles mapping technologies' potential for imagining a return of Palestinians. Saglier suggests that multiple understandings of layers—layers of digital imaging, layers of the land as an archive itself, and layers of participatory activity that mapping apps encourage—enable us to visualize the land not as a tool of colonial control but as a practice of recovering and reviving Palestinians' ancestral connections, and thus part of a broader ecology of (participatory) images that Palestinians have been producing around the architectural traces of Palestinian life. The constant layering underlines the physicality of symbolic representations, the effective social relationships that these configure, and their tangible consequences on spatial and political realities, while also offering a "counter-forensics" to colonial destruction.

The case "Virtual Returns: Rehearsing and Remediating Return in Palestinian Vidoes" by Kareem Estefan examines projects by Palestinian artists Razan Al-Salah and the team of Basel Abbas and Ruanne Abou-Rahme which visualize and refract possible returns to Palestine through virtual spaces and speculative abstractions. Estefan shows how these artists' videos and multimedia installations do not depict return to historic Palestine in concrete terms, as a movement toward material and territorial reclamation that must be realized through acts of resistance. Rather, these explore possible modes of return and multilayered images of Palestine through the "virtual," which not only denotes technologies of sensory simulation but more broadly refers to what remains fictional and potential.

Taking the story of the life and afterlife of a Syrian martyr from the Golan as its focus, Aamer Ibraheem's "Reincarnated: Common Sense and the Poetics of Elsewhere" invites readers to question spatial and temporal assumptions of a clearly defined Palestine. Ibraheem highlights movements in space and time across a landscape that figures as a reminder and remainder of Palestine as part of Syria, thus reflecting on the fluidity not only of time and space but also of "homeland."

Nadeem Karkabi and Kiven Strohm's "Fugitive Crossings: On the Condition of Being Palestinian" engages with fugitivity as a mode of flight that offers an anti-colonial practice which evades representational politics. The authors examine three instances of flight—the return of Palestinian refugees to their homeland between 1948 and 1951, the "infiltration" of West Bank Palestinians across the Separation Wall, and the escape of Palestinian prisoners from Israeli incarceration—as offering possibilities of creative dissonance within/against colonial enclosure.

Sary Zananiri, in his visual case "Marking Bodies: A Catalogue of Keffiyehs," demonstrates how Palestine has been a significant site of documentation and reproduction even before the advent of image reproduction technologies. Zananiri literally traces the keffiyeh across changing contexts and networks of circulation that have created new, often contradictory meanings of the Palestinian body in popular culture. By reducing the keffiyeh from each element from which it was drawn—such as postcards and Hollywood films—what's left of the garment provides the space for re-reappropriation.

Lara Khalidi's "'We are still alive, so remove us from memory': Asynchronicity and the Museum in Resistance" alludes to the absurdity and limitations of museumification practices that commodify Palestinian cultural artifacts. She proposes that the museum in resistance is not a material structure and archive of a past struggle of emancipation but a generative collective disintegration of this material in the struggle for forging collective myths, an archive which does not (p)reserve a record or a trace but a shared knowledge in continuous circulation and transformation.

In "Forging Revolutionary Objects," Stephen Sheehi introduces us to a handful of popular objects as techné of liberation: social and subjective practices that emerge from knowledge-production that operate within a culture of settler-colonialism, exile, and liberation. He argues that these materialize from a culture of popular resistance within Palestinian life, whether in the village, the city, the refugee camp, or the prison, and thus demonstrates how a spoon, stone, kite, and bullet are not simply technological objects but techné that surface from the psychological-subjective-social fabric of Palestinian community and identity.

Anne Meneley's case, "Cooking Online with Chef Fadi," analyzes how cooking shows and food preparation are used in contemporary Palestinian media outputs on Facebook and YouTube as a subversive implement to bring distinctive Palestinian culture to a wider audience, using the ability to "eat with your eyes" as a means, along with online narratives, to bring Palestinian stories to the center.

Dale Hudson, in "Producing Palestine as Layers of Historical Evidence with Interactive Documentaries," examines mobile apps and documentaries, such as

Zochrot's iNakba and Dorit Naaman's *Jerusalem, We Are Here*, that prompt audiences to reflect upon power asymmetries by mapping Palestinian geographies that have been rendered invisible. Hudson shows how digital tools can use remapping as an effort to counter dominant power and shape not only meaning but a rendering of Palestine.

"Palestine and the Question of Queer Arab Becoming" by Sophie Chamas offers a close reading of the music video of the song "Cavalry," by renowned Lebanese indie-band Mashrou' Leila, to consider the role that Palestine, and a commitment to Palestine, plays in defining and distinguishing queer Arab identity, not as a hyphenated identity that assumes the stability of "queer" and "Arab" but as a mode of becoming that destabilizes both.

Helga Tawil-Souri's "Refractions" takes representations of Palestinian "icon" Ahed Tamimi, as a mural on the Separation Wall and a series of social media posts, to unpack the relationship between the real and the virtual. Contending with how graffiti on the wall changes once it becomes part of a social media post, she addresses media's role in the creation and transcendence of multiple spaces.

The case "Terra ex machina," by Hagit Keysar, Ariel Caine, and Barak Brinker, visualizes the invisible wall around Jerusalem's Old City created by a regulatory no-fly zone called "Temple Mount." By taking footage through a camera-equipped drone to "crash" against this geofence, Keysar, Caine, and Brinker create a multidimensional vision of the aerial ban, showing us, through images from the drone's control panel and street images, where the invisible controls on everyday (digital and aerial) life in Jerusalem extend. In the text that accompanies this visualization, they discuss how this no-fly zone acquires theological and ethno-political meanings and suggest new forms of state/corporate sovereignty in Jerusalem, the epicenter of conflict and colonization.

Producing Palestine, we hope, provides multiple imaginations and contra-imaginations of Palestine and Palestinians, unsettling dominant regimes of representation and production while exposing the inherent tension between representation and production exacerbated by digital technologies and new modes and aesthetics of seeing and producing. *Producing Palestine*, we hope, raises questions about, while also asks you to partake in, the intersecting spaces of signification that defy classification.

Notes

1. William J. T. Mitchell, "Holy Landscape: Israel, Palestine, and the American Wilderness," *Critical Inquiry* 26, no. 2 (2000): 207, 199.
2. Cindi Katz and Neil Smith, "An Interview with Edward Said," *Environment and Planning D: Society and Space* 21 (2003): 642.
3. Anne Swidler, "What Anchors Cultural Practices," in *The Practice Turn in Contemporary Theory*, ed. Theodore R. Schatzki, K. Knorr-Cetina, and Eike von Savigny (London: Routledge, 2001), 74–92.
4. Michel Foucault, "The Subject and Power," *Critical Inquiry* 8, no. 4 (Summer 1982): 777–95.
5. Raymond Williams, *Marxism and Literature* (Oxford: Oxford University Press, 1977).

6   Rashid Khalidi, "The Journal of Palestine Studies in the Twenty-First Century: An Editor's Reflections," *Journal of Palestine Studies* 50, no. 3 (2021): 7.
7   Khaled Furani and Dan Rabinowitz, "The Ethnographic Arriving of Palestine," *Annual Review of Anthropology* 40 (2011): 475–91.
8   Salamanca et al's special issue of Settler Colonial Studies is both a powerful example and a theorization of this. Omar Jabary Salamanca, Mezna Qato, Kareem Rabie, and Sobhi Samour, "Past Is Present: Settler Colonialism in Palestine," *Settler Colonial Studies* 2, no. 1 (2012): 1–8.
9   Ann Stoler, "Archiving as Dissensus," *Comparative Studies of South Asia, Africa and the Middle East* 38, no. 1 (2018): 49. It is worth noting that certain global connections are not new. For example, Palestinians have been implicated in the so-called migration problem not of their own will but through expulsion from their homeland, a process that continues in the contemporary period. The Palestinian strategy of liberation in the 1960s operated in a global and comparative landscape, spatially linking Palestinians politically, socially, and culturally to other colonized peoples struggling against similar processes of oppression and dispossession—processes that themselves are global. Palestine's implication in indigenous and marginalized movements and struggles worldwide and has been called upon as a witness and a force in activist practices against subjugation worldwide.
10 Richard Seymour, "The Equanimity of Lunatics," *Verso Blog*, October 17, 2023, https://www.versobooks.com/blogs/news/the-equanimity-of-lunatics.
11 Helga Tawil-Souri, "Cinema as the Space to Transgress Palestine's Territorial Trap," *Middle East Journal of Culture and Communication* 7, no. 2 (2014): 169–89.

1

A Place Called Return

Rayya El Zein

Return

My family doesn't talk about Return. Mostly, reference to Palestine is a discussion of the depravity of Israel and US foreign policy. Sometimes, there is some tenderness around new films, theater, or music produced by Palestinians. We are very precious with that tenderness; we are quiet and gentle with it, as if it would scamper off if spooked. So these cultural interventions largely don't spark heated conversation. They are appreciated quietly and we listen anxiously to the younger generation's reactions—eager to hear that they have both enough interest and enough respect. Like a formal dining room we rarely use, Palestine is a room in the house of ourselves we hold aside, to be lit and warmed and set with festive faces—one day, but not today. Like all survivors, we move and work in the kitchen. We keep the kids and the mess of everyday life from spilling too far into the rest of the house.

The silence around Palestine is noticeable because we argue about everything. We are not quiet because we don't know how to be otherwise. And, of course, we know why: it hurts too much. Why revisit that pain? Why conjure it? Why pick at that wound aloud for all to see? Just finger that pain like the edges of a lace tablecloth, quietly.

After college I was somewhat surprised to learn that in other families there was, what I perceived to be, more talk about that table to be lit and warmed and set with festive faces—about return. Elders talked about what they would cook, and how the earth and the sun would feel, and how those things would be set on the table, and who would be there and so on. I imagined in those conversations that Palestine was like the more formal dining room tablecloth being used all the time, in the actual kitchen. It was comforting that Palestine felt closer somehow. But still, it seemed, Palestine was to be listened to when it escaped someone's reveries and seeped into spoken speech. Hush greeted it, lest our tenderness, or our resolve, be jolted and scared away by too many questions or divergent dreams.

When I traveled to Palestine I realized that I hadn't ever heard any actual details about return. How would we manage it? What would it actually look like? How would we treat the soft and hard parts of each other we would actually displace? I am assuming that the return of Palestinian refugees to homes and territories displaced since the

Nakba is an eventual reality. And I am speaking of its dynamics among Palestinians. How will we reconcile the dreams, exhaustions, and imaginations nurtured in the diaspora and on the ground? How will we confront our disappointments in each other? Where will we file resentment about each of the endless compromises we have all made to survive? What will we do about the disparities in resources between us that were there when some of us left and will continue to exist when some of us return?

Obviously, my observation that in my family we don't talk about return is not a refutation of our or any Palestinian's ability to imagine the future. Our deferral of conversation to the depravity of Israel and US foreign policy is a way of channeling imagination about the future into a zone of criticality, anger, or righteousness that evades, in its way, the very tender parts of dreams, memories, and futures stolen over three generations. There is a vibrant tradition of writing, mobilizing, art, and other cultural production that imagines a Palestinian future as sovereignty, as autonomy, as return, or otherwise.

Taking to heart Nayrouz Abou Hatoum's observation that for Palestinians, "the idea of the future is much more tethered to the ways in which the everyday is inhabited," in this chapter I am pursuing a specific meditation on our eventual returns, and the alienations, navigations, and struggles that may accompany them.[1] Sleeping in rented beds in Yaffa, Haifa, Jerusalem, and Ramallah, the distance between Return as the political horizon where Palestine will be realized and return as a practice of millions packing suitcases and arriving to read unfamiliar street signs and staking claims to the land opened up like the night sky—impossibly beautiful, impossibly full, incredibly real. Messy, empty, alive.

* * *

I am a second-generation Palestinian raised in the diaspora. My grandfather and his siblings fled Yaffa as young men in 1948. My grandfather returned to Jerusalem with my grandmother once before 1967. Between then and 2014, no one in our immediate family returned. With the exception of my mother and I, an entire generation—my mother's brothers, sisters, and cousins—have not stepped foot in Palestine.

In 2014, I was awarded some research funding for my PhD and made my way to the West Bank. I turned thirty that fall. I flew into Tel Aviv. I went to Yaffa and searched Jamal Basha street for remnants of the family apartment. I went to Wadi Hunayn and found the family estate. Exhausted, sweaty, and disgusted with mankind, I meandered Jerusalem. In a kind of exalted daze, I walked and walked and walked the hills of Haifa. I lived in Ramallah and sifted through the layers and layers of closeness and distance, and clarity and contradiction familiar to so many there and who pass through there. I was greeted with incredible warmth and palpable sadness. I was met with immediacy and urgency and distance. I lay on and worked in the solid ground. And I walked threadbare paths around a gaping abyss, where nothing but the sweat from my palms connected one patch of dust to another.

I took notes and shuffled them away. I moved apartments eight times in three countries in the two years that followed. I finished a degree and scrambled onto an academic job market that promised more moving. In the eerie and abrupt stillness that the confluence of the global pandemic and the birth of my daughter brought in the early 2020s, I am returning to my return to Palestine in 2014. Conscious now of the practice of building worlds with her, I am trying to understand the painful silence that greets Palestine and consider how not to recreate it. I start by reflecting on moments of my own return. In doing so, I am trying to shift my weight. I am looking to understand a collective horizon called Palestine, imagined and embodied in visions, memories, and dreams of return. What does the creative power necessary to hold on to Palestine look like? Where are its politics? Who does it call? And what does it call them to do?

A Plate of Watermelon

When the intelligence officer in Tel Aviv airport in July of 2014 finally told me, OK, they were going to let me in, he attempted small talk. He asked me several times for the address at which I would stay, which I had of course already furnished. It was a shared rental on Shivtei Israel Street. He was kind of quiet and then told me twice to be careful, and not to walk outside at night.

It took me a long time to make sense of what he said. If he was afraid of an Arab neighborhood, fine, but he did remember I was Arab, right? But he wasn't only talking about that. Racist, sure, but he was also talking about money. About tourism and money. About gentrification and the edges where our ideas about places bump up against the realities of them.

Of course, at that time, I could not have imagined that Yaffa was a ghetto. I mean that I could not have imagined it was an underdeveloped suburb of somewhere else. I could not have relied on a quantitative analysis of it as Tel Aviv's gentrification ground zero, ripe for the speculation of Israeli artsy, techy social entrepreneurs, nor was I ready to rely on accounts of the sporadic but collaborative struggle against that gentrification. I had read such analysis documented by researchers more disciplined than me, but all of it settled in my mind as debris. How could Yaffa—Yaffa of the orange groves, Yaffa of "ahla nass"—be a run-down, neglected neighborhood, with all the trappings of urban blight of any other millennial city? It didn't make sense.

I found the rental, Yafo Creative House, on AirBnB (Figure 1.1).[2] At the time it was run by three friends, Amnon, Tzlil, and Anna—a videographer, a musician, and a graphic artist, respectively. Amnon (Israeli-Australian) bought the second floor of the three-floor Ottoman-style villa some years prior and he and the two women were running the property (where they also lived, at least part of the time) as a collective arts space, production house, and hostel with the help of two interns. Tzlil is the granddaughter of a rabbi, of Moroccan descent. Anna moved to Israel with her parents from a Russian-speaking town on the Black Sea in Ukraine when she was ten. When I first arrived I was alone in the house except for a friend of Amnon's who was staying in his room while Amnon was on holiday in Australia. My third night, a German couple, both actors, arrived on summer vacation to occupy one of the four guest rooms.

Stepping outside the complicated reality of which it is a part, which I managed in fleeting moments throughout my stay, the space is gorgeous. It's been tastefully redone; the original windows and tiles are still there. The hosts identify on the cultural left,

Figure 1.1 Yafo Creative House. Photograph courtesy by Amnon Ron.

including of liberal Zionism. In eight years, they have occasionally hosted (though never promoted) Palestinian artists. My first evening there, Tzlil met me at the apartment and then took me out for a bite and a drink in the Flea Market—a hip and not cheap area of bars and restaurants. On the way home she warned me not to walk west past the property alone at night. In my room, I looked at a map to find that Ajami district lay to the west. I logged her quiet voice next to the airport security guard's.

I had come to Yaffa on my way to the West Bank to look for my family's property and where they used to make their home. While I did so, I had elected to stay in a villa that was undoubtedly also once owned by an Arab family. And to do *that*, I was paying young Israelis rent that their Arab neighbors obviously could not afford. As if to comment on the absurd precarity of all of that, the Israelis I interacted with reminded me just how close to the edges of legibility I was moving. How invisible I was as a returnee in economies such as these and how the pleasures and aesthetics that pulled me visiting even *this* new city identified me as part of a globalized cosmopolitan consumer much more readily than any family history identified me as coming home.

It touched everything in Yaffa. My first full day, I went to locate a family apartment on Jamal Basha street (Sderot Yerushalayim). I had been told it was in the vicinity of the Al-Hambra building, close to the Spinneys supermarket, across the street from the Rashid Cinema. I found the Al-Hambra building easily. Looking for friendly allies in this search for what the Rashid cinema might be today, I happened upon an Arab butcher shop—marked on the outside in Arabic. I asked the clerk at the register at the door, who pointed me to an older man behind the counter. He started answering in Hebrew, but the clerk corrected him, and the butcher smiled and switched to Arabic. He told me the building of the Rashid cinema still existed, but was now operating as a discotheque. I'd find it on the left, at the third *ramzor,* past the bank and the post office. When I asked him what a ramzor was, an Arab client listening—a man about the age of the butcher—scoffed and retorted, "So, you *don't* speak Arabic!" The butcher didn't say anything. My own throat turned to cement. But I smiled and nodded and thanked them and carried down the street in the direction he had pointed.

I found the cinema-disco where the butcher said. I walked around the building next to the cinema from the back and found the faded sign of the Spinney's supermarket. Across the street from both, where I was directed that the family residence had been, were three things. The Chelsea theatre—a new, white-washed building with modern text and a fountain; a residential building made of stone and stucco with a bustling cafe on the ground floor; and, a covered mall of sorts that could house small shops. No shops were open, but there was a sign that read, "The Israel Falafel. Since 1950" (Figure 1.2). I crossed the street and stared at the residence above the cafe. I approached a metal door and studied it. How could you tell how old a building was by just looking at it? Did I know how to do that?

The cafe on the ground floor was full of young people in tight shorts and flowing tops. There were small dogs and multiple kisses as greetings. I sat down and ordered a plate of watermelon with feta cheese. I didn't know if I should cry or be happy. If I should be disgusted by the cafe and its summery vibe or relieved it was there—so I could sit precisely here, near this entryway of our home, and breathe in the afternoon light as long as I could. And what the hell was that word for stoplight, *ramzor*? I sat

Figure 1.2 The Israel Falafel. Photograph by the author, July 4, 2014.

in the cafe for a long while, WhatsApping the photos I'd just taken to the Family chat. Nobody could recognize anything in the pictures I sent.

The next day, eager to be near the sea, I left the rental and headed for the shore. Approaching it, I was confronted with an expanding boardwalk enterprise, in which the first of several very new cafes promised fancy coffees and a cooler holding five-dollar popsicles. Inside the cooler, the flavors were written in Hebrew on cardboard pieces in front of each of the dozen or so red, orange, yellow, and deep-purple piles.

I stopped a teenager in a black T-shirt and an apron after a barista called out to him in Arabic. I asked him if he could translate the flavors for me. He looked with me down through the glass door of the cooler, his brown, nail-bitten finger pressing on the glass. He got through *manga*, *bateekh*, *toot*, and *joz hind* before telling me he didn't know the names of the other fruits in Arabic. He stopped another busboy to ask him what something was in Arabic; his colleague shrugged and responded with the same word in Hebrew. They both left. It was the second time language would not pass as currency, as familiarity, or as trust in Palestine. *The names of fruits*. It would have crushed me if I had understood it more completely. I picked *manga* and took the popsicle outside, where the sea had no interest in unraveling the coil of live wires in which I saw myself entangled.

A Villa Near the Sea

After the search on Jamal Basha, I received a WhatsApp message from my mother's cousin F. It read,

> N is telling me if u find villa Abdel Rahim in Ajami area then take pictures because her father's house was in front of it (where she grew up). Up on some hill.

The next day, I went to look for the Abdel Rahim villa. A Google search informed me that the villa, built in the 1930s, was now the residence of the French ambassador to Israel, located on Toulouse street. The story behind the building starts in 1934 with the founding of the Tel Aviv Rotary club. I walked west from Yafo Creative on Shivtei Israel until it merged with Yefet Street. I turned right on Mendes-France and then left on Toulouse. The villa and the French embassy were right on the corner, at the very top of the hill. When I got there I realized I didn't know what I was looking for. I went back to the WhatsApp message. The request was to take pictures. I walked north of the villa and took pictures. I came back to the villa. I walked east of the villa and took pictures. I came back to the villa. I walked south of the villa and took pictures. I came back to the villa and I faced west and I walked down toward the sea, taking pictures.

It was a Saturday. The streets were empty as I walked. It was quiet. None of my pictures show people. By 1:00 p.m., I sat myself in a seafood restaurant, ordered a beer and a small plate of hummus. I watched the restaurant manager, a bald man with a round belly in a fitted black T-shirt, and his staff, in matching T-shirts, interact. In the restaurant, no one talked to me and I found comfort in being near the sea, in its constancy. I sat there in the anonymity of foreignness and read some studies of class and coloniality I had earmarked for the summer.

And, I sent F the pictures. No one recognized anything.

＊

I didn't know what to make of the shifting foreignness of Palestine when I had been (unreasonably perhaps) hoping, dreaming for the familiarity of home. What I found and what I've been trying to describe is an unsettling set of familiarities, comforts, alienations, and feelings at ease—quite different from that of which I had dreamed or romanticized my tiny return to consist. When my mother came to visit me in Ramallah several months later, we went to Bethlehem together as part of her visit. In one of the alleyways of the Old City, a group of young Palestinian boys followed and lightheartedly taunted us, the way local kids do visiting tourists. They kept asking where we were from, to which my mother insisted on responding in Arabic and with no little indignant pride, we're from here, we're one of you, from Palestine. Confused, the boys retorted we must be Israeli—which cut my mother so resoundingly that it clipped her words and her steps short. While she faced the twin impossibility of responding to the child and of swallowing such a slap in the face, the boys ran past us. Long seconds later she called after them, *fashartou*!

Nobody called me Israeli to my face in Yaffa. Perhaps there were too many other easily identifiable trajectories on which I might be located. Perhaps it doesn't have currency the way it does in the West Bank. But I can't say that anyone assumed, or cared, really, that this half-hipster walking around wondering if she was in the right place and periodically seeking refreshment was Palestinian, either.

Perhaps I am trying to locate a practice of return in the everyday practices of what might otherwise be recognized as tourism. More specifically, I am wondering what the role of micro returns like mine—distinctly marked by economic privilege and access to travel, in many ways ignorant of and out of touch with local, material dynamics (how could they be otherwise)—can play in a collective "protocol of recognition" in the current chapter of Palestinian imagining a horizon called Palestine.[3] More specifically still, in relating to a horizon where Palestine appears as interwoven with other destinations, dissolutions, and desires, how can the particular alienations and familiarities, like the ones I've pointed to here, help reposition Palestine in conjunction with plans and dreams and struggles for access and equity in the other places we have also called home?

Mango in a Green Tin Can

The day after meandering in Ajami, I set out to try to find remnants of the family estate in Wadi Hunayn (Ness Ziona). And while this was outside of Yaffa, in this search there was more than WhatsApp messages: there was research and oral history, and proper archives to help. I had started with the memoir of a cousin of my grandfather's and the Wadi Hunayn page on *Palestine Remembered*.

I took a shared taxi toward Rehovot and asked to be dropped off in Ness Ziona. I knew from the good work at *Palestine Remembered* and from Taj Farouki's biography that a house, once surrounded by citrus groves, should still be standing.[4] Taj (a cousin of my grandfather) recounts that they moved into the house when he was seven or eight years old. Before I left, I downloaded these pictures onto my phone for reference (Figures 1.3 and 1.4).

The shared-taxi driver asked me where I'd like to get off in Ness Ziona. I hadn't the foggiest idea. I knew from *Palestine Remembered* that there was a synagogue in the town that used to be a mosque. I got out in front of it, on Herzl St. and walked around it. Herzl St. is kind of a bustling street. There was no sign of an estate anywhere.

Under a tree, near the bus stop, I spotted a young man and a young woman in a hijab sitting together. I approached and I asked them if they'd ever seen the house in the photo. They both nodded yes but couldn't tell me where. "Walk past the synagogue and turn right," the man offered. Maybe I'd find it way off in that direction.

It seemed as good a start as any. I walked and turned right at the stoplight as he indicated. Right there was a real-estate office. I entered and a young man in a fitted blue T-shirt at a computer greeted me. I showed him the photo on the phone. He didn't recognize it, but he took the phone to his father, seated in an office in the back. The tan, balding man looked at it quietly and then nodded slowly. Yes, he knew the building. It was around here and it was a hospital. "Where is it?" I asked. He turned to his son and gave him directions. "I can take you," the son offered.

I accepted, thanked him, and he waved a gesture of "it's my pleasure" and said *bi kaf*. I guessed he was about my age. In the car as we drove down a street parallel to

Figure 1.3 Estate at Wadi Hunayn. Photograph from Palestine Remembered.

Figure 1.4 Close-up from the photograph of the Estate at Wadi Hunayn from Palestine Remembered.

Herzl, back in the direction I had come, he explained in broken English that he didn't know as much as his father did, who was born here. "Were you born here?" I asked. He nodded. But, he joked, not as long ago as his father. We veered off to the right and began winding up a hill. He asked me where I was from. "Do you know someone in this hospital?" he asked. I shook my head no. "So you came all the way from New York for this building?" "Not only this building," I answered. At the top of the hill, he told me this was it. A metal gate and a security guard office stood in front of us. I got out of the car and the real-estate broker's son drove back down the hill.

Inside the small security office I took out my phone again. "Is the house in the photo here?" I asked. Two guards in gray polo shirts tucked into black cargo pants, with pistols in leather holsters around their waists, and yarmulkes on their shaved heads crowded over the phone. The first one, looked up, surprised.

> "Wow, it looks like it!" He said.
> I beamed. "Great!" I said. "I just want to see it."
> "You can't," he answered.
> "Just from the outside—"
> "It's not permitted," he said. "Why do you want to see it? You know someone here?"
> "I just want to see if it's the same house." I answered.
> "No."
> The two guards conversed in Hebrew and the first one relented. "Ok but no pictures," he said. "And he'll come with you." He pointed to his colleague.

I nodded OK. The second guard led me through the security office and onto a paved pathway leading up to a yellowing building. As we approached the house, it was pretty clear it was the same building in the photo I was carrying. But sight was no longer the sense that preoccupied me. All my other senses clamored for my attention. A breeze picked up and flitted through the trees just so, a scent lifted up from somewhere, the sun stopped being so hot, and an astounding familiarity washed over me. I felt like I was at the land above Tyre in Lebanon, the *biyarra* that my great uncle had bought upon fleeing Palestine and that mother's cousins now tended—the same feeling, an almost exact replica down to the slope of the land, the calm under the trees, the scent of the ground.

As if he could see me floating there, tethered to but no longer standing on the ground, held just by the breeze off the Mediterranean, the guard got nervous and started talking into his radio. Scratchy voices responded and he told me urgently it was time to go. One photo, I asked again, pulling out the phone. "No," came the reply and he gestured firmly back toward the security office.

I walked straight through the security office without stopping or saying anything and stopped under a tree a hundred meters or so from the front gate. I looked out at the rolling landscape in front of me and tried to hold all the smells and sounds inside me. I tried not to think of the absurdity of everything. I tried to formulate how I'd explain how I came and left. I tried to be still and patient, but sometimes, nothing works. Inside, a dam broke. Water and air stopped and started flowing in the wrong directions.

A few minutes later, it occurred to me I could ask to speak to a director, or someone in charge. I went to pull out the bottle of water I had in my bag to help compose myself first when I noticed that the first security guard was standing quietly nearby with a plastic cup full of water. "No thank you," I said. "I have some." "But this is cold," he said, putting the cup in my hand.

When I took it, he started to ask me what was wrong. I interrupted and asked to speak to the director of the hospital. He told me the director wasn't there today. I asked if we could call him. He shrugged and said, "But you have to tell me what for." I took a deep breath, and, not keen to go into the details of my family tree with an Israeli security guard, told him this was my grandfather's house. "Grandfather?" he said, his eyebrows raised. I nodded and he said the word again in English. Then he said it to himself in Hebrew, as if thinking out loud, *saba*. He told me to come with him and we went back to the security office. I waited outside. He explained to one guard, and then a second, and then a third, gesturing to me, then to the house, and repeating the word *saba* each time. Smiles and bemused confusion disappeared from their faces. They got quiet and looked more at the ground than before. He picked up the phone.

Thirty or forty minutes and a dozen or so calls later, he told me, "OK we are going to go speak with the onsite director." I followed him to a building to the right of the house. A woman asked me why I didn't have an appointment. Another woman explained to me, "You see we have rules here." I showed them the photo. They stewed and looked at me and each other and the floor.

A half hour later, they put me on the phone with some high-up head of security. His English was perfect. "I can't just let anybody on the property," he said, "out of respect for our patients." I told him I understood his concern. "When do you think your family was here?" he asked.

"They left in 1948."
Pause. "And when did they move here?"
"I'm not sure. He (I meant Taj, my grandfather's cousin) says he was seven or eight when they moved here. Maybe 1930."
The line went silent. I almost asked if he was still there. "OK I'll allow it," came the voice, "but the guard stays with you."

I handed back the phone. The first woman introduced me to the guard, the first security guard, whose name was Elie. He'll take you around.

Elie walked me around the house and waited while I took photos (Figure 1.5). He took my photo on the steps. Walking around the back of the house, he showed me inside the building, explaining it was a kitchen. Inside the kitchen, we ran into a rabbi. Elie stammered, then looked at me, and took a breath, stopped, and explained. The word *saba* came again and with it the rabbi's face dropped. He looked at me without saying anything. I turned to leave, and he stopped me, asking if I'd like something to drink. I thanked him and declined. We continued walking around the rest of the house.

Back at the front gate, Elie said, "It's good, you can sleep now." I didn't answer. I asked how I could get a bus back to Tel Aviv. "Give me a minute and I'll take you," he said. He dropped me off in front of the mosque-now synagogue, on Herzl St. There, I approached a falafel stand and asked for a mango juice.

The falafel guy said, "English?" I nodded.
"Why you don't speak Hebrew?"
"Oh, I don't know Hebrew," I said.
"Are you staying, or are you visiting?" He asked.
"Some of both."
"Good, then, you'll learn."

I sat under an umbrella that the wind seemed hell-bent on knocking over. I drank a mango juice from a green tin can and WhatsApped the photos to the group.

I must have got a shared taxi back to Yaffa though I can't remember it. Back at Yafo Creative, Tzlil and the German actors were smoking cigarettes on the balcony. Tzlil was eager to hear about my day—I had asked her before about the shared taxis. I told her where I had gone and what happened. The actors got up awkwardly. Tzlil was quiet and rolled us both another cigarette.

For a long time, I kept thinking about the Arab couple under the tree whom I had met when I first got out of the taxi. Who did they think I was or did they care? How is it they came to point me in the opposite direction of the house (which, given the security apparatus, they likely would never have seen), but directly onto the steps of two generations of real-estate agents? Was the feeling of familiarity on the hill real? Maybe it was just the actual similarity of the geography? Why didn't I feel anything so certain anywhere else in Yaffa?

Figure 1.5 Estate at Wadi Hunayn. Photograph by the author, 2014.

That night I had a long conversation with a friend who, while usually quick to opine, was uncharacteristically quiet as I recounted the events of the day. We'll buy it, he said, finally. The hospital, the house. We'll buy it back. Buy it? I thought. Buy an estate-turned-mental-hospital? Buy it with that security house out front and the gate? Buy it with the basement kitchen where the rabbi sat? Enlist the real-estate broker's son and buy it? Buy it, *back*? How absurd, I thought. How perfectly absurd.

Toward Return

Incidentally, one of the things I can't explain about my photo archive and my field notes in Yaffa is about a dozen photographs of property for sale. I have no recollection of why I thought those signs or those properties were worth documenting or what I thought connected them to each other. They're not connected to notes about searches for family property or notes I took about gentrification patterns in my own informal research on the subject. Photos of property for sale don't appear in my archive from my visits to other cities in Palestine. Most, but not all, are near the port, as if another version of me was subconsciously scouting for ocean-front property. The rest of my notes from July 2014 are full of links to press on gentrification patterns in Ajami, quick reflections on religious sites in Jerusalem, and then the beginning of my research on the Iron Dome system as Israel began its brutal bombardment of Gaza later that summer.

These two fantastical speculations about buying—the suggestion from my companion via WhatsApp call the night I came back from Wadi Hunayn, and my subconscious interest in the subject manifest in my personal archive—are fundamentally relevant in an exploration of an "affective ecology" of return.[5] I am arguing for a recognition of this material crassness, a class- informed vision of the world, in an imagination about returning to Palestine. Not because either Palestine or return can be bought. But as a recognition of the transactional economies of which our returns may also consist. That is, Palestine is already connected, replicated in, and woven into every other place we are. It does not and cannot, by virtue of being homeland alone, undo flights and flows of capital. It cannot expect, by virtue of being wished for and dreamt about, to avoid the material fall outs of these speculations as the land and the cities and the buildings themselves twist and tear and call out to accommodate the births of three and a half generations in absentia.

This begs the question: What is the vision of the future that our returns to Palestine help shape? As Abou Hatoum advises, "Palestinian struggle for liberation from the settler-colonial condition requires intense forms of imagination of the future of the everyday."[6] There are many articulate, engaged efforts to imagine return as reconstitution, as rebuilding, as regrowth, as celebration, as imminent reality—from occupations of destroyed villages, to spontaneous gatherings, to the collective commitment to the recurring Great March of Return, calling and connecting the range of the Palestinian diaspora from Gaza to the South of Lebanon and across oceans to the Americas.

I have tried to mobilize accounts of the most basic of alienations, pleasures, surprises in only the very initial steps of return as an opening to consider how to build an "affective infrastructure" that locates the practice of everyday return as a physical and affective reorientation. This is a reorientation inextricable from myriad other economies, aesthetics, which we as Palestinians, as travelers, as returnees will also be and are already inevitably a part.[7] In reviewing my notes from nearly a decade ago, I am struck by just how much I seemed to be consuming Palestine in that first, life-changing week of return. Absorbing sights, sounds, smells, emotions but also literally, physically, materially eating, drinking, sleeping in exchange for cash. I am struck by how much the aesthetics of these consumptions—their banality—has lodged in my memory and my personal archive as somehow significant.

In lingering in these moments I have wondered: Can return, itself, become a place? A place where expectations, visions, imaginations, memories, dissolve into other realities that are all too familiar but which have not been allowed to touch dreams and reveries and commitments called Palestine. A place whose infrastructure needs to be built—whole boulevards on which to project fantasies and flush them out, all while considering them together—to call out and laugh at these fantasies and each other, correct them, argue over them, without fear they might scamper off or disappear, knowing they are both as real and as pliable as the earth we will sit on and scramble over. And I suppose this too is a speculation.

In these pages, I haven't offered proof for it, only gestured toward its necessity in the chasms that caught me when I ventured the tiniest of returns. I have tried to log and project the fantasies and the pleasures and the alienations of my own return as an invitation to others to do the same. To convene in a place called return, and linger.

Notes

1. Nayrouz Abou Hatoum, "Decolonizing [in the] Future: Scenes of Palestinian Temporality," *Geografiska Annaler: Series B, Human Geography* 103, no. 4 (August 2021): 3.
2. For more on Yafo Creative, see: AirBnB listing https://www.airbnb.co.uk/rooms/1829019?source_impression_id=p3_1655566839_EJthtxmJwmUrGsYT; Facebook page https://www.facebook.com/yafocreative/photos/?ref=page_internal; Production site https://www.yc-roomservice.com/roomservice; Website http://www.yafocreative.com/; all accessed June 26, 2022.
3. Rebecca Stein, *Itineraries in Conflict: Israelis, Palestinians, and the Political Lives of Tourism* (Durham, NC: Duke University Press, 2008), 3.
4. Taj Farouki and Cheryl Nathan, *My Life Story*, https://thelibrary.org/lochist/els/farouki.pdf; Palestine Remembered, "Wadi Hunayn," https://www.palestineremembered.com/al-Ramla/Wadi-Hunayn/index.html, account here referenced 2014, link accessed June 29, 2022.
5. Lena Jayyussi, "The Time of Small Returns: Affect and Resistance during the Nakba," in *An Oral History of the Palestinian Nakba*, ed. Nahla Abdo and Nur Masalha (London: Zed Books, 2018), 91.
6. Abou Hatoum, "Decolonizing," 5.
7. Ibid.

2

Imagining Return: Countless Palestinian Futures

Danah Abdulla and Sarona Abuaker

Imagining Return

How is return imagined, and in what ways is return conceptualized in a landscape dominated by the materiality of territory, home, and nationhood? We see return practiced in a multiplicity of ways: the Great March of Return, the Intifadas, the images and videos showing Palestinians running toward Palestine from Jordan and Lebanon chanting, "We will return" cutting through barbed-wire fences that make a border. We see it reflected in literature in a linear singular conceptualization through Ghada Karmi's *Return*,[1] Salman Abu Sitta's *Mapping my Return*,[2] while stories such as "Returning to Haifa" by Ghassan Kanafani pose the point:

> I always imagined that the Mandelbaum Gate would be opened some day, but I never imagined, never imagined that it would be opened from that other side [...] maybe I'd be crazy if I told you that door should always open from one side only, and that if they opened from the other side they must still be considered closed.[3]

We are moved to expand collectively the conversation surrounding return. Return is often seen only as "we go back" and the conversation stops. But what happens afterward? What would return look like? Is going back to Palestine a return if we are re-subjugating ourselves and perpetuating the oppressive systematic practices (such as racial capitalism) that we experience in exile? Return should not be about reproducing debt, racism, neoliberalism, and patriarchy under a different flag. These modes of domination already exist and are part and parcel of systematic practices—they will not cease to exist when Palestinians return to live in that space. These are modes of domination we need to destabilize.

How can we talk about Palestine without involving ourselves in heated arguments, or having to go to a lecture or read a dense book or to be an expert? How can Palestine become a quotidian conversation? What if we took Palestine out of exclusive spaces and enabled people to talk about ideas in a safe space? Grappling with, thinking through, and reckoning with the different ways of returning is an invitation to explore what Arturo Escobar describes as "the politics of the possible ... our notions of what is real and what is possible determine both our political practice, from the personal to the collective, and our sense of hope ... what he calls 'sentipensar' (what is possible)."[4] Conversations around Palestine are often framed either in historical or present terms. But what and where are the tools that help us think through what a return to Palestine could be?

This case looks at the process of developing and playing *Countless Palestinian Futures* (CPF), a discussion-based game we developed that attempts to answer this question. The aim of CPF is to stimulate the imagination by helping people develop tangible outcomes and ideas around Palestinian futures—to empower players to not limit themselves by the political imagination of others. We wanted to develop a tool that did not frame Palestinians as victims but rather as people who take ownership over their own narratives. This does not mean to replicate the past—return is often seen as a backward motion, a going back to something/someplace—but to create discussions that materially look forward—world(s)-building—not imaginary worlds but situations in our own world. Our goal is educational and to elicit debate.

In this case, we discuss the process of creating CPF, featuring photographic documentation, reflections, and analysis of the process and the pilot event in October 2021 at the Mosaic Rooms in London, where Palestinian and Arab cultural producers, policy makers, activists, and academics were invited to participate. We discuss the multiple understandings and ideas brought forward by participants through the questions that were played and the feedback they shared which challenged them to orient their ideas toward the future and emphasizing the role of imagination, demonstrating the necessity of unpacking what return would materially look like. In other words, what and who are we—as Palestinians—after the struggle?

Gamification and Iteration

While thinking through what a tool could be, we realized how the questions we posed ourselves drew us to gamification. Gamification is a strategy used in education and training to help make learning more motivating and engaging. The process can help a person retain knowledge and promote problem-based learning. Games are often open-ended rather than fixed; they have the possibility of creating connections, and are an easy way to start a conversation, particularly around Palestine. The game is centered on imagination: using imagination as a tool to build ideas of liberation, to cultivate alliances and material developments between the very people who are systematically denied their return. CPF humbly offers possible ways of orienting liberation not as a given practice or discourse but as something that should be explored beyond the limits presented in resolutions set out by hegemonic global governance institutions such as the United Nations.

The title was influenced by Umberto Eco's idea of the open work, because it can be read in an infinite number of ways depending on what the user brings, enabling more audience/user participation into the process.[5] Therefore, we do not see this game as a fixed entity but as something open to interpretation and iteration, and why the name itself emphasizes futures rather than a singular future—to demonstrate a space not of singular solutions but of multiple possibilities. For example, it can be Countless Afghan Futures or Countless Lebanese Futures or Countless Arab Futures.

In developing the questions, we first established six broad themes: culture and media, economy, governance and policy, infrastructure, geography, and people and society. We then contacted prominent Palestinians working in these areas to contribute questions and developed our own. Questions are framed around near

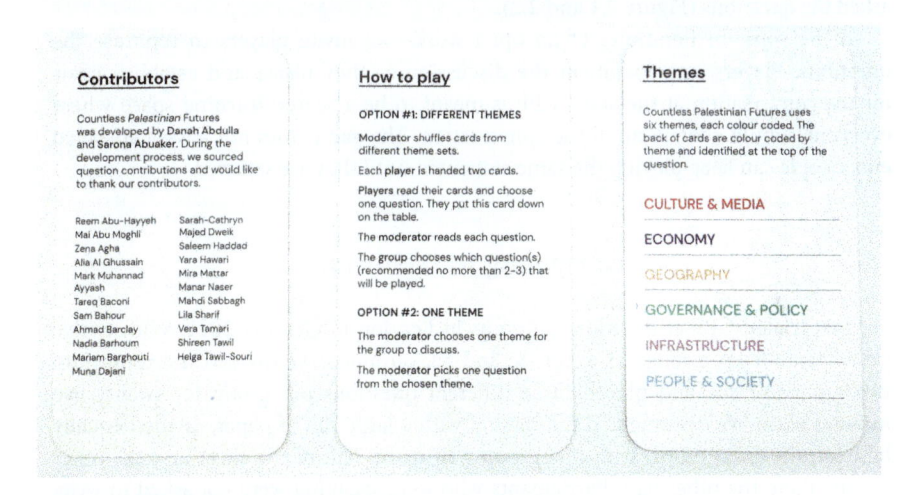

Figure 2.1 Countless Palestinian Futures game. Image by Danah Abdulla.

Figure 2.2 Countless Palestinian Futures game. Image by Danah Abdulla.

medium- and long-term futures that spark conversations, and challenges players to consider Palestinian futures. The game features over sixty different questions and is designed to be played in different formats with three to six players or as a conversation prompt between two people. Players can choose questions drawing on either different themes or within one theme. One player acts as a moderator, whose responsibility it is to decide how different voices/perspectives are to be heard, while other players are asked the questions (Figure 2.1 and 2.2).

In the spirit of iteration—of an open work—we invite players to rephrase the questions. Players can document the discussion as they please and establish goals for the conversation at the start. CPF is meant to be a shared learning space where everyone should contribute to the conversation. The game does not have a specified end: people can keep playing the same statement until they are satisfied.

Imagining with Others

We first trialed CPF at the Mosaic Rooms in London in October 2021. With twelve participants from a range of expertise and backgrounds, we divided the room into two groups of six, and played three different questions per group for twenty-five minutes each. We documented the session with a large roll of paper, divided equally between the two groups, with one group writing on half of the sheet and the other group taking the other half. Participants who were speaking were not asked to write their thoughts with the markers but those next to them had to document some key comments. In this section, we present the responses from participants in both groups to the questions played.

Would Liberation Include a Palestinian Ruling Class?

In addressing this question, participants debated between working with the ruling class, reforming the working class, redistribution of wealth and wealth being taken back. Themes that were touched on included abolition, forms of governance and participation, accountability, and gender. The discussion led to further questions, such as: How do we encounter and confront the ruling class if we are concerned with democracy and democratic practices? What do we do with the people who do not want to change? Who governs the government? Who is held accountable? Participants referred to current political parties such as Hamas and the Palestinian Authority. For example, one participant wrote: "If Hamas were to [form a] government, would Palestinians want to live under their regime?" In another instance, participants identified how much influence the current Palestinian ruling class has on what happens on the ground.

What Radically Transformative Policies and Ideas Could Palestine Implement?

The questions introduced themes such as composting, policing, restorative justice, passports and borders, bureaucracy, the role of technology, resource distribution, surveillance, gender, and patriarchy. The themes led to ideas around each of these, including curfew for men (which was challenged by participants), and then evolved into a conversation around abolishing the patriarchy and notions of masculinity and femininity, with interesting points a future Palestine could develop including a society that does not center gender identity or the adult. From this conversation, there were ideas proposed, including nonbinary bathrooms, sex education, all genders and expression, an inclusive healthcare and therapy system for all, the abolition of marriage, and questioning what happens to the nuclear family.

The theme of policing and borders revolved around challenging the police, methods of restorative justice, which led to exploring passports, and the role of bureaucracy. Participants asked if Palestine would be borderless and what the distribution of land and resources to everyone could look like, or the introduction of farming plots for neighborhoods, and if Palestine would have a military. The conversation then moved toward the sustainable design of cities with ideas proposed such as bike-friendly cities, free public transportation, a frequent flyer levy, bullet trains, cities with no cars, and zero-waste policies. Other discussions arose around freedom of speech in the press, mandatory civil service, and free education.

What Strategies Could a Liberated Palestine Put in Place to Address the Climate Emergency?

The participants discussed ideas of decolonization and decarbonization, connecting themes like control of resources, reparations, migrants, and refugees. The logistics of taking in refugees was discussed, specifically questions around health, personhood, and rights, but also if Palestine would send ships to bring refugees, and what materials they would bring to greet them upon arrival. There was a balance between participants thinking of solutions from a logical and material level and others from a decarbonization level. How can we ensure migrants are allowed in and live sustainably, and will Palestine become uninhabitable?, participants asked. Helping the land was a recurring idea with questions being debated like: Do we endow the land with personhood rights and what are the policy implications of doing so? Do we provide all living things in Palestine with personhood and legal protection?

The participants agreed that a future Palestine would draw on ideas from decolonial studies and decarbonization, where Palestine can become a leader in climate policies and technology. They discussed Israel's planting of non-native species (which are harmful and destructive), desalination, the use of technology (renewable and solar energy), the destruction of colonizing architecture, weapons, and the removal of trash (such as the debris of the apartheid wall and settlements). Militarism, as one participant highlighted, is responsible for 70 percent of global emissions and is a root cause of the global climate emergency.

Future thinking, however, quickly returned to a present context where participants discussed the role of BDS (Boycott, Divest, Sanctions), specifically if BDS can become a frontrunner of action against climate change and be an effective campaign in calling for the boycott of companies and corporations culpable for the most emissions. The conversation returned to the future with the recurring debate around Palestine's role as a destination for climate refugees: What if Palestine became a route for climate refugees to access the Mediterranean? How can Palestine be an example for other countries—as a place to settle refugees making their way to Europe? This was followed by another participant asking if Palestine can become a plausible destination for people and provide them with access to a better life.

How Will Palestinian Society Remember and Commemorate Our Culture of Collective Resistance after Liberation?

This question induced participants to think through collectivity, the language(s) created to memorialize resistance, and how the historical role of resistance will function in everyday life "after liberation." The big concepts held within the question are unpacked as the first step by participants: highlighting the word "collective" and putting "individual" as a way of re-addressing the question, picking apart and attempting to identify what will society be liberated from—capitalism? The themes of discourse and discourse formation, with group members deliberating if there should be an "official narrative" to the role of resistance, were weaved continuously throughout the conversation while considering the structures of narrative-building such as education, materiality, and how return could build a story "to tell our histories to build a nation for all."

The question of space, and how space can be used to commemorate resistance, was prominent. Namely, the distinction between public and private spaces, and the ways in which they would hold space for remembering the resistance it took to return: Is it a commemoration to be held in both private and public spaces? Participants focused on materials and forms of remembering that are often absent and/or were

Figure 2.3 Countless Palestinian Futures game. Image by Danah Abdulla.

erased such as textbooks, memorials, and oral testimonies from older generations. Questions participants debated included: What do we teach in school that goes beyond the mainstream narrative? How do we get the older generation(s) to talk about the past? How do we include the diaspora as a relic of remembrance? Will there be a day dedicated to commemorating resistance? (Figure 2.3)

Not only were the materials of remembrance considered but participants unpacked the methodologies that will enable remembering to take place as participants navigated between thinking through non-extractive ways of remembering resistance and thinking through methods of commemorating resistance that would avoid replicating neoliberal state-building practices. In other words, the character, texture, and language of the space of a future return – and how what is remembered – will be agreed on collectively: Will a truth and reconciliation commission be institutionalized that collectively agrees on a discourse of resistance? Do we include the bad stories? What kind of language do we use to commemorate without perpetuating oppression? How do we avoid fetishizing resistance?

This was followed by questions that point to what happens to a society when it no longer has to resist and struggle: How and what do younger generations look forward to? In reclaiming history what sort of regime will exist after liberation? How do we show we have culture and destiny beyond the narrative of resistance? When we are no longer resisting, what will our identities be? How do we support the struggles that supported us?

How Would Palestine's Foreign Policy Enable and Advance the Freedom of Other Oppressed and Colonized Peoples?

Participants approached this question by exploring themes relating to governance, the functionality of foreign policy, the shape and form of sovereignty beyond the nation-state, and looking back at how foreign policy was historically created through Palestinian leadership.

Considering the future of foreign policy, participants first looked to the use of it: foreign policy as a form of making connections. Following this, the conversation moved toward the body from which foreign policy will be created and implemented and questioned potential ways of self-governing: Is it assumed that return will entail a state? If a state is not the agreed upon form of self-governing and exercising sovereignty, then how can foreign policy come out of grassroots organizing? What kind of movements form? What would making these connections look like without the nation-state?

Participants began thinking through how to build power within a nation without falling into the trap of a nation-state, and the civic actors that do not need formal institutions to implement foreign policy such as students. This thread of thinking brought into the conversation decentralized forms of making connections, namely how foreign policy in return should not entrench existing power models such as the Palestinian Authority. It also brought into account and cautionary thinking around forming connections with the IMF and World Bank, with participants noting self-governance should be sustainable and not rely on these institutions.

Establishing the necessity of sustainability implemented through foreign policy, participants moved toward thinking through how foreign policy as connection-making could help build that very sustainability and stability, such as methods to cultivating the land, environment and farming strategies, creating a trade system, economic resistance, looking at protection of minorities in a liberated Palestinians, cultivation and protection of indigenous rights, and climate policy to safeguard Global South.

Foreign policy was discussed and thought through as a generative form of making transnational links where nation-state governance has failed, and by moving away from the state as the producer and embodiment of foreign policy creation. Participants then reoriented foreign policy as coming out of Global South links—making references to the non-aligned movement and how the Palestine Liberation Organization (PLO) crafted its foreign policy through links developed with the non-aligned movement—and connecting ideologies from a different world. The group repurposes the role of civic society within this framework as creators and generators of these foreign policy connections, moving Palestinians as co-producers and building stability in their connections rather than foreign policy being a top-down consolidated approach. This led to a few ideas of student exchange groups from allies such as Ireland to Palestine and supporting Palestinians who choose to remain in the diaspora.

What Would Be Done with the Apartheid Wall?

Participants addressed this question very directly at first by noting down "demolition party." There was a playful aspect presented with suggestions to transform it into a maze, which weaved into more practical solutions around land ownership, who has a right to say what to do with the wall, public spaces, and transforming its uses toward care or tourism (e.g., rehabilitation or community centers, museum, public art). Participants moved between building structures and institutions that would stand as testimony to the Apartheid Wall's history and what it accomplished and wanting to completely upheave the structure to create something that is new without forgetting the struggle. Suggestions included engraving names and stories, audio archives of crossing checkpoints, and creating a statue of liberty.

Once the moderator discovered that the responses were direct, participants were invited to think about the usage of material itself. This then developed into further ideas of what can be done with the material: using concrete to build education centers (such as a center for dismantling borders worldwide), building houses and community and art centers, theaters, or street furniture (which led to a discussion on the gendered nature of public spaces in Palestine), rebuilding homes for displaced Palestinians and those Palestinians who were originally from destroyed villages—where participants acknowledged the unintended consequences of mass housing—re-affirming roots (e.g., planting an olive tree grove orchard), and donating material to other countries. The conclusion of the session centered on the necessity of reimagining the apartheid wall without forgetting or denying the struggle that came before.

The responses had a series of recurring themes and ideas, but most noticeably, they demonstrated tensions and hesitation with participants imagining other possible worlds. Many responses were grounded in present-day realities, and only when prompted did discussions move toward more radical forward-thinking propositions. For example, when discussing the question *would liberation include a Palestinian ruling class*, participants referred to the Palestinian Authority and Hamas, which signaled an inability to think of future political parties/alternative governance that could come into existence, where the thinking in addressing this question was grounded in the present. This was a big tension throughout the second group's responses and discussion during the session.

Similarly, in responding to *what radically transformative policies and ideas could Palestine implement*, participants debated the present role of the BDS movement, and when they moved to debate the role of Palestine in hosting climate refugees, they imagined Palestine as a route toward settling in Europe, where Europe was viewed as the space for a better way of life. Finally, in addressing *how would Palestine's foreign policy enable and advance the freedom of other oppressed and colonized peoples*, the responses demonstrated clear gaps in engaging the imagination. What is interesting is there is no mention of leadership, but instead they stressed the indigenous connection made through grassroots organizing and solidarity. It looked back historically at what had been done but what is absent is envisioning forward. The questions themselves produce more questions, and multiple relationships between the questions, which is a feature by design. This exercise shows that one of the goals of our game is to generate alternative questions that help drive and develop actions and different ways of thinking. As one participant put it, "It only just hit me how invigorating it was to imagine the complex and mundane aftermath of a liberated Palestine with other Palestinians."

Toward Imagined Return(s)

Palestine-Israel is often referred to as "complicated," or a wicked problem (problems with many interdependent factors making them seem impossible to solve). We believe that what solutions to Palestine lack is imagination. What we—as Palestinians—have is an inability to imagine beyond what is in front of us, beyond the damaging ideas and decisions set out by state governance institutions. Instead, we legitimize these institutions. Israel's constant settlement building and ethnic cleansing is not only destructive to Palestine's physical appearance but a politicide that fixes the Palestinian imagination. How can Palestinians utilize the ultimate human resource—imagination—to get what they want, to see real change, and take it back into their own hands?

Instead of using the power of imagination to confront situations in our own world and frame them in reality—real possibilities, real imagined futures—we tackle imaginary worlds. But even science fiction, as Fredric Jameson states, becomes a testament to our incapacity to imagine the future and to the limits placed on our political imagination.[6] One only needs to look at the metaverse to understand how empty or innovative these images of the future are.

Projects such as Udna by Baladna (whose aim is to educate the youth about the Nakba and use 3D modeling to create actual models for return) and BADIL's "Putting the Right of Return into Practice" are important for visualizing return.[7] However, they remain within specific concepts of return—returning to something that was once, in a modern form, rather than what could be.

The effect of global governance organizations and the concept of international law in particular have shaped the Palestinian imaginary; it has hijacked the Palestinian imagination to think only within these strict definitions and ideas. In reflecting on action,[8] trialing CPF illustrated how little people discussed practical questions about return, and seeing them on a card where the goal was not to produce a resolution but working through the question was a rare occurrence because Palestine is often confined to certain contexts and reserved for experts. Moreover, it demonstrated the power in presenting return differently—as something that you can create with other people—not as a solution to a problem but a realm of possibilities—possibilities that could materialize in the future. The concept of CPF is not to force people to be imaginative; rather it is an invitation to think about Palestine differently and in a way that considers return seriously. What happens beyond the statement of "Palestine will be free"? How will Palestine be free? We start to reckon with return as world-building through these questions, which then hopefully encourage us to learn more about things we did not know, incorporate new things into our works, and to possibly build networks that may then enact change. We hope CPF is a minor gesture in starting to think beyond what we already know, and to imagine changes that develop our thinking around return and the multiplicity of everyday life.[9]

The strengths of CPF are its open-endedness: it is different from the usual forms of engagement—not an awareness campaign, nor about collecting signatures, or attending a protest and posting on social media. It invites people to approach Palestine in a new way by bringing them together in dialogue and exchange. The groups themselves represent little microcosms of society—in the sense of seeing how people's professional and life experience informs how they approach the questions differently. Another strength is how the questions present a lot of nuance and connections, leading to further questions that start to stimulate people's imaginations and how they begin to draw off others. But CPF is also challenging because it is not designed to be outcome based. Our idea around the duration, or outcome or continuity of the game, is that the CPF session will end, but with this there is some sort of ongoing conversation. In many ways that solidifies the idea of imagination.

Why do we play games? What do we get out of them? What is produced? In a way, CPF is something to enjoy with friends by engaging in a good discussion. While some participants suggested providing a reward at the end of each iteration to entice people, we think the reward is in playing a game that opens your mind to new possibilities. And in many ways, this goes back to that question: What does it look like to produce Palestine? As a place that is not only under erasure but also as people who are not there.

Notes

1   Ghadi Karmi, *Return: A Palestinian Memoir* (London: Verso, 2015).
2   Salman Abu Sitta, *Mapping My Return: A Palestinian Memoir* (Cairo: The American University in Cairo Press, 2017).

3   Ghassan Kanafani, *Palestine's Children: Returning to Haifa and Other Stories*, trans. Barbara Harlow and Karen E. Riley (London: Lynne Rienner Publishers, 2000), 150.
4   Arturo Escobar, *Designs for the Pluriverse: Radical Interdependence, Autonomy, and the Making of Worlds* (Durham, NC: Duke University Press, 2018), 2.
5   Umberto Eco, *The Open Work* (Cambridge, MA: Harvard University Press, 1989).
6   F. Jameson, "Progress versus Utopia; Or, Can We Imagine the Future? (Progrès contre Utopie, ou: Pouvons-nous imaginer l'avenir)," *Science Fiction Studies* 9, no. 2 (1982): 147–58.
7   BADIL, "Papers of Palestinian Youth Conference Right of Return: Towards a Practical Approach," in Papers of Palestinian Youth Conference Right of Return: Towards a Practical Approach (Palestine: BADIL, 2019). https://www.badil.org/phocadownloadpap/badil-new/publications/research/in-focus/RoR-Conf-Papers-2019-en.pdf.
8   Donald Schön, *The Reflective Practitioner: How Professionals Think in Action* (London: Routledge, 2017).
9   Danah Abdulla and Pedro Vieira Di Oliviera, "The Case for Minor Gestures," *Diseña* 22 (2023).

3

Re-centering Palestine and Palestinians in Poster Art

Dina Matar

I began writing this piece during the intense escalation in violent Israeli armed interventions in Palestinians' daily lives in the Occupied West Bank and the Gaza Strip in May 2021 and revisited it again during the full-scale Israeli war against Gaza that started in October 2023, bringing even more destructive violence against the Palestinians. Throughout this "conjuncture" marked by artificial and imposed arrangements of interrupted space and the dislocation of disturbed time, the global and local media as well as digital spheres were animated with stories and images of life and death, despair and hope, along with creative and subversive images, videos, graffiti, emojis, music, and graphic and poster art that together, I suggest, constitute what Kraidy termed revolutionary creative labor[1] entailing the convergence of expression, production, and revolution intended to mobilize meaningfully around Palestine and what it means to be Palestinian, Palestinian identity.

Such contemporary, mostly digital, creative labor recalls an older agentive and productive "conjuncture"[2] in Palestinian history—the Palestinian revolutionary period of the 1960s and 1970s—that, too, saw Palestinians' public and private spaces animated with creative imagery of Palestine and Palestinians in media, film, art installations, music, and popular culture that responded to lived conditions and experiences and the traumas of dispossession, conflict, and suffering and to the spirit of popular resistance and revolution. In this intervention, I limit the discussion to poster art as an example of Palestinian revolutionary creative labor in two conjunctures: the Palestinian revolutionary period of the 1960s and 1970s and in the recent tumultuous mediated and overrepresented Palestinian present. While acknowledging that revolutionary creative labor in the older period quantitatively differs from that of the contemporary digital era, mainly because of the monumental expansion and accessibility of "new" technologies and digital platforms to diverse populations as well as the increasing militarization of violence against the Palestinians in the contemporary period, I contend that both conjunctures can be understood as liminal times of extreme political ferment and flux during which everything is up for grabs and in which local and global imaginations of Palestine and Palestinians are productive in terms of the possibilities they offer for Palestinians, as colonized and oppressed subjects, to imagine their futures and themselves.

My focus on these two conjunctures does not assume that other tumultuous periods in Palestinian history—such as the first and second *intifadas* (1987 and 2000), the post-Oslo phase and Israel's regular violent incursions in the Occupied Palestinian Territories and Gaza, among numerous others—are not worthy of attention; nor do I suggest that Palestinians' creative revolutionary labor and intervention in popular culture are episodic and only responsive to tumultuous historical "event times," such as the two periods mentioned above. On the contrary, Palestinian revolutionary creative labor must be understood as a continuous temporality of practice that intervenes in personal and public lives to articulate Palestinians' changing lived experiences as "dynamic and articulated social presence(s) in the world"[3] through and in which structures of feeling shape cultural meanings and values that have been, and continue to be, "actively lived and felt."[4] Furthermore, Palestinian revolutionary creative labor, understood broadly as a field of social practices, a form of work, or negotiation between individuals and globally defined fields of possibility, is by necessity diverse and multi-sited, appearing in immaterial and material forms, such as public spaces, museums, film, art, music, graffiti, and in a variety of media and popular cultural genres. For the purpose here, I limit the discussion to poster art as the most ubiquitous, visible, translatable, trafficked, and shared product of Palestinian revolutionary creative labor and, as such, its possibilities for imaginations and emancipation.

The PLO's Revolutionary Creative Labor

Like many Palestinians growing up in the Middle East, I experienced Palestinian poster art, along with many other forms and genres of Palestinian cultural production, in my everyday life—I saw poster art on walls, lampposts, in newspapers, and in books—to the extent that I almost no longer saw it. Later on, I encountered Palestinian political poster art in my field research on the Palestine Liberation Organization's political communication strategies and media practices which ran hand in hand with its political activism during its heyday in the 1960s and 1970s.[5] It was during that period of local, regional, and global flux, which Susan Sontag described as entering a "period of renaissance"[6] against repression and colonial power, that the poster format became the medium par excellence for the global production of anti-colonial sentiments and for ordinary people to engage in political life.

There is no doubt, as several scholars have suggested, that the so-called long 1960s—a period of global anti-colonial ferment—enabled the convergence of expression, production, and revolution witnessed in the plethora of Palestinian cultural and artistic output, just as there is no doubt that this convergence was also the product of the global meeting of art and politics. In the Palestinian context, the period saw the emergence of what many now consider highlights of "classical" Palestinian art forms, such as Ghassan Kanafani's literature, Mahmoud Darwish's poems, and Suleiman Mansour's paintings, most of which reflected the nationalist and emancipatory aspirations of the Palestinian people despite their trauma of refugeehood, dispossession, and exile. At the same time, it was during this period that the PLO initiated a veritable revolution in Palestinian cultural production, particularly in the proliferation of print media, radio, music, art, film and poster art as the main cultural platforms for the dissemination of the ideologies and aims of the resistance movement, while also attracting Palestinian talent along with Arab and global actors. As I had argued elsewhere, as part of its overall political communication strategies, the PLO instrumentalized popular culture and popular iconography to mobilize a *Palestinian-centric revolutionary aesthetic* in language and image, mediate an agential visibility for the Palestinian people, and help transform the PLO into the most potent contemporary social and political movement in the Arab world and beyond.[7]

Print media at that time was the main PLO cultural platform for the dissemination of the Palestinian revolutionary aesthetic in different written and visual forms, including poster art, which would become the most important communicative popular genre in myriad local and transnational reproductions and representations of Palestine and the Palestinians. Newspapers, periodicals, and communiqués also provided spaces for the inscription of the Palestinian struggle within a global evocative map of revolutionary ferment in a collective battle against colonial and imperial forces.[8] But it was poster art, with its capacity to make meaning accessible and contestable, that became the most ubiquitous medium for Palestinian cultural activism, aided by the PLO's financial and manpower investment. For example, as soon as it was formed in 1964 as the representative of the Palestinian people and as part of its broader political communication strategy, the PLO appointed Palestinian graphic artist Ismail Shammout (1930–2006) in charge of production of experimental political and revolutionary poster art. Shammout, who came to be known as the artist of the Palestinian revolution, headed the Artistic Culture Section at the PLO's Department of Information and National Guidance and designed the first set of PLO posters, such as those in Figures 3.1 and 3.2. Shammout also created a logo for the PLO, with a Palestinian flag drawn above a map of Palestine (Figure 3.1). Shammout was one of several prominent artists, including Taman al-Akhal in Beirut, Suleiman Mansour in the West Bank, and Naji al-Ali in Beirut and Kuwait, who helped develop an organic Palestinian-centric visual vocabulary reflecting Palestinian identifications, struggles, and nationalist consciousness and combining symbols and icons of the resistance movement with more traditional imagery associated with Palestinian handicrafts, calligraphy, folklore, music, and poetry.

The new vocabulary and imagery were representative of a period of aesthetic creativity in what is often called Palestinian resistance art, supported by global actors and revolutionaries who contributed to creative acts of solidarity with Palestine within a multiverse constituted by numerous types of solidarity in a spectrum of participation, commitment, belonging, and identification to a constantly shifting global community of anti-colonial revolution. However, what differentiated Palestinian creative cultural production and labor from that of other global anti-colonial and liberation movements was the foregrounding of Palestinian poster art as a mode of a Palestinian-specific revolutionary struggle, which, as Zeina Maasri writes, served to alter the visuality of Arabic militant periodicals,[9] constituting an affective avenue for a visual episteme that drew on repressed memories and lived experiences of the Palestinians.

A large number of the PLO's poster artwork of the revolutionary period is accessible for viewing, downloading, and sharing at the Palestine Poster Project Archives[10]

Figure 3.1 All For the Resistance. Ismail Shammout. Accessed from "Liberation Graphics of the Palestinian Poster" (https://www.palestineposterproject.org/search/site/shammout).

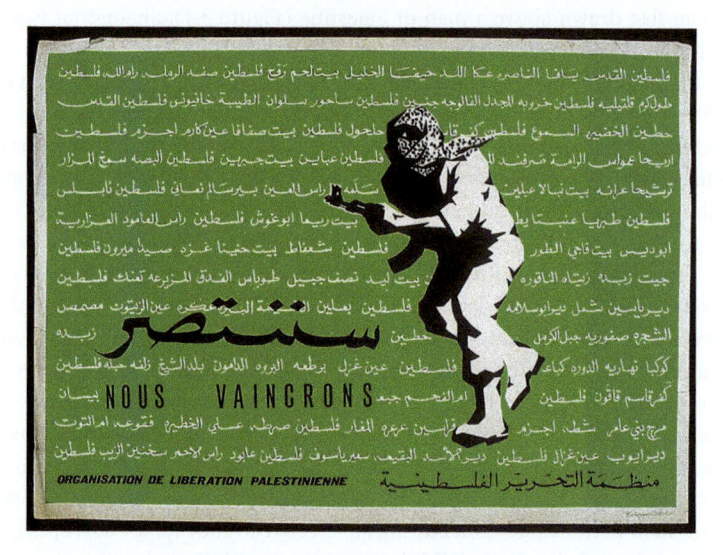

Figure 3.2 Nous Vaincrons (We Will Win), by Ismail Shammout. Accessed from "Liberation Graphics Collection of Palestine Poster" (https://www.palestineposterproject.org/poster/nous-vaincrons).

website, where it is grouped under an all-encompassing genre (thematic) titled the *Liberation Graphics Collection of Palestine Poster*. The site functions as a meta-archive bringing together poster art produced by the PLO, Palestinian artists, and ordinary people as well as other poster art related to Palestine, including Zionist posters and other posters produced by entities and actors denying Palestinians their rights. Founder Dan Walsh claims that the grouping provides a more complex and complete history of modern Palestine[11] and a rich canvas from which to consider the battle over popular iconography. Liberation graphics was submitted to UNESCO's Memory of the World program during its 2014–15 and 2016–17 rounds, but despite receiving unanimous support for inscription, the nomination was effectively vetoed twice by UNESCO's director-general who makes the final decision on submissions.

Icons of Revolution; Symbols of Palestine

The prolific poster art of the 1970s and early 1980s when the PLO had its base in Lebanon offers a visual and productive optic and language for addressing Palestinian revolutionary creative labor as a significant temporality of practice through which a radical imagination of Palestine and what it means to be Palestinian (Palestinian-ness) was continuously produced, distributed, shared, and appropriated. Palestinians' radical imagination of Palestine and themselves took many forms and styles but acquired a specifically agential and emancipatory anti-colonial significance after the battle of Karameh in 1968, a turning point in the Palestinian revolutionary history. Since that battle, Palestinian poster art depicted Palestinian refugees, men, and women not only as victims, dispossessed people, and refugees but also as anti-colonial freedom fighters rising together from the squalor of refugee tents and exile. Along with other genres of popular culture, the poster art depicting Palestinians as agents in charge of their lives and futures serves to underline the important dynamics between aesthetics and politics particularly in uncertain times, as well as art's capacity, as Jacques Ranciere had argued, to disrupt the senses, by dislodging the commonsensical and the normal and by performing the political in new radical ways.[12]

Poster art's potential to perform and imagine the "Palestinian" political in new and radical ways is particularly visible in the countless images, renderings, and poster art of what has become the quintessential revolutionary Palestinian icon, the "freedom fighter" (the *fedayee*), a Palestinian man/woman often depicted with gun in hand and in active mode, confirming the transformation of the Palestinian subject into an active agent and the construction of a productive and agentive Palestinian identity that ruptured older and traditional nationalist representations of what it means to be Palestinian.[13] Images and poster art of the *fedayee* along with other representations of Palestinians, men and women, rising together in armed struggle against Israel, circulated on leaflets in the camps and in newspapers were plastered on walls and buildings, at the same time as *fedayee* military operations were celebrated as the defining moments in Palestinian sociopolitical history. By most accounts, the *fedayee* icon signified the birth of the Palestinian revolution and helped a radical transformation in the Palestinian refugee camps and the diaspora, while also finding resonance in the global community because of the revolution's ability to lay claim to global concepts of human rights and national sovereignty. In fact, the prolific poster art of the Palestinian *fedayee* circulated in newsletters and publications of many anti-capitalist, and national liberation movements, student groups, and unions globally.

Palestinian poster art of the revolutionary period, like much poster art, was experimental, spontaneous, and crude at times, but spoke to Palestinians' chaotic lived experiences while reflecting the complexity and diversity as well as the constant uncertainty of Palestinian lives during a period of extreme flux and possibilities. Poster art of that period was also generative and agentive, and, as such, managed to retain its popular and productive status as the most recognizable, translated, communicated, copied, commodified, and politically empowering Palestinian poster art even after the demise of the PLO following its expulsion from Lebanon in 1982 and its transformation into a quasi-state with official institutions after the 1993 Oslo agreement. Indeed, dominant iconography of the revolutionary period, including the icon of the *fedayee*, as well as other symbols associated with the Palestinian landscape—olive groves and orange orchards—and icons from material culture, such as the key and the *kufiyyeh*, continue to be reproduced, reappropriated, and adapted to new contexts. During different historical junctures in Palestinian history—such as the first and second *intifadas* (1987 and 2000, respectively), Israel's repeated military and violent attacks against Gaza and the Occupied Territories, the 2021 Israeli attacks in East Jerusalem, and, more recently, Israel's war against Gaza—new icons embodying Palestinian lives, aspirations, and losses began to emerge. One example is the mediated and re-communicated iconic image of twelve-year-old Mohamed al-Durra as he cowered in his father's arms during the second Palestinian intifada of 2000 and the mediated image of Palestinian-American journalist Shirin abu Akleh, who was killed by Israeli soldiers in June 2022. However, the revolutionary and productive imaginations of Palestine and the Palestinians that the icon of the fedayee produced have continued to inform every phase of the Palestinian history and struggle for rights.

Palestinian Poster Art in the Digital Age—Emergence of New Icons

Like poster art of the revolutionary period, contemporary Palestinian poster art is organic, indigenous, dissenting, speculative, as well as purposeful, enterprising, and progressive, underlining its role as a site for knowledge production as well as a space for memory production, documentation, and subversion. Like its predecessor in the revolutionary period, poster art in the contemporary period draws on contemporary Palestinian lives, his-stories, and experiences to produce diverse creative imaginations of Palestine and the Palestinians through the production of new symbols, icons, and figures that resonate with ordinary people's lived experiences and lives while also borrowing the global language and symbols of contemporary anti-colonial global movements, such as Black Lives Matter. Some of the contemporary poster art has also creatively recycled and reappropriated the meanings and significations proposed in the poster art of the revolutionary period, particularly the commitment to liberation of Palestinians. These reappropriations are particularly evident in the poster art of the Palestinian Youth Movement, a transnational movement whose purpose, as stated on its website and its work, is inscribed within anti-colonial mobilization and which is committed to mobilizing the Palestinian diaspora around Palestine and the liberation struggle (https://palestinianyouthmovement.com/).

Most of contemporary Palestinian poster art is born digitally and produced by a variety of actors, including ordinary people, and has become the most visual and prolific cultural genre of creative revolutionary labor intended to mobilize meaningfully around the idea of Palestine and what it means to be Palestinian through the production of new symbols and icons. One of the most prominent and affective new symbols that has provoked subversive and powerful imaginations of Palestine and what it means to be Palestinian since May 2021 is that of the lowly watermelon which, unlike other fruit, such as oranges, the prickly pear, and citrus fruit, had not been prominent in popular Palestinian nationalist iconography nor had featured in much of the PLO political poster art. Public lore has it that the watermelon was used as a symbol of Palestinian resistance following the 1967 Israeli occupation of the West Bank and Gaza Strip and Israel's prohibition of the public display of the Palestinian flag or its colors. In response, Palestinians would carry watermelons in defiance of military orders and as a sign of resistance, with the story becoming a popular myth talked about in gatherings and circulating in social media platforms, with its true origins buried in various retellings and reposts.

Some well-known Palestinian artists have, too, instrumentalized the watermelon as a symbol of Palestinian peoplehood and as a tool subverting traditional national symbols, including the Palestinian flag. Indeed, the urge to "dissent from (subvert) the flag" and go beyond the forms and content of classical nationalist resistance art marks, among many others, the artwork of Palestinian artist Khaled Hourani's silkscreen series (2013), titled "The Story of the Watermelon" and that powerfully subverts Palestinianism (Palestinian nationalism) through subverting the Palestinian flag and imagination of Palestinian futures. The series appeared in *The Subjective Atlas of Palestine*,[14] a project by Dutch designer Annelys de Vet that showcases creative designs of the Palestinian flag by Palestinian artists and designers. Hourani later isolated one silkscreen and titled it "The Colours of the Palestinian Flag" (2013) a variation on the Palestinian flag.

Since May 2021, when clashes broke out in East Jerusalem following Israel's forced eviction of Palestinians from their homes in the Sheikh Jarrah, the watermelon has emerged as an unlikely, meaningful, and popular Palestinian icon etched, produced, and imagined by a variety of artists, cultural producers, and ordinary people, and trafficked through the internet and social media, such as Instagram posts, TikTok videos, websites, emojis, YouTube clips. Creative and meaningful renderings of the watermelon have also appeared in public spaces, on placards carried by pro-Palestinian activists against Israel's attacks in Gaza in 2021, and in 2023, painted on bodies and produced in material culture, such as in T-shirts, cups, and other memorabilia. These emotive, affective, funny and meaningful renderings, I suggest, evoke and invoke creative imaginations of Palestine and Palestinians that differ from older imaginations, and also underline poster art's potential as an affective space of creative *visual thinking* that, as Jonathan Fineberg writes, can bypass the conscious control of language in articulating experience and to tap directly into the language of primary processes—the uncensored cauldron of repressed memory, body experience, and metonymic logic.[15]

For this piece, a search for the word "watermelon" from the Palestinian poster archive brought up a page with thirty-eight posters of, or related to, the watermelon (https://www.palestineposterproject.org/search?search_api_fulltext=watermelon). The works displayed on the page are those of different cultural producers, including Zionists, from different periods of Palestinian history, some of which predate the 1948 Nakba. Among these posters are early Zionist poster artworks of the watermelon co-designed by Otte Wallish, a Czech of Jewish descent known for his scroll of Israel's Declaration of Independence. Wallish worked with the Jewish National Fund, the agency that consistently intervened in private and public domains with its posters using explicit Zionist rhetoric, and with United Israel Appeal, another pro-Zionist organization. On the same page, what might be described as subversive posters of the watermelon recall the famous "Visit Palestine" poster designed by the Austrian Jewish immigrant Franz Krausz in the 1930s to attract tourists to Israel as part of several other graphic designs for Zionist organizations already functioning in Palestine.

Some of the more recent creative imaginations of the watermelon produced by a variety of creators since May 2021 are also displayed on the page, producing agentive anti-colonial imaginations of Palestine and what it means to be Palestinian that subvert older nationalist signs and symbols while also imagining a future of a Palestine free from colonial control. These imaginations of liberation come across most strikingly in the "Palestine Uprising Hues" series of poster art of the watermelon by Sama Gheith published in 2023 and seen in Figures 3.3 and 3.4 that interestingly use a vocabulary of liberation and return (*we will return, and her total liberation has begun*) reminiscent in terms of its agentive potential of the language used during the revolutionary period and seen in Figure 3.2 (*we will win*).

As an icon, the watermelon, like any other icons, is not produced in vacuum nor did it emerge overnight—it is the product of creative revolutionary labor as active imagination understood as an organized field of social practices, or a form of work and negotiation between sites of agency, including individuals and globally defined fields of possibility. The watermelon icon is unstable and fluid, subject to contestations and re-colonization. As an icon, it might not immediately conjure an image of Palestinian resistance as much as the older icon of the fedayee did, but like its revolutionary predecessor, its emancipatory and epistemic potential comes from its potential for meaningful grassroots mobilization around Palestine and what it means to be Palestinian in an age of continued and persistent settler colonialism. Like the icon of the fedayee, the watermelon icon has become the most recognizable symbol of meaningful global Palestinian mobilization against colonialism and oppression, politically intervening in the space and conditions of visibility and the restricted spatial temporalities and practices within which it emerges as an image. Space, as Henri Lefebvre has suggested, embodies the tension between visibility and invisibility; bounded and unbounded imagination; community and identity, and between conceived, perceived, and lived spaces.[16]

Re-centering Palestine and Palestinians in Poster Art 47

Figure 3.3 Palestine Uprising Hues: We Will Return, 2023, Sama Geith, Courtesy of the artist.

Figure 3.4 Palestine Uprising Hues, Her Total Liberation Has Begun, 2023. Sama Geith, Courtesy of the artist.

Concluding Thoughts

I conclude by thinking through WJT Mitchell's idea of landscape-as-ideology and the notion that insofar as the "landscape way of seeing" is ideological and, therefore naturalizes meaning, meaning is still deconstructed and revealed through contestation.[17] Poster art as fluid, malleable, adaptable, and unstable is perhaps the accessible popular cultural material and symbolic space for deconstructing old meanings and for producing new meanings, for subversion and resistance, and for providing the medium for the making new national icons of mundane material objects, such as the watermelon.

Ultimately, however, as this intervention has shown, poster art functions as a necessarily *political space of appearance* that helps re-center Palestine and Palestinians in the imagination not as a bounded predetermined national entity but as a productive and generative landscape and people. As Helga Tawil-Souri has argued in relation to the 2011 Arab uprisings,

> No matter their eventual political outcomes, what the uprisings confirmed—both on streets and on screens—is that places, and presence and action in places continue to matter .... where, when, and for how long people gather, what they choose to do in their immediate and shared presence in a specific location is a fundamental requirement for political change.[18]

Palestinian poster art, this case has shown, can be discussed as a politically productive genre for producing and imagining Palestine in different forms, and for framing and reframing the conditions of visibility within which politics is subverted. While the relationship between politics and visibility/invisibility and between power and resistance is complex, addressing Palestinian poster art in critical conjunctures allows us to consider how these conjunctures provide the conditions and possibilities for creative labor and meaningful mobilization and imaginations of subjectivities and futures. Importantly, examining Palestinian poster art in moments of extreme flux and tension can help us address its potential for solidarity building across spatial enclosures and borders and consider how Palestinians engage with anti-colonial politics of liberation that allows them to reconfigure place, space, and knowledge and violence against them. Finally, borrowing from Hannah Arendt's conceptualization of power,[19] this case suggests poster art re-centers Palestinians as creative laborers and agents confronting their consignment to conditions of non-appearance and invisibility. It also re-centers a Palestine imagined beyond utopian pasts that have prescribed Palestinian identity as singular and fixed, while confirming that anti-colonial liberation struggles are about the narratives people attach to place and landscape imagined and reimagined in pasts, presents, and futures while also contenting with possible and impossible horizons.

Notes

1. M. Kraidy, "Revolutionary Creative Labour," in *Precarious Creativity: Global Media, Local Labour*, ed. M. Curtin and K. Sanson (Berkeley, CA: University of California Press, 2016), 231–40.
2. Stuart Hall used the term "conjuncture" to denote different elements in a sociopolitical situation during crisis moments which he applied in his seminal work on Thatcher's Britain. In this intervention, I use the term "conjuncture" as a time/space orientation to anchor my argument about the potential of Palestinian cultural production in mediating a new visibility for the Palestinian people and in redefining their imagination of themselves while locating this imagination in lived experiences of displacement and struggle against injustice.
3. Raymond Williams, *Marxism and Literature* (Oxford: Oxford University Press, 1977), 37–8.
4. Williams, *Marxism and Literature*, 132.
5. For a detailed account of Arab artistic practices in that period, read Zeina Maasri's *Cosmopolitan Radicalism* (2020).
6. S. Sontag, "Posters: Advertisement. Art, Political Artefact, Commodity," in *The Art of Revolution: 96 Posters from Cuba*, ed. D. Stermer (London: Pall Mall Press, 1970), vii–xxiii.
7. D. Matar, "PLO Cultural Activism: Mediating Liberation Aesthetics in Revolutionary Contexts," *Comparative Studies of South Asia, Africa and the Middle East* 38, no. 2 (2018): 354–64.
8. P. Chamberlin, *The Global Offensive: The United States, the Palestine Liberation Organization and the Making of the Post-Cold War Order* (Oxford: Oxford University Press, 2012).
9. Z. Maasri, *Cosmopolitan Radicalism: The Visual Politics of Beirut's Global Sixties* (Cambridge: Cambridge University Press, 2020).
10. https://www.palestineposterproject.org/
11. Walsh, D. (2011). *The Palestine Poster Project Archives: Origins, Evolution and Potential*, 16.
12. Rancière, *Dissensus: On Politics and Aesthetics*, 2010: 152.
13. https://www.palestineposterproject.org/search/site/shammout
14. de Vet. (2007). Subjective Atlas of Palestine.
15. Jonathan Fineberg, *Modern Art at the Border*, 73–6.
16. Lefebvre, H. (1991). The Production of Space, 38.
17. William J. T. Mitchel, "Holy Landscape: Israel, Palestine, and the American Wilderness," *Critical Inquiry* 26, no. 2 (2000): xiv.
18. Tawil-Souri, H. (2012). "It's still about the power of place," *Middle East Journal of Culture and Communication*, 2012: 95.
19. See Hannah Arendt, 1963 (reprint 1990). *On Revolution*, and Hannah Arendt, 1968, (ed.) "What Is Freedom?," in Between Past and Future: Eight Exercises in Political Thought and and Hannah Arendt, *The Origins of Totalitarianism* (New York, NY: Harcourt Brace Jovanovich, 1973).

4

Becoming *Al-Mulatham/a*: *Fedayee* Art, Abu Oubaida, and Palestinian TikTok

Nayrouz Abu Hatoum and Hadeel Assali

Introduction

Abu Oubaida is the masked spokesperson of the 'Ezzedeen Al-Qassam Brigades (or Qassam Brigades or Qassam for short), the military wing of Hamas. In response to their censorship on Twitter, Qassam created their own parallel Twitter-like feed on their official website. This feed features the "tweets" of Abu Oubaida from 2012 until today, in what is essentially an archive of their messages that counters Twitter censorship (see Figure 4.1). Here are example translations of the earliest two "tweets" from December of 2012:

> *2012-12-24:* We do not own modern, precise and accurate weapons that enable us to strike military targets with precision. #QassamBrigades #Hamas #Resistance

> *2012-12-26:* #QassamBrigades works for the sake of the mighty goal that has been agreed by the laws of the sky and the laws of humanity, and this goal is liberation of #thehuman #theland #theholysites.

The appearances and statements of Abu Oubaida operate through a carefully curated media strategy. This is a part of the larger Hamas media operation in the face of increasing Israeli containment through the siege on the Gaza Strip, which includes surveillance of all communication infrastructures. Qassam's media strategies are not necessarily one and the same, for although the Qassam Brigades is a wing of Hamas, it has its own website and spokespersons. Much of the Qassam Brigades' official discourse centers on resistance, and more recently, on the practice of unity in resistance. While there is a certain "official" curation by Hamas and the Qassam Brigades, the image of Abu Oubaida, the masked figure, gets picked up and appropriated through social media in other forms of popular curation that blend image and sound. In part this draws on the long history of "the masked figure"—*al-mulatham*—a nickname also given to Abu Oubaida.

Palestinian resistance has a history that precedes the emergence of Hamas, Qassam, The Palestinian Authority, and even the Palestinian Liberation Organization (or PLO).

Figure 4.1 Screenshot of Abu Oubaida's "Tweets" on the Qassam Brigades' website (https://alqassam.ps/arabic/twitter).

Part of that resistance has often entailed the practical and aesthetic act of wrapping the head with a *kufiyyeh*, which is the act of becoming *mulatham/a*.[1] The image of *mulatham/a* and the spirit it entails became part of the everyday for Palestinians—whether through wearing it for protests or armed resistance or through other everyday practices such as art-making and social media posts, often in subversive and satirical ways. Everyday acts of resistance bring a sense of collectivity and joy, and these acts proliferate in creative ways across Arabic-speaking networks on platforms like TikTok through humorous skits, memes, and songs celebrating the resistance. While both Hamas and Qassam carefully control and curate their resistance media, the figure of Abu Oubaida has been taken up much more broadly on social media platforms, revealing the popular, even if underground, identification with the figure of *al-mulatham/a*. Palestinian resistance has long mobilized opacity in different ways, such as Qassam's use of underground tunnels to evade Israeli surveillance.[2] In this chapter, however, we focus on how this opacity is mobilized creatively, playfully, and more popularly in the virtual world of TikTok in ways that subvert Israeli surveillance and algorithms.

In this case, we examine TikTok and other social media platforms as sites of archival practices. David Beer argues that the power of social media archive lies in its ability to build collective memory and create what Long et al. describe as an "affective archive".[3] Hashtags are the archival mechanism for classifying and indexing, which users create with future uses in mind.[4] Indeed, we consider TikTok as an archival form of documenting and presenting political expression and resistance. What makes TikTok more efficient is that the archival mechanisms of classifying rely on text as in hashtags, images, and most importantly sound, in the form of audio-memes. As such, we consider these modes of visual and audio engagements as a form of counter-archives to official media narratives.

Relatedly, when TikTok users employ hashtags to feed algorithms, they are engaging in the act of curation. We too, in this chapter, carefully chose material in order to place Abu Oubaida within a border historical trajectory of Palestinian resistance and the deployment of the figure of the *mulatham/a*. The root word for curation is "caring for," as Gayatri Gopinath reminds us. This connection requires us to rethink curation from a practice of selection, re-arrangement, and positioning to a practice of care-taking and an intimate and intersubjective way of dealing with the past. Caring for the past, as she continues, can take the form of attending to aesthetic practices through writing and through placing them in relations to one another.[5] We take Gopinath's conceptualization of curation to think about our chapter as carefully attending to the Palestinian practice of curating videos on TikTok. These videos offer new modes of thinking about liberation in the future and the radical potential of images and sound in generating different forms of resistance, which we identify as becoming *al-mulatham/a*. We also view these selected visuals as a form of curation that presents a rather unintelligible visual text for non-Arabic speakers. These visuals might otherwise be dismissed, but are actually fleeting moments of subversion that demonstrate how Palestinian TikTok, through sound, image, editorial, and curatorial practice, nurtures an affective space for imagining liberation. In the following, we briefly trace the aesthetic history of *al-mulatham/a* and its ubiquitous presence. We then explore Abu Oubaida's role in official media strategies, and we focus on how his image is taken up popularly and proliferates through the popular and viral nature of TikTok. We conclude with brief reflections on these acts as collective archival practices that reappropriate *al-mulatham/a* for everyday people.

Al-Mulatham/a: A Brief History

The notion of *al-mulatham/a*, the masked figure, picked up a renewed life in Palestinian social media after the appearance of Abu Oubaida. However, the masked figure has long been a popular image in Palestinian visual aesthetics, such as photography, film/video, and art. For example, historically, Palestinian Fedayeen (freedom fighters)[6] portrayed themselves as masked as can be seen in Figure 4.2. Images of the first intifada, the second intifada, and the marches of return in Gaza and beyond also capture Palestinians who are masked. When searching images of Palestinians throughout different demonstrations and confrontations with the Israeli army, the masked figure is often at the center of these visuals. This can help explain why the popularity of Abu Oubaida extends beyond Hamas supporters: *al-mulatham/a* is a popular figure that precedes the creation of Hamas (which was only created in the 1980s) and, as such, precedes Abu Oubaida. *Al-Mulatham/a* is a unifying figure that exceeds religious boundaries and political factions.

Importantly, the masked figure symbolizes the everydayness and readiness of the act of resistance. This has been taken up by Palestinian artists, such as in the works of

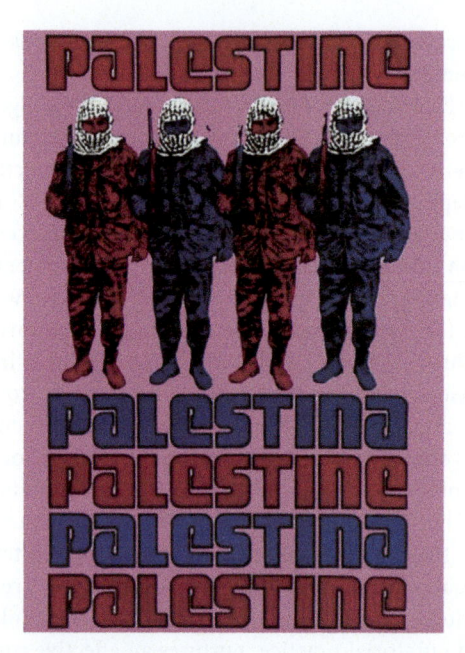

Figure 4.2 Poster from Cuba, 1975. YaHala Studio Archive (https://www.palestineposterproject.org/poster/palestine-palestina-0).

Monther Jawabreh ما كان يعرف *As Once Was Known* (2012) (Figure 4.3), which depict a series of painted masked figures carrying out ordinary actions, like sleeping, reading a book, playing cards, or dressing up in fancy outfits.[7] Jawabreh's series depicts the image of the masked figure in Palestinian aesthetics as a ubiquitous image, as if stating resistance has a presence in everyday life for many Palestinians. Through this work, the artist reinterprets the figure of *al-mulatham/a* allowing for playful ways to make a political statement. For example, some of his paintings feature *al-mulatham/a* in a business suit, which is on the one hand a critique of the neoliberalization of the Palestinian struggle post-Oslo but, on the other hand, signals to the inextricability of resistance, as if it were an inherent part of everyday life.

In another work, Leila Shawa, a Palestinian artist from Gaza who recently passed away in the UK, engaged with the image of Palestinian resistance through the figure of the *mulatham/a*. She titled this work *Fashionista Terrorista* (2012) and used mixed media in campy or kitschy aesthetics to criticize the flattening of Palestinian resistance symbols (see Figure 4.4). The *kuffiyeh* turns into a commodity emptied of meaning and mass-produced to be sold as scarfs in American or European markets.[8]

Importantly, the figure of *al-mulatham/a* outlived the commodification and the attempted neoliberal containment of its aesthetic. The *kuffiyeh* did not lose its historical significance nor its revolutionary potential. As we will see, while it was taken up politically by Qassam and other official resistance groups, it was again reappropriated for popular use in the collective curatorial archiving on social media *and* for other everyday practices of becoming *al-mulatham/a*.

Becoming Al-Mulatham/a 55

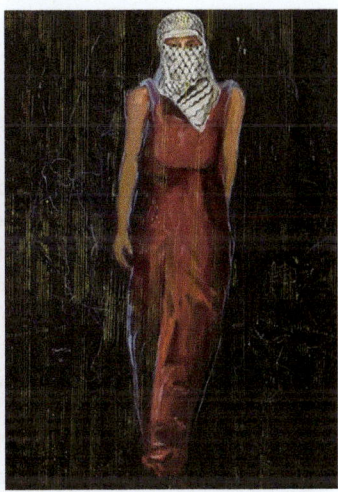

Figure 4.3 Monther Jawabreh. *As Once Was Known*. Acrylic on canvas, 2012. Courtesy of the artist.

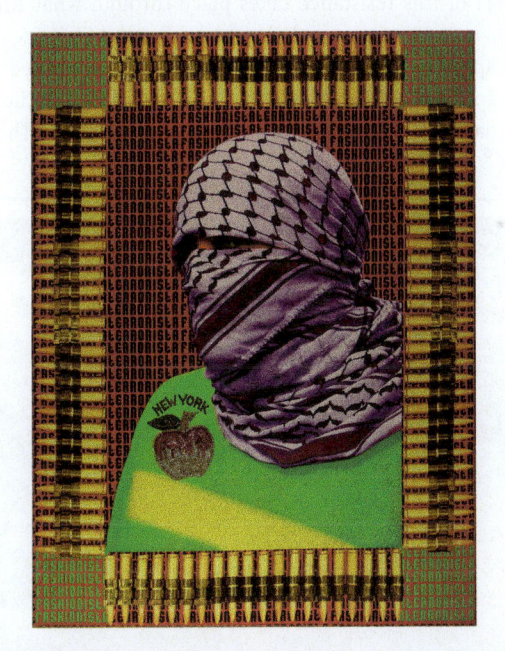

Figure 4.4 Laila Shawa. *Fashionista Terrorista II*, 2011. Courtesy of the artist and October Gallery, London.

Professionalizing *Al-Mulatham*: Abu Oubaida

Both Hamas and Qassam, the official leadership in Gaza, have demonstrated media proficiency through extensive video productions that are archived on their websites. Many of these videos have a professionalized look and are in collaboration with large media outlets such as *AlJazeera*, thus giving "official" legitimacy to different forms of resistance, including armed resistance.[9] Moreover, through close readings of Hamas official statements and interviews with various officials, Wael Abdelal argues that their media strategy has two main objectives.[10] The first is to mobilize, with varying target audiences in order of the following hierarchy: Hamas members, the Palestinian public; the Arab and Muslim public; followed by international opinion; and lastly, Israeli opinion. In other words, their primary audience is an Arabic-speaking one. The second objective is to counter the psychological warfare meted out by the state of Israel to establish a counter-media that also targets an Arabic-speaking audience.

This strategy recognizes and even formalizes the everydayness of Palestinian resistance through what the Hamas project calls the creation of a *mujtama'a muqawim* (resistance society). Hamas's notion of resistance is one that encompasses all aspects of life, both military and civilian matters—"social, religious, political, economic, and culture."[11] Part of this resistance takes place through what Abdelal describes as *al-ia'lam almuqawim* (resistance media), which Hamas recognizes as a fundamental and "decisive weapon."[12] The importance of media is mentioned multiple times in Hamas's charter, and from its inception, Hamas established a radio station, a satellite channel, and a daily newspaper as state-building practices. Their military wing,

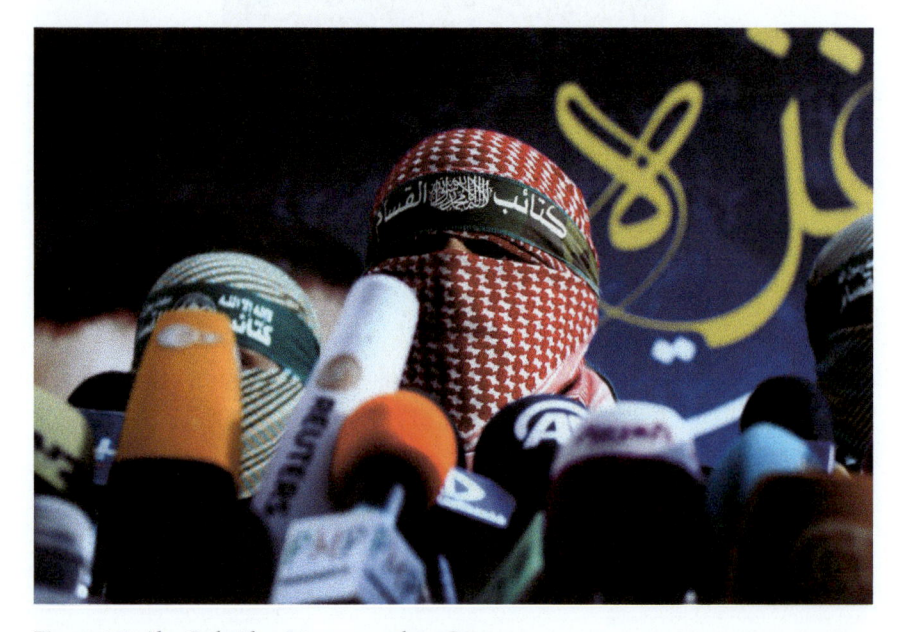

Figure 4.5 Abu Oubaida giving a speech in Gaza.

Qassam, established its own media presence through an active official website that has significantly expanded in content over the past several years. It serves as an extensive archive, as if operating in official state military capacity. It also features official military statements, carefully curated and released videos of their military operations, an "oasis of martyrs," a list of Qassam members in Israeli prisons, and much more (Figure 4.5).

While *al-mulatham/a* has long existed in Palestinian imaginaries in varied forms, the most prominent contemporary version is Abu Oubaida, whose identity is unknown and whose first appearance was in 2006. Sometimes referred to as *al-mulatham al-majhool* (the anonymous masked person), his face and most of his head are wrapped with a red *kuffiyeh*, leaving only his eyes visible. A green bandana around his forehead features the logo of the Qassam. He dons military attire with a Palestine flag patch on his left shoulder and a name tag on his chest with the title "the military spokesperson." He is most often seen in front of a cluster of microphones and a podium, his right hand pointing to elaborate his points, often flanked by other Qassam members. He was especially widely visualized and popularized during the 2014 Israeli aggression on Gaza and again more recently during the Israeli aggression on Gaza in 2021, particularly after his speeches which addressed Palestinians citizens of Israel and Palestinians in the West Bank insisting on the unification of resistance against Israeli colonization.

During this moment in 2021, the resistance was operating in a "joint operations room" shared by all of the Palestinian political factions. Abu Oubaida issued a message to the Palestinians in the rest of Palestine calling for unity during what came to be known as the Unity Intifada. In the rare moments of Abu Oubaida's appearances, his popularity—and the general popularity of the aesthetic of *al-mulatham/a*—as well as the growing calls for Palestinian unity led to a proliferation of his image through social media platforms like TikTok. This also led to ordinary people themselves embodying *al-mulatham/a*. In the same year, especially in May during the Sheikh Jarrah protests, Palestinians in Jerusalem would taunt Israeli soldiers or police by chanting *Abu Oubaida badereckh*, Hebrew for "Abu Oubaida is on his way." The informal and playful ways Abu Oubaida was evoked and even appropriated by ordinary Palestinians are more poignant when considering the professional presentation of Abu Oubaida as part of a larger, careful Hamas and Qassam media strategy. As such, the proliferation of Abu Oubaida on social media platforms might be seen as a means of reclaiming *al-mulatham/a* for popular everyday subversive acts, thus giving this figure an afterlife beyond the contained and rare appearances of Abu Oubaida himself.

Palestinian TikTok: Becoming *Al-Mulatham/a*

The "everydayness" of resistance in Palestinian contexts merged almost seamlessly with the ability of Palestinian TikTok users to appropriate official narratives of resistance, whether through popular music at weddings or through social media networks, thus making them legible and danceable to a wider Arabic-speaking audience. This phenomenon gave the resistance a life of its own on social media outside of Israeli surveillance and outside of official Hamas and Qassam accounts. Like other popular appropriations of *al-mulatham/a* in other contexts, these playful TikTok clips of Abu

Oubaida also exceeded the heavily masculine representations. Because of the masked figure's history in Palestinian imaginaries, the merging of Abu Oubaida with the features of TikTok enables Palestinian users to enact their own version of a virtual masking through which they evade surveillance algorithms.

TikTok was initially released in China in 2016 and became officially available almost all over the globe in 2018.[13] In 2020, it was the fastest growing social media app with 850 million global downloads[14], and it continued to grow faster than others well into the first quarter of 2022.[15] Several academics and tech-expert journalists attribute the app's large success over other social media to the fact that it was one of the first to introduce the ability to share videos as short as six seconds.[16] This feature made it more popular with younger demographics: shorter videos would most likely be replayed multiple times, thus allowing more views.[17] TikTok enables everyone to be a creator and encourages users to "share their passion and creative expression through their videos."[18] This particular feature makes it more accessible for everyone with a smartphone to become a creator and to showcase what is going on around them, including activists in war-torn areas documenting what is being done to them without having to rely on mainstream media's coverage or worrying about how their lived experiences might be framed to serve a bigger political agenda.

From its inception, audio was a main component of TikTok, and its early uses involved music for lip-syncing and dancing.[19] This audio focus has also been taken up by activists who overlaid the cheerful and trending music jingles onto political messaging. This playfulness blurs the lines between official political messaging and subversive expressions.[20] This also serves to evade typical forms of surveillance and algorithmic censorship. Users on the app have used trending topics, such as make-up techniques, to start their videos discussing their make-up and then turn the conversation—either through audio or visual messaging—to political matters that might otherwise be censored or shadow-banned. For example, in the context of Palestine, when commenters ask for an "Israeli make-up look," the content creator might start a make-up routine to evade censorship, and then end the video with a Palestinian flag painted on their face. These methods offered Palestinians a way to get their messaging across while tricking the algorithm, and it has become a widespread form of broadcasting their struggle in the face of mainstream media censorship.[21]

While TikTok features visual filters similar to Snapchat and Instagram, the videos are built around the sounds themselves. Users choose to include a particular sound, even if it has very little to do with the video's contents, in order to get more exposure and attempt to land on the "For You" page. Sounds in and of themselves become the viral meme and everything else is secondary. These were recently referred to as "Audio Memes" by *The New York Times*, which predicted that we are now in an "audio era" in which audio has become more impactful than text and visuals.[22] Videos often go viral because the audio chosen for the visuals is what creates "brainfeel"—that which "makes a sound compelling beyond musical qualities or linguistic meaning." This quality of TikTok creates affective registers and playful reactions to the videos and sounds shared on the platform. This playful and nonserious nature of TikTok, as Abbas et al. argue, "obscures its actions as a playfield for political persuasion."[23] These playful ways of performing politics allow for reaching wider audiences while escaping surveillance that, as in our examples, proliferate the afterimage of Abu Oubaida—effectively turning the supportive users themselves into their own everyday version of a virtual masked figure, or into *al-mulatham/a*. While previously, *al-mulatham/a* was taken up popularly by Palestinians through visual means, TikTok's introduction of the aural component opened up new ways for the proliferation of everyday acts of resistance.

"Algospeak" is another clever way to evade typical forms of censorship. Algospeak is defined as "the changing of words to avoid automated content moderation systems [...] a combination of the words 'algorithm' and 'speak.' It refers to the abbreviation, deliberate misspelling, or substitution of words."[24] For example, in Palestinian TikTok (and on other social media platforms), words are often modified with numbers and spaces such that they would remain recognizable and legible enough to other Arabic speakers but undetected by the algorithm. For example, Qassam is written like this in Arabic القسام. However, in "algospeak" it could be written as ال ق س ا م, while resistance (مقاومة) becomes م&اومة. There are many different iterations of these words which native Arabic speakers can read and understand.

The social media proliferation of Abu Oubaida's image, audio memes, and algospeak effectively counter Israel's efforts to contain images of resistance from Gaza. On the one hand, there is a controlled and curated image production, and on the other, there is the popular and symbolic image that circulates on social media with associated sounds (like songs and statements), and both use different tactics to escape traditional surveillance or containment. Consider two songs that became popular through social media in 2021. Both songs celebrated Abu Oubaida and were then circulated on YouTube. They were then edited as soundtracks to innumerable social media posts, most notably on TikTok. These soundtracks became audio memes, which, through the editing features on TikTok, then proliferated in innumerable different ways.[25] Wedding songs turned into Abu Oubaida homages, which turned into TikTok jingles that were circulated and shared in humorous posts. The first song by Oudai Zagha, a Palestinian singer from Nablus, has the following lyrics:

> Our leader[26], the guard of honour and men
> You protect us with your eyes
> If you ask for my blood and soul, it is yours
> For your eyes Abu Oubaida
> Abu Oubaida, pride of the universe, Abu Oubaida,
> Your history honors the young and the old
> At difficult times, we call you for protection
> You're the dream and the knowledge
> And you and God are great.[27]

While the song originally was written to express an appreciation for a father figure, in May 2021, Zagha addressed Abu Oubaida to replace the "father figure." The Abu Oubaida version of the song became more popular than the original lyrics, with over

18 million views on YouTube. The song was spliced and used as an audiomeme in TikTok, where users and content creators edited it into many visual forms. For example, a Palestinian elder filmed herself dancing to this song and posted on TikTok with the hashtags #ArabPride, #AbuOubaida, and #Palestinianandwearingakuffya.

Around the same time, another song and homage to Abu Oubaida came from another part of Palestine. Mu'ain Al Aa'sam, from Tal As-Sabea', sang a *dahiyah* (Bedouin) style song for Abu Oubaida. The video was published on YouTube and similarly popularized on TikTok and other social media platforms. The main lyric line from the song translates: "Abu Oubaida is torturing them, every night he is scaring them." Palestinian TikTok creators filmed themselves driving past Israeli police cars while blasting the song, and as a result, the song turned into another audio meme.

Both Zagha and Al Aa'sam's songs are sung and filmed during what might seem to be a wedding party that turned into a *dahiyah*, essentially an all men's rave, where they riffed on popular Palestinian folk singing. Al Aa'sam was arrested by the Israeli police, but the song circulated widely nonetheless. The fact that these songs were popularized by both Bedouin and sha'bi (popular/folk) musicians demonstrates that Abu Oubaida's image transcends the divisions sowed by the Israeli occupation between Palestinians in the West Bank, Gaza, and inside Israel. These songs, by providing an aural component that merged well with the unique platform of TikTok, offered another way for ordinary Palestinians to become *al-mulatham/a*.

Conclusion: The Non-containment of *Al-Mulatham/a*

Al-mulatham/a as a symbol of resistance was not successfully commodified, nor entirely neoliberalized by the PA, nor is it a symbol of resistance solely for Hamas and Qassam. The image endures (space/time/politics/capital) and is constantly reclaimed by ordinary Palestinians. *Al-mulatham/a* is anonymous yet ubiquitous; it lends itself to different forms of resistance and metamorphosizes from the literal to the virtual utilizing different sensorial registers such as aurally on TikTok. In other words, *al-mulatham/a* can be embodied by anyone. This allows it to proliferate through the viral nature of TikTok and, as a result, allows Palestinians to subvert media surveillance while also constructing an archive of resistance that would otherwise be censored.

This archive is often replete with history lessons embedded in the messaging; this is but one example of collective archival practices as pedagogical methods. For example, we saw another form of *al-mulatham/a* when young men shaved their heads to obscure the targeting of a bald Palestinian by the Israeli occupation in Shu'fat refugee camp, which was documented and widely circulated on social media, and which should thus be seen as yet another archival practice. Other examples since 2021 include the recent Giloba prison break taken up on social media platforms to educate about the history of Palestinian prison breaks. We also learned of the history of banning Palestinian symbols such as the flag, and its reincarnation through the symbol of the watermelon. In other words, the everyday Palestinian social media *mulatham/a* is an archivist and a teacher, one that deserves further attention and study.

Notes

1. The masked figure as masculine is *al-mulatham* and as feminine is *al-mulathama*.
2. Nayrouz Abu Hatoum and Hadeel Assali, "Attending to the Fugitive: Resistance Videos from Gaza," in *Gaza on Screen*, ed. Nadia Yaqub (Durham, NC: Duke University Press, 2023).
3. David Beer, "Archive Fever Revisited: Algorithmic Archons and the Ordering of Social Media," in *Routledge Handbook of Digital Media and Communication* (Amsterdam: Routledge, 2020), 99–111.
4. Ibid.
5. Gayatri Gopinath, *Unruly Vsions: The Aesthetic Practices of Queer Diaspora*. Perverse modernities (Durham, NC: Duke University Press, 2018), 4; P. Long, S. Baker, L. Istvandity and J. Collins, "The Labour of Love: The Affective Archives of Popular Music Culture," *Archives and Records* 38, no. 1 (2017): 61–79; Harry McCracken, "Twitter's Big Bet on Topics and Lists is just Getting Started," *Fast Company* (2019). https://www.fastcompany.com/90446827/twitters-big-bet-on-topics-and-lists-is-just-getting-started
6. Loubna Qutami, "Unsettled Debts: 1968 and the Problem of Historical Memory| Reborn as Fida'i: The Palestinian Revolution and the (Re)Making of an Icon," *International Journal of Communication* 16 (2022); S. Schechner, "You Give Apps Sensitive Personal Information. Then They Tell Facebook," *The Wall Street Journal* (2019). https://www.wsj.com/articles/you-give-apps-sensitive-personal-information-then-they-tell-facebook-11550851636
7. Rana Anani, 2022, "Monther Jawabreh: A Story of an Artist who Threw Stones in a Shallow pond." Palestine Studies. *Art and Culture* (blog). July 13, 2022. https://www.palestine-studies.org/ar/node/1652935.
8. Mustafa Mustafa, "Laila Shawa Draws on Top of a Landmine," *Al Akhbar*. July 12, 2014. https://al-akhbar.com/Literature_Arts/34566; C. Newton, "Why Vine Died," *The Verge* (2016). https://www.theverge.com/2016/10/28/13456208/why-vine-died-twitter-shutdown
9. Abu Hatoum and Assali, "Attending to the Fugitive."
10. Wael Abdelal, *Hamas and the Media: Politics and Strategy* (London: Routledge, 2016).
11. Ibid., 50.
12. Ibid., 57.
13. K. E. Anderson, "Getting Acquainted with Social Networks and Apps: It Is Time to Talk about TikTok," *Library Hi Tech News* 37, no. 4 (2020): 7–12. https://doi.org/10.1108/LHTN-01-2020-0001; C. Shane, "Why Do We Love TikTok Audio Memes? Call It 'Brainfeel,'" *The New York Times* (August 17, 2022). https://www.nytimes.com/interactive/2022/08/17/magazine/tiktok-sounds-memes.html
14. DigiView, "All about the Fastest Growing Social Media App – TikTok," (2020). https://digiview.se/articles/everything-you-need-to-know-about-tiktok/; Ezzedeen Al-Qassam Brigades. https://alqassam.ps; H. Farrell, E. Lawrence and J. Sides, "Self-Segregation or Deliberation? Blog Readership, Participation and Polarization in American Politics," *Perspectives on Politics* 8 no. 1 (2008). DOI:10.2139/ssrn.1151490
15. Lauren Forristal, "TikTok was the top app by Worldwide Downloads in Q1 2022," *TechCrunch+* (2022). https://techcrunch.com/2022/04/26/tiktok-was-the-top-app-by-worldwide-downloads-in-q1-2022/; Maryam Mohsin, "10 TikTok Statistics that You Need to Know in 2022 [Infographic]" (2022). https://www.oberlo.com/blog/tiktok-statistics.

16   Anderson, "Getting Acquainted with Social Networks and Apps"; Gabriel Weimann and Natalie Masri, "TikTok's Spiral of Antisemitism" (2021). https://doi.org/10.3390/journalmedia2040041; Mohsin, "10 TikTok Statistics That You Need to Know in 2022 [Infographic]."
17   Shahira Tarrash and Craig Brown. "How TikTok Is Exposing Dissent and Repression in Israel-Palestine," *Resistance Studies* (2021). https://wagingnonviolence.org/rs/2021/06/tiktok-dissent-in-israel-palestine/; Helga Tawil-Souri, "Digital Occupation: Gaza's High-Tech Enclosure" in *Journal of Palestine Studies,* 41, no. 2 (2012): 27–43; "What Does ALGOSPEAK Mean?" *Cyber Definitions: An Academic Look at "Cyber Speak."* https://www.cyberdefinitions.com/definitions/ALGOSPEAK.html
18   tiktok.com, 2022.
19   tiktok.com, 2022; A. Zulkifli, "TikTok in 2022: Revisiting Data and Privacy," in *Computer* 55, no. 06 (2022): 77–80. doi: 10.1109/MC.2022.3164226
20   Tarrash and Brown, "How TikTok Is Exposing Dissent and Repression in Israel-Palestine"; Weimann and Masri, "TikTok's Spiral of Antisemitism."
21   Tarrash and Brown, 2021, "How TikTok Is Exposing Dissent and Repression in Israel-Palestine."
22   Shane, "Why Do We Love TikTok Audio Memes? Call It 'Brainfeel.'"
23   Abbas, Laila, Shahira S. Fahmy, Sherry Ayad, Mirna Ibrahim and Abdelmoneim Hany Alim "TikTok Intifada: Analyzing Social Media Activism Among Youth" Online Media and Global Communication, June 8, 2022, 714.
24   Cyber Definitions. n.d. What Does Algospeak Mean? Systems. https://www.cyberdefinitions.com/definitions/ALGOSPEAK.html#:~:text=Algospeak%20is%20a%20combination%20of,as%20TikTok%2C%20Instagram%2C%20Facebook%2C.
25   Shane, "Why Do We Love TikTok Audio Memes? Call It 'Brainfeel.'"
26   The literal translation is "Our father."
27   The full song is on YouTube here: https://www.youtube.com/watch?v=em7DD0xvP_A

5

Vertical Visions of the Nakba: Toward a Topography of Layers

Viviane Saglier

Layers versus Maps

In Annemarie Jacir's road(block) movie *Milh hadha al-Bahr/The Salt of This Sea* (2008), Palestinian American Soraya returns to Palestine for the first time. She experiments with various ways to assert her inherited relationship with the land, first by attempting to retrieve the money her grandfather left in the bank before being expelled from Jaffa in 1948, then by re-occupying the spaces that make Palestine her legitimate home. After an unsuccessful stay at her grandfather's house, now inhabited by a young Israeli leftist who refuses to admit her participation in the ongoing Nakba, Soraya and her accomplice and lover Emad drive to his ancestral village of al-Dawayima, destroyed in 1948. The Israeli neighbors do not recognize the name, which does not figure on the colonial maps. For the Israeli guide touring visitors on site, the village's remains can be reduced to "ancient ruins" from a different era that prove Israel's biblical history. Soraya and Emad set camp in a well-preserved Palestinian house, and reactivate the landscape and its function as a living environment with the potential to host a future Palestinian family. Absent from the map, the destroyed village endures as a living trace on the land's surface.

This case looks at the layers that bring maps to life. Maps are inanimate objects and symbolic representations that produce forms of relationship to the land through their rendering as territory. As colonial tools, maps are both border-making agents and cement historical processes of domination and rule. In Palestine, maps always risk reifying power relations due to what they erase/leave out and foreclose alternative modes of inhabiting space and community beyond colonial fragmentation. And so, when considered as finite delineations of land claims, they often feel insufficient not only for the speculative work of imagining liberated futures but also for the materialization of return through the transformation of colonial relations. Maps are unable to convey tensions between representations and lived experience, as well as temporal changes, dynamic projections in time, and contradictory, yet coexisting alternatives.[1] Conversely, the layers that we may affix on maps are in movement; they enable the shift from one temporal unit to another in ways that often also include material changes, technological adaptations, and glitches. Through their instability, layers reconfigure modes of indexicality—how the image becomes both *a part of* and *an inscription into* the material world. As a result, they also materially inform our social and symbolic relationship to landscapes and their temporalities.

The visual layers that interest me can be found in different technologies, from digital mapping applications and experimental digital filmmaking to community map-making projects captured in film. What unites these multiple media explorations is the vertical vision induced by an investigation of layers that supplements maps' inherent horizontality and flatness. A re-structuration of the image and the land through layers prompts a reconfiguration of space and plane figurations as potential archives, memories, and modes of participation.

This chapter establishes a *topography* of layers of images that also informs Palestinians' material and symbolic relationship to the land. Topography is the study of how relief is distributed over a landscape. When applied to layers, it signals the various affordances of a vertical vision for weaving new relationships with the land, which may include the return of Palestinian refugees. Excavating Palestinians' buried histories enables us to visualize the land in its verticality not simply as a tool of colonial control but also as a practice of building new solidarities and reviving Palestinians' ancestral connections. While films and interactive projects are often considered to "intervene in digitally mediated realities,"[2] this chapter insists on the politics of collaborative layering across mobile apps, cinema, and video that may enable Palestinians' *material* return. In other words, investigating layers' vertical vision asks us to think about the physicality of symbolic representations, the effective social relationships that these configure, and their tangible consequences on spatial and political realities.

Layer as Forensics

Developing a vertical vision of Palestine's land proved crucial to its very colonization. Israel's strategy of occupation since 1967 relies on building layered infrastructures of circulation and separation such as elevated roads, tunnels, and walls that obscure Palestinians' persisting presence on the territory and reinforce settlers' violent claims to the land.[3] A distinct yet complementary colonial practice of verticality, the archeological dig plays a role in producing ancient material objects as supporting evidence for Israel's colonial-historical claims to the territory. The function of Israeli museums and intermediaries such as the tour guide in *The Salt of This Sea* is then to institutionalize this history and legitimize these claims. The archeological focus on excavation participates in what Nadia Abu el-Haj calls "making place," the reconfiguration of the territory through a direct intervention into the land and its meaning.[4] However, the practice of verticality organizes the past in ways that are not inherently colonial. When applied to images, it provides Palestinian artists with the forensic tools to investigate the making of history in the materiality of the land.

It is archeology's verticality and destruction that Dima Srouji explores in her experimental film *Sebastia* (2020),[5] which focuses on the eponymous town in the Northern West Bank renowned for its Roman city and monuments. The film mixes grainy-textured home-movie shots of the old city, drones' digital bird's-eye view captures of the site, 3D rendering of the Roman forum, as well as a variety of archival footage from a 1930 British archeological expedition in Palestine, 1940s American promotional films, and a 1960s British television show. Through the combination of those distinct image materials, the film exposes how the making of Zionist history led to the unmaking of Palestinians' historical relationship with the land.

The larger exhibition, *Depth Unknown*, in which the video is inscribed,[6] highlights how the Zionist quest for artifacts as proof of Israel's millenary existence privileges re-historicized objects. This occurs at the expense of other artifacts that do not fit the desired narrative, but also at the detriment of the layers from which these have been extracted. Indeed, the nature of the excavating process is that "each layer needs to be destroyed by removal before the next one can be accessed."[7] The annihilation of these strata of soil and cultural remains—the process by which history becomes material through the geological and cultural sedimentation of situated power relations—constitutes one material manifestation of Israel's historical erasure of Palestinians.

The film's first function is thus to act as a counter-forensics by analyzing the colonial process of destruction. In the face of the eradication of the soil's layers through the excavation process, the film proposes a reconstruction through the very layering of images. Layers constitute a methodology to deconstruct Zionist discourse. After introducing the different tools that it will use—namely, the distinct image materials mentioned earlier—the film proceeds to articulate the Zionist logic of land claim: on the flat layer of an aerial view of the city of Sebastia, which breaks into two separate images to reflect the contemporary fragmentation of the city into an Area B and area C of colonial control, the film superimposes another, smaller, frame that shows an old manuscript (Figure 5.1). The audio commentary, taken from a 1967 American documentary on biblical anthropology,[8] identifies this book as the Bible, which carries stories dating back 2,000 years and more. How can we certify their veracity? the

Figure 5.1 Dima Srouji, *Sebastia* (2020). The Bible is laid over the map of Israeli-controlled Area C where the Roman forum is located. *Sebastia* by Dima Srouji commissioned by Het Nieuwe Instituut and e-Flux.

voice-over asks. The answer "is buried in the land where the book itself was written." As the mystery gets resolved by this assertion, the image of the Bible is substituted by a close-up of two trowels digging into the ground. By combining footage of 1930 excavations, 1967 documentary images, and, later in the film, contemporary footage of the IDF's night expedition to steal St John Baptist's baptismal font from a crypt in the Palestinian village of Taquu, the film's exposé demonstrates the longue-durée of the ongoing Nakba through complementary practices of extraction and looting. After 1967, the colonial authorities identified Sebastia's Roman forum as an archeological site, which justified the site's following registration as an Israeli National Park, whose access could be restricted for Palestinians. Through incremental land takeover and processes of legitimation, the nearby military base turned into a settlement, and the exclusive extraction of natural resources such as water quickly followed, and, importantly, *complemented*, the extraction of archeological artifacts.

The film's multilayered show of evidence is mediated by Palestinian officials and inhabitants with a status of expert: Zaid Azhari, historian and tour guide from Sebastia; Muhammad Azem, mayor of Sebastia; and Ahmad Kayed, local farmer. Taken in its totality, the film performs the *prosopopoeia* which Weizman identifies at the core of the practice of forensics: the ability to make material objects or landscapes speak.[9] As the landscape becomes a witness of the totalizing violence perpetrated by colonial organizations, the film, the larger exhibition project, and the events where these circulate become the forums where Palestinians can present new historical claims, with the hope that these will lead to material reconfigurations of the land. Images, artifacts, and discourses, the film argues, have deeply material consequences; they enable, but may also dismantle, land grabs and forced displacement.

One of the film's preoccupations is to highlight the epistemological importance of layers as opposed to objects in the process of historicization. Colonial authorities (be they Zionist or, earlier, British) are keen on looting archeological artifacts because this mode of extraction also represents a form of de-contextualization that can negate local histories and communal practices. The relocation of the looted objects in museums effaces the layers that the excavation process had already started to expunge. *Sebastia* uses the layering of images to reinscribe the stolen artifacts in their soil, and also to illuminate the condition of production of these objects as museum pieces. As Azhari explains, the Harvard excavations were only made possible because the expedition recruited the inhabitants of Sebastia as cheap labor at a moment when they were financially vulnerable. The film de-fetishizes the museum artifact by adding a supplemental layer over a documentary that praises institutions for their new supply of archeological items. The layer showcases the hard labor of Palestinians at the dig. Because it belongs to a later expedition in the 1930s, this layer makes the broader argument that colonial museums are entirely built on the theft and exploitation of local communities, who unwittingly aid the eradication of their own history as they work on those digs (Figure 5.2).

The longue-durée articulation of these different colonial narratives materializes in the grain and color of the footage at hand. The 1940 footage with green inflections—a promotional film for the University of Pennsylvania Museum of Archeology and Anthropology[10]—naturalizes museums' looting and conceals the violence of the

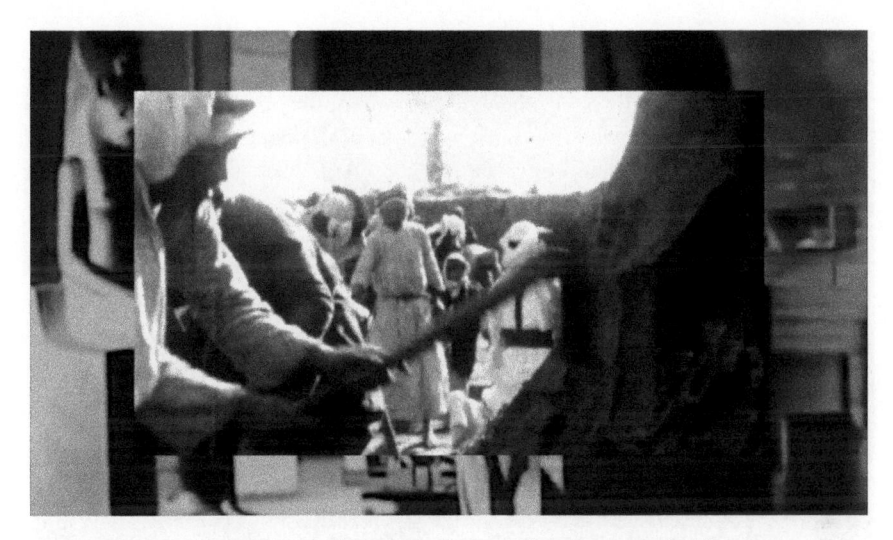

Figure 5.2 Dima Srouji, *Sebastia* (2020). The footage of Lankester Harding's 1930 excavation (smaller layer) reveals the exploitation and dispossession of Palestinians that made colonial museums' wealth possible (green layer underneath). Courtesy of Dima Srouji.

archeological expedition. British historians of archeology have described British archeologist Lankester Harding's recording of the 1930 expedition as a celebration of the British team's work. Less convincingly, they have also argued for a supposed friendship between the archeologists and the Palestinian Bedouins whom they exploited.[11] Privileging a more critical view of those recordings, *Sebastia* shows how colonial violence is continuously both evident and obscured across colonial empires— in other words, normalized. No wonder that, for example, a British television network would casually air an interview of former Haganah member and Israeli military leader Moshe Dayan, where he shares his two "passions": archeology and the "art of war." Rather than distinct, these two disciplines are intimately linked in destruction through the desire for material conquest (Figure 5.3), so that the archeological site effectively becomes a military zone. The film's layering thus recasts relationships between British, American, and Israeli archeological teams, Palestinian villagers, and the land as being profoundly shaped by material concerns over labor, history, and territory in ways that become identifiable in the very materiality of the image.

The relationships that the film's layers draw are not of mere causality. They point to the intricate mechanisms of colonial power and the reorganization of history through material intervention into the land and its symbolisms. Yet, such relations are not immutable, and, as *Sebastia*'s investigation unfolds, the play with layers also unearths and restores Palestinians' relationship to the land beyond colonial mediation. The home movie footage at the beginning points to another practice of the archeological site that is not militarized. Similarly, the drone footage, while also a tool of surveillance, is here used to provide a panorama of Palestinian life. As Dima Srouji writes, "the Roman forum was historically used as a threshing ground and community gathering space where families would sing songs as they threshed wheat during the harvest season."[12]

> as he was holding an ancient coin and said: "This is the coin of my ancestors"

Figure 5.3 Dima Srouji, *Sebastia* (2020). Moshe Dayan's two passions: archeology, and the art of war. Courtesy of the artist.

The Roman forum, where friends, families, and lovers still meet, now continues to exercise its function as a place of gathering where Palestinians congregate to perform their shared belonging. The 3D rendering of the forum shows both how the site used to be before attacks by settlers and the Israeli army, and what it can become, that is, a site of leisure with umbrellas, chairs, tables, and a football cage where children can play. It also serves as an "active battleground"[13] when the youth plant the Palestinian flag on a monument as an act of resistance. What the film suggests, and what the rest of this chapter explores, is that visual layers enable new forms of material relations to the land.

Layer as Collective Labor

When digitized photographs of the actual 1908 Harvard excavation are introduced in *Sebastia*, the screen scrambles for a second. How to move from one layer to the other? The temporal and material passage from the contemporary 3D rendering of the Roman forum to the early colonial documentation of land destruction cannot be a smooth one; instead, it is rooted in a violence that also affects the image itself. The glitch is the moment of malfunction in the conversion of digital material that allows for its wider circulation. As a "bruise of the image or sound," it signals the work involved in switching platforms and adapting to new technological contexts.[14] In other words, the glitch points to the issue of accessing layers and the material transformations this implies. In this section, I move on from the epistemological work of layers to their capacity of carrying us from one reality to the other. Yet, I ultimately argue, this journey—and the possibility of return for Palestinian refugees—becomes truly material only if we learn from *Sebastia*'s teachings about the collective labor involved in exploring archeological layers. If the land remains intangible for those whom borders continue to exclude, the very work of establishing layers is what reinforces the social relations that sustain the material reclaiming of the land. In this specific context, the slow materialization of return shouldn't be only thought horizontally as the ability to travel across the flat plane of the map. Return also refers to the vertical exploration of what it takes to establish presence over time, through the participation in and the strengthening of the community, and via visual layers.

Several artists and activists have explored the capacity for layers to contest the rigidity of maps and present alternatives to colonial representations of the landscape. Since the mid-2000s, many have taken advantage of Google's early mapping explorations and navigation tools. Linda Quiquivix reminds us how, in 2006, Palestinian refugee Thameen Darby initiated a "Nakba layer" that could be added to Google Earth. The layer enabled displaced Palestinians to envision a counter-geography to the existing colonial map and to reposition the 530 destroyed Palestinian towns and villages in their rightful place. Most recently, Palestine Open Maps, with the cooperation of the design collective Visualizing Palestine, has launched an open-source mapping project where users can affix a similar layer over a variety of historic map sheets from the Ottoman era until today.[15] These projects show that mapping technologies can be instrumentalized and reappropriated outside of colonial visual regimes. For example, Darby's geo-mapping from below proposes a space that evades the military history of Google Earth and its inscription within the Cold War race for surveillance. As Quiquivix explains,

> Google retains no control over a layer's content. Users can create place marks, superimpose images, control and update map content across the web, and manage large data sets. A layer can be shared, uploaded, and worked on simultaneously on collaborative projects.[16]

The Nakba layer, later augmented by Salah Mansour, is now accessible via the website Palestine Remembered (launched in 2005), a Palestinian, grassroots-led, participatory database and extensive archive which includes interviews with Palestinian elders; thousands of pictures before and during the 1948 war which are divided into sectors, towns, and villages; a variety of still maps until today; and various forums where contributors can discuss the material they upload. The website "becomes a virtual space through which people can re-territorialize themselves onto the lost (historical, physical, distant) spaces of Palestine."[17] The database offers distinct entry points but the most evident one remains the list of Palestinian cities, refugee camps, and searchable destroyed villages, the majority of which derive from Palestinian historians' census.[18] Each village webpage includes some statistics and historical facts, pictures, articles, oral history videos, video documentation, a discussion board, and a list of contributing members to each topic. It is also from the village webpage that users can access the Nakba layer by viewing the satellite map (Figure 5.4). Further exploration into the map can lead to other village and city pages. The website aims to educate a broad

Figure 5.4 Palestine Remembered. The satellite view of al Dawayima. Courtesy of Palestine Remembered.

audience about the Nakba, preserve memories and archival material, and facilitate communication and organization amongst Palestinians.

If the layer contributes to the website's invaluable archive (mostly in Arabic), its interface remains oriented toward a computer use and makes no promise of moving from the virtual layer to the physical one.[19] The mobile application iNakba (trilingual Arabic, English, and Hebrew), launched in 2014, follows a similar impulse by overlapping a layer of destroyed Palestinian villages and towns over the digital map. Yet this time it is also, but not only, suited for an audience that is able and allowed to travel to the sites under inquiry through its use of the Waze navigation app. Conceived by the anti-Zionist Israeli organization Zochrot (est. 2005), which comprises Palestinian citizens and a majority of Jewish Israelis who support the return of Palestinian refugees, iNakba can be used onsite or offsite. Based on GPS navigation technology, it locates Palestinian sites destroyed and depopulated since 1948 and provides an interactive interface where users can both "learn about these localities, but also share their own content, videos, photographs, impressions, and stories."[20] Here, the navigational capacity of the app brings the transformational power of layers to another level: the layer no longer simply enables the passage between two image materials as was the case in *Sebastia*, it also a priori facilitates the bilateral move between the physical landscape and the virtual rendering (Figure 5.5). At the time of writing, the app is waiting to be relaunched and therefore cannot be accessed. But for Israeli scholars Norma Musih (co-founder of Zochrot) and Eran Fisher, who have experimented with the first version on location, the app functions as a form of digital mapping that is relational and has "reciprocal effects."

Figure 5.5 Trailer for the iNakba app in 2014. Courtesy of Zochrot.

Instead of creating a representation of the territory, the radio signals sent from the GPS satellites creates a system of coordinates that overlap and co-occur with the physical terrain, constructing a different relationship between users, landscape, and sovereignty.[21]

The app re/produces space in ways that echo Dima Srouji's experimental work of reinscribing layers within the material formation of histories and land relations. iNakba partly materializes a response to colonial excavation by forging new physical relations to the land that are mediated through the virtual layer's expanded information about the past. If space is always constructed, then the app's onsite feature contributes to "creat[ing] a new spatial reality."[22]

Yet, the condition for the app's layer to perform its *distinct* political and epistemic work is physical, onsite access. Digital mapping can only promise new relationships to historicized landscapes and the revival of destroyed Palestinian lives for the limited users who *already* have primary access. This includes Palestinians with Israeli citizenship, Jewish Israelis, and some members of the Palestinian diaspora who may occasionally (and temporarily) visit historic Palestine providing that their current passport allows them to do so and that they fulfill the selection criteria arbitrarily activated at the Israel-controlled border. In that sense, the onsite use of the app perpetuates the fragmentation of the Palestinian people, and the promise of return both remains exclusionary and reinforces the territorial divide. Fabio Cristiano and Emilio Distretti reach a parallel conclusion in their embodied study of the augmented reality (AR) game *Pokémon GO* in Jerusalem, in which users move across the physical space in order to catch creatures located in the virtual layer. For them, the app's imaginary normalizes colonial segregation by promoting a vision of Israeli sovereignty over the entire city that denies Palestinian claims.[23] In other words, by embracing the fantasy of seamless access in the city, the app erases the very possibility that Palestinians might be digital users. Recognizing their existence would demand a reshaping of the game's logic and its acknowledgment of very material divides.

This brings us to the inherent limitation of notions of access that are considered from a navigational perspective (through the horizontality of the map). For some, envisioning iNakba as digital mapping and approaching the presentation of destroyed villages as a layer posited as "ontologically secondary to the 'map,'" "falsely assumes that there is a fixed ontological entity on top of which layers can be placed."[24] But if, instead, we continue to center the critical work of the layer as established in *Sebastia*, we may reconfigure what sort of return layers enable. This form of return is one that is incrementally, and prefiguratively, built through the struggle of making history available, shared, and lived—and which is thus always already entrenched in the continued violence of colonial power structures. Thinking about return through the perspective of the *onsite* app's users always already excludes Palestinian refugees as well as Palestinians in the West Bank and Gaza who face the double limitation of restricted mobility and weak internet infrastructures.[25] Instead, the transformational aspect of iNakba is the one that doesn't discriminate between onsite and offsite. Like for the website Palestine Remembered, it is the process of gathering stories and images that gives the layers their informational texture and their potentiality to slide from one world to the other. The vertical work of the layer does not legitimize the primary layer as an "ur-map"; rather, it makes, unmakes, and remakes the terrain of history and land-based relationships. Access, and return, can only happen through the long-term work of building new relations and the material struggle that reconfiguring power structures implies.

It is interesting that the temporal imaginary of the iNakba app has changed over time, and with it, the very function of its layers. In 2014/15, the Arabic coverage of the app's initial launch, which seemed to draw from the website's then-description,[26] emphasized iNakba's orientation toward the past and its focus on remembering life before displacement. The very name of Zochrot (Hebrew for Remembering) showcases a primary investment in rewriting history. The relaunch of the improved and updated app, later called iReturn, carries a new subtitle, "The Invisible Map of the Future."[27] By shifting the users' expectations for the app toward what is to come rather than what has been, the website suggests that the work iNakba performs is prefigurative—enacting now the future of Palestinian return. It wouldn't make sense for Zochrot's imagined future to reproduce the life before the Nakba as it is represented in the virtual layer. Instead, as the organization examines what the right of return means in practice (rather than simply in principle), they ask, "what might return actually look like on the ground? What needs have to be met for refugees to be re-absorbed?"[28] The app prefigures a future enabled by the very labor of the core team and the multiple participatory interventions by Palestinians and allies, from which the layer itself originates. It is the *present* of collaboration that constitutes the layer's material possibility as well as the eventual passage from present to memory, and from virtual return to physical return. More than the navigational functions of the app, it is the *ongoing* participation in reorganizing the imagined space of sovereignty and the solidarities that it builds that materially prefigures return.

For Zochrot, this mode of collaboration reshapes the promise of coexistence beyond a dialogue between the "two sides of the conflict" promoted by agents of normalization, which the young Israeli leftist who invited Soraya into her grandfather's house represented in *The Salt of This Sea*. Zochrot's advocacy for Palestinian return is intimately tied to abolishing the power structure that sustains "the relationship of occupier-occupied and expeller-expellee."[29] This means, first, reckoning with Noura Erakat's reminder that "Israelis are not neighbors, or even occupiers, but colonial masters and beneficiaries of ongoing Palestinian deprivation."[30] Both iNakba and *Palestine Remembered* have committed to recruiting Palestinians and Jewish Israelis for the task of gathering information. They do so in the name of solidarity, but also pragmatically because a lot of the material, including videos, is in possession of, or more easily accessible to, Jewish Israelis who live in the 48 area. In practice, such collaboration also implies a continued engagement—the mobilization of resources and energy—in educating Jewish Israelis who might be entrenched in their support for Israel yet curious to hear alternative views, as some of the forum posts on Palestine Remembered indicate.[31]

The layer becomes a pedagogical interface, which translates more analogue modes of exchange that perdure alongside the app.[32] The genealogy of iNakba's layer should be traced back to the in-person tours organized by Zochrot and led by internally displaced Palestinians who share stories about their disappeared villages. These stories are later translated into Hebrew. As Musih and Fisher explain "some of the tours were also recorded in a video format, and, for most of the tours, booklets were produced with information about the place from different archival material as well as oral histories of Palestinian refugees and Jewish neighbours."[33] This collective work includes those who do the labor of sharing material, of coordinating the archives, and of setting the digital layer, but it also accounts for the learning process of positioning oneself within a history of dispossession, or one in which some families have gained from the dispossession of others. Nasser Abourahme, who relays Erakat's call for "co-resistance," insists on describing it as a "joint struggle [that] will only open up genuine newness by connecting future redress to past dispossession, by returning to another time altogether."[34] Through their refashioning of the landscape and the relayering of the land's meaning, the various digital layers evoked in this section introduce a vertical vision that proves expansive and elastic, and that produces a new temporality that does not simply reproduce the lost past. We should however question Zochrot's use of the Waze app, launched by former Israeli intelligence officers who profited from Israel's militarized tech boom. Co-resistance must reject the colonial digital infrastructures actively developed to deny the very possibility of Palestinian sovereignty and continued existence.[35] The labor of layering becomes a tool of mobilization; it solidifies a network of present relations if—and only if—those forces are also redirected against colonial state and ideological structures and their neoliberal ramifications. The framework of co-resistance however appears increasingly frail as we witness the overwhelming Israeli support for Israel's ongoing genocide in Gaza at the time of proofreading this chapter.[36]

Conclusion: An Ecology of Layers

While excavation constituted a material and symbolic intervention into the land to change its meaning, the visits that Zochrot organizes and the archival material shared across virtual layers emphasize the protuberant traces of Palestinian life. Even when left in ruins, these remainders persist on the surface. In the *Depth Unknown* exhibit that included *Sebastia*, Srouji and her team produced models (maquettes) that play with the inversion of volumes. These models "restitut[e] the context destroyed in excavation," so that what was carved out and expunged can "make space" again.[37]

I propose to think about those various layers across media—be they archeological, architectural, archival, onsite, offsite, or even offline—as an ecology. Taken together, these layers draw a topography of distinct land relations and strategies of co-resistance specific to the contexts in which they operate. Not all strategies hold the same implications across fragmented Palestine. The imaginary of co-resistance figured by Zochrot, whose educational work tends to focus our attention onto Jewish Israelis, may represent a crucial intervention in the 48 area. However, such collaboration takes a specific meaning in the West Bank or Gaza, where the structures of occupation are more directly visible and operate as a constant reminder of the violence necessary to sustain hierarchies of life between Palestinians and Israelis. In the city of Sebastia, Srouji explains, "when Palestinians living in archaeological sites refer to 'Israelis' they mean both the IDF and settlers as a single body". Mindful of context, layers weave a variety of flexible modes of participation and solidarities among Palestinians and beyond that simultaneously function on different strata.

And so, I end this case vertical investigation by centering Palestinians' present practice of those layered spaces and their preservation of the ruins that still live. Dima Abu Ghoush's personal documentary *Emwas* (2016) follows the collaborative reconstruction, as a model, of the village of Emwas where she was born, but which Israel destroyed and depopulated on June 6, 1967, during the Six-Day war. The film is guided by the director's quest for the meaning of home and how we shape our relationship to place. The model, whose photogenic relief opens and punctuates

Figure 5.6 The model of Emwas in Dima Abu Ghoush's *Emwas* (2016). Courtesy of the artist.

the film, materializes the entire network of social relations that she mobilizes to concretize the village's memory (Figure 5.6). Through the work of collective remembering, Abu Ghoush contributes to reactivating the space in the present. She rides alongside the former residents of Emwas on the yearly pilgrimage towards the fence that separates the West Bank from the village, where their protests are met with the IDF's tear gas. Equipped with a permit, she visits the rubble with her mum, uncle, sister, and nieces, and starts creating a working map of the village. Soon, the whole family is recruited according to their skills (from engineering to coloring to building the model to sharing memories). Former Israeli soldiers who participated in the village's destruction, elder priests of the neighboring monastery who hid villagers during the 1967 bombings, and elder residents now based in Amman are also enticed into this ecology of layers.

Like the Roman forum of Sebastia, Emwas was turned into a natural park by Israeli authorities, with the financial support of the Canadian branch of the Jewish National Fund. The Park authorities covered the village's ruins with pine trees that reproduced a European, non-native ecology which would also impede the growth of local herbs. And yet, the director's mother forages and collects the plants that survived. Throughout the film, the model grows with each social interaction, with each shared memory. The film's editing emphasizes this temporal continuity between past and present. An older footage shows an interview of the director's late father on the grounds of the destroyed village years after 1967, where he describes the local life before the expulsion. As his hand extends to the square where celebrations and commemorations were held, the scene cuts to the contemporary footage of the park, where dispersed houses and stones mark Palestinians' persisting presence.

The passage from the map to the model drives the film, which is almost processual—it instructs us about the different steps toward return, from drawing the map to layering the landscape to building the model to adding more layers. In the latest stages, the model circulates from Palestine to the diaspora where former residents can identify the houses where their family used to live. The importance of the model format might lie in its capacity to reinject life back into the map. The model, *mujassam* in Arabic, is that which is embodied (from *jism*, body). And in fact, the layering work that the film performs re-animates the community spirit and hope for return. Since 1967, this hope has been enacted through various acts of militancy, from the protests mentioned earlier to membership in the revolutionary Democratic Front for the Liberation of Palestine (DFLP). These layers of resistance aggregate in one of the last scenes of the film, when the family gathers around the product of their communal work that lies on the table. As he contemplates the model, an elder man joyfully declares: "The people of Emwas have become socialist; when we return, we will divide and share equally." This prophetic claim can be interpreted in various ways, either as an echo of some of the residents' socialist inclination as part of their DFLP militancy or as a logical conclusion to the collective journey that constituting the model has represented. Either way, return cannot be restricted to a virtual imaginary that solely intervenes in the realm of representations. Instead, return emerges as the inevitable endpoint of a process enabled by collective resistance and mediated by a vertical vision of the ongoing Nakba.

Notes

1. Nasser Abourahme and Laura Ribeiro, "Re-weaving Fragmented Space-Time: Notes from a Mapping Project in Palestine," *Lo Squaderno* 15 (2010): 37–43.
2. Dale Hudson, "Mapping Palestine/Israel Through Interactive Documentary," *Journal of Palestine Studies* 50, no. 1 (2021): 54.
3. Eyal Weizman, *Hollow Land: Israel's Architecture of Occupation* (London and New York, NY: Verso, 2007), 11.
4. Nadia Abu el-Haj, *Facts on the Ground: Archeological Practice and Territorial Self-Fashioning in Israeli Society* (Chicago: University of Chicago Press, 2001).
5. Available online at https://vimeo.com/463782519, last accessed June 30, 2022.
6. The team involved in the larger project, which was presented at the Sharjah Architecture Triennial, includes aforementioned anthropologist Nadia Abu el-Haj.
7. Depth Unknown, "Let the Ground Speak," https://depthunknown.com/depthuknown, last accessed June 30, 2022.
8. This footage is from Glen Bernard's documentary *The Book and the Spade* (1967) produced by the University of Pennsylvania Museum of Archeology and Anthropology. Available at https://archive.org/details/upenn-f16-4027_1967_Book_and_the_Spade, last accessed June 30, 2022.
9. Eyal Weizman, "Introduction: Forensis," in *Forensis: The Architecture of Public Truth*, ed. Forensic Architecture (Berlin: Sternberg Press, 2014), 10.
10. Available at https://archive.org/details/upenn-f16-4015_1940_Ancient_Earth_Making_History, last accessed June 30, 2022.
11. This is the reading that Amara Thornton and Michael McCluskey propose of Lankester Harding's footage. https://www.youtube.com/watch?v=nVkvLiKIvUw, last accessed June 30, 2022.
12. Dima Srouji, "Vignettes of Subterranean Palestine," *The Avery Review* 56 (April 2022). http://averyreview.com/issues/56/vignettes-of-subterranean-palestine See also: Dima Srouji, "A Century of Subterranean Abuse in Sabastiya: The Archeological Site as a Field of Urban Struggle," *Jerusalem Quarterly* 90 (Summer 2022): 58–74.
13. Ibid.
14. Hito Steyerl, "Artifacts: A Conversation between Hito Steyerl and Daniel Rourke," *Rhizome*, March 28, 2013, https://rhizome.org/editorial/2013/mar/28/artifacts/
15. Palestine Open Maps, last accessed June 30, 2022, https://palopenmaps.org/
16. Linda Quiquivix, "Art of War, Art of Resistance: Palestinian Counter-Cartography on Google Earth," *Annals of the Association of American Geographers* 104, no. 3 (2014): 447.
17. Helga Tawil-Souri and Miriyam Aouragh, "Intifada 3.0? Cyber Colonialism and Palestinian Resistance," *The Arab Studies Journal* 22, no. 1, Special Issue: Cultures of Resistance (Spring 2014): 125.
18. Salman Abu Sitta's *The Palestinian Nakba, 1948: The Register of Depopulated Localities in Palestine* (2000) and Walid Khalidi's *All that Remains: The Palestinian Villages Occupied and Depopulated by Israel in 1948* (1992).
19. As Helga Tawil-Souri and Miriyam Aouragh have demonstrated, the virtual layer is enabled by very physical internet infrastructures embedded in global capitalism, international aid dependency, and Israel's colonial structures. For the purpose of clarity, I am here using a simplified dualism. Tawil-Souri and Aouragh, ibid.
20. Zochrot, "Our Newly Designed Application Is Coming Soon," last accessed June 30, 2022, https://www.zochrot.org/articles/view/56528/en

21 Norma Musih and Eran Fisher, "Layers as Epistemic and Political Devices in Mobile Locative Media; The Case of iNakba in Israel/Palestine," *Continuum* 35, no. 1 (2021): 156.
22 Musih and Fisher, "Layers as Epistemic and Political Devices in Mobile Locative Media," 162.
23 Fabio Cristiano and Emile Distretti, "Along the Lines of the Occupation: Playing at Diminished Reality in East Jerusalem," *Conflict and Society: Advances in Research* 3 (2017): 130–43.
24 Musih and Fisher, "Layers as Epistemic and Political Devices in Mobile Locative Media," 166.
25 As of June 2022, Israel continues to delay Palestinians in the West Bank access to the 4G while only the 2G network is available in Gaza.
26 For example, Al-Jazeera (communicate from Anadolu Agency), "iNakba…Tatbeeq el-Ajhaza el-Zakia Yanquluk li-Filasteen qabla el-Tahjeer," *AlJazeera*, May 12, 2015, https://tinyurl.com/4sbaduew Nahed Derbas, "Itlaq Tatbeeq 'el-Nakba' li-Ahia el-Quraa el-Filastiniyya 'el-Muhajira,'" *Al-Araby*, May 5, 2014, https://tinyurl.com/8eydr4mt
27 Zochrot, "Our Newly Designed Application."
28 Zochrot, "Return," https://www.zochrot.org/sections/view/19/en?Return_Vision, last accessed June 30, 2022.
29 Ibid.
30 Noura Erakat, "The Case for BDS and the Path to Co-Resistance," in *Assuming Boycott: Resistance, Agency, and Cultural Production*, ed. Kareem Estefan, Carin Kuoni, and Laura Raicovich (New York and London: OR Books, 2017), epub.
31 Palestine Remembered, "Mission Statement," https://www.palestineremembered.com/MissionStatement.htm, last accessed June 30, 2022.
32 Musih and Fisher, "Layers as Epistemic and Political Devices in Mobile Locative Media."
33 Musih and Fisher, "Layers as Epistemic and Political Devices in Mobile Locative Media," 163.
34 Nasser Abourahme, "Boycott, Decolonization, Return: BDS and the Limits of Political Solidarity," in *Assuming Boycott: Resistance, Agency, and Cultural Production*, ed. Kareem Estefan, Carin Kuoni, and Laura Raicovich (New York and London: OR Books, 2017), epub.
35 Matthew Kalman, "Israeli Military Intelligence Unit Drives Its Hi-Tech Boom," *The Guardian*, August 12, 2013, https://www.theguardian.com/world/2013/aug/12/israel-military-intelligence-unit-tech-boom
36 Laura Silver and Maria Smerkovich, "Israeli Views of the Israel-Hamas War," *Pew Research Center*, May 30, 2024, https://www.pewresearch.org/global/2024/05/30/israeli-views-of-the-israel-hamas-war/
37 Depth Unknown "Let the Ground Speak."

6

Virtual Returns: Rehearsing and Remediating Return in Palestinian Video Practices

Kareem Estefan

Virtual Possibilities and Limits

Expelled and exiled, living in diaspora or under occupation, separated by militarized borders and checkpoints, Palestinians would seem precisely the subjects for whom new media technologies from the internet to virtual reality (VR) hold the utopian promise of escaping a carceral actuality. Well into the twenty-first century, however, we know that online space is never disconnected from offline space; the structural inequalities of the real world remain present at every level of the virtual world, from algorithms to infrastructure. In Palestine, internet use is circumscribed by a constellation of political forces and factors that include Israeli settler-colonial control over Palestinian land, Palestinian elite capitulation to the occupation, and US and international profiteering from a development-oriented economy that benefits donors more than Palestinians.[1] The reality of apartheid in Palestine/Israel, belatedly recognized by Human Rights Watch in 2021 and Amnesty International in 2022, suffuses the digital sphere as well. Even as we reject the premise of a borderless, egalitarian virtual space removed from the real, however, can digital media nonetheless afford means for Palestinians to experience their homeland at a spatial remove?

In recent years, a variety of digital mapping platforms, interactive documentaries, virtual (reality) tours, and new media artworks have staged spatiotemporal returns *to* and *of* Palestine, opening portals to the land and to the repressed past-that-is-present of the ongoing nakba. Take, for example, Zochrot's iNakba, an app that maps the hundreds of Palestinian villages destroyed to create Israel, incorporating user-generated images and histories on an interactive map of present-day Israel. Similarly, there is the palimpsestic Palestine Open Maps, which digitally overlays maps of Palestine from the 1870s, 1940s, 1950s, and the present to create open-source, searchable versions with which users can interact. Or consider the interactive documentary *Jerusalem, We Are Here* (2016), directed by Dorit Naaman, which invites web users to tour the contemporary Qatamon neighborhood of Jerusalem—guided by the director and Palestinian researchers Anwar Ben Badis and Mona Hajjar Halaby—prior to the 1948 expulsion of Palestinians and other non-Jewish Jerusalemites. Live, virtual tours of

Jerusalem are offered by the Palestinian civil society organization Grassroots Al Quds, which since the start of the Covid-19 pandemic, has complemented its on-the-ground tours with online tours for people around the world to learn about Palestinian experiences of Jerusalem and Israeli policies designed to displace them from the city.

These projects use digital media tools to excavate histories hidden by Israeli settler colonialism while offering "*virtual transportations* for Palestinians, unable to travel due to Israeli restrictions," as Dale Hudson writes of iNakba and *Jerusalem, We Are Here*.[2] In this case, I explore a similar notion of "virtual returns" in two digital video works by Palestinian (diasporic) artists that both *represent* and *enact* return: Basel Abbas and Ruanne Abou-Rahme's *At Those Terrifying Frontiers Where the Existence and Disappearance of People Fade into Each Other* (2019) and Razan AlSalah's *Canada Park* (2020). Amplifying recent marches of return undertaken by Palestinians as acts of commemoration and protest, these videos perform virtual returns by digitally accessing land from which the artists are separated. Importantly, they do not enact "virtual" returns in opposition to "real" returns; rather, they use digital media to explore imaginaries and acts of return that are rooted in offline political practice. The artists' insistence on tethering the possibilities afforded by digital media to the material realities of settler colonialism and anti-colonial resistance distinguish their engagement with the "virtual" from VR projects that address political conflict through frameworks of humanitarianism and empathy.

Contemporary discourse surrounding VR stresses the technology's allegedly unprecedented capacity to transport its users to distant places and immerse them in ultra-realistic surroundings.[3] Given these qualities, it should be no surprise that VR has been employed increasingly by humanitarian organizations, activists, and journalists in their efforts to stimulate empathy by bringing people into startling proximity with war-torn cities, refugee camps, or impoverished and disaster-stricken rural areas.[4] Even as liberal values of empathy and understanding are the stated aim of many humanitarian VR documentaries, their emphasis on the exposure of unfamiliar victims in distant sites of conflict—particularly when considering who has access to VR today—is ethically and politically troubling.

If immersion, or "access without accountability," is uncritically championed in much humanitarian VR discourse, it is closely intertwined with the portmanteau concept of *immediation*.[5] In this case, I call upon *immediation* as a critique of humanitarian media that conceal the means by which catastrophes are (re)produced in order to elicit shock and sympathy from relatively privileged spectators. For media theorist Pooja Rangan, immediation consists of "audiovisual tropes that are mobilized when documentary operates in the mode of emergency—that is, when it seeks to redeem dehumanized lives as a first-order principle."[6] Through the concealed mediation of a situation presented as requiring immediate intervention, the figure of the human (victim) emerges as political actors and structures of violence recede. In the context of an NGO-ized post-Oslo Palestine, anthropologist Lori Allen argues, immediation circumscribes Palestinians to the role of "sympathy-deserving suffering human."[7]

AlSalah and Abbas and Abou-Rahme's videos are significant as practices that rehearse ways of sensing Palestine and Palestinians otherwise. Unlike VR works that strive for immersion, they emphasize cuts and glitches, foregrounding and disrupting processes of mediation, precisely to highlight the inability of "virtual returns" to substitute for real returns: of Palestinian refugees to their land, of expropriated lands to Palestinians, and of the right to build and forage on land to those living under Israeli colonial rule. Notably, they also operate at more poetic and affective registers than the largely expository new-media works aimed at raising awareness among Israeli and international publics. Rather than uncover realities that should already be evident, or seamlessly transport audiences into an immersive environment, the videos considered here act as opaque portals to a potential Palestine, performing return as an ongoing possibility while maintaining a representational unknowability and impasse that can only be overcome through material, collective acts of decolonization.

Rehearsing Return

Against tendencies to fetishize new media technologies as primary agents of political activism, I want to foreground the fact that Palestinians, like other exiled people, have long enacted virtual returns *without* the use of digital media. If we consider the virtual as a space of potential, unmoored from virtual reality technologies per se, we understand imaginative and practical modes in which Palestinians have been continually performing return since the moment of their exile. What is today called "telepresence"—action at a distance, of the sort we are accustomed to in the age of remote work and remote war, an era of drone warfare, telehealth visits, Zoom meetings—has long been foreshadowed by the cognitive condition of diaspora, of living both *here* and *there* at once.[8]

The importance of *rehearsing* return can be seen in the centrality of return to Palestinian cultural production ever since the nakba. Ghassan Kanafani's 1969 novella *A'id 'ila Hayfa* ("Return to Haifa") is probably the most well-known Palestinian narrative of return, a landmark of "committed literature" that sensitively depicts both the tragedy of the nakba and the necessity of revolutionary struggle. Notably, *A'id "ila Hayfa* represents return as simultaneously temporal and spatial, with the characters" return from Ramallah to the Haifa home from which they were forced to flee also necessitating a return to 1948, which Kanafani renders through flashbacks. Kanafani narrates a concrete spatial return to a house expropriated by the Israeli state, but also a dream of returning home, in which "the homeland is the future."[9] The 2008 film *Salt of This Sea*, directed by Annemarie Jacir, echoes Kanafani's novella in a pivotal scene in which a young Palestinian American woman (played by poet Suheir Hammad) enters the Jaffa home that belonged to her grandfather and demands that the young Israeli woman living there recognize it as stolen. But it is Jacir's subsequent film *When I Saw You* (2012) that conveys the exhilarating and unresolved potential of return, with its final scene of a young boy and his mother running back home that ends in a freeze frame before they reach the perilous guarded fence separating Jordan from occupied Palestinian land. Alongside these examples in cinema and literature, one might think of Emily Jacir's celebrated photo-and-text series *Where We Come From* (2001–3). To create this work, Jacir (Annemarie's sister), who holds a US passport, asked Palestinians forbidden from accessing different parts of Palestine (depending on the ID cards they hold), "If I could do anything for you, anywhere in Palestine, what would it be?" The artist visited a woman's Jerusalem grave for her son with a West Bank ID in Bethlehem, took a photograph of a Jaffa home for a refugee whose family was expelled in 1948, and played soccer on the streets of Haifa for the son of exiles from that city, among other actions she documented.

In evoking such rehearsals, it is important to emphasize that Palestinian refugees have not only imagined and demanded but indeed *practiced* various forms of return ever since 1948. Immediately following the nakba, tens of thousands of Palestinians—labeled "infiltrators" by Israeli authorities—walked back to their villages across newly divided Galilee lands. This "War on Return," as historian Shira Robinson recodes David Ben-Gurion's "War on Infiltration," entailed both the deportation or execution of returnees and regular raids on Galilee villages to root out Palestinians without state-issued identification cards.[10] In 1949, Robinson writes, "an average of a thousand refugees crossed into Israel each month, a flow that continued even after a free-fire policy issued in April 1949 turned the country's truce lines into killing fields that left a thousand dead by the end of that year."[11] Importantly, Robinson calls attention to the *failures* of these military operations. As protests against Israel's border policies led by Galilee clergy members and Communist politicians mounted, expelled Palestinians continued to reunite with family members, hiding in "underground railroad stations."[12]

Return is not only a dream but also a dangerous, even deadly, act of defiance. Return therefore depends on collective vision and solidarity. Palestinians are frequently inspired by refusals performed by each other across the borders and political fragmentations imposed by Israel. In Abou-Rahme's view, Gaza's Great March of Return was in part "an answer to the marches of return that young people had been doing to the sites inside '48, at that point for years, in a large-scale way."[13] Many such examples exist. In the summer of 2012, a small group of Palestinians whose grandparents were displaced from Iqrit decided to return to the depopulated Galilee village in a sustained way after many years of meeting there for annual summer camps, weddings, and burials. Creating the Iqrit Community Association, they publicly asserted their history and right to return, inspiring other '48 Palestinians to follow suit. The year 2013 saw a "Summer of Return," during which descendants of Palestinians displaced from the villages of Kufr Birim, Ghabisiya, Saffuriyya, Miar, Malul, and Lajjun participated in the *Udna* (Our Return) project, which "aims to educate the new generation with family connections to these villages of their history and rights, with film screenings and storytelling featuring residents who survived the expulsion."[14] As members of Udna returned to their villages, they projected possible futures of return both materially and virtually, building on-the-ground structures and also producing digital rendering of villages to which Palestinians had returned en masse.[15] Israel demolished the new structures that these young returnees built, but this only strengthened the latter's conviction that their resistance was part of a long history of refusing settler-colonial authority.[16] Moreover, the media produced by Udna endures as concrete documents of return, past, present, and future. Their efforts are testament to how "[r]eturn to Palestine is both a virtual, imagined future and a planned, substantive present."[17]

Beneath the Pine Trees, the Undercommons: Razan AlSalah's *Canada Park*

In *Canada Park*, Razan AlSalah narrates a virtual excursion to the video-essay's titular site, an Israeli national park built on the land of Palestinian villages near Jerusalem that the Israeli army destroyed in 1967. A touristic area in which Israelis regularly hike, picnic, and take historical tours, Canada Park becomes, in AlSalah's virtual visit, a site of radical haunting. The artist layers glitchy moving images from Google Earth with photographs of a return march undertaken by Palestinians to the destroyed villages, over electronic music and sonic manipulations of her spoken narration that establish an uncanny balance between the familiar and the otherworldly. AlSalah's voice-over, distanced and distorted by heavy reverb, poetically evokes the sensory disorientation that the video performs; as she intones early on, *'aynee la thuqubbu lil-noor fiha, 'aynee al-takseer* ("my eye has no iris, my eye is a glass prism").[18] Opening with this first-person declaration of a fantastically defamiliarized organ of sight, lacking that which controls the flow of light and breaking apart all the light that flows through it, AlSalah both undermines the idea of a neutral technology of vision and proposes a potent mode of perceiving otherwise. Even as it employs Google's mapping software to visualize a virtual return to Palestine, then, *Canada Park* suggests that it is a decolonial, surrealist eye/I that can see Palestine—past, present, and potential—beneath the pine trees Israel has planted to hide its remains.

Before engaging AlSalah's video in further depth, some context about the site after which it is named is needed. Canada Park is located to the north and west of Jerusalem in a strategic area, formerly known as the Latrun salient, that Israel failed to conquer in 1948 but seized during the June 1967 war. Meeting no resistance, the Israeli army occupied three villages in Latrun (Imwas, Yalo, and Beit Nuba), expelled several thousand Palestinian inhabitants, and forced them to walk roughly 30kilometers to Ramallah without food or water.[19] Following orders from then commander-in-chief Yitzhak Rabin, it demolished hundreds of homes in each village to prevent their inhabitants from ever returning.[20] Soon after, the Mevo Heron settlement was erected atop the ruins of Beit Nuba, while Canada Park was established over the remains of Imwas and Yalo. Built by the Jewish National Fund (JNF), which has planted millions of pine trees and other nonindigenous species over scores of destroyed and depopulated Palestinian villages, Canada Park is so named because the JNF's Canadian branch funded it with roughly 15 million dollars—equivalent to some 100 million dollars today—in donations.[21]

The expulsion and erasure of Palestinian life around Latrun, and the JNF's erasure of that erasure, echo similar stories from 1948; indeed, many of the refugees of Latrun had been forced to flee their homes two decades prior. If there is anything exceptional about this episode of ethnic cleansing, it is that Canada Park's land lies beyond the "Green Line"—unbeknownst to most Israeli and international visitors—and has been effectively annexed by Israel.[22] Thus, when Palestinians from the three destroyed villages, together with members of Zochrot, undertook a procession of return in summer 2007 to mark forty years since their expulsion, the separation wall cut them off from Canada Park as they stood near the Mevo Heron settlement, even though the land on both sides of the wall is the West Bank.[23] In addition to organizing this march, Zochrot campaigned to have signs erected within Canada Park that would testify to the histories of Imwas and Yalo. Following a long legal process, Zochrot compelled the JNF to erect two signs that acknowledged the existence of the two Palestinian villages "until 1967"; however, these did not so much as mention the events of that year or use the words "occupation," "expulsion," or "refugees."[24] Within weeks, one sign was soon removed and another defaced and subsequently removed.

Canada Park incorporates images of the return march organized by Zochrot, showing masses of people holding Palestinian flags and protest signs emblazoned with the names of the three villages. But AlSalah's aims as an artist, and a Palestinian, are distinct from the documentary exposure of the villages' histories Zochrot undertakes largely to raise critical awareness among an Israeli public. *Canada Park* is not expository. Its images do not uncover a hidden truth but blur, enlarge, juxtapose, and glitch motley visual layers, as the artist drops into various "street views" within and perspectives of Canada Park offered by Google Maps and its affiliated user data. Photographs of the return march are themselves presented as one layer among others, digitally faded, recolored, and superimposed over the virtual Canada Park landscape. An image of a protest sign from the march, which reads *Lam w lan nasmah b'al-musawamah 'ala qurana 'Imwas, Yalo, Beit Nouba* and is translated in the subtitles as "we will not concede to the erasure of our villages," is the only explicit allusion to the destroyed Palestinian villages. By contrast, AlSalah's voice-over consists of first-person poetic phrases that perform the artist's spectral digital presence in Palestine as they evoke a psychic and political reality concealed by Canada Park (and amplified by the alternately eerie and entrancing soundtrack by Nabihah Iqbal). The aforementioned line *'aynee al-takseer* repeats at least three times in the video, alongside other statements beginning *'aynee* that name refusals both sensory and political: "my eye has no tears/to feed the monstrous pines." These accompany the artist's distortions of Google Street View imagery of Canada Park, subverting the notion of the software as a transparent window onto the world. Early in the video, the park's pine forests appear to melt away into abstraction, as the artist manipulates the digital imagery into over-exposed contours of dark green and white. Dissolving and reconstructing images of "the monstrous pines," the artist identifies her defiant, tearless eye with a decolonial "I," as her voiceover continues: "I'm not from the public, I'm the undercommons."

Both critically reflexive and surrealist in its exploration of space, *Canada Park* substitutes psycho-geography for cartography. As if on a situationist dérive, AlSalah rejects an algorithmically efficient path for a set of disorienting movements and defamiliarizing perspectives, carving out spaces that elude those mapped by the Google software she employs. Rather than heighten the immersive quality of a virtual visit to Canada Park through spatiotemporal continuity—that is, by recording click-by-click movements along routes with clear imagery and ample information—AlSalah cuts across distinct user perspectives and discontinuous spaces while foregrounding processes of mediation that structure both Google's mapping software and her own video. If immersive VR offers users the illusion of access, proximity, and presence, *Canada Park* continually emphasizes partiality, distance, and absence. The video's opening glimpse of an informational sign in Hebrew, for example, is too brief to situate the park geographically, historically, or cinematically; the artist quickly tilts upward to the sky, and circles amid the blur of sunlight and clouds, as if searching for a space beyond the mapped reality. When the view tilts back to ground level, we see a tourist bus, the road in front of it, and the emblematic "X" and arrow icons that designate where the Google Street View user stands and where she can move. The arrow is then seen superimposed on the helmet of a bike rider whose blurry, jolted movements we follow and then abandon. These opening images both establish the contemporary functions of the national park—tourism and leisure—and gesture at evading them, suggesting a user resistant to the software she employs as much as the site she explores.

Situationist tactics of détournement supplement AlSalah's dérive in an interactive work the artist created alongside *Canada Park*. Commissioned by the Canadian art publication *C-Mag*, *No Man's Land* invites people to overlay images of the Latrun return march within the Google Maps view of Ayalon-Canada Park. *C-Mag*'s website and AlSalah's artist website link to a Google Drive folder with a document titled "counter-mapping instructions" (uploaded by the user "digital spectre"), which enjoin visitors to "disrupt the normalization of occupation and ethnic cleansing in Palestine." The instructions read, "download the images of the *March of Return to Latrun* (June 16, 2007) in this folder, locate 'Ayalon Canada-Park' on Google Maps and reupload the images onto that location." *No Man's Land* both foregrounds *Canada Park*'s critique of Google's allegedly objective cartography and opens it up for interaction and discussion, in ways similar to the collaborative (counter)-cartographic projects *Palestine Open Maps* or iNakba.[25]

Imagining Palestinian return, AlSalah suggests, requires ways of sensing that are foreclosed by the visuality of Google's platforms. Despite the avowedly apolitical character of Google Maps or Google Street View, these tools are not neutral, but rather reproduce the divisions and hierarchies of a settler-colonial reality, not unlike nineteenth-century and early twentieth-century photographs of the Holy Land that bolstered an imperial imaginary that rendered Palestinians absent or mere objects in the background of a biblical landscape. AlSalah highlights this as she visualizes the human icon on Google Street View hopping across landmarks within Canada Park like "cave" and "Roman bath" to Emmaus Nicopolis, a touristic site whose signposted Roman structures, together with signposted stories of a reincarnated Jesus walking, eclipses the unmarked remains of the Palestinian village 'Imwas. Paradoxically, AlSalah continually employs Google's mapping software to critique its naturalization of colonial power; in this sense, *Canada Park* is a work of détournement as much as *No Man's Land*.

AlSalah's previous video, *Your Father Was Born 100 Years Old, and So Was the Nakba* (2017), also employs Google Street View to digitally return to Palestine while underscoring the platform's ideological limits. For *Your Father Was Born ...*, the artist simulates a walk through the Haifa neighborhood from which her grandmother was displaced. Layering Google Street View with photographs of the pre-nakba Palestinian city, she performs a spatiotemporal return to a Haifa whose buildings and street names have changed, in an extended allusion to Kanafani's "Returning to Haifa" that the artist underscores by closely paraphrasing it: "I can't even see it, they're showing it to me."[26] Where Kanafani referred to the opening of the Mandelbaum Gate directly after the June 1967 war, in AlSalah's video it comes to suggest the appearance of Haifa, via Google, as an Israeli city.

Canada Park is distinct from AlSalah's previous work with Google mapping software, however, in at least two respects. First, in addition to performing a virtual return for the diasporic artist, it also visually represents a collective march of return by Palestinian refugees to the destroyed villages from which they were expelled. In so doing, it disrupts the virtual sphere she uses with images documenting a material practice of return by Palestinians living under occupation. Second, it reflects on the artist's own implication in settler-colonial processes, with the choice of Canada Park as site and subject through which AlSalah thematizes the similar settler-colonial histories that have displaced her ancestors and those of the people whose land she occupies as an artist living in Montreal. "I find myself on unceded indigenous territory in so-called Canada, an exile unable to return to Palestine," AlSalah writes.[27] Her statement helpfully explicates the video by providing some of the political context to which it alludes, but it also poetically complements the video as much as it describes it. Opening with the surreal assertion, "I walk on snow to fall unto the desert," AlSalah performs a collapse of time and space that dramatizes the political proximity of the two geographically far-flung settler states as she virtually transports herself to a home that is no longer home: "I trespass the colonial border as a digital spectre floating through Ayalon-Canada Park, transplanted over three Palestinian villages razed by the Israeli Occupation Forces in 1967."

By concluding *Canada Park* in present-day Canada, AlSalah refuses a unidirectional critique or a focus on her digital return to Palestine that would conceal her embodied location "on unceded indigenous territory in so-called Canada." Indeed, the scene features a body—for the first time in a video constructed through screen-captures of Google Street Views—standing on a snowy hill, at a distance, between two communications towers, as if visualizing the artist's position, both *here* and *there* within

Figure 6.1 Still from Razan AlSalah, *Canada Park* (2020). Courtesy of Razan AlSalah.

Figure 6.2 Still from Razan AlSalah, Your Father Was Born 100 Years Old, and so Was the Nakba (2017). Courtesy of Razan AlSalah.

a settler-colonial network. Here, the figure starts to clap her hands and dance, as the voiceover concludes—"My eye has no lid / to close for prayer / my eye is a glass prism / an incantation for rain"—and the sounds of a traditional Arabic song emerge from the electronic soundtrack. The camera zooms in on her during this rain dance, but she does not come into focus; instead, her dark coat fractures into kinetic pixels, dissolving the snowy scene into black-and-white abstraction until a view of the Canada Park desert fades in behind the pixels. *Canada Park* concludes with this evocation of an interconnected settler-colonial present and an invocation, through dance and haptic imagery, of the power to bring about another future.

Opaque Portals: At Those Terrifying Frontiers

Throughout this case, I have emphasized return as a structure continually imagined and performed by Palestinians. Even within this framework, Gaza's Great March of Return stands as an extraordinary demonstration of collective will and political refusal.[28] Having lived under a brutal siege for more than a decade, tens of thousands of Palestinians in Gaza performed the lethal act of converging on a heavily guarded border fence *as if* returning to their homes, though they understood that debility or death likely awaited them. In Azoulay's words, "The Great March of Return is not only a matter of defiance; literally and physically it potentializes history, makes these claims present, ensures that they have not and can never be buried, even as many bodies are buried."[29] Like countless other practices of return from 1948 to the present, the Great March of Return both asserts the ongoing reality of Palestine as a nation not bounded by the borders imposed on it and renews return as an urgent right that exceeds its legal framework in UN Resolution 194.

Abou-Rahme and Abbas's *At Those Terrifying Frontiers* represents Palestinians who participated in Gaza's Great March of Return through avatars generated from their images and from the artists' own bodily movements. Abstracted into virtual, but still expressive and mobile human figures, the avatars appear—one, two, three, or four at a time—framed in tight squares or vertical rectangles with cellphone camera features at their bottom, as if confined in or trying to escape their visual mediations. These frames are superimposed over images of fields, mountains, and roads, or on black screens, across which the artists' signature bold on-screen text flashes. Gaza, the March of Return, and its violent repression are *not* visualized, effectively reframing a de-historicized media focus on climactic violence to address a broader history of Palestinian aspiration and action, even an ontology of the Palestinian condition. The artists sample text from Edward Said's 1986 book *After the Last Sky: Palestinian Lives*, a collaboration with the photographer Jean Mohr, in which Said's reflections on Palestinian subjectivity complement and address Mohr's images of daily life in a range of Palestinian locales, across historic Palestine as well as refugee camps in the region. Through the artists' acts of sampling, remediation, and performance, *At Those Terrifying Frontiers* transmutes Said's poetic text into a mournful song sung by these avatars, creating a virtual, transhistorical collectivity that reflects on what it is to be Palestinian, to be uprooted from one's land and way of life, and to dream of returning home.

Abbas and Abou-Rahme conceived of *At Those Terrifying Frontiers* in the early weeks of the Great March of Return, while working in Ramallah. The West Bank city is roughly 50 kilometers away from the northern Gaza Strip, but this short distance is unbridgeable. Unable to approach, let alone enter Gaza, the artists witnessed the march from a mediated distance. The project began, then, as an "effort to break [this] forced separation."[30] Abbas and Abou-Rahme collected images of Palestinians participating in the march taken by Palestinian protesters and photojournalists in Gaza. Subsequently, they input these images into software that generated three-dimensional human figures from the images, abstracting their features, and enabling the artists to smooth the texture of their skin, reconstruct or remove their hair, and place them in simple monochrome T-shirts. The Palestinian returnees become anonymous avatars, shedding their individual identities. But they remain expressive in their poses, gazes, gestures, and "wounds." In the process of rendering, missing data produced blurry deformations that appear as bruises and cuts—glitches that evoke the injuries suffered by the Palestinian demonstrators. To animate the avatars, Abbas and Abou-Rahme recorded themselves re-enacting gestures they witnessed in footage of the march. After feeding video of their performance to the software, the avatars "adopted" the movements of the two artists and some of their distinct facial features. In this process of "disembodiment and re-embodiment," the artists merged with the protesters they could not join, making themselves present affectively and virtually through their rendering of the avatars.[31]

Through their opaque mediation of the March, Abbas and Abou-Rahme generate proximity to Gaza outside the logics of humanitarian optics and violent spectacles. Bridging the distance to Gaza for themselves and their viewers, Abbas and Abou-Rahme use embodied performance to connect with the Great March of Return. But far from hiding mediation to present an immediate, immersive sense of *being there*, one intended to produce the sympathy of distant spectators, they puncture the illusion of proximity with cuts, glitches, and delays. Virtuality is not, here, about the poignant simulation of presence at a distant site of conflict.

The opacity of *At Those Terrifying Frontiers* establishes a relational mode of witnessing premised not on a spectator's empathy with distant subjects they come to see as *human* or *just like us* but on an engagement with social practices and histories of struggle that show these subjects to be *political* actors inviting (or challenging) viewers to join them in solidarity. Cognizant of the limitations of humanitarian forms of witnessing, Abbas and Abou-Rahme counter both an aesthetics of immediation and the illusion of immersion. Rather than expose victimized Palestinians to spectators, they intimate oblique elements of Palestinian struggles to shape their own identity, image, and narrative. In the artists' practice, the *cut* emerges as a key gesture against immediation and immersion. This includes the cut in the cinematic sense of montage, as the artists dispense with continuities of space and time through their editing. A logic of the cut is also emphasized in the artists' installations, for which images are often projected across multiple surfaces, interrupting their wholeness and rupturing the gestalt of figures such as, for example, a human face or body. Similar fragmentation occurs through their use of screens within screens, which emphasizes the partiality of any mediation through both the interrupted image and the suggestion of simultaneous planes of action. In the artist's words, "our practice makes ... the thread between different times, spaces and imaginaries visible."[32] This simultaneously connective and disjunctive logic emerges in *At Those Terrifying Frontiers* in its visualizations of impossible conjunctions between the West Bank and Gaza, and in the resonances and translations between its sources and the audiovisual forms they take.

The conceptual core of *At Those Terrifying Frontiers*, reflected in its soundtrack and on-screen text, emerged from Abbas and Abou-Rahme's experience reading Said's *After the Last Sky* as the March was unfolding.[33] The video is constructed around sampled phrases from Said's poetic meditation on Palestinian subjectivity, which the artists sing in Arabic—having translated excerpts of the text themselves—as the original English text flashes on screen, in short lines synchronized with their vocals.[34] Over the course of ten minutes, they sing and intone, separately and together, in solemn, lamenting, and at times declarative cadences. Their words resound as they are both swallowed and amplified by heavy reverb, often looped to generate echoes and grooves, and sometimes interrupted by effects that produce noisy stutters. Produced with the dense sonic layering common to the artists' videos, the complex soundscape conveys as much as the lyrics. It is also distinctly and disarmingly personal, as the artists' first video to feature their own voices.

After the Last Sky likewise marked a departure for Said, a personal reflection that was, then, a far cry from the scholar's typically assertive argumentation. It is an inward-looking book, full of doubt, melancholy, and vulnerability. These qualities emerge, in large part, from Said's collaboration with the Swiss photographer Jean Mohr, to whom Said was introduced by their mutual friend John Berger. *After the Last Sky* is Said's response to the intimate photographs that Mohr took during visits to Palestine/Israel and Palestinian refugee camps in the region in the late 1970s and early 1980s, during which he documented quotidian Palestinian experiences in streets, markets, schools, and domestic spaces.[35]

Said's text focuses on questions of how to represent Palestinians in this context, how to narrate the Palestinian condition to a world steeped in negations of Palestinian

Figure 6.3 Still from Basel Abbas and Ruanne Abou-Rahme, *At Those Terrifying Frontiers Where the Existence and Disappearance of People Fade Into Each Other*, 2019, Video/Sound Installation view at Fisher Center, Bard. Photography by Maria Baranova. Courtesy of the artists.

Figure 6.4 Basel Abbas and Ruanne Abou-Rahme, film still from *At Those Terrifying Frontiers Where the Existence and Disappearance of People Fade into Each Other*, 2019, Video/Sound Installation view at Fisher Center, Bard. Courtesy of the artists.

identity, not to mention in the shadow of disappeared archives and across the social fragmentations imposed by Israel. The first words the artists cite from Said's book (in song and text) announce these themes: "We have experienced a great deal that has not been recorded. Many of us have been killed, many permanently scarred and silenced, without a trace. And the images used to represent us only diminish our reality further." In these lines, distinct forms of violence converge to convey Palestinian existence as threatened by physical force, by representation (in images), and by the absence of representation ("has not been recorded").

Said takes the book's title from a well-known Mahmoud Darwish poem, using as its epigraph the couplet, "Where should we go after the last frontiers? / Where can the birds fly after the last sky?" If Darwish's poem is a classic expression of Palestinian displacement and dispossession, of spatial and spiritual confinement, Said plumbs these themes further but adds the sense of being confined by images and narratives of one's identity. The artists translate this confinement visually, at times circumscribing the avatars' images with tight frames as if to ask: What frames are capacious enough to hold and to transmit Palestinian experience? Which frames do not bring Palestinian life closer, but contain it? Is visibility a trap? Or as Said asks, "Can we see what we are, have we really seen what we have seen?"[36] These are some of the questions artists take up as they grapple with the question of how to bear witness and mediate that witnessing to a world saturated with images of violence.

As mentioned previously, Gaza does not appear in this video. Nor do images of tear gas, burning tires, or bloodied bodies. The artists show a few fleeting, nighttime views of border fences in the West Bank that evoke a sense of incarceration shared by Palestinians living under occupation. Other than these images, however, there is only a general sense of place, as the avatars are superimposed over monochrome screens, fields of thistle, and mountainous landscapes. In light of the vocal soundtrack, sung in the style of an Islamic *nasheed* or chant, it is as if the avatars are lifted into a spiritual plane. This sense is heightened by following the gazes of the avatar, as they look upward or into the distance, perhaps at the viewer, or through them. But this spiritual quality is not deliverance; it is imbued with doubt, and yearning, that registers across image, text, and sound.

When Said wrote *After the Last Sky* in 1985–6, he had not been to Palestine since his family fled Jerusalem in 1947, under the duress of Zionist and British fighting. Palestine/Israel was mediated for the world's most famous Palestinian scholar as a faraway if intimately familiar place, utterly inaccessible to him even when he was geographically and culturally proximate, as he often was, in Beirut. It was not until 1992—after Said had resigned from the Palestinian National Council—that he was able to return to Palestine, forty-five years after his family's exodus. Until then, it was arguably Mohr's photographs that brought him closest to imagining everyday life in Jerusalem, Gaza, Nablus, or Hebron. In this sense, *After the Last Sky* itself marks a virtual return, before the event of the author's individual return, before the return of thousands of PLO members that followed the Oslo Accords, and before the collective return that Palestinians insist will come.

Past the video's midpoint, *At Those Terrifying Frontiers* visualizes avatars, within the frame of smartphone screens, superimposed over night skies and mountainous landscapes. The avatars join the artists on the road, in the West Bank, evoking a sense of a virtual return for these marchers who are not able to cross the border fence. But of course, the West Bank too is occupied, and the artists and protesters can only reach one another through their virtual merging, so the enforced separation remains. For now, it can only be transcended through virtuality, which, as I suggest, does not imply high-tech immersion in a simulated reality, or escape into *unreality*, but something closer to emergence: a combination of actuality and potentiality, of *what is* and *what could be*.

What *is* are ongoing practices of Palestinian *sumud* and resistance: holding steadfast on one's land and rehearsing return. What *is*, in other words, is the ongoing effort to come home that is halted, within 1948, by army demolitions and arrests, and in Gaza, by being tear gassed and shot down. What *could be* is a return like the one visualized as the avatars become unmoored from Gaza's siege and are lifted virtually into spaces from which they might return home. Abou-Rahme and Abbas forge a multisensory, embodied form of witnessing that opens onto this potentiality that can be felt but is only fleetingly glimpsed, that is immanent in the here and now but rarely visualized. It is in these opaque openings that the Palestinian condition can emerge as a struggle for freedom that invites not humanitarian sympathy but political solidarity, on the basis not of Palestinians' identities as victims but of our collective becoming at those terrifying frontiers where the existence and disappearance of peoples fade into each other.

Notes

1 Miriyam Aouragh and Helga Tawil-Souri, "Intifada 3.0? Cyber Colonialism and Palestinian Resistance," *Arab Studies Journal* 22, no. 1 (2014): 102–33.
2 Dale Hudson, "Mapping Palestine/Israel through Interactive Documentary," *Journal of Palestine Studies* 50, no. 1 (2021): 71. Italics in original.
3 As media scholars have argued, VR technology is in fact far from novel in its underlying drive to represent an ever-wider scope of reality and to minimize perceptions of mediation. For a critical genealogy of (humanitarian) VR that traces its links with the cathedral, the planetarium, the panorama, and cinema, see Sasha Crawford-Holland, "Humanitarian VR Documentary and Its Cinematic Myths," *Synoptique* 7, no. 1 (2018): 19–31.
4 On humanitarian uses of VR, see Eszter Zimanyi and Emma Ben Ayoun, eds., "In Focus: Humanitarian Immersions," *Journal of Cinema Studies* 61, no. 3 (Spring 2022): 154–94.
5 Sabrien Amrov, "Virtual Reality Encounters at the Israel Museum," *Jerusalem Quarterly* 84 (Winter 2020): 96.
6 Pooja Rangan, *Immediations: The Humanitarian Impulse in Documentary* (Durham, NC: Duke UP, 2017), 4.
7 Lori Allen, "Martyr Bodies in the Media: Human Rights, Aesthetics, and the Politics of Immediation in the Palestinian Intifada," *American Ethnologist* 36, no. 1 (February 2009): 162.
8 See Kris Paulsen, *Here/There: Telepresence, Art, and Touch at the Interface* (Cambridge, MA: MIT Press, 2017).

9   Ghassan Kanafani, *Palestine's Children: Returning to Haifa and Other Stories*, trans. Barbara Harlow and Karen Riley (London: Lynne Rienner: 2000), 187.
10 See also Azoulay on the fabrication of the category "infiltrator" as part of Israel's constituent violence, maintained through citizens' complicity in accepting the state's photographic records and archival classifications. Ariella Aïsha Azoulay, "The Imperial Condition of Photography in Palestine: Archives, Looting, and the Figure of the Infiltrator," *Visual Anthropology Review* 33, no. 1 (Spring 2017): 5–17.
11 Shira Robinson, *Citizen Strangers: Palestinians and the Birth of Israel's Liberal Settler State* (Stanford, CA: Stanford University Press, 2013), 78.
12 Robinson, *Citizen Strangers*, 74–82. The phrase "underground railroad stations" was used by an unnamed Israeli spokesman, cited on 78.
13 Personal conversation with Abbas and Abou-Rahme, February 21, 2022.
14 Nadim Nashef, "Palestinian Youth Assert Right of Return with Direct Action," *Electronic Intifada*, September 11, 2013, https://electronicintifada.net/content/palestinian-youth-assert-right-return-direct-action/12760. Accessed March 7, 2022.
15 For an incisive reading of Udna's engagement with media in envisioning return, see Meryem Kamil, "Postspatial, Postcolonial: Accessing Palestine in the Digital," *Social Text 144* 38, no. 3 (September 2020): 69–72.
16 George Ghantous, an activist from Kufr Bir'im, recalled the eviction of returnees to his village four decades prior, and stated, "We wish to become a front for Palestinian return." Nashef, "Palestinian Youth."
17 Kamil, "Postspatial, Postcolonial," 75.
18 The video's script is spoken in (formal) Arabic and translated with English subtitles.
19 Rich Wiles, *Behind the Wall: Life, Love, and Struggle in Palestine* (Washington, DC: Potomac Books, 2010), 19. Figures range from 5,000 (Cook) to over 10,000 (Wiles).
20 Ghazi-Walid Falah, "War, Peace, and Land Seizure in Palestine's Border Area," *Third World Quarterly* 25, no. 5 (2004): 967. I am grateful to Sasha Crawford-Holland for this reference.
21 Jonathan Cook, "Canadian Ambassador Honored at Illegal Park," *The National*, June 18, 2009, https://www.thenationalnews.com/world/mena/canadian-ambassador-honoured-at-illegal-park-1.522327. Accessed October 29, 2022.
22 Eitan Bronstein Aparicio, "75% of visitors to Israel's Canada Park believe it is located inside the Green Line (it's not)," *Mondoweiss*, June 15, 2014, https://mondoweiss.net/2014/06/visitors-israels-located/. Accessed October 29, 2022.
23 Zochrot, "Procession of Return to the Villages of Latrun," https://www.zochrot.org/activities/activity_details/52157/en?Procession_of_Return_to_the_Villages_of_Latrun
24 Eitan Bronstein Aparicio, "Restless Park: On the Latrun villages and Zochrot." Translated by Charles Kamen. Zochrot, undated. https://www.zochrot.org/publication_articles/view/51029/en?Restless_Park_On_the_Latrun_villages_and_Zochrot
25 See Olga Blázquez Sánchez, "Collaborative Cartographies: Counter-Cartography and Mapping Justice in Palestine," *Journal of Holy Land and Palestine Studies* 17, no. 1 (2018): 75–85.
26 Early in Kanafani's story, when Saffiya remarks, "I never imagined I'd see Haifa again," her husband Said retorts, "You're not seeing it, they're showing it to you." Kanafani, *Palestine's Children*, 151.
27 Razan AlSalah, "Canada Park." Razanalsalah.com.

28 The Great March of Return began on March 30, 2018, a day Palestinians commemorate as Land Day, and continued to grow every Friday through May 15, 2018, a Nakba Day that marked seven decades since the State of Israel's founding. The protests were initially meant to end then, but with tens of thousands of Palestinians joining week after week, the marches continued through December 2019.

29 Ariella Aïsha Azoulay, *Potential History: Unlearning Imperialism* (London: Verso Books, 2019), 128.

30 Basel Abbas and Ruanne Abou-Rahme, "Being in the Negative." Cooper Union talk, September 21, 2021.

31 Abbas and Abou-Rahme, "Being in the Negative."

32 Fawz Kabra, "Ruanne Abou-Rahme and Basel Abbas in Conversation with Fawz Kabra," *Ocula*, January 18, 2018, https://ocula.com/magazine/conversations/basel-abbas-and-ruanne-abou-rahme/. Accessed November 22, 2021.

33 The artists take their video's title from a poignant passage in Said's text, in which he describes the doctoral dissertation of the Palestinian feminist activist and former PLO representative Hanan Ashrawi: "Thus our need for a new consciousness, as Hanan Ashrawi reminds us […] is that of a people whose national experience belongs, with that of the Armenians, the Jews, the Irish, the Cypriots, the American blacks, the Poles, the American Indians, at those terrifying frontiers where the existence and disappearance of peoples fade into each other, where resistance is a necessity, but where there is also sometimes a growing realization of the need for an unusual and, to some degree, an unprecedented knowledge." Edward Said, *After the Last Sky: Palestinian Lives* (New York, NY: Pantheon Books, 1986), 159.

34 Remarkably, unlike most of Said's books, *After the Last Sky* has yet to be translated into Arabic.

35 Said commissioned many of the photographs in the book, through his request that the United Nations sponsor Mohr's travel to Palestinian locales ahead of the UN's 1983 International Conference on the Question of Palestine. Some of the photos, however, predate this trip.

36 Said, *After the Last Sky*, 159.

7

Reincarnated: Common Sense and the Poetics of Elsewhere

Aamer Ibraheem

Prelude

It's December 27, 1976. A strong wind blows outside while rain pours. Nazih Abu Zeid, resident of Majdal Shams in the occupied Golan Heights, walked across a minefield that was set up by Israel following the Separation of Forces Agreement with Syria three years earlier. Nazih, who was only seventeen years of age and working for the Syrian Intelligence Forces, had embarked on a secret mission earlier that evening, and he was on his way back home to the Golan after having delivered sensitive reports about Israel to Syrian agencies, years before the arrival of telephones and fax machines. Nazih was gifted with a remarkable navigational skill, for he was thoroughly familiar with the border area; he knew it too well and crossed there too often. But that night of December 1976 was deadly for Nazih, as it brought his "national duty" to an end when he accidentally stepped on an Israeli landmine, and tragically, breathed his last the next morning upon a night of suffering. Entangled in the minefield with a bleeding leg and serious injuries, Nazih slowly died in front of the eyes of dozens of his community members and residents of Majdal Shams, who had promptly gathered after hearing the landmine's explosion. Helplessly, the witnesses stood a few meters away from the minefield's fence, not able to get in and rescue their dying comrade, relative, and acquaintance. Among them, that night is painfully remembered. It was only after his death that the Israeli army entered the field and claimed Nazih's body, which was released back to his family four days later.

Years of political uncertainty followed the Israeli occupation of the Golan in 1967. A remaining small community, consisting almost exclusively of Syrian Druze, had to endure two national projects that were simultaneously unfolding. On the one hand, Israel was expanding its presence to the newly occupied landscape through Jewish settlements, agricultural farms, and a few industries where local Druze

---

I am grateful to Helga Tawil-Souri, Dina Matar, Khaled Furani, and Adrien Zakar for their helpful comments, and to the Palestinian American Research Center (PARC) for their support in funding parts of my fieldwork.

were to be incorporated as a workforce. On the other hand, the Syrian authorities were repurposing already-existing networks of Druze kinship and political affiliations in the Golan, deploying military intelligence through civilian presence. The story as well as legacy of Nazih was part of this latter political reality, through which dozens of other men and women among his contemporaries emerged to political life in the Golan. Together, they helped shape an anti-colonial scene in the Heights, which culminated in 1982, when the local Syrian community refused the impositions of Israeli citizenship following the Knesset's decision to fold this territory under its sovereignty. Expectedly, this political moment of refusal has been celebrated across different parts of Syria, often as a way of staging a semantic national commitment orchestrated by the Syrian government.[1] In 2008, for instance, the city of Jaramana in the south of Damascus, celebrated the inauguration and naming of a school after the martyr Nazih Abu Zeid with lionizing speeches and emphatic statements, courtesy of the Baath Party.

The Golan: Reoriented

Readers of this story might wonder as to why a text about the life and afterlife of a Syrian martyr from the Golan appears among other cases that explore Palestine. My answer is rather simple. There lies in that very mode of questioning an assumption of a Palestine that is clearly defined. Both spatially and temporally, such an assumption imagines Palestine as a place with strict boundaries, beginnings, and endings; a territory with fixed centers and peripheries; a land with tenacious claims about an inside and outside. This case aims at disrupting these enclosed and enclosing assumptions, or at least at creating moments of dissonance in them. It does so by highlighting particular scenes of life in the Golan, a landscape that often figures as both a reminder and remainder of a Syrian presence in Palestine, and more precisely, of Palestine as part of Syria as well as its extension. Put differently, I am writing this episode with a certain imagination of the Golan as itself a site of mediation from which to reflect on the fluidity of the homeland by looking simultaneously on Palestine and Syria and recognize in them what otherwise could be seen as isolated and fragmented.

The minefield where Nazih was killed is part of a larger history. It is an enclave, with a width of 20 kilometers (12 mi) and a total area of 400 square kilometers (150 sq. mi), that materialized the so-called Agreement on Disengagement between Israel and Syria that was signed in 1974, officially ending the 1973 war. This minefield is at a distance of 40 kilometers (25 mi) from Damascus, a capital city, a center, and a destiny to which many locals in the Golan were attached not long ago. Prior to 1967, the Golan was Syria's most southern province, but after the military defeat of the Arab regimes in June of that year, it was occupied by Israel. Within a month, the Golan—with its 130,000 inhabitants and 139 villages—was almost emptied out. With only 6,396 people remaining in the official record,[2] it was transformed from a populous region integral of the Syrian nation-state into a sparsely populated borderland in a settler-colonial landscape. Five primarily Druze villages remained: Aīn Qinīa, Buqʿāthā, Ghajar, Majdal Shams, and Masʿada.

Examined either through their colonial relationship with Israeli settlements or through their attunement to Syrian authoritarianism, local protagonists such as Nazih, and the politics of commemoration around their legacy, are sites where citizenship, attachments, and political desires are constantly incited by state discourses and persistently reworked by local residents. Here, I pursue a different direction by looking at another site of relations, one that despite being located within clear national boundaries is less dictated by them. It is a site where relations themselves, and the way they come to appear, mediate distant landscapes with political temporalities that have been for long deemed unrelated. Such mode of examination, as I explain below, requires not only a political sensibility but also, and more importantly, a theological one. To do so, we have to head further south, toward Palestine, approximately 75 kilometers away from the Golan's center to the Galilean village of Hurfeish.

Hurfeish is the hometown of Mazen Halabi, who was born to a Druze family on the very morning following December 27, 1976. For his Galilean community, as well as for that of the Golan, Mazen is believed to be the reincarnation of Nazih Abu Zeid. To put it simply, when Nazih was killed in the minefield of Majdal Shams his soul transmigrated into Mazen's body at the moment of his birth in Hurfeish. What gave his parents indications of his soul's journey was that Mazen spoke about the Golan and shared particular details of Nazih's life as he started uttering his first words, at the age of two. He "kept on talking about a fence, obsessively mentioning a landmine and an explosion."[3]

I look at the entanglement of two life histories through the reincarnation narratives of Nazih in the Golan and of Mazen in the Galilee. My aim in following these stories is not to investigate how and if they accurately complete and continue one another but rather to track how the social contexts and political landscapes within which these stories emerged are affected by histories in ways that do not appear to have anything to do with reincarnation theology. I start by teasing out a possible conversation between having and speaking of past-life memories and the work of mediation. Within such a conversation, reincarnation is understood as a mundane organizing activity, one that creates an infrastructure of knowledge against which more elaborate and abstract religious ideas become credible. I then show how past-life memories become part of the givenness of a Druze reality as they imbue ordinary knowledge and everyday habits. Here I offer that we look at such knowledge of past-life as a "common sense" that mediates the relationship between humans, and the places and times they have inhabited in the past or still inhabit in the present. I suggest that narratives of reincarnation hold a radical potential for opening up political and geographical horizons as they necessarily encapsulate histories beyond the immediate context of the here and now. As such, narrating one story from the Galilee would be incomplete without relating it to another story from the Golan, and similarly, making sense of Mazen's trajectory as a Palestinian in Israel in the present won't be fully graspable without linking it to Nazih's past life as a Syrian. My ultimate argument is that reincarnation could be approached as a mode of mediation; a repository of indexed relations that intimately and alternately document and reassemble larger political geographies, structures, dynamics, and realities. Past-life memories, in other words, are history in another form.[4]

Reincarnation and the Question of Mediation

Historically, Islamic traditions of the early eleventh-century Egypt were the foundation on which Druze teachings and cosmologies emerged. The concept of reincarnation in particular is mainly traced to Pythagorean and Platonic ideas that are concerned with the relation between numbers and the natural world.[5] Even today, the veneration of the sage Pythagoras in Druze cosmology and history remains central. Described in scholarship as well as in Druze theological discourse, reincarnation refers to the act of the soul re-entering the flesh of a (presumably) newborn at the very moment that the soul departs from the body of its current residence. Thus, "upon physical death, as defined by biological and physiological parameters, the soul departs the body of the deceased and immediately takes residence in the flesh of a newborn. At that point the old abode becomes lifeless just like any other object, while the newborn becomes a person with a *self* and an *identity* consisting of body and soul."[6] The life of the subject, therefore, never ceases; it merely persists as his or her soul continues on the journey of existence, always in conjunction with a human body.

I approach the conversation about memories of past lives and the act of remembering them as decidedly political. In a region where different regimes of sectarianism, authoritarianism, and settler colonialism shape everyday practices and rhetoric, to grapple with reincarnated memories experienced by Druze subjects is to raise the question of those subjects' own location vis-à-vis the national project under which they carry their lives.

The story that I follow in this case unfolds between the Golan and the Galilee (al-Jawlān w al-Jaleel), two geographical locations that not long ago were parts of different political realities, the Syrian and the Palestinian, respectively. Today, the remaining Druze communities of these geographies have gone through radical, and often contradictory, political transformations. While those in the Golan are gradually but carefully reorienting themselves toward life in Israel as "their" Syria has become a site of ruins and violence, many of those in the Galilee, at least since 1956, have been serving as soldiers in the Israeli army. And yet, the pasts of these places and communities, as well as their interconnectedness, could still be traced and witnessed as lived actuality if we account for and attend to the political narratives of reincarnation theology. The story of Nazih and Mazen, or the story of Nazih *as* Mazen, helps us consider the significance of this political and historical interconnectedness, by allowing two geographical and political contexts seep through to one another.

Such a story is neither unique nor exceptional, for experiences of reincarnation are lived through the quotidian rhythms of Druze realities. Such stories of relations and continuities from one's previous life to the present are rarely questioned for they speak to a centuries-old theological tradition. Instead, what is particularly unique is the different political registers that such stories voice and the political potentialities that these narratives offer. Reincarnation is a repository of lived memories that mediates different histories with geographical landscapes. One way to understand its working is by invoking the anthropological concept of the implicit. Writing in 1975, Mary Douglas argues that the implicit is the necessary foundation of social intercourse.[7] Through implicit channels of meaning, "human society itself is achieved, clarity, and speed of clue-reading ensured. In the elusive exchange between explicit and implicit meanings a perceived-to-be-regular universe establishes itself precariously, shifts, topples, and sets itself up again." The implicit is that which is understood by a speech community to be so much part of their shared assumptions that it does not need to be said in words, shown in gestures, or otherwise depicted.[8] It is, in other words, one of society's common sense. This understanding of the implicit is illuminating as it offers a framework for thinking about the work of reincarnation across Druze communities and the mode of mediation it takes. Reincarnation is a "mundane organizing activity," to borrow from Douglas, which creates an infrastructure of implicit knowledge against which more elaborate and abstract theological ideas become credible.[9]

By approaching reincarnation theology as a repository of implicit knowledge, I assume three modes of mediation to be at work. First, it is a mediation that does not abide by the given national boundaries of the nation-state. The life histories of the Druze protagonists in this case, either Nazih or Mazen, cannot be fully understood if we only narrate them as part of their immediate political positions, as a Syrian in the Golan or as a Palestinian in Israel. Here, I offer an understanding of mediation that transcends the political present. Second, it is a mediation that expands the scope of the geographical location of the subject beyond the contemporary borders of the nation-state. Accordingly, Mazen's story in the Galilee is never complete without tracing its origins in the Golan, and Nazih's legacy in Syria is never complete without following its continuity and afterlife in Mazen's life in Palestine. Such mode of mediation promises to transcend colonial or postcolonial borders. Finally, it is a mediation that is theologically reflexive. In a way that is central to this argument, I maintain that a mode of mediation understood within the finite category of "the cultural" is a mode of mediation patently reduced.[10] Culturally mediated relations are locatable among humans, animals, or among other sublunary species and even objects, ideas, and emotions, a distinctly different mediation from that articulated in reincarnation theology—wherein the relation is with a past-life. These theological relations, as I hope to show, mark various experiences of the political.

Theological Common Sense

Born in Hurfeish in the Galilee into a family of nine, Mazen was the youngest among his siblings with a significant generational gap between him and his oldest brother. This condition perhaps offered him an intimate environment where different temporalities were experienced together as part of a single unit. At the age of three, and without any specific context provided, Mazen started repeatedly bringing up the names of two persons: "Iqab" and "Saniyya." While his parents were not able to relate this pair to any familiar acquaintance, they quickly realized that their son might be offering them some verbal hints of a potential reincarnation narrative. For many Druze families, the accumulation of such verbal hints encourages what could be called an authentication process, a process of communal and social investigation through which past kinship of the reincarnated subject is traced and delineated in an attempt to reach answers as of who and where did this person figure in a past life. Mazen's parents were not particularly interested in dealing with their son's story, but his siblings got intrigued and started teasing him over the years with questions such as "who is Iqab?," "who is Saniyya?," "what are they to you?," and "who are you?." Mazen recalled very little at the time and had no sufficient answers regarding these oft-mentioned names, but all he could add to these utterances was that he vividly remembered "a huge explosion."

But these utterances, and the peculiar stories they carry, circulate in a tightly knit network of families and communities. In Hurfeish, Mazen's neighbor was a Druze woman originally from the Golan who married a Galilean man sometime after Mazen was born. As soon as she learned that a child next door was obsessively speaking of "Iqab" and "Saniyya" and of "an explosion" that took place in the past, she connected the dots and made new sense of the story, for she had witnessed Nazih Abu Zeid's death the dark morning of December 27, 1976. Not only that but she had also known that Nazih's siblings were named "Iqab" and "Saniyya." With clues that resonated too familiarly, the neighbor decided to visit Mazen's family, and following a brief conversation she was able to confirm that Mazen's date of birth precisely coincided with the day on which Nazih was killed in the minefield. As soon as these nuances and other details are traced, revealed, and, more importantly, matched, they become connective markers between at least two life histories: that of the present and that of a past-life. With sufficient answers in hand, it became locally authenticated that "when Nazih was killed in the Golan his soul transmigrated into Mazen's body at the moment of his birth in Hurfeish."

The reality I describe here is often taken for granted in Druze communities. Neither was it odd for Mazen to mention seemingly unfamiliar names at such an early stage nor was it peculiar for his siblings to follow up with attentive questions, nor unusual for the neighbor to inquire more, make sense of these details on her own, and interpret them as part of "another" story that took place elsewhere. This is a theological "common sense" that shapes everyday life in Druze towns and villages in the sense that it constructs a language, directs feelings, instructs ways of asking and paying attention, and informs a certain logic that allows the connection between different temporal relations. It is a form of quotidian perception and mediation.

By common sense I draw mainly, but not exclusively, on Mark Rifkin's work to think about how relations among a certain community help generate forms of understanding through which they become imbued with a sensation of everyday certainty.[11] Examined within a particular political context where the two Druze communities in the Galilee and the Golan are officially assumed by the Israeli state discourse to belong to seemingly two different national histories, such quotidian common sense, practiced and sustained by experiences of reincarnation, can be understood as a normalizing presence, opening up one's own present to other past collectives, histories, and landscapes. As a matter of fact, as I will show in the following paragraphs, not only Mazen's personal life but also that of his family, relatives, and friends in the Galilee became certainly linked to the Golan's political past and present and vice-versa through an apprehension of an unfolding story of reincarnation. The common sense here is not only Mazen's reincarnated memories themselves but also the local conversations taking place around them, the questions people follow up with, and, most importantly, the intuitive world of references that becomes available to mediation. In other words, if reincarnation mediates at least two lives, two places, and two temporalities, then it is through reincarnation as a common sense that other national histories and political territories come to be lived as given, as simply the unmarked, generic conditions of possibility for association, history, and personhood.

At the age of five, Mazen took the bus with his parents and left for a casual trip to the Golan. They first arrived in Qiryat Shemona (formerly, al-Khalsa) in northern Palestine. From there they took a taxi straight to Majdal Shams. It was Mazen's *first* time in the Golan. On their way, he was able to identify some remarkable spots along the road and name them out loud. The taxi driver, himself a Druze resident of Majdal Shams, noticed that this five-year-old kid had a particular attachment to and a close familiarity with the vicinity. Knowingly, the driver tried to playfully trick Mazen by mis-calling some place names along the road, but Mazen was quick to respond and correct these inaccuracies. It is in these spontaneous moments that the driver, the parents, and Mazen drew on a Druze theological common sense to interact and investigate Mazen's own relationship with the place they were traversing.

As they entered Majdal Shams, Mazen's father tried to trick him one last time by declaring that they had arrived in "Mas'ada," one of the other remaining Syrian villages in the Golan. But Mazen was quick to insist that the town they entered was in fact Majdal Shams, and that this was *his* town. Mazen, five years of age at the time, asked the taxi driver to drop him and his family off on the town's main square for he wanted to walk toward his house, namely Nazih's house. Followed by his parents, Mazen arrived there and knocked on a backyard door. It was Nazih's family house, where Mazen had grown up in his past-life. Expectedly, Nazih's parents had anticipated such a visit, for the word that their late son, Nazih, was reincarnated in the Galilee had circulated. One of the details that Mazen still speaks about today is when he entered the house for the first time and noticed that the backyard was missing an old fig tree under which he used to rest. During that visit, Mazen shared many other memories of his past childhood and life as Nazih.

While the content and details of these memories are unique in that they show the generative work of common sense, I am more interested in tracing the political and sometimes radical possibilities and relationships that these memories ignite, bring together, and deem viable. What does it mean to say that Mazen's and Nazih's realities are closely connected? And even more so, what does it entail to assume that together they constitute the same continuous narrative? How do these reincarnation stories entangle two different political experiences: a Syrian community in the Golan and a Palestinian one in the Galilee? What prompts me to ask these questions is the simple fact that, as a Galilean Druze male, Mazen would later receive an official letter at the age of eighteen directing him to register for selective service in the Israeli army. He will have to do so despite his journey of reincarnation, and his awareness of himself being a Syrian agent in his past life. Common sense, as I suggest here, allows us to account for these entangled political spheres and grand national constructions but without being confined by them. It will allow us to understand how multiple, and sometimes contradictory, temporalities work concomitantly with varying hierarchies.

Theological common sense often appears "at odds with national narratives": rooted in highly localized ways of knowing and authenticating, inscribed in bodied selves and their spontaneous utterances, and "regarded as irredeemably subjective, seemingly out of sync with the urgency of politics."[12] However, it is a mode through which people, and in this case Druze communities, come to terms with their present and understand the radical historical transformation that has taken place in their lives over the years. It's necessarily an effect, lived by individual-in-relation-to-others, but at the same time, it undeniably reflects a historical condition.[13]

Common sense, as Antonio Gramsci put it, is a collective noun.[14] "It is a product of history, and part of the historical becoming." It is not something rigid and immobile, but it is "continually transforming itself, enriching itself with scientific ideas and with philosophical opinions which have entered ordinary life." Common sense is the folklore of philosophy.[15] It creates a folklore for the future, which becomes a relatively stable phase in the making of popular knowledge in a given place and time. And despite Gramsci's "apparent contradictory attitude to folklore," and his argument that common sense (and religion broadly speaking) cannot be reduced to unity and coherence,[16] I still want to suggest that the theological common sense at play here functions as an everyday social habit of communication and reasoning that mediates between different political registers.

Porous Palestine: The Poetics of Elsewhere

Narratives of reincarnation, as I have illustrated, enable relations to unfold in time and across space in ways that are radical. In sticking to moments in Mazen's life it becomes possible to notice how Druze individuals, through stories of reincarnation, always live (and become) in relation to *an* elsewhere. This mode of unfolding evokes Édouard Glissant's errantry, for it captures the notion of movement, wandering, and relationality that suffuses everyday life.[17] In his *Poetics of Relation*, Glissant argues that through the practice of errantry individuals gain fuller identities, which are based on not only their roots but also their relations with others. Such relational identity enables individuals' capacities for dialectics, relying on both dialectic's connotations of discussion and tension. Errantry, Glissant writes, is "wandering but with a sacred motivation," and thus constructing relations "not merely an encounter, […] but a new and original dimension allowing each person to be there and elsewhere."[18]

One afternoon during the summer of 2022, I met with Mazen at a Majdal Shams café. He is now forty-five years old, married, and a father of two, and while officially based in the Galilee, Mazen and his family have rented a place in the Golan, where they spend most of their time. As soon as we sat for coffee, I was preparing to ask him a few questions about Nazih's personal and political life. I was interested in learning more about that historical period in the Golan during which Nazih was politically active, a period that witnessed a strong anti-colonial scene, including a large network of local intelligence agents who operated under cover on behalf of the Syrian state. I was aware that by speaking with Mazen about what he remembers of his past-life I would gain unique access into Nazih's life story. I had read archival documents and interviewed local residents who knew Nazih very well. However, I realized that by conversing with Mazen himself, I was *actually* interacting with the late Nazih Abu Zeid.

The point here is not to search for "origins" but to trace the erratic and unpredictable way by which pasts became the present. Attending to the life of those who reincarnate entails an acknowledgment of a plurality of realities and selves that are closely knitted and intertwined. Such an acknowledgment is neither paradoxical nor mere rhetoric but rather a call for a different order of engagement and scholarship.

"What was it like for you to work for the Syrian secret intelligence services at the time?" I asked Mazen. "Well," he responded:

> as a young man [referring here to himself as Nazih], I used to cause lots of trouble in town. I was a trouble-maker and I would get myself regularly arrested and put for short periods of time into [Israeli] prisons. People here would think that I just had uncontrollable manners, but little did they know that getting myself caught was my secret technique to spend time inside these places to observe and study how that system [...] works from within. This was one kind of information that I would collect at the time and then convey [to the Syrians].

Understandably, Mazen was generous but very careful with the information he shared with me. On occasions, he would request that I refrain from writing down certain notes. Other times, he would respond abstractedly to my questions so that I understand that the topic I am inquiring about is a sensitive one that we better leave vaguely unaddressed. Mazen gave me the impression that I was talking simultaneously to multiple characters from multiple time periods. He would speak about his time spying for Syria, and weave this with informed details about the local politics in the Golan at the time. He would mention names and map some local drama very meticulously. For instance, at one moment during our conversation Mazen interruptedly received a phone call from a friend in the Galilee. It was only in this intermission, as he slightly switched accent and used a few Hebrew words, that I was abruptly reminded that Mazen was actually not from the Golan but from the Galilee. Ethnographic moments like this one provided a gateway into how the temporality of reincarnation, that is, the interplay between past and present, can make itself felt through powerful impressions in daily conversations, including in the experience of the ethnographer.[19]

My conversation with Mazen was certainly a journey in time and historical periods that throughout felt unusually malleable. I was talking to someone who bears witness to an anti-colonial past which no longer exists in the Golan—a past to which very few have direct access today. But navigating through time and through the different historical periods of the past and present was not the only journey unfolding here. In taking Mazen's reincarnation seriously, geographical imaginations become more accessible, and different landscapes are reconnected. One could ask how Mazen's past-life in Syria and the Golan seep through his present in the Galilee. How does one's past-life elsewhere remain woven into the current life here and now?

As a Palestinian Druze who was born in the Galilee, it was expected from Mazen to fulfill his duty and enroll in the Israeli army at the age of eighteen, a mandatory military conscription for Druze men that was established and officially recognized by the Israeli government as early as 1956. But for Mazen, this was and is an impossible duty. With a life history of reincarnation, whereby he grew up with a living memory of himself having been a Syrian agent in a past-life, it was inconceivable for Mazen to now join the Israeli military. Mazen successfully sought alternative ways to avoid military service in Israel and secure an exemption, and while his refusal was not officially framed by him or others necessarily as a political act, it is still important to trace its political and theological underpinnings. Those in Druze societies, and particularly those who reincarnate, realize that who they are today and what they do are details shaped largely by who they were and what they did in their past lives. It is a form of continuity, both temporal and geographical, which rarely attaches itself to an official narrative, yet very often determines the course of events. Understanding reincarnation as operating as a form of embodied "common sense" suggests that the normalized realities of past histories and geographies function largely as backdrop, and sometimes as the unacknowledged condition of possibility for political and social becoming.

When we grapple with this form of common sense more critically, we quickly realize that it always relies on a set of human relations and social dynamics that took and are still taking place elsewhere. If we look back at Mazen's story, although he lives in the Galilee he is aware of the fact that much of his past-life dynamics and contexts are still happening in the Golan. In other words, although Nazih was killed in the late 1970s, his parents and siblings, Iqab and Saniyya, are still alive and have their ordinary life and families in the Golan. Nazih's parents acknowledge Mazen as a family member, that he is the reincarnation of their late son, Nazih, and they treat him as such. However, Nazih's parents and community understand that today Nazih is part of a different life trajectory (which is Mazen's), and that he belongs to another (new) family in the Galilee. It is this realization, and to some extent the daily maintenance of the connectedness between the here and the elsewhere, that is at the heart of the living relations of reincarnation. Put differently, only by attending to a certain history in the Golan are we able to understand a certain present in the Galilee. Mediation, as the story I bring here shows, entails not only attending to the political and theological common sense of a community but also attending to the geographies and landscapes beyond its current visible location. And still, this mode of mediation, to borrow from Glissant, "maintains the idea of rootedness but challenges that of a totalitarian root."[20]

Later that summer of 2022, I was driving back to the Golan from Haifa and decided to drop by Mazen's house in Hurfeish. He was excited to debrief and I was surprised that he had prepared something to show me. We went into their living room, his son was there, and they pulled out a videotape and turned on the screen. It took me a minute to realize that this was a TV recording from 2008 of the inauguration ceremony of the school in Jaramana that was named after "the martyr Nazih Abu Zeid." Apparently, some relatives who knew of Mazen's reincarnation story had informed him in advance of this event, so he could watch and record it live from his home in the Galilee, while it was streaming on the Syrian channel. As I stood there, next to Mazen, watching the recorded event, it took me a few seconds to register this multilayered reality. An ethnographic description would have to be flexible enough to capture an experience that took place in Baathist Syria, had an anti-colonial past in the Golan, and unfolds today in a colonial present in Palestine. It is here where a political sensibility to reincarnation theology can serve as guide.

While the daily reality of tens of thousands of Palestinian Druze is mainly seen through Israeli state discourse and its accompanying grammars of collaboration, military service, and loyalty to the state, among others, more critical and nuanced aspects of life are still waiting to be unearthed. Understanding Mazen's narrative and life choices in the here and now entails that we go beyond them to look for answers. Reincarnated memories have a radical dimension to them; they are an extended notion of what things were or could be. Tracing these reincarnated lives, and letting them seep through the present, means that we challenge the quotidian forms of national settlements that locked contemporary temporal and geographical horizons.

Notes

1   Aamer Ibraheem and Adrien Zakar, "Jawlān," *Middle East Journal of Culture and Communication*, Vol. 15, Issue 4, Special Issue: Keywords in Contemporary Syrian Media, Culture and Politics (2022): 358–66.
2   Uri Davis, *The Golan Heights under Israeli Occupation 1967–1981* (Durham, NC: University of Durham, Center for Middle Eastern and Islamic Studies, 1984).
3   Interview with Mazen Halabi (January 2022). Upon the interviewee's request, I have modified some details in this story that could otherwise be revealing.
4   In rethinking historical forms, here I draw heavily on Diana Allan's work on embodied experiences and the ways in which habit, routine, and embodiment are themselves modes of knowing that shape how people comprehend and ascribe meaning to their material and social environment over time. See Diana Allan, "What Bodies Remember: Sensory Experience as Historical Counterpoint in the Nakba Archive," in *An Oral History of the Palestinian Nakba*, ed. Nahla Abdo and Nur Masalha (Bloomsbury Publishing Plc, London: Zed Press, 2019), 66–87.
5   Adnan Kasamanie, "Druze Gnosis and the Mystery of Time," in *The Gnostic World*, ed. Garry W. Trompf, Gunner B. Mikkelsen, and Jay Johnston (New York, NY: Routledge, 2018), 349–57.
6   Anis Obeid, *The Druze and Their Faith in Tawhid* (Syracuse, NY: Syracuse University Press, 2006), 145.
7   Mary Douglas, *Implicit Meanings: Selected Essays in Anthropology* (New Fetter Lane, London: Routledge, 1999).
8   Douglas, *Implicit Meanings*, 95.
9   Ibid.
10 Khaled Furani, *Redeeming Anthropology: A Theological Critique of a Modern Science* (Great Clarendon Street, Oxford, UK: Oxford University Press, 2019).
11 Mark Rifkin, *Settler Common Sense: Queerness and Everyday Colonialism in the American Renaissance* (Minneapolis, MN: University of Minnesota Press, 2014).
12 Allan, "What Bodies Remember," 67.
13 Lauren Berlant, *Cruel Optimism* (Durham, NC: Duke University Press, 2011).
14 Antonio Gramsci, *Selections from The Prison Notebooks*, ed. and trans. Quintin Hoare and Geoffrey Nowell Smith (New York, NY: International Publishers, 1971), 325.
15 Gramsci, *The Prison Notebooks*, 326.
16 Kate Crehan, "Gramsci's Folklore Bundle," *Anuac* 11, no. 1 (2022): 55–64.
17 Édouard Glissant, *Poetics of Relation* (Ann Arbor, MI: University of Michigan Press, 1997).

18 Glissant, *Poetics*, 34. More about the "sacred motivation" in translator's (Betsy Wing) note in Glissant, *Poetics*, 211.
19 For a discussion of relevant encounters during fieldwork, see Alireza Doostdar, "Sensing Jinn," *Critical Muslim* 43 (2022): 75–89.
20 Glissant, *Poetics*, 34.

8

Fugitive Crossings: On the Condition of Being Palestinian

Kiven Strohm and Nadeem Karkabi

Life which has been stolen steals away ...

Fred Moten, Stolen Life

In the opening scene of Hany Abu-Assad's acclaimed film *Omar* (2013), the viewer is presented with a close-up of the face of the principal protagonist of the film, Omar himself. The camera then shifts to a wide-angle side view showing us his profile as he stands in front of the Separation Wall. Behind him we can make out a rope lightly moving against the surface of the wall. After a few moments, he turns, grabs the rope, and climbs. He scales the wall rapidly, suggesting this is not the first time he's crossed it. As he reaches the top, shots are fired at him by Israeli forces. He immediately descends before absconding into an alleyway on his way to see his girlfriend, Nadia. Omar seems to know precisely where to cross the wall and when. Indeed, we can surmise that it is an established crossing point for Palestinians from the West Bank to the '48 Territories. Such scenes are quite common within Palestinian cinema, with the protagonists often depicted transgressing the imposed boundaries that brutally separate Palestinians from each other and their lands. More significantly, these are scenes of hope for Palestinians.

As Rashid Khalidi once poignantly noted, the crossing of borders and checkpoints is the "quintessential Palestinian experience."[1] The ubiquitous, formal and informal, borders across occupied Palestine are designed to halt, discipline, and enclose bodies in motion.[2] As such, they are forms of colonial captivity. Under the Israeli regime of selective (im)mobility, Palestinians find themselves separated and confined in small, fragmented spaces. Our interest here is with those crossings that are considered "illegal" and in which Palestinians are defined as "illegal infiltrators" according to the colonial occupier. In this chapter, we look at these crossings as instances when the refusal to acknowledge Israeli colonial authority opens a line of fugitive movement that, we argue, is the condition of being Palestinian.

Slipping through the fissures of the fortified Israeli regime, Palestinians have a long history of "illegally" crossing borders and walls that separate them from each other and remove them from their lands. In this sense, they not only refuse the arrest of their movement and of life itself but also refuse to recognize the authority of the settler colonizer and their assigned role of subordinates. However, Palestinian crossings are not necessarily moments of resistance, insofar as one is not literally fighting back in opposition, and refusal is not sufficient in and of itself to "reconstruct a creative sense of liberated being."[3]

Still, the act of refusal opens itself to a condition of fugitivity, as a mode of action. By examining acts of "illegal" and transgressive crossing, we explore fugitivity as a strategic mode for evading colonial capture. Central to Black studies, the concept refers to "fugitive slaves, fugitives from the law, or fugitivity as an abstract subject position."[4] In this sense, fugitivity not only is about being ungovernable, disobedient, and unruly but invites us to consider "another way of living in the world […] in and out of this one"[5] to actively regenerate and preserve forms of sociality.

We contend that when Palestinians participate and cultivate modes of escape and evasion of colonial enclosure, they practice a fugitive sensibility, or a mode of doing, that can be inhabited through repetition. It is this aspect that distinguishes fugitivity from mere refusal (albeit being a condition of it) and mere escape and fleeing (though it is this too). Therefore, an embodied practice sustained by intentional repetitions, fugitivity is a corporeal practice of multiplicity; a repetition that multiplies itself and becomes generative. Based on this, we invoke the concept of "crossing" in both its material and metaphorical modes to think about fugitivity as both an act of evasion and an imagining of another world. We argue that fugitivity is a condition of being Palestinian, situated alongside other conditions such as statelessness and suffering. Yet, fugitivity is distinctive in that it is generative and invites the repairing and sustaining of Palestinian sociality from within confinement. As such, the foreclosing of escape from the Israeli regime is less about extirpating escape as such, as it is with crushing the sociality that such fugitive crossings ignite.

In what follows, we present three instances of fugitive crossings. We begin with Palestinian refugees who returned from nearby Arab states to their homeland in the first years after 1948. We continue with Hamza Younis' remarkable prison escapes and subsequent wanderings, instances where repetition meets planning and improvisation. We then examine Khaled Jarrar's film *Infiltrators*, which depicts practices of fugitivity while crossing the Separation Wall. Here we focus on the repetition of images of crossings as an invitation to new crossings, networks, and forms of sociality. Finally, in the conclusion, we turn to the escape from Gilboa prison in 2021 and the future possibilities of fugitive crossings for Palestinians, in light of increased Israeli surveillance.

Crossing Back: The Return of Refugees from 1948 to 1956

The desire of Palestinians displaced in 1948 to return to their homeland is undoubtedly one of the most tenacious instances to think about fugitive crossings. For people torn asunder, internally displaced, and divided across newly established borders and neighboring countries, to return was to reclaim and repair a shattered sociality.

Demographic considerations played a central role in establishing Israel as a home for the Jewish people. The displacement of Palestinians to neighboring Arab countries began already in 1947, yet the issue of their return alarmed the Israeli authorities as soon as the state was declared in May 1948. Amid the instability that prevailed, the prevention of the refugees crossing the porous borders demanded immediate attention. Besides patrols, Israeli authorities cleansed Palestinian border villages and quickly resettled some with Jews. In addition, Israeli authorities installed military rule in October 1948 with constant curfews on Palestinian villages. Individuals who attempted to cross the borders back to Palestine were deemed "illegal infiltrators." Many were arrested, followed by imprisonment and deportation across the borders. Others were injured or killed by lenient Israeli use of firearms.[6] In addition, the Israeli government conducted a swift seven-hour census in November 1948 to survey the population in the lands that it occupied. The remaining Palestinian population was then issued identity cards in order to be distinguished from expelled refugees, especially those who attempted to return.[7]

While Israel quickly prevented Palestinians from crossing the border back from Egypt, Jordan, and Syria, the border with Lebanon remained porous in the first years of Israel's independence. A lush mountainous landscape adjacent to Lebanon, the Galilee region provided opportunities for refugees to hide while returning to their homes. More importantly, as the Galilee was still not fully occupied in 1948, many Palestinian villages in the region remained inhabited after the establishment of Israel. This meant that the returning refugees, who sought to reunite with their families and regain their livelihood, still had family members who could support them upon their return. However, during these years, and even after the armistice agreements between Israel and neighboring Arab countries in 1949, the Galilee was still facing ethnic cleansing, including massacres and collective expulsion to Lebanon. This led to a chaotic situation of heightened movement, whereby Palestinians moved in opposite directions: some to Lebanon and others back to Palestine.[8]

The relatively long duration of the porous Israeli-Lebanese border allowed thousands of refugees to return. Some even made the crossing several times, moving back and forth, often to help other family members to return. Stories about crossing the Lebanese-Israeli borders and return of refugees to their homeland can be found in many Palestinian literary texts.[9] While most mention these crossings in passing, the journalist Elias Nasrallah provides an exceptionally detailed account of his family's return from Lebanon to their Galilean village Shefa'amr. In his autobiography,[10] he admits that he was only a one-year-old during these events, so he could not possibly remember the experience himself, yet the family story was so formative that it was told to him numerous times by several involved relatives who did not spare the smallest details.

Elias, his parents, and brother left Shefa'amr in July 1948, when Zionist militias violently raided the village and scared people off. The family headed to Lebanon in their private car, it being the nearest safe haven and the birthplace of his mother. They stayed in a house that belonged to his mother's family in the village of Kufr Sheima. A few months later, they were reunited with Elias' paternal uncle Na'im and maternal uncle Philip, who were initially expelled to Jenin. Then from there, they continued to Amman, where they received identification cards allowing them to make the journey to Lebanon.

Without a source of income, and with the spread of success stories of people who crossed the borders back, the family decided to return to Shefa'amr. To overcome the dangers of the journey, most returnees had to rely on a *dallul* (or *dalil*), a local guide familiar with the area, in this case Abu Ma'rouf, a Lebanese man who used to live in Shefa'amr before the war and who was well acquainted with the family. They decided that Elias' paternal uncle, Na'im, would embark on the return journey first with his wife and three children. A few days later, they left with Abu Ma'rouf and his two donkeys. Leaving after sunset from the border village of Rmesh, they arrived to Shefa'amr the following night just before dawn. There they were received by Elias' other paternal uncle, Boulous, who remained in Shefa'amr with his family.

Na'im immediately wrote a reassuring letter to the family waiting in Kufr Sheima, urging them to follow suit. Abu Ma'rouf delivered Na'im's message a week later, along with other letters to Palestinians in Lebanon. However, upon his arrival, Abu Ma'rouf also warned the family that on his way he came across an Israeli trap near Rmesh, where some solders noticed him and opened fire. While he survived, one of his donkeys was killed and the other ran away with the supplies. Abou Ma'rouf went west in search for another safe trail across the border to Lebanon, by chance finding his lost donkey along the way.

When night fell, it was time to go. Abu Ma'rouf seated Elias and his older brother in the panniers at both sides of the donkey, while he and Elias' parents went on foot. Leaving on Thursday night, they planned to arrive to Shefa'amr on Friday night, hoping that Israeli patrols would lessen during Shabbat. They crossed the border within hours and soon met another group of returnees with their *dallul* and his two donkeys and continued together. A few hours later, they decided to rest and tied the donkeys at a distance. In full darkness, the group heard the engine of patrolling Israeli soldiers and caught glimpses of torches. The soldiers focused on the area where the three donkeys were tied and soon began shooting, killing them all. The group remained paralyzed in fear until they heard them leave. Elias' parents had to carry him and his brother in their arms and march fast in order to cross the dangerous area. After an hour, Elias' mother was exhausted and Abu Ma'rouf took Elias' brother on his shoulders. As they advanced south, the families headed in different directions.

On Friday afternoon Elias' family reached the village Bqi'a. Suffering from increasing back pain, and due to the long way ahead, his father decided to check on his old friend Na'im to ask for help. Not knowing what the fate of Bqi'a in the war was, the family waited until darkness to enter. Once in the village, they knocked on the first door they found to ask for Na'im. Soon they were directed to his house and spent the night there. The next day, they found a taxi driver willing to risk taking them to Shafa'amr. To avoid checkpoints, the driver took a longer route, driving first to Tarshiha, the driver's village, then to Abu Snan, where he had relatives, before finally arriving in Shafa'amr in the evening.

After a festive reception, Elias' family still had to secure their stay, since as "infiltrators" with no Israeli identity cards they were at risk of deportation. With the Galilee undergoing a bureaucratic unsettlement, many Palestinians were expelled to Lebanon, while others in the region took refuge in nearby villages.

Internally displaced Palestinians were officially termed by Israeli authorities as "present absentees," absent from their homes during the 1948 census, but present in the country. To the advantage of Palestinians, Israeli authorities had difficulty distinguishing "legally" remaining Palestinians from "illegal infiltrators," whereby the latter were able to immerse among the remaining population, while legalizing their status as "present absentees." However, this ambiguous state of affairs also allowed Israel to expel "present absentees" who were falsely declared as "infiltrators," including entire villages in the Galilee even after the war was over.[11]

Elias' family was among the lucky. After arriving to Shefa'amr in early December 1948, Elias' father went with the village mayor to see the Israeli military governor. The mayor convinced the governor to issue the family identity cards, claiming that they were "present absentees" who missed the census that just took place a few weeks earlier, because they were working in the fields outside the village. Yet, as with all other "present absentees," their properties and land were confiscated by the state. Abu Ma'rouf was unable to replace his dead donkeys. Afraid to cross the border again, he remained in Shafa'amr, where the mayor offered him a job at the municipality. He never reunited with his family in Lebanon.

In the aftermath of these events, it is estimated that around 20,000 Palestinian refugees returned to the Galilee and were successful in acquiring Israeli citizenship. Nevertheless, several thousand lost their lives trying and many more were deported. Israel allowed around 3,000 Palestinian to officially return by way of family reunification, but expelled around 10,000 others to Lebanon between 1949 and 1956.[12] When Palestinian refugees in 1948 refused their dispossession and displacement, they decided to cross back and return to their homes. They became fugitives who had to secretly move back, against colonial closures. Yet their movement was not just a matter of return tout court. Returns, such as those undertaken by Elias' family, were about re-establishing networks of social relations and forms of sociality that would be cultivated and endured throughout many of the future returns of Palestinians to their homeland.

Breaking Out of Israeli Captivity: The Three Escapes of Hamza Younes

In addition to violent border closures and bureaucratic governmentality through ID cards and censuses, incarceration has been a common Israeli practice to confine Palestinians and crush their attempts to resist. Mass imprisonment was already introduced with the establishment of the Israeli state, as in the early case of the returning refugees turned "infiltrators." Israel inherited this brutal practice of governance, along with the existing network of prisons, from the British Mandate.[13] While Israeli military rule over Palestinians who remained in its borders ended in 1966, it was established in the West Bank and the Gaza Strip in 1967. From this point on, imprisonment only increased. During the first intifada (1987–93) and the Second Intifada (2000–2004), it peaked so that almost every Palestinian family in the '67 Territories had at least one member in prison throughout the ongoing Israeli occupation, including minors, women, and "administrative detainees" who were never tried in court.[14] Indeed, prisoner population has become so significant that it has been recently termed Palestine's "sixth geography."[15]

Any political prisoner would consider breaking out, especially when his or her incarceration is not regarded as a correcting form of justice. Over the long period of Israeli occupation, there have been several attempts by Palestinian prisoners to escape Israeli jails, most of whom were caught or killed during flight. Nonetheless, some managed to achieve durable freedom, in some cases rejoining Palestinian resistance where it was still active.[16]

Such was the outstanding case of Hamza Younes, who not only escaped three times from Israeli incarceration but remained alive, and free, to tell his story in a detailed autobiography.[17] In his crossings, Younes challenged Israeli borders with neighboring Arab countries and also the Green Line that internally separates Palestine into different regimes of Israeli governmentality. Yet his story also demonstrates the expanding Israeli control over Palestinian territories, changes to Arab regional attitudes toward Palestinians, and the shrinking possibilities for Palestinians to reach safe havens.

Younes was born in 1942 in the village 'Ara, located inside Israel near to the north of the West Bank. A lad of strong posture, Younes won Israel's national championship in boxing for Welterweight in 1963.[18] A year later, Younes and his cousin Makram got into a fistfight with some Jewish Israeli young men, and Younes severely injured one of them. Afraid of arrest and likely imprisonment, Younes and Makram fled to Gaza, then under Egyptian rule. They took the bus to Ashkelon ('Asqalan in Arabic) and crossed the Green Line by foot. The Egyptian authorities in Gaza deported them back, so that they were eventually caught by Israeli authorities and sent to Ashkelon Prison.

Facing the possibility of substantial charges that would lead to long imprisonment, the cousins began planning their escape. A few weeks later, during the night count, they overcame the guards and ran through the front door. They headed to the sea and walked by the shore to hide their tracks. Four hours later, they reached Gaza again. This time they turned to Palestinian *fedayee* (freedom fighters) who helped them settle their status with the Egyptian authorities, in exchange for offering their service as translators of the Israeli press. During the three years spent in Gaza, Younes resumed his secondary education. However, the 1967 War caught him at the examination room, writing his eleventh-grade finals. He joined the Palestinian resistance but injured his foot during a close combat with the Israeli army. He was taken as a prisoner of war to the English hospital in Gaza City, which fell under Israel control. After two operations and a few weeks of hospitalization, Younes was ready for his second escape.

While expecting a visit by some Gazan friends, Younes went to the yard to meet them. When they arrived, it turned out that one of them knew the hospital employee guarding the main door. He convinced him to allow Younes to meet his mother, who was supposedly waiting outside on a wheelchair and couldn't enter the hospital. Once out, another friend helped Younes take a taxi to a pottery workshop in Shajariyya area. As a measure of safety, he then moved to an orange orchard where he spent his days in a pit that he dug in the ground, while at nights he went out walking to strengthen his injured leg. A month later, his parents came to visit. They took him home to 'Ara, where he met his family and friends. The next morning, Younes left on a donkey to the West Bank. After crossing the Green Line, he took a taxi to Amman, using a fake ID card at the Israeli border and eventually joined the PLO in Jordan.

After the "Black September" events in 1970, Younes left with the exiled Palestinian leadership to Lebanon, where he joined the resistance as a smuggler delivering arms to Palestinians inside Israel. His smuggling strategy was simple. He used a map that indicated the location of mines near the border and a ladder to climb across the barbed wire. To confuse the guard dogs, he splashed spices to mask his tracks. His knowledge of the area and its natural habitat helped him make the journey multiple times without ever being caught by Israeli patrols.

In October 1971, Younes joined a special PLO unit of divers, which was supposed to kidnap Israeli soldiers to be exchanged for Palestinian prisoners. On its first mission, however, the unit was captured in the Mediterranean Sea, near the Israeli city of Nahariya. After several months of investigation under severe torture, Younes was sentenced for life and sent to Ramleh Prison.[19] Initially built by the British and fortified by the Israelis, it was the most secure prison in the country.

Two years into his incarceration, Younes teamed with two other Palestinian inmates to escape. It took them six weeks to cut the bars of the small window at the laundry room, where one of them was working. Choosing a rainy day to cover their traces in mud, Younes and Mohammad were able to slip through the small window, while their friend got stuck. The two fugitives climbed over the barbed-wire fence and reached the external security wall. Dodging heavy shooting by the guards, they used the scaffolding that was temporarily installed to build a watch tower and crossed over to their freedom.

However, their journey to a safe haven had just begun. Leaving footstep traces as if they were heading east to the West Bank, they marched directly to the north. They walked under the heavy rain in water channels and natural streams, until reaching a forest near Tel Aviv around midday. As the sun came up, they took some rest, buried their prison uniform in the ground, and hung their civilian clothes (which they wore under) to dry. They took the day to explore the area and found an orange orchard to quell their hunger.

Considering their options, they decided to head to Lebanon. In preparation for the long way ahead, Younes went in the evening to the nearest neighborhood in Tel Aviv, and with the money he had, he bought some food, shaving equipment, a newspaper, a small transistor radio, a man's outfit for him, and a green dress with red headscarf for Mohammad. The next morning, they disguised as a couple and marched through the fields. They walked during the day and rested at night, sleeping on their covered campfires to subdue the cold. When they arrived in the Triangle area, they decided to visit a friend, who gave them a ride to the Galilee, where their journey became easier thanks to the lush forests. Finally, six weeks into their journey, they arrived at the Lebanese border in mid-April 1974. They climbed across the barbed wire and walked to the nearest Lebanese village, where they took a taxi to PLO offices in al-Burj al-Shamali refugee camp.

Younes resumed his work with the PLO until it was forced into exile from Lebanon in 1982. He joined the PLO offices in Saudi Arabia, where he could meet his family members who traveled over the years to Macca for Haj. He also married and was blessed with three daughters. Yet this too did not last for long. During the Gulf Crisis (1989–91), Younes was imprisoned by the Saudi authorities, along with other

Palestinian officials, because they supported Saddam Hussein's regime in Iraq. He was released two years later but lost his residency rights in Saudi Arabia. In the following decade, he traveled across the Arab world in a desperate search for asylum. He couldn't return to Ramallah with the PLO after the Oslo Accords in 1993 as Israeli security personally blacklisted him. Only in 2000, he reunited with his wife and daughters in Algeria, where they stayed for a few years, until finally moving to Sweden as recognized asylum seekers.

Younes' story offers a regretful account of how opportunities of durable freedom for Palestinians have dwindled over the years. His first two escapes demonstrate the existence of pockets inside the historical homeland in which Palestinians could disappear from colonial captivity. His third escape took place in 1974, after Israeli colonization expanded over the entire Palestinian homeland. Under such circumstances, he had to cross the whole country to find refuge in Lebanon. Yet this story of fugitive crossings also reflects regional politics, in which Arab regimes betrayed Palestinians. Spaces of freedom gradually narrowed as Younes was driven out of Jordan with the PLO in 1970, then of Lebanon in 1982, and then again of Saudi Arabia in 1991, leaving only Algeria and Sweden as options for asylum.

Nevertheless, Younes' autobiography tells an inspiring story of multiple escapes from Israeli captivity. It is a story of indigenous intimate knowledge of the nature and land, as well as of close communal networks. Although well-planned and exceptionally daring, his fugitive crossings and survival technics were strikingly simple. He depended on basic natural resources, such as rain to hide his tracks, night to conceal his movement, fruits for nutrition, and fire for heat. Another fascinating aspect is how Younes configured his strategies to evade Israel's carceral grasp again. In a sense, each capture was a reflective moment to reimagine his mode of fugitivity and repeatedly consider a new experimental variant for embarking on a different series of crossings and cultivation of social networks.

Image and Repetition: Jarrar's *Infiltrators*

A black screen. The rustling of feet moving across stones and earth, accompanied by heavy breathing and the occasional muffled thuds. We then begin to hear dim voices as the image slowly reveals the darkness within which a celerity of bodies walking and running, crouching low so as not to be seen, peaking into the horizon, exchange glances. The image is shaky as it immerses itself in and within the movement of bodies. We see lights in the background blending with lights from the screens of the cell phones of those walking, running, and hiding. So starts Khaled Jarrar's film *Infiltrators*. It is tempting to discuss the film in terms of its documentation of Palestinian bodies moving over, under, across, and through the Separation Wall. The scale and complexity involved in these crossings are astounding, including their dangers, excitements, and disappointments. While ostensibly this is what the film is "about," we should appreciate it as something more than a representation, as itself a production of fugitivity.

In taking the crossing of barriers as quintessential experiences within Palestinian life, *Infiltrators* sits within two Palestinian film genres: roadblock cinema[20] and cinéma verité,[21] which emerged with the growth of security and surveillance dispositives under the Israeli settler colonial regime since the Second Intifada.[22] Alongside the acceleration of Israeli surveillance and displacement of Palestinians, roadblock films contended with the shifting geographies for Palestinians in a post-Oslo world. As Tawil-Souri notes citing al-Zobaidi, "films of this period were 'impulsive, passionate films, bad quality films, homemade, homegrown, desperate,'" in which "film was 'a passage, a crack, a flight, a leap' [...] beyond the confines of territoriality."[23] Jarrar's film also works in the cinéma verité genre in which the filmmaker is located within the situations he is observing. Throughout the film, Jarrar's presence is felt in the movement of the camera, his proximity to those crossing, and the sense of intimacy in which subject and object become transposable. In a scene in which Palestinian women are assaulted by Israeli forces using teargas, we can hear Jarrar coughing, gasping, and screaming as he runs with the women to escape. Moreover, we are never comforted with an authoritative narrative or commentary explaining what we are seeing, nor interviews with subjects reflecting on what they are doing. Rather, we are immersed with Jarrar in the constant motion of these fugitive crossings.

When watching Jarrar's film, it quickly becomes apparent that the crossings which we are witnessing are not random events but planned happenings at specific moments and places. They are strategic improvisations that create passages across the Wall. Throughout the film we witness Palestinians crossing to see loved ones, access medical care, pray at al-Quds, or simply find work. They are daily activities, part of the making of everyday life. Yet, these crossings, as well as Jarrar's film, are also refusals of enclosure and a making of new forms of sociality in the face of colonial "immobility [that] cements displacement."[24]

Indeed, Jarrar's *Infiltrators* is itself a repetition of these crossings, though it is not repetition in the sense of restating the same, a process of mimesis or representation. On the contrary, we are presented with a series (not a sequence) of images, a flow of bodies that are "passing across" not in the same way again and again but in an experimental, innovative, and creative repetition. There is no beginning, as there is no end, either to the film or to the movement of Palestinians crossing. To repeat is to begin anew. This is underscored in the last image in the film where we see a young man through the front door of his home at dusk, kissing his mother and grandmother goodbye, presumably on his way to make his own crossing.

To be sure, images are never innocent. As a maker of crossing images, Jarrar is not re-presenting a world out there but enacting a new spatiotemporal reality through repetition. Jarrar's images in the film are creative acts of transformation. They participate in the making of worlds that they depict. As such, images of Palestinian crossings, as repetitions that are not unidirectional, are a poetics of fugitivity. In this sense, Jarrar's film is a multiplicity, a series of images oriented toward a network of excess. It is an asignifying assemblage that initiates the reparation and creation of forms of sociality over and against the continuing Israeli settler colonial project of sociocide.[25] As movement against separation and displacement, fugitivity here becomes oriented toward the repair of the Palestinian social fabric and daily life.

Conclusion

On September 6, 2021, six Palestinians escaped from the Israeli maximum-security Gilboa prison and "disappeared into the morning darkness."[26] Using spoons, they had dug a 22-meter-long tunnel below their cell toilet, making their way underground to a hole outside the prison walls. Palestinians across the homeland and beyond celebrated the heroic cunningness of the prisoners in thwarting Israel's security apparatus. "Like thousands of fugitives and exiles and maroons throughout the centuries, they have illustrated that the oppressor's notion of security is tenuous."[27]

A great deal of speculation took place among Palestinians as to where the prisoners would go after their escape. The longer they stayed in Israel, the greater the risk of them being arrested, punished, and possibly even killed. Would they head back to their families in the nearby West Bank, which Israel military controls with a tight network of intelligence? Would they cross to Jordan and risk deportation by the Hashemite Authorities back to Israel? Would they take the long way north to Lebanon, crossing around a 100 kilometer of densely populated areas inside Israel? Or, would they try to cross the highly secured borders with turbulent Syria? None of options was ideal, but many Palestinians prayed that the fugitives would reach a safe haven. Their freedom, however, did not last long. Two of the fugitives were captured in the outskirts of Nazareth after four days, another two were found the next day near a village in the vicinity, and the remaining two were caught around a week later in the West Bank.

Some falsely accused the Palestinian population in the area to have tipped the Israeli authorities for their whereabouts. Others suggested that the fugitives should have better planned the later stage of their flight, maybe making their way north in a car driven by a comrade. However, though many people were sad about the turn of events, no one was particularly surprised about the success of the Israeli forces in their hunt. Over the decades of expanding settler colonialism, the possibilities and a durability of Palestinian fugitive crossings have severely diminished.

As demonstrated through the case studies in this paper, Israeli surveillance of Palestinians' movement has become almost hermetic, employing physical barriers, bureaucratic means, technological advancements, and even diplomatic partnerships with complicit neighboring governments. Yet, fugitivity is not necessarily to be settled by its outcomes or achievements. Rather, it is a state of mind and a practice. If a captive will imagine his escape as long as he is still alive, so will Palestinians as a nation struggling for liberation and freedom of movement. As will be recalled from *Omar*, such scenes of transgression and possible escape, even when thwarted, nonetheless ignite a popular imagination by holding out the hope of a life otherwise. It is in this sense that acts of fugitivity are a condition of being Palestinian. Such acts may not always include a physical crossing; they may well be the mental imagination of the future possibility of escaping. "Where do the birds fly after the last sky?" Edward Saïd asks.[28] But birds don't have to fly to know they are still birds. As long as they have wings, they can remain nested in the potential of spreading them one day. Therefore, it is not only about clearing the sky but about clearing the mind to continue inhabiting the moment of refusal until a possibility, a crack in time, manifests for an actual flight. Thus, Israeli surveillance will ever be only *almost* hermetic. If there is a refusal to accept captivity, moments of fugitive flight will be sought through the repetitive reminder of past, present, and possible future crossings.

Although the Gilboa fugitives failed to reach a safe haven, their brazen escape reignited the imagination of Palestinians to the possibility of fleeing settler colonial captivity and hold out the hope for a life otherwise. "They emerged from the earth like precious resources, like natal organisms, like seeds determined to initiate life."[29] After being recaptured, they admitted that the escape was worth it, at least to taste the fruits of the land that they picked from the fields they were crossing. The imagination of life otherwise, outside of colonial capture, of a Palestinian life as it might yet be, is that which ignites the desire for fugitivity as a generative practice of repair and perseverance of sociality, that state or quality of being social that furnishes the creating of community and a future.

The escape of these six Palestinians and their recapturing were not received by Palestinians as a failure but a cause for celebration of a fulfilled possibility to locate the crack in the *almost* hermetic wall. "There is a crack in every wall/ In every land there is a hole," Jowan Safadi sings in *Heroes of Spoons*, a tune produced to honor the escapees from the Gilboa Prison. "Don't let the hope die/ Every time the hero dies/ Or gets arrested again [...] The prisoners didn't reach/ But their message reached."[30] Cracks are everywhere; they are invitations to improvise with a spoon, a moving image, or a laughing sound, so as to embrace hope in the "lawlessness of imagination."[31]

Notes

1 Rashid Khalidi, *Palestinian Identity: The Construction of a Modern National Consciousness* (New York, NY: Columbia University Press, 1997), 1.
2 Rema Hammami, "Destabilizing Mastery and the Machine Palestinian Agency and Gendered Embodiment at Israeli Military Checkpoints," *Current Anthropology* 60, Supplement 19 (2019): S87–S97.
3 Nadeem Karkabi and Aamer Ibrahim, "On Fleeing Colonial Captivity: Fugitive Arts in the Occupied Jawlan," *Identities* 22, no. 5 (2022): 691–710.
4 Nick J. Sciullo, "Boston King's Fugitive Passing: Fred Moten, Saidiya Hartman, and Tina Campt's Rhetoric of Resistance," *Rhizomes: Cultural Studies in Emerging Knowledge* 35 (2019).
5 Fred Moten, "Blackness and Nothingness (mysticism in the flesh)," *South Atlantic Quarterly* 112, no. 4 (2013): 737–80.
6 Nadera Shalhoub-Kevorkian, "Infiltrated Intimacies: The Case of Palestinian Returnees," *Feminist Studies* 42, no. 1 (2016): 166–93.
7 Anat Leibler and Daniel Breslau, "The Uncounted: Citizenship and Exclusion in the Israeli Census of 1948," *Ethnic and Racial Studies* 28, no. 5 (2005): 880–902.
8 Adel Manna, *Nakba and Survival: The Story of the Palestinians Who Remained in Haifa and the Galilee (1948–1956)* (Berkeley: University of California Press, 2022).
9 See Anton Shammas, *Arabesques* (Berkeley, CA: University of California Press, 1988); Email Habibi, *The Secret Life of Saeed the Pessoptimist* (London: Zed Books, 1985); Fahed Abu Khadra, *Al-Layl wa-al-Hudud (The Night and the Borders)* (Nazareth: Al-Hakim [Arabic], 1964).

10. Elias Nasrallah, *Shahadat 'ala al-Qarn al-Falastini al-'Awal* [Testimonies on the First Century of Palestine] (Beirut: Al-Farabi [Arabic], 2016), 63–98.
11. Manna, *Nakba and Survival*.
12. Ibid.
13. Esmail Nashif, *Palestinian Political Prisoners: Identity and Community* (London: Routledge, 2008).
14. "On Administrative Detention," *Addameer: Prisoners Support and Human Rights Association*: https://www.addameer.org/israeli_military_judicial_system/administrative_detention (Retrieved on 20.6.2022).
15. Abdul-Rahim Al-Shaikh et al., "Nadwa al-Kharaka al-Filastiniya al-Asira: Al-Jugrafiya al-Sadisa" [Symposium on the Palestinian Prisoner Movement: The Sixth Geography]. *Majallat al-Dirasat al-Filastiniyya* 128: 9–59 [Arabic], 2021.
16. "A short history of escaping prison in Palestine [in three parts]" (19.4.2017) *Bab el-Wad*: https://babelwad.com/ar/%d9%81%d9%84%d8%b3%d8%b7%d9%8a%d9%86/houroub-men-elsejen/ [Arabic] (Retrieved on 20.6.2022).
17. Hamza Younes, *Al-Hurub Min Sijn al-Ramleh* [The Escape from Ramleh Prison] (Self-published [Arabic], 1999).
18. Tamir Sorek, "'The Only Place Where an Arab Can Hit a Jew and Get a Medal for It': Boxing and Masculine Pride among Arab Citizens of Israel," *Sport in Society* 12, no. 8 (2009): 1065–74.
19. Also known as Ayalon Prison since 1980.
20. Nurith Gertz and George Khleifi, *Palestinian Cinema: Landscape, Trauma and Memory* (Edinburgh, UK: Edinburgh University Press, 2008).
21. Hannah Sender, "'Putting Me in Jail Would Be Their Biggest Mistake'—Palestinian Artist Khaled Jarrar Talks to Art Radar," *Art Radar*, July 7, 2013. https://artradarjournal.com/putting-me-in-jail-would-be-their-biggest-mistake-palestinian-artist-khaled-jarrar-talks-to-art-radar/ (Retrieved on 1 July 2022).
22. Helga Tawil-Souri, "Cinema as the Space to Transgress Palestine's Territorial Trap," *Middle East Journal of Culture and Communication* 7 (2014): 169–89.
23. Ibid., 170–1.
24. Amahl Bishara, *Crossing a Line: Laws, Violence, and Roadblocks to Palestinian Political Expression* (Stanford, CA: Stanford University Press, 2022), 8.
25. Saleh Abdel Jawad, "A Palestinian Sociocide?" Russell Tribunal on Palestine, 8 January. New York, 2013. https://youtu.be/fd_tx9-r25s (Retrieved on 5.7.2022)
26. Steven Salaita, "Architectures of Delusion," *Mondoweiss*, 13 September 2021. https://mondoweiss.net/2021/09/architectures-of-delusion/ (Retrieved on 5.7.2022)
27. Ibid.
28. Edward Saïd, *After the Last Sky: Palestinian Lives* (New York, NY: University of Columbia Press, 1988).
29. Salaita, "Architectures of delusion."
30. A link to the video clip of the song: https://www.youtube.com/watch?v=aqVLKBmj6Ak (Retrieved on 4.7.2022).
31. Fred Moten, *Stolen Life* (Durham: Duke University Press, 2018).

9

Marking Bodies: A Catalogue of Keffiyehs

Sary Zananiri

This case analyses the keffiyeh as a marker of the Palestinian body, mapping its changing uses and meanings. This visual cataloguing acts as means to visually hone in on the specific importance of the keffiyeh as a marker. It traces the nature of the garment and the ways in which changing contexts, deployments, and networks of circulation have mobilized the keffiyeh as a marker to create new, often contradictory, meanings of the Palestinian body in popular culture.

It catalogues a chronology that shows the changing trajectory of the keffiyeh and, implicitly, the changing trajectories of performing Palestinian-ness by Palestinians and non-Palestinians alike. In doing so, it engages with a series of keffiyehs drawn from a range of twentieth-century source material to consider the confluence of nationalism, indigeneity, religion, class, gender, and transgression through the keffiyeh as a marker. Each keffiyeh is isolated as a constituent element of various modes of marking Palestinian-ness through a process that homogenizes them as archetypes in producing this "catalogue."

Marking Bodies: A Catalogue of Keffiyehs

As the introduction to this volume attests, Palestine has been "produced" in multiple, sometimes contradictory ways, but also within the scope of a mythologized "national past." If we are to create a "New Vision" of Palestine, this necessitates understanding the fraught context of representation in such a complicated cultural landscape that extends far beyond the territoriality of Palestine and narrow readings of "Palestinian-ness."[1] This needs to take into account many diverse and divergent groupings—including both outside of Palestine but also the many communities within different epochs of Palestinian society that are far from homogeneous—and how they impact the many ways in which Palestinian bodies were and are projected and propagandized, criminalized and valorized, read and understood.[2]

The keffiyeh, a cloth men's head covering, though not uniquely Palestinian, has come to have particular associations with the Palestinian body in different, though highly specific, ways through the course of the twentieth-century. Although particularly associated with men's bodies, notable examples such as Laila Khaled's famous image[3] debunk a purely gendered reading of the keffiyeh.

Indeed, tracing the humble *fellah*'s (masculine, villager or "peasant") keffiyeh gives us many insights into the Palestinian body and the ways in which the garment marks it. The garment appears repeatedly in many different places often involved in claims and counter-claims of indigeneity in various modes of romanticized imagery relating to the landscape, but also in murkier contradictory spaces such as the confluence of Third Worldist revolutionary imagery and its liberal counterpart of Hollywood filmic aesthetics of terror.[4]

Tracing the humble keffiyeh, both literally and figuratively, this catalogue of images reduces the garment to its constituent elements—including removing the body it surrounds—from each of the photographic or filmic contexts from which it was drawn. This comparative vision lays out how each of these "instances" of a keffiyeh's appearance build, conflate, appropriate and reappropriate one another visually in constructing the many conflicting representational narratives of the Palestinian body. While far from an exhaustive listing of instances of the keffiyeh's visual appearances in media, it does create a methodology that traces ligatures across a broad set of visual sources from relatively diverse geographies that have been chronologized.

These instances of keffiyeh mark the Palestinian body in many different ways, even when it is wrapped around a non-Palestinian body. The specter of the *fellah*, though it is often buried between murky layers of cultural strata, still haunts each disembodied instance. Each instance speaks to a globally connected system of imagery hinging on the *fellah*, from which we can extract information on both local and global identity, the ways in which identities are projected in both positive and negative ways, and the processes of meaning-making that are embedded such complex transnational remediations.

The keffiyehs on the following pages are drawn from souvenir postcards, documentary photos of events, films, political posters, and even amateur theatre. Some instances are of famous figures like PLO chairperson Yasser Arafat or TE Lawrence better known by his moniker "of Arabia." This catalogue reflects as much on classed intra-Palestinian dynamics as it does to more global appropriations. It reflects on romanticizations of the keffiyeh by Marxist anti-imperialists as much as its significations of early Christianity in Hollywood biblical epics. In considering the contradictions inherent to the keffiyeh's representation as a type object, tracing these instances of keffiyehs provides one tangible way of analyzing the shifting meaning of the Palestinian body as it became increasingly dematerialized during the course of the twentieth century, while also excavating the traces of its presence.

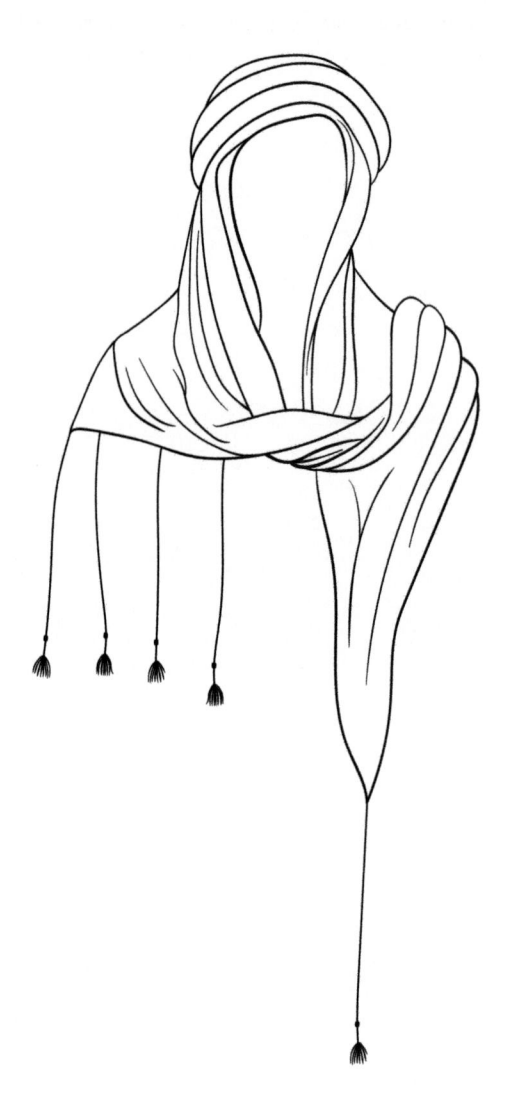

Figure 9.1 Keffiyeh of "A Nazarene." Drawn from a touristic photograph made for the souvenir market c. 1900–20.

The photographic souvenir market for putatively authentic images of the "Holy Land" was lucrative and heavily projected Palestine as an ancient and "biblical" land.[5]

This keffiyeh purports to represent an authentic Nazarene. Such images were commonplace and often utilized models for studio portraits sold to the tourist market as photographs or postcards.[6] Typically, they were couched in ethnographic terms that conjured the link between Bedouins and the *fellahin* as continuities of the ancient, biblical past.[7]

Rarely did such photographs show the modern, urban life of Palestine, which demonstrates a classed approach to the ways in which images of Palestinians circulated through global networks.[8] This keffiyeh can be seen as typifying such *biblified* imagery, which conjures the pre-modern past.

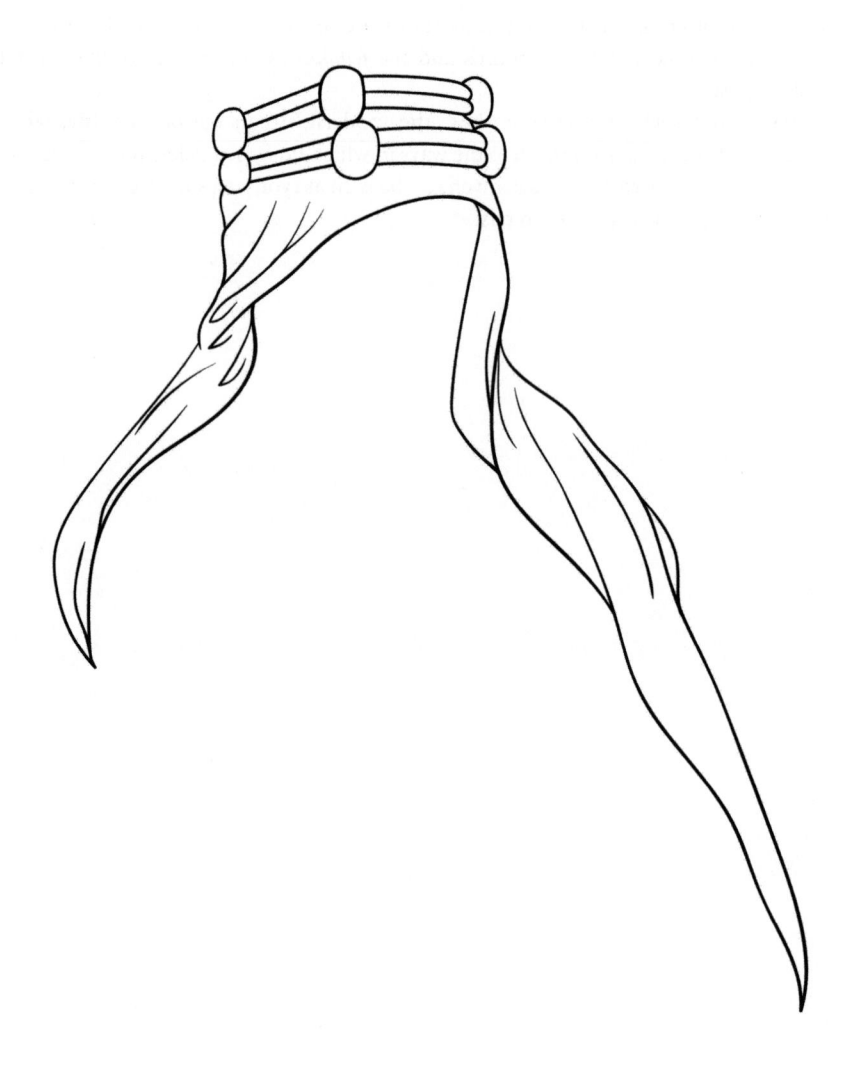

Figure 9.2 T.E. Lawrence's Keffiyeh. Lawrence in Palestine, 1918.

T.E. Lawrence was an archaeologist and military officer with the British Army during the First World War, immortalized in the 1962 film *Lawrence of Arabia*.[9] He is well-known for his role in galvanizing Arab support for the British against the Ottomans during this period and is often regarded as a spy.[10] Lawrence was often photographed wearing a Saudi-style keffiyeh, contributing to his moniker.

Lawrence's role in the First World War paved the way for the Franco-British colonization of the region through the Mandate system. This was best embodied by the Sykes-Picot Agreement, which delineated many of the modern Arab states that exist today, despite Lawrence's assurances to Faisal Al-Hashemi, the son of the Sharif of Mecca, that if the Arabs sided with the British against the Ottomans, the British would support the creation of an independent Arab nation.[11] This keffiyeh can be seen as embodying the ambiguities of British positions toward Arab nationalist aspirations.

Figure 9.3 A Bedouin Keffiyeh. Nabi Rubeen 1922.

This keffiyeh was drawn from an image of a Bedouin man riding on horseback at the *Mawsim Nabi Rubeen* (Prophet Ruben Festival) in 1922.[12] The annual event had historically been a religious celebration, but by the 1920s had evolved into a yearly social event in the summer in which those celebrating flocked to Nabi Rubeen for festivities which included music, performances, horse racing and pageantry.[13]

Each year a tent city was swiftly constructed on the sand dunes near the Mediterranean. Period sources note that women of urban backgrounds would threaten to divorce their husbands if they did not take them to the festival,[14] though it attracted the young and the old from a diversity of class and urban-rural backgrounds for the celebration in which fun parks and other activities were specifically constructed.

This keffiyeh, rather than hailing from a touristic image, can be seen more as a mode of ethnographic documentation.

128 *Producing Palestine*

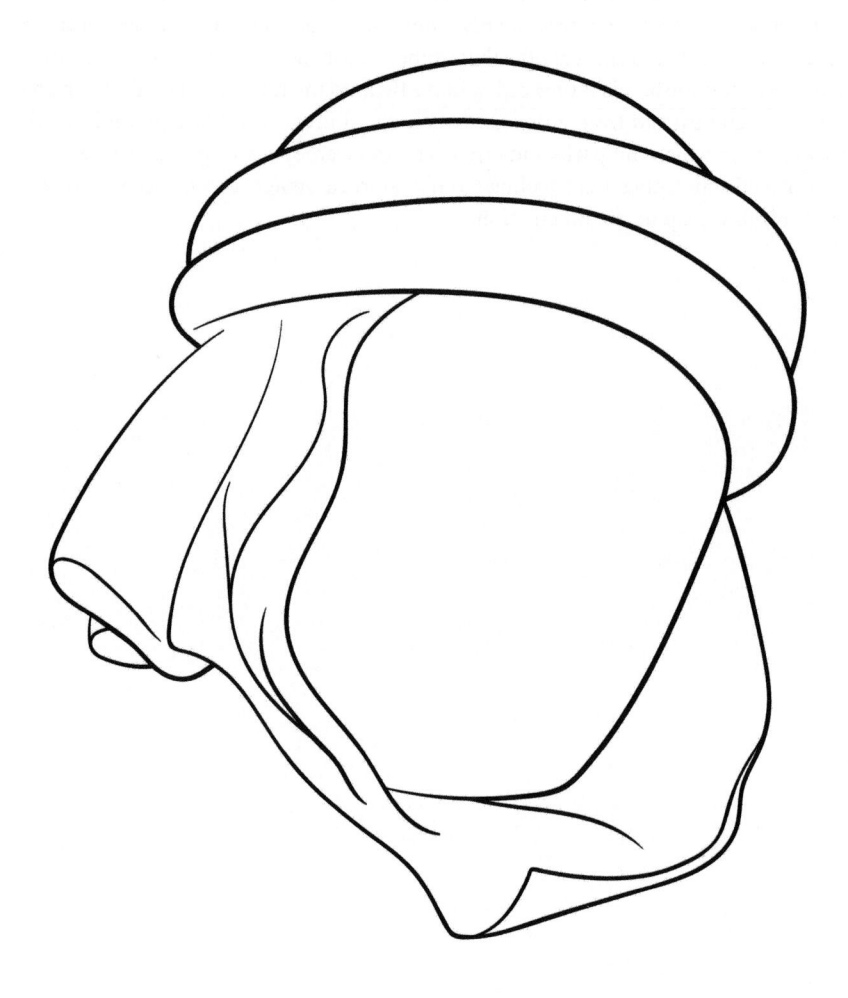

Figure 9.4 Costume Keffiyeh: Simon the Cyrene. Hollywood film, 1927.

This keffiyeh was made as part of a costume for Simon the Cyrene in the Hollywood biblical epic in 1927.[15] Simon the Cyrene is said to have helped Jesus carry the cross en route to his crucifixion.[16]

In the 1920s there was broad consensus that the *fellahin* were contemporary traces of the peoples of biblical times. This perspective was supported by a range of viewpoints across political and confessional divides including the Palestinian anthropologist Tawfik Canaan as well as Zionists like David Ben-Gurion.[17]

Such presumptions of *fellahin* biblical indigeneity had significant impacts on the ways in which costuming was deployed in Hollywood biblical epics, with the keffiyeh a strong feature of men's costuming.[18] This keffiyeh is an early filmic example of such coded costuming practices.

130 Producing Palestine

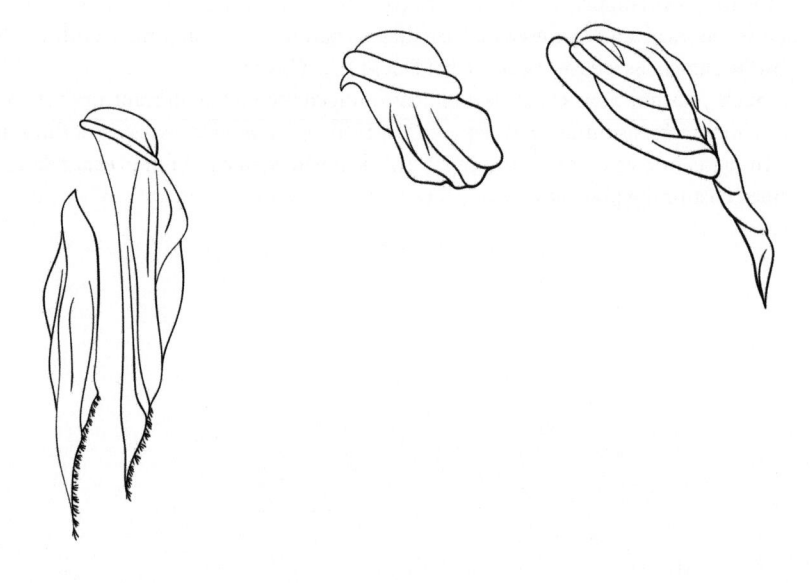

Figure 9.5 Costume Keffiyehs: The Three Wise Men. From a Passion Play held at the Jerusalem YMCA 1934–9.

These three keffiyehs are also costumes that were used in a Passion Play that was performed at the YMCA in Jerusalem in the mid- to late 1930s.[19] The keffiyeh-clad Three Wise Men show that there was a clear confluence between urban middle-class Palestinians and their global counterparts in how they perceived the biblical authenticity of the *fellahin*.

The timing of the play was on the eve or during the Great Arab Revolt (1936–9). This also hints at the idea that the keffiyeh was deployed as a nationalist symbol in the context of such a religious performance.[20] During the Revolt, urban Palestinians were known to wear the keffiyeh—typical of the rural sphere—to confuse British authorities who were cracking down on protestors.[21] These keffiyehs, though each in a slightly different style, mark a nationalist reappropriation of the garment, a shift in nationalist Palestinian cultural diplomacy and self-perception.

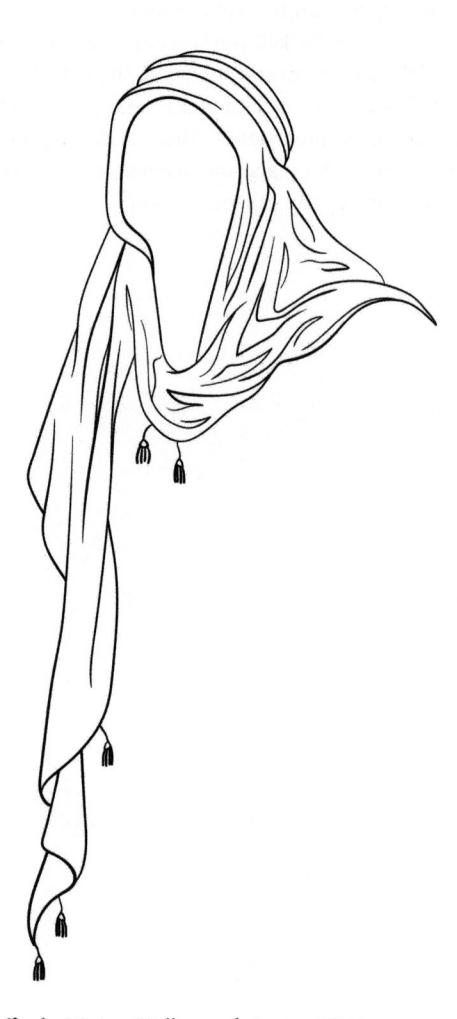

Figure 9.6 Costume Keffiyeh: Moses. Hollywood cinema 1956.

This keffiyeh is a costume drawn from another Hollywood biblical epic.[22] It was made for the character of Moses in a 1956 film. This keffiyeh can be seen as marking a shift in Hollywood identification with Jewishness as the site of biblical indigeneity in the years after the Nakba and the creation of the State of Israel.

The context of many Hollywood biblical epics of the 1950s and 1960s constructed Jewishness as a mode of proto-Christianity that was conflated with liberal-democracy.[23] This had two primary effects. First, it reascribed indigeneity to Jews, rather than Arab Palestinians in the period after the creation of Israel. Second, it constructed Christianity as a force of liberation in the context of the Cold War, drawing a correlation between religion and politics in US-Israeli relations.[24] This keffiyeh marks a different attitude to the question of indigeneity.

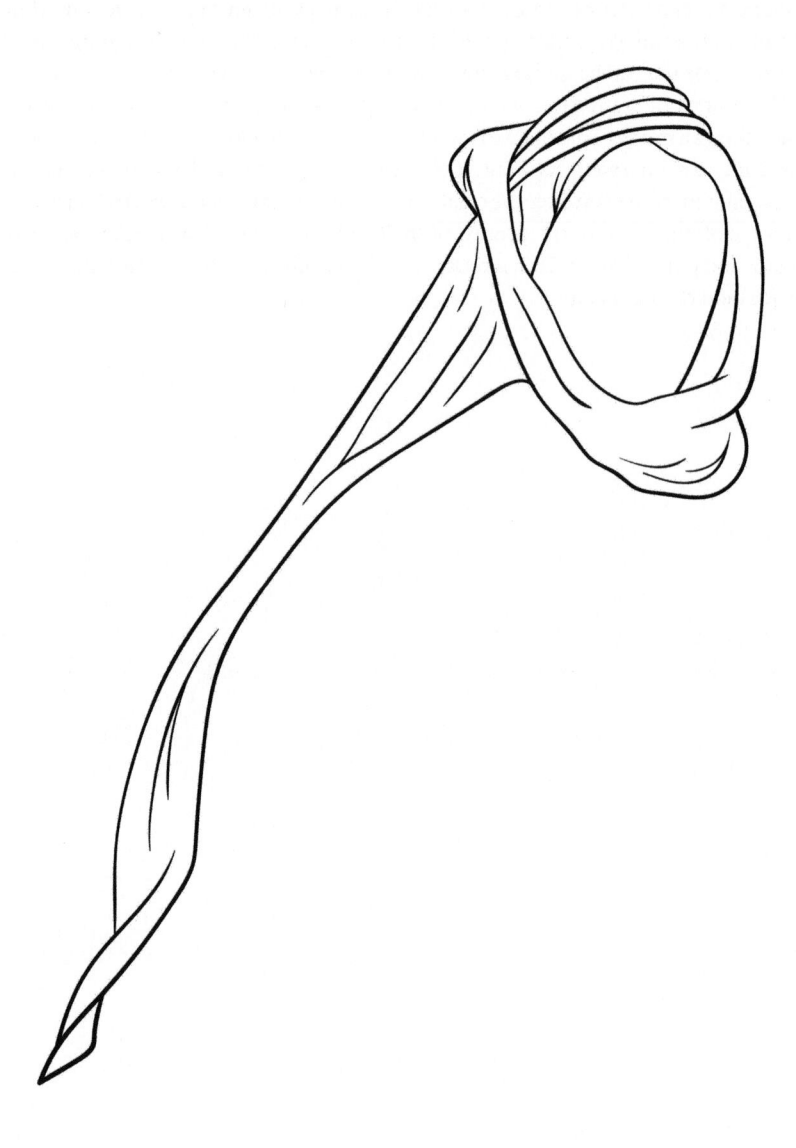

Figure 9.7 Costume Keffiyeh: Disguise. Hollywood Cinema, 1960.

This keffiyeh is also a costume drawn from Hollywood cinema. It was used to disguise the main protagonist, a member of the *Haganah*, from a 1960 film.[25] It was used in a scene when he broke into a jail used by the British to rescue Zionist militants who had executed the bombing of the King David Hotel in Jerusalem. This keffiyeh operates not only as a costume but as a disguise—a costume that was performed as a costume during the jail break sequence.

Arabness, in the homogenized form of the keffiyeh, is used to mask Jewish difference from the general Palestinian populace within the Zionist narrative of the film. Underlying the deployment of this keffiyeh is a notion of veiling to obscure differentiation between individuals. The cross-cultural adoption of the keffiyeh-as-disguise in this context hints at a classed assumption of what constitutes Palestinian identity (with a subtle reference to the Great Revolt), but also makes assumptions about Arab cultural homogeneity.[26] It also re-genders orientalist ideas of deviance regarding the politics of veiling. This costume keffiyeh-as-disguise embodies orientalist assumptions of the homogenizing role of the garment.

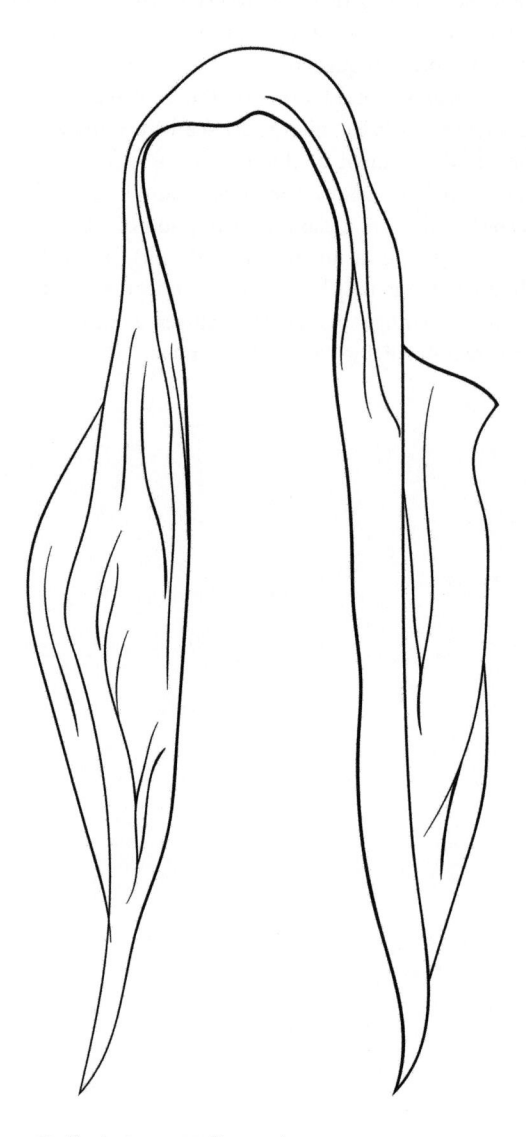

Figure 9.8 Costume Keffiyeh: Jesus. Hollywood cinema, 1965.

This keffiyeh is drawn from the costuming of Jesus in a 1965 biblical epic.[27] The escalation of tensions in the lead up to the Six Day War in 1967 can be seen as a cementing of the politics in earlier Hollywood films of the 1950s and early 1960s.[28] Within the highly politicized context of the 1960s we see the geopolitical relationships of the period applied through the narrative of the life of Christ.[29]

While many keffiyehs appear in the film, this costume for Jesus underscores a particular gentleness. Without an 'agal (head band), it slightly feminizes the figure of Jesus in a way that tempers the more typically masculine reading of the garment. In this respect, it mimics tropes of veiling that are associated with depictions of the Virgin Mary. Given the politics of the mid- to late 1960s, the feminization of this keffiyeh underscores the benevolence of Christianity, and hence liberal democracy, within the Cold War context.

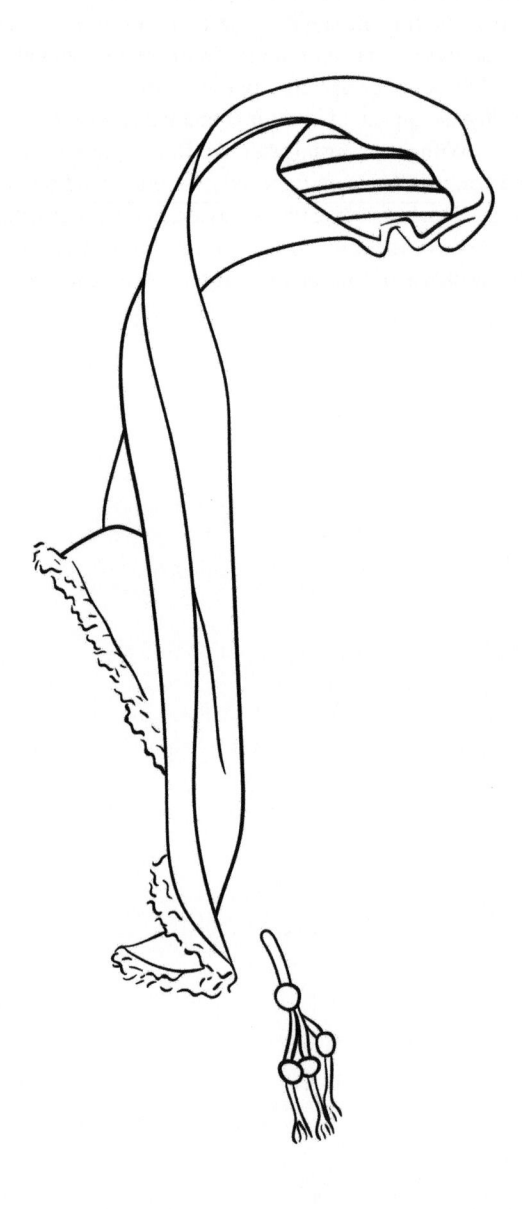

Figure 9.9 Arafat's Keffiyeh. Organization of African Unity conference, 1975.

This keffiyeh was worn by Palestine Liberation Organization's chairman Yasser Arafat to the Organization of African Unity conference in 1975, with whom both the Arab League and the Palestinian Liberation Organization had close relations.[30] Arafat often wore a keffiyeh and it is one of his defining iconographies along with military fatigues and sunglasses, particularly in his younger days.[31]

The keffiyeh, in this context, becomes a nationalist statement of indigeneity. When combined with sunglasses and military clothing, we see a mixing of markers of indigeneity with markers of modernity. This paralleled the leftist, Third-Worldist politics of the period. Here the keffiyeh is cast as a symbol of revolutionary modernity within a vernacular of traditional *fellahin* aesthetics.[32] This can be seen as a continuity of aesthetics of resistance that developed during the Great Arab Revolt of 1936–9. This keffiyeh is nationalist symbol, but also a re-conception of Palestinian modernity.

Figure 9.10 Solidarity Keffiyeh. Image of Cuban solidarity with Palestine, 1980.

This keffiyeh is drawn from a Cuban solidarity poster produced in 1980 by Gladys Acosta.[33] Here, the revolutionary aesthetics that had begun to emerge from the late 1960s onward can be seen as part of a formal Palestinian revolutionary iconography by the 1980s.

Such aesthetics often anonymized the figure of the *fedayee* (freedom fighter), but also drew heavily on the image of the *fellah* as an archetype. This anonymization often obscured or removed the face of the individual,[34] but also multiplied *fedayee* bodies through the reproduction of solidarity posters in public spaces.[35] This has parallels with the homogenizing use of the costume keffiyeh-as-disguise within the narrative of the 1960 film previously discussed.

This keffiyeh, however, is mobilized as protective through its anonymization. It functions on a propagandistic level with the guerilla tactics that marked much of the PLO's military action[36] from the late 1960s to the 1980s.

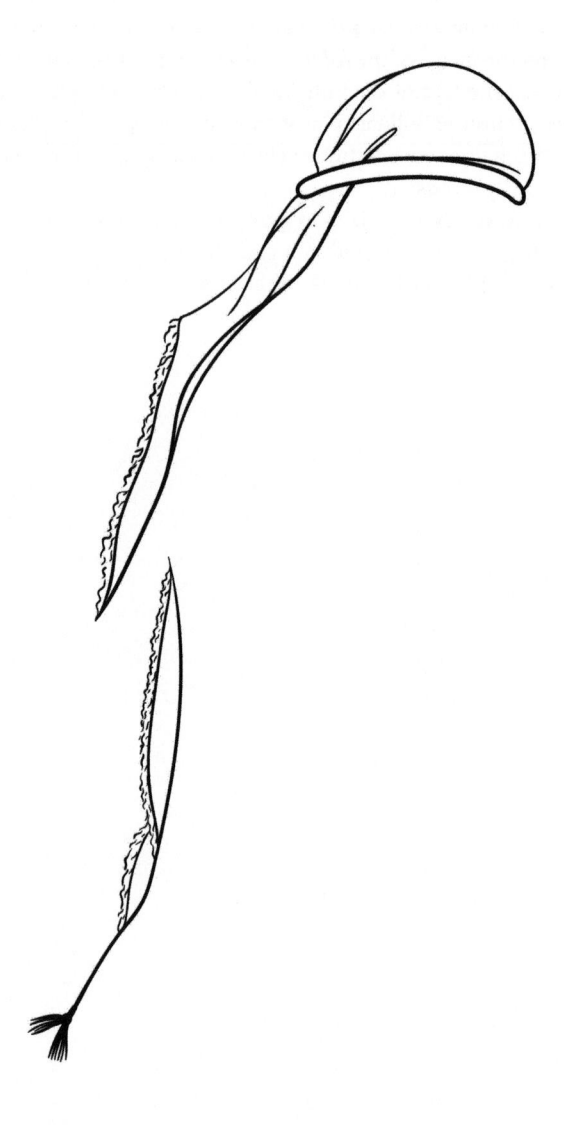

Figure 9.11 Costume Keffiyeh: Terrorist. Hollywood cinema, 1994.

This keffiyeh is also a Hollywood costume. It is drawn from a minor character within a 1994 film about a terrorist organization that threatens to blow up various American cities if the United States does not withdraw troops from the Persian Gulf.[37]

The costuming of members of the terrorist organization plays with a mixture of military fatigues and keffiyehs that strongly references Palestinian revolutionary aesthetics.[38] Here, we see the figure of the *fedayee* re-embodied as terrorist, with both identities rooted in the same archetypal figure.[39] This keffiyeh is utilized in a propagandistic manner against Palestinians in juxtaposition to the keffiyehs of Arafat and Acosta's 1980 solidarity poster. This keffiyeh marks a sense of threat to liberalism.

Notes

1. Helga Tawil-Souri, "Cinema as the Space to Transgress Palestine's Territorial Trap," *Middle East Journal of Culture and Communication* 7, no. 2 (2014): 169–89.
2. Chrisoula Lionis, "Peasant, Revolutionary, Celebrity: The Subversion of Popular Iconography in Contemporary Palestinian Art," *Middle East Journal of Culture and Communication* 8, no. 1 (2015): 69–84; Issam Nassar, "'Biblification' in the Service of Colonialism: Jerusalem in Nineteenth-Century Photography," *Third Text* 20, no. 3-4, 317–26. Jack Shaheen, *Reel Bad Arabs: How Hollywood Vilifies a People* (North Hampton, MA: Olive Branch Press, 2001). Edward Said, *Orientalism* (New York, NY: Vintage Books, 1979).
3. Leila Khaled is often photographed wearing a keffiyeh. One iconic image taken by Eddie Adams depicts her in a keffiyeh with an AK-47, which has been reproduced repeatedly in political murals and posters as well as contemporary artworks.
4. Ariella Aïsha Azoulay, "Photographic Conditions: Looting, Archives, and the Figure of the Infiltrator," *Jerusalem Quarterly* 61 (2015): 6–22; Sary Zananiri, "Indigeneity Transgression and the Body: Orientalism and Biblification in the Popular Imaging of Palestinians," *Journal of Intercultural Studies* 42, no. 6 (2021): 722–3.
5. Nassar, "'Biblification' in the Service of Colonialism," 317–26.
6. See for instance the studio portraits produced by Maison Bonfils.
7. Sary Zananiri, "Costumes and the Image: Authenticity, Identity and Photography in Palestine," in *The Social and Cultural Histories of Palestine: Essays in Honour of Salim Tamari*, ed. Sarah Irving (Edinburgh: Edinburgh University Press, 2023), 73 and 91.
8. Sary Zananiri "Imaging and Imagining Palestine: An Introduction," in *Imaging and Imagining Palestine: Photography, Modernity and the Biblical Lens, 1918-1948*, ed. Karène Sanchez Summerer and Sary Zananiri (Netherlands: Brill, 2021), 11–12.
9. *Lawrence of Arabia* (1962), dir. David Lean.
10. Scott Anderson, *Lawrence in Arabia: War Deceit, Imperial Folly and the Making of the Middle East* (New York: Doubleday, 2013), 609; John James Moscrop *Measuring Jerusalem: The Palestine Exploration Fund and British Interests in the Holy Land* (London: Leicester University Press, 2000), 205–8.
11. A detailed account of secret dealings including the Franco-British Sykes-Picot Agreement that delineated new colonial "protectorates" after the war, the McMahon-Hussein Correspondence in which the British guaranteed an independent Arab state after the war, and the Balfour Declaration, in which the British declared support for a Jewish homeland in Palestine, can be found in Christopher Simon Sykes *The Man Who Created the Middle East: A Story of Empire, Conflict and the Sykes-Picot Agreement* (Great Britain: William Collins, 2016).
12. Frank Scholten *Man on a Horse* digitized nitrate negative, NINO F Scholten 2: 19, Netherlands Institute for the Near East and Leiden University Library https://digitalcollections.universiteitleiden.nl/view/item/3427811?solr_nav%5Bid%5D=bfe3ecc338f51da01e25&solr_nav%5Bpage%5D=0&solr_nav%5Boffset%5D=13
13. Mahmoud Yazbak, "The Muslim Festival of Nabi Rubin in Palestine: From Religious Fesitval to Summer Resort," *Holy Land Studies* 10, no. 2 (2011): 169–98.
14. Yazbak "Nabi Rubin," 190–3.
15. *King of Kings* (1927), dir. Cecil B. DeMille.
16. Simon the Cyrene was compelled to carry the cross as Jesus was sent to be crucified. He is mentioned in Matthew 27:32, Mark 15:21, and Luke 23:26.

17 Khaled Nashhef, "Tawfik Canaan: His Life and Works," *Jerusalem Quarterly* 16 (2002): 16; Jonathan Marc Gribetz, *Defining Neighbors: Religion, Race, and the Early Zionist-Arab Encounter* (Princeton, NJ: Princeton University Press, 2014), 123–4.
18 See for instance costuming in *King of Kings* (1927), *Ben-Hur* (1959), *The Greatest Story Ever Told* (1965), and more recently *The Passion of the Christ* (2004) as examples.
19 The Christmas Story, Y.M.C.A. tableaux. [The Tidings to the Shepherds III] American Colony Photo Dept. 1934–39, digitized nitrate negative, Matson Collection Library of Congress. https://www.loc.gov/pictures/item/2019710696/
20 Zananiri, "Indigeneity Transgression and the Body," 722–3.
21 This reached a peak in August 1938, when the Arab leadership of the revolt commanded all urban Palestinians to wear the keffiyeh, rather than the middle-class tarboush. See Ted Swedenburg *Memories of Revolt: The 1936–1939 Rebellion and the Palestinian National Past* (Minneapolis, MN: University of Minnesota Press, 1995), 31–3.
22 *10 Commandments* (1956), dir. Cecil B. DeMille.
23 Sary Zananiri, "From Still to Moving Images: Shifting Representation of Jerusalem and Palestinians in the Western Biblical Imaginary," *Jerusalem Quarterly* 67, Autumn (2016): 76–8.
24 Bruce Babington and Peter Evans, *Biblical Epics: Sacred Narrative in the Hollywood Cinema* (Eugene, OR: Wipf and Stock, 2009), 33–4.
25 *Exodus* (1960), dir. Otto Preminger.
26 This operation can be seen as an inversion of what Ariella Azoulay has theorized as the figure of the Infiltrator. See Azoulay "Photographic Conditions," 6–22.
27 *The Greatest Story Ever Told* (1965) dir. George Stevens.
28 Melani McAlister, *Epic Encounters: Culture, Media and U.S. Interests in the Middle East, 1945–2000* (Berkeley, CA: University of California Press, 2001), 43–7.
29 Zananiri, "Still to Moving Images," 72–8.
30 Mario J. Azevedo, "The Organization of African Unity and Afro-Arab Cooperation," Africa Today 35, no. 3/4 (1988): 68–80.
31 This mix of keffiyeh, sunglasses, and military fatigues was particularly so in the 1970s.
32 Zananiri, "Indigeneity Transgression and the Body," 729–31.
33 Gladys Acosta *Day of World Solidarity with the Struggle of the Palestinian People* poster produced for the Organization of Solidarity with the People of Africa, Asia and Latin America (1980). https://www.palestineposterproject.org/poster/day-of-world-solidarity
34 Zananiri, "Indigeneity, Transgression and the Body," 727.
35 Laleh Khalili, *Heroes and Martyrs of Palestine: The Politics of National Commemoration* (Cambridge, MA: Cambridge University Press, 2007), 238.
36 See for instance Rosemary Sayigh *Palestinians: From Peasants to Revolutionaries* (London: Zed Books, 1979), 152–4.
37 *True Lies* (1994), dir. James Cameron.
38 Khalili, *Heroes and Martyrs*, 416.
39 Zananiri, "Indigeneity, Transgression and the Body," 726–31.

10

"We're Still Alive, so Remove Us from Memory": Asynchronicity and the Museum in Resistance

Lara Khaldi

Take One: The Museum Object in Battle

In her essay "A Tank on a Pedestal: Museums in an Age of Planetary Civil War," Hito Steyerl writes about a military tank that was stolen from the pedestal of a Second World War monument in Ukraine and used in battle during the 2014 conflict.[1] Borrowing from Giorgio Agamben's work on the relationship between civil war and stasis, Steyerl accuses the museum of being the site—perhaps even the engine—for a history which keeps returning and remains stuck in a loop. She defines the kind of history that returns by the reuse of the tank as "partial, partisan, and privatized, a self-interested enterprise, a means to feel entitled, an objective obstacle to coexistence, and a temporal fog detaining people in the stranglehold of imaginary origins."[2] In other words, the exhibition of the tank on a memorial site is complicit with this history, as it embodies it, makes it available and visible, causing its return. Following her argument, the museum functions as a time travel machine that hurls us back in loops of violence: "The museum leaks the past into the present, and history becomes severely corrupted and limited."[3] National museums work under the assumption that their objects are representative of its citizens, tacitly equal and homogeneous. However, this only continues to aggravate residual tensions. Civil wars thrive on historical tensions and are usually propelled by national, ethnic, or religious binaries, which mask class struggle and injustice caused by the ruling national bourgeoisie.[4] Still, museums present themselves as public institutions and the objects within them as owned by the citizens of the state. Exhibitions in this sense become a means for the representation of the nation. Thus, it is not illogical for citizens to reuse its objects. Once the objects are exposed and reused, the museum's time seeps out of its doors, infecting all its citizens, trapping them into a loop.

The birth of the modernist museum has always been associated with revolution, with the Louvre as the emblem of this history. If the museum is postrevolutionary, it is

---

The quote in the case title is from the poem "The Exiles Don't Look Back" by Mahmoud Darwish: *Now, As You Awaken*. Transl. Omnia Amin and Rick London (San Francisco: Sardines Press, 2006).

also postcolonial, as it is often one of the first institutions to be built postindependence. In the Palestinian context, however, time outside the museum is still under settler colonialism, and resistance to this is still underway. So, while the debate around decolonizing the museum is rooted in a "postcolonial time," the colonialization of Palestine continues, and the struggle against it ensues as an elongated present. We therefore find ourselves in an uncanny situation where we suffer the symptoms of a new postindependence nation-state, with new national museums, local authorities, and a neoliberal economy, while still under settler-colonial rule and without sovereignty over land, people, or infrastructure. Considering this asynchronicity with the temporal rhythms of the national and modernist postrevolutionary museum, what happens to the objects within them, and how do they remain active in the present?

Take Two: Fugitive Objects

The Yasser Arafat Museum in Ramallah exhibits a number of weapons, some with symbolic provenance. One such weapon is the personal pistol of the late Yasser Arafat. Another gun belonged to the late Khalil Al Wazir (Abu Jihad), cofounder of the Palestine Liberation Organization and commander of the armed wing of Fatah. Yet there is a stark difference in the ways the two pistols are exhibited. While the pistol of Arafat is displayed behind museum glass, near the famous speech he gave at the 1974 UN General Assembly, Abu Jihad's is only represented by a photograph. Arafat's pistol has had a symbolic function ever since he spoke the most famous lines from his 1974 speech: "Today I have come bearing an olive branch and a freedom-fighter's gun. Do not let the olive branch fall from my hand."[5] Almost fifty years later, encased in museum glass in Ramallah, the pistol is evidence of the death of that revolutionary era for the leadership. It represents the trigger for the museum's present-day politics: collaboration with settler-colonial powers through censorship, repression, and security coordination.

The picture of Abu Jihad's pistol, on the other hand, is like a hole in the museum. From this crack, present-day reality seeps in. Underneath the photo, the label reads: "The gun was obtained from the family of the martyr but the museum has not yet been able to bring it from Gaza." Abu Jihad was assassinated in 1988 in Tunis by the Mossad. The pistol carries traces of the assassination, as the handle is shot off. The reason why the museum cannot physically obtain the pistol is because it is impossible for his widow to transport it through Erez, one of the Israeli checkpoints encasing Gaza in an impenetrable siege for over ten years.[6]

Every time I visit the Yasser Arafat Museum, I wonder why the photo of Abu Jihad's pistol is exhibited, since the museum is an obvious site for claiming the death of a revolutionary era and setting the stage for the narrative of the present political regime: peaceful negotiations, security coordination, and political complicity with the Israeli settler-colonial regime. The photo of Jihad's weapon posits an opposing narrative of the museum. Naturally, we all know that the museum (and any other conduit for hegemonic ideology for that matter) is not omniscient and that it leaks, breaks, and falters. However, this looks like a very deliberate curatorial decision: a photo of the pistol behind museum glass. I would postulate that it is an attempt at de-functionalizing the pistol even while it is outside the museum. The museum would like to capture both militant past and present and put them to their death, thus situating resistance to settler colonialism in the past in an attempt to frame everything in a postcolonial time. The photograph of the pistol, therefore, carries with it the contradiction and tension within this museum.

However, contrary to the desire of the museum, the photo of the pistol has invoked various stories, rumors, and myths as to why the pistol is missing. In fact, the photo looks like a wanted poster. The museum wishes to capture the fugitive pistol, but as sometimes happens with wanted posters, its purpose backfires, transforming the outlaw into a popular figure of rebellion. In *The Undercommons*, Stefano Harney and Fred Moten write of the fugitive as the outlaw, as the rebel, the one who stands their ground against the settlers.[7] Evading the relationship between the powerful and the powerless, the fugitive is the one who transgresses this relationship of binaries by refusing "to be corrected." Similarly, some objects are compelled by colonial powers to refuse to enter the museum, to refuse to be transformed into pure postcolonial form, into corpses of colonial time.

Take Three: The Museum Before or After the Revolution?

As stated above, the Louvre is considered by many to mark the birth of the modern museum. The conversion of the palace into a museum was propelled by the French Revolution. As discussed by Boris Groys, the decision by French revolutionaries whether to destroy the palace or not was resolved by converting it into a museum, an iconoclastic response which turns everything in the museum into material evidence of the death of the past regime/s.[8] This irrevocable death marks a new political era outside the museum, de-functionalizing its objects, transforming them into art.[9] So, the museum's time, according to Groys, is after the end of a revolution. The museum in this way functions to deem not only what is inside of it irrevocably dead but also the revolution itself. Revolutions are defined by the present, as they are usually the moment of destruction of the present regime. Once this regime is destroyed, the revolution is destroyed along with it. Museums are built to commemorate those revolutions; they become both evidence of the death of a past regime and guarantor that another revolution is unnecessary. This is precisely the case with the Yasser Arafat Museum; it commemorates the history of the militant era, or what Palestinians refer to as the Palestinian Revolution, subsequently hurling it into the past. With the postrevolutionary museum in place, there is no longer a reason to revolt. Time in the modernist museum moves between history and the future. The present is only a tunnel. History is employed to determine the future, and the future is rather posited as the present.

Take Four: *The Secret*

There is another notorious gun in the Palestinian imagination. During the—continuing—Nakba of 1948, many Palestinians buried their valuable belongings (ranging from photos to gold) in their backyards or secret locations, so that they would be able to retrieve them once they return, not knowing that many of them would remain buried for decades. However, the stories of those underground remainders keep circulating in the diaspora and across generations. In the satirical novel *The Secret Life of Saeed: The Pessoptimist* by Emile Habibi, there is such a story. The novel centers on the strange time of the Nakba aftermath. Chronicling the struggles and transformations of the anti-hero Saeed and his family, the story spans two generations, wherein his son is empowered by the buried objects. Two secrets haunt the novel: the first is that Saeed is a collaborator with the new regime, and the second is a buried treasure box that his wife's family hid in a cave in their village, Tantoura, before they were forcibly expelled in 1948. Eventually, their son finds the treasure box, which contains guns and gold, and becomes a *fida'i* (resistance fighter).

The Nakba of 1948 defined the Palestinians as a collective through the shared experience of death and expulsion. The moment of death and burial is simultaneously the moment of birth and reproduction.[10] Therefore, the novel's return to the buried treasure follows this form of movement. Throughout the novel, the buried treasure functions like a promise of salvation, a reminder of a possible return, the potential for some kind of emancipation. Indeed, the story of the treasure box enables the son to become a resistance fighter. The act of burial produces life; the stories of the buried objects circulate among the Palestinians, and they are kept alive through continuous oral chronicling.

Take Five: What About the Present?

In *All Shall be Unicorns*, Marina Vishmidt writes about the notion of the commons and art activism in relation to time. She juxtaposes communist time with commonist time. Vishmidt argues that the fulfilment of communism takes place after the revolution; thus, it exists in the future while commonist time takes place in the present. Commonism is rooted in the present because, instead of waiting for the future revolution or political mobilization against the state, or making demands of the state, it launches its affirmative projects in the here and now. In the modernist conception of time, and its association with progress, the present and the future become binaries, as we resist the present and work toward a "better" future. According to Vishmidt, the commons is still "future oriented" but embodied rather than using time as a medium for its realization. The commons "does not oppose the present, but proposes an active reconstruction of it from within."[11] Moreover, this idea of progress, which sees the present as the tunnel for the future, is at the very core of capitalism, as financial markets are based on future projections and speculation. Postponement and delay are tactics of the market and a means to control the present. According to Timothy Mitchell, even the construction of infrastructure is built to delay and accumulate interest and profit.[12] However, the future orientation of the solution to come is futile in the case of settler colonialism. For the oppressed, the present and the everyday are determined by struggle and resistance. Thus, a deferral into the future constitutes self-denial.[13]

Practices of the commons are also rooted in the everyday. Capitalism pervades every aspect of our lives; its violence is slow. Vishmidt discusses the different discourses of the left around the fight with capitalism, and a futurist orientation seems to pervade. Those discourses are set after the destruction of capitalist institutions opens the way for communist living. Commonism is instead situated in the present and is rather affirmative, building communities and support structures which are based on alternative economies, slowly and silently leaving those hegemonic institutions to falter and fall. So, is the time of the museum in resistance to the present?

The museum in struggle needs to be a site of burials. As Groys writes, contrary to the prevalent narrative of calling the museum a graveyard, the graveyard is a space full of possibilities.[14] Stories about graveyards abound. Death in the graveyard becomes generative. Spirits inhabit the present. In popular culture, there are many stories about corpses awakening at graveyards, less so at museums.[15] The secret and promise of finding the treasure box in *The Pessoptimist* function in the same way. The buried treasure box reminds the son of his mother's village and the necessity for return. Similar to Abu Jihad's missing pistol, the story of the object, and its emancipatory powers, survives because of its lack of exposure.

Take Six: Archives in Resistance

The museum of resistance is a museum engaged in struggle. Therefore, it is a museum outside of time. During the first intifada in Palestine, underground communiqués were discarded by burial; they were deemed illegal by the Israeli military, and any Palestinian caught reading or in possession of one was arrested. So, the communiqués had to disappear after they were read. Burning was not an option since the traces were incriminating, so it is said that they were dumped in wet concrete construction sites or buried underground. The future material exposure of these documents implicated their readers and authors. This is precisely the danger of the exhibition of a material archive during a struggle. Any record is incriminating. To be outside of time is to be outside the reaches of the archive and surveillance. It is through the collective practice of struggle and resistance that a community can attempt to be outside of time. It is through preserving a secret together.

The late 1980s in Palestine were distinguished by collective emancipatory knowledge production and radical imagination. Another form of an archive in resistance is a book titled *Falsafat al Muwajahah Wara al Qudban* or *The Philosophy of Confrontation Behind Bars*. This book was smuggled in fragments inside of capsules by political prisoners and circulated outside and inside of Israeli prisons to educate Palestinians about how to confront political imprisonment. The book does not contain any publishing information; neither the author, the publication date, nor printing information are mentioned. Scholar Esmail Nashif writes about the deliberate absence of this information:

> The main characteristic of the space/time of the no-naming practice is the fact of being out of reach of the colonizer's surveillance practices. But in the case of

Philosophy of the Confrontation Behind Bars this being out of reach is not a passive fragile insulation. On the contrary, the invisibility is capitalized on to resist the colonizer whose eye is blinded by the secrecy. The act of no-naming blinds the colonizer's eye/discourse.[16]

The absence of the information places the book outside of a record of time and space which the colonizer controls. To achieve this resistance to the time and space of the colonizer, authorship should encompass the collective: "The author is the collectivity ... By not naming it, one reproduces the myth of the We."[17] The record of knowledge by the Palestinian collective body was materialized and circulated because it was necessary to share in and for resistance. However, the way it was disseminated protected the collective instead of exposing it. The absence of a date places this body of knowledge outside of time, making it impossible to capture yet available to everyone. The underground authorship and circulation of collective knowledge is one of the aspects of a museum in resistance. The medium of this museum is continuous collective dissemination rather than a building made of concrete with an immovable collection about resistance.

Notes

1 Hito Steyerl, "A Tank on a Pedestal: Museums in an Age of Planetary Civil War," *e-flux*, February 2016, www.e-flux.com/journal/70/60543/a-tank-on-a-pedestal-museums-in-an-age-of-planetary-civil-war/
2 Steyerl, A Tank.
3 Steyerl, A Tank.
4 Madi Amel, "Al Thaqafa Wal Thawra," *Al Hiwar Al Mutamadden*, Al Hiwar Al Mutamadden, May 23, 2016, www.ahewar.org/debat/show.art.asp?aid=518075.
5 Yasser Arafat "Yasser Arafat's 1974 UN General Assembly speech." United Nations General Assembly, New York (November 13, 1974).
6 The Palestinian police cannot even move with their weapons between different zones and ghettos, as connecting roads are under Israeli control.
7 Stefano Harney and Fred Moten, *The Undercommons. Fugitive Planning & Black Study* (New York etc: Minor Compositions, 2013).
8 Boris Groys, "On art activism," *e-flux journal*, no. 56 (2014): 1–14.
9 Groys even suggests that it is the modernist museum which marks the transformation of design into art.
10 Esmail Nashif, *Images of a Palestinian's Death* (Beirut: Arab Center for Research and Policy Studies, 2015).
11 Marina Vishmidt, "All Shall Be Unicorns: About Commons, Aesthetics and Time," *Open! Platform for Culture, Art & The Public Domain*, September 3, 2014, www.onlineopen.org/download.php?id=128
12 Timothy Mitchell, "Infrastructures Work on Time," *e-flux architecture*, January 28, 2020, www.e-flux.com/architecture/new-silk-roads/312596/infrastructures-work-on-time/

13 Joseph Massad uses the term "postcolonial colony" to describe Palestine with which he presents a historical argument where Zionism presents Israel as a postcolony: Joseph A. Massad, *The Persistence of the Palestinian Question. Essays on Zionism and the Palestinians* (New York, NY: Routledge, 2006).
14 Groys, On Art Activism.
15 Groys, On Art Activism.
16 Nashif, Images of a Palestinian's Death.
17 Nashif, Images of a Palestinian's Death.

11

Forging Revolutionary Objects

Stephen Sheehi

Shadia Mansour and DAM's "All of Them Have Tanks" repurposes a traditional Arab children's song into an anthem of defiance, refusal, joy, affirmation, and love.[1] They rebuff military violence of the settler state now known as Israel with sacrifices and commitments of the Palestinian Resistance (*al-muqawimah al-falastiniyah*). In the face of tanks and bombs, the stories of women, men, and children form the fabric of Palestine, especially in besieged Gaza. Palestinian weapons are stories and stones, pens, songs, and poems, minds, will, commitment, and their bodies. The chokepoints fail in the face of a defiant population of mothers, fathers, and children. In this asymmetrical cruel settler occupation, the feebleness of Zionism is accentuated by the dignity and willfulness of "the people." The lyrics emerge from Palestinian life and life worlds and resonate with innumerable poems of defiance within a *culture of* Palestinian resistance including Tawfiq Ziyadah's "Here We Remain":

As if we are twenty impossible
In Lydd and Ramlah and the Galilee
Here on your chests, we remain.
In your throats
Like a shard of glass, like a cactus
In your eyes,
A cyclone of fire
Here on your chest, we remain like a wall,
We are hungry, we are stripped naked, we defy.
We compose poems
We fill the streets with the anger of demonstrations
We fill the prisons proudly
We create children, rebellious generation after generation.[2]

Pairing Mansour-DAM's song and Ziyadah's poem presents us with the "infrastructure" of *objects* that organize and structure Palestinian cultural productions. The objects circulating within an affective economy bind psychic worlds to material realities, while this infrastructure connects psychic structures of Palestinian life to the shared social formations within their communities. Against the backdrop of Mansour and DAM's song and Ziyadah's poem, this chapter explores how people under oppression "attach to" and "internalize" particular "objects"—things, people, social formations in the psychoanalytic meaning—that facilitate survival and resistance under seemingly overpowering conditions of settler colonialism.

In the following pages, then, I approach a handful of popular techné of liberation that operate within a culture of settler-colonialism, exile, and liberation. Techné is not only about technology. Rather, it is an object of social and subjective practice that emerges from knowledge production, from bringing knowledge into the world. This knowledge operates within and as a product of the material, social, and lived worlds—in other words, as a consequence of *being-in-the-world*.[3] Techné of liberation emerge as the social organization and the sociogeny of marginalized peoples, as Frantz Fanon would say. In the case of the Palestinians, these techné materialize from a culture of *popular resistance (al-muqawimah al-sh'abiyah)* that Mansour/DAM and Ziyadah narrate within Palestinian life, whether in the village, the city, the refugee camp, or the prison. Rooted in the internal worlds and material realities of coloniality, *popular resistance* "is a set of processes, procedures, and technologies for decolonizing the imagination."[4] Whether a spoon, stone, kite, bullet, or a poem, this chapter demonstrates how technologies of self-liberation surface from a psychological-subjective-social fabric of Palestinian community and identity.

The Spoon

On September 6, 2021, a spoon was the object of liberation for six Palestinian political prisoners who escaped using it to dig out of one of the settler-colonial Apartheid state's most impermeable gulags. Gilboa Prison was built hastily in 2004 because the settler-colonial regime quickly filled up its archaeology of prisons during the Second Intifada, also known as the *Intifadat al-Aqsa*. Mohammed al-Ardah, Yaqoub Qadri, Ayham Kamamji, Munadil Nafi'at, Zakaria Zubaidi, and Mahmoud al-Ardah, the architects of the escape, crawled to freedom through a tunnel that took nine months to excavate. They dug through 6 inches of concrete wall, metal plates in the floor, and 100 feet of dirt.

The settler colony now known as Israel was in nervous breakdown until all six *fida'iyin* (freedom fighters) were recaptured. Upon arraignment, Ayham Kamamji yelled defiantly in the settler court:

> We will leave the prison upright, through the door, above the ground just as we defeated them from under the ground. We see clearly the Resistance's promise (*w'ad al-muqawimah*) to us is close at hand: The victory is coming -despite the nose of the occupier.[5]

Upon further recent sentencing, Yaqoub Qadri affirmed:

> We don't care about the Israeli sentence. For us, what is important is that we created the impossible. We dealt a blow. What Israel and its security apparatus considered impossible, we made happen![6]

What is this power of a spoon to have licensed the defiance of these prisoners, six men who should have been broken by the dominance of the state now known as Israel? The spoon became a transformative object that transubstantiates into a techné of liberation and an object through which the "promise of the Resistance" can be heard and enacted. Thinking about technologies of liberation as a techné challenges settler-colonial myths of the supremacy of the Apartheid state and Palestinian helplessness. In order to comply with settler "reality-bending" that insists upon the compliance of the subjugated to acknowledge one's subordinated position as natural, Israel as a settler-Apartheid state requires Palestinians to *dissociate* and *disassociate*.[7] In other words, Palestinians are not only required to see themselves as vanquished people but required to willfully act as vanquished people. Regularly commanded to "commit national suicide" by high-ranking Israeli politicians, they are required to disassociate from historical and material realities, particularly their relationship to their land and the communities on it in order to become colonial subjects worthy of political "autonomy."[8] Collapsing the claims of technological superiority, state supremacy, and settler sovereignty necessitates absolute disassociation not only from the past but from the present and the future by acquiescing to the naturalness of racial hierarchies that instigates "racial dissociation."[9] Whether understood psychoanalytically as dissociated "self-state" or schizoid condition, "there is a persistent scission between the self and the body," where one's "true self is experienced as more or less disembodied and ... felt to be a part of the false-self system."[10]

Techné of popular liberation emerge, however, out of a culture of refusal to disassociate from the will to collectively affirm Palestinian identity.[11] The six Palestinian heroes of the Freedom Tunnel are fostered and nurtured in communities of care—whether they are in the camps of Jenin or among political prisoners in the Apartheid carceral system. They are buoyed by a culture of solidarity, *sumud* (stalwartness), and care.[12] Yaqoub al-Qadri's and Ayham Kamamji's statements make willful affirmation and self-assertion clear. Their statements are not about *re*-association in the face of dissociation. They are about a sustaining and affirming identification with Palestinian selfhood in the space of Occupied Palestine. Their statements are about *association*.

Al-Qadri's and Kamamji's statements reflect the clarity of *disalienation*, as Fanon would call it. Al-Qadri's and Kamamji's statements transform the spoon into a techné of liberation, an instantiation of disalienation and a vehicle for association. Transforming the spoon as an implement for liberation makes whole worlds visible in the same way poesis creates meaning in the material world. The spoon, taken from that empty plate by the disalienated political prisoner, makes "happen" what was "considered impossible." This is the same "impossible" of another of Tawfiq's Ziyadah's poems, "As if we are twenty impossibilities."

Good Objects/Good Attachments

"We see clearly the Resistance's promise to us is close hand: The victory is coming." The statement must be located within a historical, subjective, and psychological topography of the Palestinian struggle. It is about *objects* that sustain oppressed peoples under systemized and unrelenting structural oppression. R.D. Laing tells us, "objects are the what not the whereby of experience."[13] The idea of psychic objects is a central feature of Melanie Klein and the Object Relational school. "Object relations theory" is "fundamentally a theory of unconscious internal objects in dynamic interplay with current interpersonal experience." Analysis of these objects "centers upon the exploration of the relationship between internal objects and the ways in which the patient resists altering these unconscious internal object relations in the face of current experience."[14] In considering objects of art, economy, and sociability as techné, psychoanalytic theory coupled with anti-colonial and anti-racist approaches to Marxist historical materialism, affect theory, and a queer-decolonial feminist methodology reveal how material, social objects work in relation to communal subjectivity and the individual's psychic interiority. This psychoanalytic method discloses much about the internalization of objects, which gives contours to a "specific kind of *relatedness* of the individual to the world," in the words of Erich Fromm.[15] Internal objects are "capable of generating meaning and experience" within processes of "an identification of an aspect of the ego with the object."[16] But also, they are relational, interpersonal, social, and rooted in *material experience.* Therefore, at the center of cultural resistance, positive identifications with objects are organized and fostered between people and communities, while these communities and individuals are subjected to sustained conditions of alienation, disavowal, dissociation/disassociation naturalized by racial capitalism, cisheteronormativity, ableism, and settler colonialism.

Central to my argument then is to track how "good objects" stand in the face of violent settler-colonial structures that aim to grind down communities by specifically targeting Palestinian internal worlds (i.e., mental health, social and family bonds, self-view, etc.).[17] If Fanon shows how the colonized internalize "bad objects," projected into them by the colonizer, Palestinian resistance divulges how anti-colonial subjects maintain *association* with their families, their communities, their land, and their present under the overwhelming power of the colonizer. In other words, Palestinian artists, poets, and militants share a practice essential to a politics of refusal and a culture of national liberation. They find agency in "good objects" that emerge from "good attachments," which, in turn, anchor the *mechanics*, healthy defenses, and networks—psychic and social—that facilitate Palestinian life, livability and revelry.

Culture of Popular Revolution

"We see clearly the Resistance's promise to us is close at hand: The victory is coming": Whether in the words of Qadri and Kamamji, Mansour/DAM, or Ziyadah, the Palestinian Revolution itself is an object, an object around which affect, action, and thought coalesce. The Apartheid archipelago of prisons are filled with "proud" Palestinians, as Ziyadah tells us. Rooted in the Palestinian Revolution, the spoon became an apparatus for the "line of flight," an apparatus that held a "complete commitment hailing freedom." The spoon became an object that condenses Palestinian selfhood, negating the "impossible," and liberating inevitable possible futures. It condensed selfhood in the moment when the very possibilities of flight and exit from colonial hegemony became eventualities. In the moment of escape and thereafter, the spoon transformed into an object of *association* that makes the world upright again, where healthy internal objects emerge from a worldliness that is otherwise marked as "impossible" by carceral settler Apartheid.[18] The spoon becomes a good object, associated with good attachments. As a techné of liberation, it organizes a larger interiority of Palestinian psyche and subjectivity. A spoon can become invested with this psychosocial power because it is connected to the Resistance, a sustained culture of subjective, cultural, and social affirmation of the Palestinian subject-qua-individual, but also a community, a collective, and a people subjected to sustained violence.

The insights of this chapter are inspired by radical Black feminist and psychotherapist Gail Lewis. Lewis teaches us how social and communal formations may themselves become "good objects" around which we are able to organize and make visible lives of livability and joy. Black feminism, Lewis says, was curated as an "object," a positive object, around which Black women engaged with the world not as Othered but as part of the world itself. Specifically,

> scholarship by black feminists on black feminism brings forth an ensemble of artefacts that become material and intellectual objects (books, articles, exhibitions, etc.). These are acts of curation bringing about artefacts that are then available for scrutiny/characterization and enable documentation and theorisation of the situated specificity of black feminism as political praxis, artistic creation, academic inquiry and pedagogy. The objects these curations produce address, but are not to be confused with, the black women subjects (individual and collective) whom they centre as full/meaningful persons living their lives/producing and engaging in forms of sociality that are about life living for itself.[19]

Lewis turns Donald Winnicott's theory of "object use" upright to radically reconsider how racialized subjects hold analysis, action, and experience of their own life world *in relation to* their own subjectivity. She offers a theory where we develop a "capacity to know" one's self in a world that otherwise positions Black folks as Other and "to quietly hold [our] own authority and legitimacy without recourse to solipsism, narcissism or triumphalism yet still recognize the quiet authority and legitimacy of" the relationship between the racialized subject to others in the world.[20]

The spoon is the *actualization* of psychosocial "unthought known," the "knowledge derived from the dialectic" between one's "true self" and their social worlds, as Christopher Bollas tells us.[21] Lewis' "capacity to know" operates with a dialectic of knowledge contained and processed by the "Popular Resistance" of the "Palestinian Revolution," which holds material truths and communal memory. Approaching the spoon as a fulcrum for a psychic organization of the Popular Revolution (a parallel to Lewis's black feminism), it becomes an object produced by the psychosocial fabric of Palestinian identity, emerging from history, from unknown memories, from good attachments and good objects, which themselves mobilize other objects. We can then understand the potential of every spoon in the hands of a Palestinian, and as one of a series of quotidian techné that sustains life because it emerges from a process of social reproduction and collective and individual subjectivity. In this way, objects materialize to produce emancipation in the face of military and political hegemony that tries to incarcerate the Palestinians within "the impossible" of liberation.

Palestinian defiance, their "will to live" and their creation of and attachment to good positive internal objects that affirm their place in a negated world, does not mean they are delusional and deny the brutal and crude force of the Israeli colonial state. In other words, considering the military character of Fortress Israel and the economic and military subsidies provided by the settler-colonial United States that underwrites the very viability of Apartheid Israel, the Palestinian Resistance quite explicitly has acknowledged, since 1967, the overwhelming military might of the settler state now known as Israel. Rather, just as Lewis notes that Black feminism is a positive internal object that works in relation to the ways in which Black folks relate to themselves, one another, and their community in a world of white supremacy and anti-Blackness, the history and culture of Palestinian Resistance similarly functions as a positive internal object for Palestinians under Israeli settler Apartheid or in forced exile. With the inception of the Palestinian Resistance, especially after 1967, new *techné* emerge from a culture of popular resistance in Palestinian life that would defy Israeli technological and military hegemony, whether in the camp, the village, the city, or in the prison.

Therefore, popular culture of resistance and the culture of the popular Resistance, or *al-muqawimah*, are co-created by and bind Palestinian communities from the Jordan River to the Mediterranean Sea to the Rafah Crossing to the Palestinian camps in exile. This is not a rhetorical assertion but needs to be understood as a mass cultural and social formation within Palestine. This mass popular culture of resistance and affirmation of Palestinian livability is also what binds these localities. Historically, the culture of *al-muqawimah* emerged in concert with a program for Palestinian Revolution (*al-thawrah al-falastiniyah*) and the People's War as a national and international project. While that revolutionary movement, politically, has largely been marginalized in the Palestinian polity, the popular culture and the psychological, social, and cultural identifications it has forged remains at the bedrock of Palestinian national identity. These identifications are made coherent through the internalization of "good objects" within Palestinian national consciousness and "genuine" mass culture of *al-muqawimah*, which "had a profound and lasting effect," according to Rosemary Sayigh. Sayigh shows us that the Palestinian National movement "sensed" that the popular revolution was the "road to the Return" and "a path into the future" that pointed "a way out of the limbo of the camps, a restoration of their humanity."[22]

The Palestinian Resistance became "a symbol of the life and destiny of the Palestinian people." This symbol, however, performs critical psychic-social work in inaugurating a social and subjective *process* by which the Palestinian revolution itself could become a psychic-subjective object of stability, dignity, and fortitude for people living under occupation and in exile. In other words, objects take on emotional and affective resonance when put in active relationship with an "identity of struggle," of affirmation linking and galvanizing a "permeant *identification*" of Palestinians to their land, Arab identity, and to collective struggle for liberation.[23] Therefore, this is how the spoon has now been internalized as a good internal object for Palestinian selfhood, internalized as a metonym for Palestinian liberation and resistance, circulating freely in murals, poems, and, even, as an emoji deployed on social media across occupied Palestine and transnational Palestine.

The Bullet and Gun

Resistance is not about technology; it is about techné, and the creation of objects by the men and women of the Resistance. Objects and knowledge are produced through social relations, through relationships between selves and their communities. If the armed struggle is the crystallization of a "struggle-identity," we understand that this struggle, whether it is personal, social, or political, does not unfold within a political economy of military superiority. Leila Khaled, who herself is described as an "icon,"[24] describes to us affective power of the "bullet" and gun. "As a Palestinian, the gun," she states, served "as an embodiment of my humanity and my determination to liberate myself and my fellow men."[25]

In 2002, a mysterious Palestinian sniper armed with an outdated antique Mauser rifle and twenty-two bullets killed seven occupation soldiers and wounded six others within twenty minutes in Wadi Haramiyah (the Valley of the Thieves) near Nablus. The Israeli security apparatus took two years to find the marksman, Tha'ir Kayid Hamad, from the village of Silwad, who now is serving several life sentences in the Israeli Gulag, Nafha Prison in the Negev. The international "counter-terrorism" community insisted that he must have been a highly trained militant, schooled by the IRA or Hizbullah. Yet, Hamad had no military training. The Mauser was a Second World War -era rifle. It belonged to Hamad's father, who had served in the Arab Liberation Army as a sniper and fought to protect Palestine against the Zionist armies in 1948. Hamad's father taught him how to shoot.

Years later, lyrics once again memorialize armed resistance. Terese Suleiman sings in honor of the murder of revolutionary intellectual and activist Basel al-A'raj, a former political prisoner and survivor of Israeli torture, who was known for his political tours and scholarship around Palestinian armed resistance, particularly in the West Bank.[26] After expending all of his ammunition, an Israeli "special counter terrorism" unit murdered him after he defiantly resisted capture. Suleiman sings, "Book and gun and Freedom neigh. Ululations arise … The military is cowardly, and bullets bear witness/The military is cowardly/Your comrades do not forget the will, my dear/Your friends don't forget your will and testament, my dear/ Knowledge is made by men's hands."[27]

Whether al-A'raj's Kalashnikov against dozens of heavily armed settler-soldiers, or the antiquated Mauser, or Khaled's militancy, the Palestinian gun and bullet do not find their value in firepower. Their power springs from the psychic-social relationship between good attachments and good objects, between fathers, mothers, and their children, generations, and heroes as Suleiman's song and al-A'raj's own writing demonstrate. The good internal objects of the oppressed and the marginalized are objects in a relational *constellation* of other objects—intra- and interpsychic—organized by and through associations. In the case of Palestinians, these constellations of objects are forged through relationality to their community, their people, their history, their present, and their Land (and I mean land not only as a nationalist imaginary but the physical land, from the River to the Sea). In this regard, the gun and bullet of the *fidayi*, like the spoon of the prisoner, or the pen of the poet-activist-intellectual, does not exist as a timeless transhistorical object always imbibed with meaning. Rather, Palestinians,

162 Producing Palestine

through their lived experience, imbibe it with meaning and birth it into this world as a techné of liberation and disalienation.

Internal objects work through *filiative* association between our selfhood and those who care for us, love us, and nurture us, and communities of care, solidarity, and meaning. Also, these internal objects take on psychic, subjective, and affective power through *affiliative* association. The gun works in tandem with the spoon and its digging of a tunnel to liberation to recall the tunnels of Gaza that serve as its lifeline to the people and Resistance of Gaza despite a brutal siege. Also, the tunnels (and spoon and gun) remind us of the tunnels built by the Resistance in South Lebanon, allowing

Figure 11.1 Night of the Gliders. Courtesy of Hafez Omar.

the "movement of people, guns and ammunition, and military vehicles between the 'Ayn al-Hilwa and Miyya-wa-Miyya refugee camps near Sidon," as Yezid Sayigh teaches us.[28] Or, perhaps, as a Lebanese, I might add the gun and spoon's association with the extensive network of tunnels built by the Lebanese Resistance under the colonial border of Lebanon and the Apartheid state.[29]

Through association, the tunnel dug by the Palestinian spoon in relation to the gun and bullet reminds us of the first commando raids that crystallized a new Palestinian consciousness in January 1965.[30] That is to say, a Fatah pamphlet tells us that an "Assifa unit [Fatah's commando unit] comprising four commandos who had set off on foot from a refugee camp located between Bethlehem and Hebron succeeded in blowing up the main water pump in Eitan, a moshav in the South near Kiryat-Gat. Six days later, 70 kilograms of TNT carried by 11 Fatah commandos ripped the main installations in the Eilabun tunnel."[31] This psychological-subjective-affective association is not just an associative game. Rather, the Fatah pamphlet that announced these New Year's attacks as the beginning of the Palestinian armed struggle specifically tells us of the psychological and material importance of commando raids and the armed struggle. Apart from the material and "practical" purpose to call attention to the illegal "diversion of the Jordan River waters," we are explicitly told by the PLO of the "intent of the Palestinian Revolution at this takeoff stage between 1965 and 1967 was to personify the practical refusal of Zionist occupation ... and mobilize the masses and instigate them to armed revolutionary action."[32]

Nasser Abourahme forcefully argues that the Palestinian Revolution was a success because the *imagination*, thought, practice, and popular participation within the Palestinian Revolution created "territory that was able to support new collective subjects and new forms of *association* that upended distinctions between governed and governing; in other words, the revolution."[33] Extending this idea to psychic territory without separating it from the spatial or geographic territory, this "revolutionary imagination" is not as an abstract, cerebral place but a material space and action that unfolds and creates revolutionary possibilities of world making. In commenting on its emergence and growth, Rosemary Sayigh specifically marks the materiality of the psychic territory of "revolutionary consciousness" in enacting a disalienated, anti-colonial, and emancipatory subjective and political program.

Conclusion

On November 25, 1987, two militants for the Popular Front for the Liberation of Palestine—General Command (PFLP-GC) flew two hang-gliders from southern Lebanon into Occupied Palestine (see Figure 11.1). The Lebanese South had been occupied by the state now known as Israel since 1978, and only five years prior to the glider attack, the Israeli national army laid siege to an occupied Beirut. Tunisian *fida'i* Mailoud Najah bin Lumah and Syrian *fida'i* Khalid Akar powered their gliders with lawn-mower engines. Despite the noise from the little motors, they succeed in entering into the northern "security zone" of occupied Palestine. Before dying, the *fida'i* operation resulted in a successful attack on an Israeli military base. This was not the first time that *al-muqawimah* used kites, but it is a celebrated event commemorated into a popular song:

The Dragonfly flew
Carrying you reclined in the pocket of a sail
Carrying a weapon
They said, the (commando) cell remains despite being wounded
The result is inevitable victory
Arms in hand, our popular masses
The tide of national unity will end Zionist machinations and colonialism.

The social and political framing of the "low-tech" tactics of the Popular Resistance differs from the prism of a state with political and military hegemony that poses annihilation as a goal. Low-techné solicits a reframe of victory. It prioritizes patience, *sumud* (stalwartness), organization, and the certainty and righteousness of *al-Qadiyah*. The value of embodied confrontation with the colonizer may rely on converting banal and quotidian objects, such as the kite or glider, into techné of liberation, transforming them into psycho-social objects of embodied revolutionary consciousness and possibility.

The *fedayeen* understood the value of not just one "operation" or even the operations in themselves. Rather, they understood that all armed struggle comes from the People's war and the popular resistance. All armed struggle is on its behalf as well as an instantiation of Popular Resistance. The Popular Resistance knew and referenced the psychological importance of the armed struggle, specifically stating that one of the "main aims and objectives of the political Struggle to foil and counter the psychological warfare launched by the enemy" and especially affirm the national identity of the Palestinian in exile.[34] Their manifestos and pamphlets name the psychological power of the armed struggle in shoring up Palestinian selfhood and, indeed, communal and individual well-being. But moreover, these manifestos became the space of imagination where "promise of the Resistance" (*w'ad al-muqawimah*) ensured new possibilities in the face of the imposed "impossible." When one pamphlet states "one victory is enough to make the fighters of a popular revolution forget several defeats," it illustrates that possibilities will not be foreclosed by the political or military hegemony.[35]

Within the context of a cumulative history, these victories are objects that draw value and meaning from their relationship and *association* with other objects within the cultural fabric of *al-muqawimah*. The glider hails the kites of Gaza, elegantly and defiantly flying over Israeli fences and guard-towers into occupied Palestine. That fence brings us to the Great March of Return and to the Jum'at al-kawtshuk, the Fridays when tires would be burned to blind the IOF snipers targeting Palestinian civilians from their sniper towers. In a long line of tactics of Palestinian popular resistance, "this tactic emerged again in June 2021 in the village of Beita near Nablus, where its natives (peasants) resisted the continuous land theft and establishment of new colonial roads and settlements."[36] The burning tires recall the "children of the stone," where Palestinian youth have been self-organizing to confront occupation forces for generations. Objects associate with one another to make meaning within a history of popular mobilization. Therefore, in this way, kites and the rising smoke of tires recall balloons with banners flying over the American president in Bethlehem, stating, "Biden you are part of Israeli Apartheid." Defiant balloons associate with the drone flying Palestinian flag over thousands of jeering settlers holding deflated Israeli flags. The drone's flag recalls all the defiant flags throughout occupied Palestine, Lebanon, Jordan, Syria, and in Diaspora. The flag recalls the flags draping Shirine Abu Akleh's coffin, as a locus for battle between occupation soldiers and the defiant population of Jerusalem.[37]

And with Abu Akleh, we recall cameras. Not the cameras of surveillance equipped with face recognition but the cameras of Palestinians, cameras which acknowledge to be seen as weapons by the occupation Army. The day of her murder, the Israeli military spokesperson Ran Kochav stated that Abu Akleh had been "filming and working for a media outlet amidst armed Palestinians. They're armed with cameras."[38] The spoon conjures the knife, the camera the flag, the flag the drone, the drone the kite, the kite the glider, the glider the antiquated rifle. They all circulate as techné of an ongoing *muqawimah* and they are all objects now internalized as "victories" of affirmation, reassurances of the "Resistance's promise" of the "inevitable victory."

This associative recounting of a series of recent victories illustrates a signification system that creates meaning for "good objects" of Palestinian selfhood and, hence, the ways objects become affectively charged. The associative map of "good objects" in this chapter charts the circuits of identification between subjects and their internalized objects, as well as the interlocking political, social, and psychic field of relations. This mapping reveals a "transformational infrastructure" that facilitates "that which binds us to the world in movement and keeps the world practically bound to itself" and, therefore, the psychological infrastructure of Palestinian life, defiance, refusal, affirmation, resistance, and, yes, Palestinian imagination.[39] The spoon, the bullet, the gun, the kite, the tire, poems, and song are all material objects that surface in the lives of Palestinians—as techné for liberation they transform into apparatuses of revolutionary, emancipated consciousness. It bears repeating that objects are not forged out of air but out of the materiality of social relations of Palestinians, from their relationship to themselves, each other, their land, and their history. Objects are perpetual techné of the moment but find coherence and affective force within a Palestinian material reality and polity: hence, transformational infrastructure upon which Palestinians build a future they can live in fully but also affirm the world that they live in presently.

Ruth Wilson Gilmore, in speaking of the "infrastructure of feeling" at the heart of building livable-worlds, reminds us that "the selection and reselection of ancestors is itself part of the radical process of finding anywhere—if not everywhere—in political practice and analytical habit, lived expressions (including opacities) of unbounded participatory openness."[40] Gilmore describes the architecture of good internal objects of manifesting livable lives among the marginalized and dispossessed. "The infrastructure of feeling is material, too, in the sense that ideology becomes material as do the actions that feelings enable or constrain. The infrastructure of feeling is then consciousness-foundation, sturdy but not static, that underlies our capacity to recognize viscerally (no less than prudently) immanent possibility."[41] In providing a parallel for the infrastructure of visceral logics within Palestinians "identity of struggle," Gilmore shows us that celebrating these good internal objects, and the ways they commute between individual psyches and shared lives of Palestinian communities, should not be regarded as polemical, fantastic, or empty sloganeering.

The scaffolding of this materialist and dialectical understanding of affect and meaning-making provides us a glimpse of the psychic-social-political infrastructure of revolutionary consciousness which emerges from the psychic relationality within social relations between Palestinians themselves. If we doubt that these techné of liberation are objects within a larger infrastructure of Palestinian selfhood and that this psychic-social constellation upends the seeming hegemony of Israeli militarism and settler-colonial logic, Mahmoud Darwish's words close this chapter with a testimonial. While never denying the "deathscapes" of Israeli settler colonialism *intentionally and mindfully* inflicts on the Palestinian people,[42] Darwish writes of affective, political, and social power of the Intifada. Writing in exile, Darwish writes how the Uprising was built around the social and affective mobilization around objects of Palestinian life—that is, the stone and the land:

> Children of the stone, bedazzlers of the world.
> Nothing in their hand, but the stone.
> They illuminate like lanterns, coming to the flame like blessed news.
> They rise up and explode. They are martyred and remain like bears …
> Rageful, you students of Gaza.
> They taught us what some of you already know and some of us already have
> forgotten.
>
> They have taught us how the stone transforms
> In the hands of children into a precious diamond
> The children of the stone transform the bicycle of the student into an explosive.
> And a silk ribbon they transform into an ambuscade.
> How the nipple of a milk-bottle
> If they are under siege, transfigures into a knife …
> The children of the stone have taught us the art of clutching the land.[43]

Notes

1 Shadia Mansour and DAM, "'They All Have Tanks,' Revolutionary Arab Rap: The Index," April 29, 2014; available at http://revolutionaryarabraptheindex.blogspot.com/2014/04/dam-ft-shadia-mansour-they-all-have.html. (All translations are authors'.)
2 Tawfiq Ziyadah, "Here We Remain," *Awad al-Nad: Majallah thaqafiyah fasaliyah*, edited by 'Adali al-Hiwari; 74;8 (2021); available at https://www.oudnad.net/spip.php?article436.
3 Martin Heidegger, *The Question Concerning Technology, and Other Essays* (New York: HarperCollins, 1977).

4   Chela Sandoval, *Methodology of the Oppressed* (Minneapolis, MN: University of Minnesota Press, 2000), 68.
5   Asra Faraj, "Prisoners of the Freedom Tunnel," *al-Mayadeen*, November 8, 2021; available at https://www.almayadeen.net/news/politics/ أسرى-نفق-الحرية:-سنخرج-من-الباب-من-فوق-الأرض-كما-قهرناهم-من
6   Muhammad Watad, "Israeli Court Sentences 5 years in Jail for the Freedom Tunnel Prisoners," Al-Jazeera (Arabic), May 22, 2022; available at https://www.aljazeera.net/news/humanrights/2022/5/22/محكمة-إسرائيلية-تفرض-السجن-5-سنوات-على
7   For a discussion of the "reality-bending," see Lara Sheehi and Stephen Sheehi, *Psychoanalysis Under Occupation: Practicing Resistance in Palestine* (London: Routledge, 2022).
8   Sheehi and Sheehi, *Psychoanalysis under Occupation*, 201–3.
9   David Eng and Shinhee Han, *Racial Melancholia, Racial Dissociation: On the Social and Psychic Lives of Asian Americans* (Durham, NC: Duke University Press, 2019).
10 R. D. Laing, *The Divided Self* (New York: Pantheon, 1960), 82. Also, Philip Bromberg, "Standing in the Spaces: The Multiplicity of Self and the Psychoanalytic Relationship," *Contemporary Psychoanalysis* 32 (1996): 509–35.
11 Sara Ahmed, Willful *Subjects* (Durham: Duke University Press, 2014).
12 Nahla Abdo, *Captive Revolution: Palestinian Women's Anti-Colonial Struggle within the Israeli Prison System* (London: Pluto Press, 2014); Ashjan Ajour, *Reclaiming Humanity in Palestinian Hunger Strikes: Revolutionary Subjectivity and Decolonizing the Body* (London: Palgrave, 2021); Lena Meari, Samera Esmeir, Ramsey McGlazer, "You're Not Defeated as Long as You're Resisting": Palestine Hunger Strikes between the Singular and the Collective. *Critical Times* 2021; and Lena Meari, "Sumud: A Palestinian Philosophy of Confrontation in Colonial Prisons," *South Atlantic Quarterly* 113, no. 3 (July 1, 2014): 547–78. Julie Norman, *The Palestinian Prisoners Movement: Resistance and Disobedience* (London: Routledge, 2021); and Esmail Nashif, *Palestinian Political Prisoners: Identity and Community* (London: Routledge, 2008).
13 R. D. Laing, *The Politics of Experience; and, the Bird of Paradise* (New York: Penguin, 1984), 44.
14 Thomas Ogden, "The Concept of Object Relations," *International Journal of Psychoanalysis* 64, (1983): 227.
15 Erich Fromm, *Escape from Freedom* (New York, NY: Rinehart & Co, 1941), 12.
16 Ogden, "The Concept of Object Relations," 228.
17 For studies of Zionist psychological warfare, see Jasbir Puar, *The Right to Maim: Debility, Capacity, Disability* (Durham, NC: Duke University Press, 2017); Hillel Cohen, *Army of Shadows: Palestinian Collaboration with Zionism, 1917–1948* (Berkeley, CA: University of California Press, 2008); and Eyal Weizman, *Hollow Land: Israel's Architecture of Occupation* (London: Verso Books, 2017).
18 Edward Said, *The World, the Text, and the Critic* (Cambridge, MA: Harvard University Press, 1983), 35.
19 Gail Lewis, "Once More with My Sistren: Black Feminism and the Challenge of Object Use," *Feminist Review* 126, no. 1 (2020): 4.
20 Lewis, "Once More with My Sistren," 9.
21 Christopher Bollas, *In the Shadow of the Object: Psychoanalysis of the Unthought Known* (New York, NY: Columbia University Press, 1987), 46.
22 Rosemary Sayigh, *The Palestinians: From Peasants to Revolutionaries* (London: Zed, 2007), 150.

23 Sayigh, *The Palestinians*, 151.
24 See Sarah Irving, *Leila Khaled: Icon of Palestinian Liberation* (London: Pluto Press, 2012).
25 Leila Khaled, *My People Shall Live*, ed. George Hajjar (London: Hodder and Stoughton, 1973), 38.
26 Matthew Demaio, "The Assassination of Basel al-Araj: How the Palestinian Authority Stamps Out Opposition," *Journal of Palestine Studies*, March 16, 2017.
27 Terese Suleiman, "Barudah wa Kitab," April 15, 2017; available at https://www.youtube.com/watch?v=3YOIapG5aeo.
28 Yezid Sayigh, *Armed Struggle and the Search for State: The Palestinian National Movement* (Oxford: Clarendon Press, 1997), 517.
29 "Tunnel Crossing between Lebanon and Israel Went 22 Story Deep," *Middle East Monitor*, June 3, 2019; available at https://www.middleeastmonitor.com/20190603-tunnel-crossing-between-lebanon-and-israel-went-22-storeys-deep/
30 For a recent history of the Palestinian nationalist movement in exile and the development of an "identity of struggle" and liberation, see Erling Lorentzen Sogge, *The Palestinian National Movement in Lebanon: A Political History of the 'Ayn al-Hilwe Camp* (London: I.B. Tauris, 2021).
31 Fath, *Revolution Until Victory*, Palestinian National Liberation Movement (Beirut, 1969), 4.
32 *Revolution Until Victory*, 6.
33 Nasser Abourahme, "Revolution after Revolution: The Commune as Line of Flight in Palestinian Anticolonialism," *Critical Times* 4, no. 3: (2021): 447 (my italics).
34 Fath, *Political and Armed Struggle*, Palestinian National Liberation Movement (Beirut, 1969), 13.
35 Fath, *Political and Armed Struggle*; 41.
36 Firas Shehadah, "Notes on the Logic of Speed," *Journal of Visual Culture* 20, no. 2 (2022): 236.
37 Patrick Kingley and Raja Abdulrahim, "Israeli Police Attack Mourners before Funeral for Palestinian American Journalist," *New York Times*, May 13, 2022; available at https://www.nytimes.com/2022/05/13/world/middleeast/shireen-abu-akleh-funeral.html
38 Zeena Saifi, "'They were Shooting Directly at the Journalists': New Evidence Suggests Shireen Abu Akleh Was Killed in Targeted Attack by Israeli Forces," CNN, May 26, 2022; available at https://www.cnn.com/2022/05/24/middleeast/shireen-abu-akleh-jenin-killing-investigation-cmd-intl/index.html
39 Lauren Berlant, "The Commons: Infrastructures for Troubling Times," *Society and Space* 34, no. 3 (2016): 394.
40 Ruth Wilson Gilmore, *Abolition Geography: Essays towards Liberation* (New York: Verso 2022), 530.
41 Gilmore, *Abolition Geography*, 530.
42 See Suvendrini Perera and Joseph Pugliese, eds., *Mapping Deathscapes: Digital Geographies of Racial and Border Violence* (London: Routledge, 2021).
43 Mahmoud Darwish, "Atfal al-hijarah," Muntada shabab Imiya, Majlis al-hukama'; available at https://kalamfikalam.ahlamontada.com/t10600-topic.

12

Cooking Online with Chef Fadi

Anne Meneley

Food is a powerful site for thinking through what it means to be human. In the contemporary era, when Palestinians are put in the rather disturbing position of having to constantly "prove" their humanity in a media world where it seems to be questioned as frequently as people need to eat, food is a potential point of entry into a site of recognition. As editors of the book, Matar and Tawil-Souri, note: "Palestinian cultural expression and production is, again implicitly or explicitly, contending with and attempting to 'correct' or readjust certain representational politics while also creating alternative ones, all of them increasingly manifested through various media and 'new' technologies." Although food is usually consumed in an embodied way, I consider here the use of media in circulating, promoting, and sharing an alternate vision of Palestinians through representations of their food. I discuss here how food is used in contemporary media to "produce Palestine," as a way of addressing the fragmentation of Palestinians in Palestine and in the diaspora. I focus here on the Palestinian chef and restauranteur Fadi Kattan, who is adept at using myriad media as a platform for promoting an alternate vision of Palestine through its food.

Chefs and Media

Circulating food knowledge through the media, particularly by professional chefs, is hardly new. Countless North Americans became acquainted with French food via Chef Julia Child's TV show, *The French Chef* (1962–72). While the "celebrity chef" platform can be mobilized for self-promotion of one's food empire, it can also be mobilized for a political cause. Chefs can mobilize disaster relief, as is evident in the work of Chef José Andrés; he uses his far-reaching media voice to widen the public's awareness of natural disaster, feeding Haitians after the earthquake in 2021, or wars producing humanitarian crises, like the Ukraine after the Russian invasion in 2022. In 2013, Anthony Bourdain opened his second season of his cooking show *Parts Unknown* with an episode titled "Israel," which included scenes from the West Bank and Gaza. This episode was appreciated by Palestinians, as it showed Bourdain enthusiastically consuming the food of his Palestinian hosts in Gaza, undermining by his very presence in the media images of Gazans as dangerous terrorists, presenting them instead as talented cooks and generous hosts. In the contemporary moment, we see Palestinians using the media to present an alternative vision of Palestine to counter the mainstream media which, at least in North America, primarily presents the Israeli version of history. Fadi Kattan mobilizes food through media to tell different stories about Palestinians and their experience of often violent displacement by Israeli settler colonialism over the last seventy-plus years.

Cookbooks preceded food television by centuries, and despite the recent fashion of searching for recipes online, they still have a relatively vibrant circulation.[1] Kattan coedited, along with Farah Abuasad and Lama Bazzari, *Craving Palestine*, a collection of recipes from notable Palestinians, including one from architect and real-estate agent Mohammed Hadid, father of supermodel Bella Hadid.[2] Kattan was educated as a chef in France, but returned to Palestine in 2016 to open Fawda restaurant, situated within his guesthouse, Hosh Al-Syrian, in the heart of Bethlehem's Old City. Fawda received a TripAdvisor's Certificate of Excellence in 2019 as well as a rave review in the *LA Times*.[3] Kattan is determined to put Bethlehem and Palestine on the world's "food map." While both his restaurant and guesthouse had to close, temporarily, due to the Covid-19 restrictions on movement of people, including pilgrims and tourists, Fadi expanded his food and media presence with a podcast, Sabah al-Jasmine. Fadi sometimes stars in this podcast, offering listeners his reflections on Palestinian food, but most often he interviews his fellow chefs. He was interviewed by Mikey Muhanna, who hosts Matbakh, a platform for podcasts and videos of Arab cookery, under the umbrella of Afikra, an international network committed to promoting knowledge about the Arab world. Muhanna introduces Fadi as the "voice of modern Palestinian cuisine" who honors Palestine's best produce with a "modern twist," transforming traditional Palestinian dishes into a gourmet dining experience.[4] Fadi is also involved in charity work, appearing in fundraising initiatives like that of the Palestine Children's Relief Fund (PCRF) in November 2020. Fadi's cooking narratives reach out to potential viewers, readers, and listeners who want to know what is going on in Palestine, from the perspective of food. Fadi posts photos of his dishes regularly on Facebook, Instagram, and Twitter. Along with entrepreneur Rasha Khouri, Fadi launched a new restaurant in London's Notting Hill district in January 2023. It is named Akub after the wild thistle beloved by Palestinian foragers and chefs.[5]

I have worked on the production, circulation, and consumption of Palestinian olive oil since 2006. More recently, I have tracked how, at this moment in time when land is inexorably confiscated from its Palestinian owners, we see a resurgence of interest by Palestinian artists and activists in the products of the land: plants, animals, and the distinctive dishes produced from it. For instance, Vivien Sansour's work on saving Palestine's distinctive seeds has inspired many,[6] as has Mirna Bamieh's work on wild plants and collective hosting as a means of celebrating Palestine's cuisine.[7] While I did most of the research for this case online while under lockdown in Canada, before its pandemic closure, I have stayed at Fadi's lovely Hosh Al-Syrian in Bethlehem, experiencing his creative cuisine in Fawda, where he brings Palestinian fresh products into conversation with global gourmet food trends. I also did a market and food tour in Bethlehem with Fadi in the spring of 2019, meeting the butchers, spice sellers, and vegetable producers whom I saw later in his cooking videos. In an interview with me, Fadi noted that the potential reach of a chef's voice is so much greater than the left-wing activists in support of Palestine or the kumbaya church voices for peace in the Holy Land.[8]

Like most contemporary chefs, Fadi already had an online presence (Facebook, Instagram, Twitter) for the promotion of Fawda, but when the pandemic began, Fadi's online work increased exponentially. He started a cooking show on the online platform, The Plate, with a subscription rate of eight British pounds a month; while this did not last long, I discuss his memorable "Hummus with Fadi!" episode below. Even a glance at Fadi's webpage[9] indicates his myriad activities. After a brief discussion of Fadi's take on Palestine's food politics under occupation, I focus on his ten-episode YouTube cooking series, *teta*'s Kitchen.

Fadi's Food Politics in the Context of Occupation

While Fadi supports the idea that food is an important means of communicating the contemporary Palestinian condition, he does not advocate the hackneyed "if they could just sit together around the table and share food, everything would be solved" platitudes about commensality and coexistence. In an interview in *The Funambulist*, Fadi states:

> Very often when a journalist wants to write about my food they'll tell me: "in Israel they do this and you do that." If you are talking about a restaurant in the southern Pyrenees in France, you would never dare to tell the chef: "oh I am going to compare you to this Spanish chef on the other side of the mountains." Cuisine is not a toy. It has its truths, and its limits. But where we are, it is often seen as an element of the conflict and only as that. We've seen in the last 20 years so many attempts of creating "coexistence cuisine" or cooking schools around the world. I remember being approached by a school in France with a coexistence program. "We have an Israeli Jew, an Israeli Christian and an Israeli Muslim, we have a Palestinian Christian and we are looking for a Muslim woman wearing hijab." It's like we're picking actors for a soap opera, it's a beautiful brand new world and everyone is lovey-dovey! This is not the reality.

However, he is committed to the idea that circulating images of Palestinians preparing their beloved dishes is a good way to get around the erasure of Palestinians themselves. Fadi is also critical of homogenization of Palestinian cuisine under the banner of "Middle Eastern foods" (kebabs and hummus) in the restaurants of Ramallah and Bethlehem as a kind of self-Orientalizing. In my interview with him in 2019, he also voiced annoyance at the facile discourse about who really "owns" hummus or falafel, foods which predate the nation-state. But he also emphasized the importance of preventing the Israeli narrative from dominating the conversation. Several food activists share this concern, noting that if one began a short media presentation, especially one limited to an hour, with the issue of Israeli appropriation of Palestinian food, it is hard to redirect the conversation to the topic of Palestinian food itself. Despite his concerns, Fadi occasionally expresses irritation at the blatant Israeli cooptation of Palestinian food. During his "Hummus with Fadi" episode, the moderator asked Fadi what his worst hummus experiences have been, given the global proliferation of strange versions of hummus. "Marmite hummus" was his first example from England, followed with a French version of hummus, which was just chickpeas and water. But his experience of seeing "Israeli hummus" on a menu in Tel Aviv was culinary appropriation that left a sting. Making a crack about the distinctive Israeli pronunciation of "khummus," Fadi notes that many Israeli chefs do not or will not acknowledge Palestinian cuisine as distinct or even acknowledge the debt they owe to it. He said he is a profoundly antiviolent person, but he lives in Bethlehem, a city surrounded by the Separation Wall famous for its graffiti, from Banksy and myriad others. He loathes the graffito on the wall that says, "make hummus not war," cracking a joke that he would like to throw a plate of hummus at it. In his view, peace comes from justice; he sums up by noting that when there is justice, they can gather to talk about hummus.

Fadi's Take on Global Food Issues

The name of Fadi's restaurant is Fawda. "Fawda," which he translates as "chaos," which for him captures the creative chaos of the beautiful world of Palestinian food products, and of contemporary Palestinian dishes made from them. Part of what he means by "chaos" has to do with his commitment to the Palestinian "local": his creativity as a cook is necessarily chaotic because what he cooks depends on what his local farmers have available that day. In several of his online presentations, he makes sure to clarify that his restaurant's name has nothing to do with the Israeli Netflix show Fauda, which has been critiqued for its presentation of Palestinians as terrorists.

While the concept of "local" appears in many food discourses as preferable to placeless industrial food products, "local" means something different when your "local" is being appropriated by an occupier. Fadi engages with wider discourses of ethical food politics, including ideas about "connecting" food producers and consumers, from the perspective of occupied Palestine. As he articulates in his Funambulist interview, Fadi is committed to using the fruit and vegetable produce of the local farmers of Bethlehem, as "they are the ones that are living the shit of the occupation. I am living the shit of occupation much less. I'm nicely in my little kitchen."[10] (He makes the same point, sans cursing, on his YouTube platform.) It is for this reason that he never bargains with the farmers, going with the prices that they set for themselves, and if it doesn't work with his budget, he finds another product. A stalwart figure of Bethlehem's market, Umm Nabil sells her foraged herbs daily; after he introduced her to me, he later told me how he appreciates her charming crankiness and honesty. She also appears various clips in his YouTube videos and in some of the promotional material for Fadi's new London restaurant, Akub.[11] The issue of the "connection" also appears in his discussion of butchers. Fadi notes how he deliberately establishes and nurtures relationships with those butchers he trusts, who can explain to him how their animals are kept and reared.[12] I met these butchers in person during Fadi's food tour in 2019, but they also appear in an episode of *teta*'s Kitchen, where the audience views their immaculate shop, with small tables where customers can drink coffee while they wait for the butchers to prepare their orders.

Teta's Kitchen

While the "cooking show" is a familiar genre, Fadi brings more to it than your average cooking show: he presents Palestine in its Covid lockdown, and in its intermittent yet perpetual sort-of state of lockdown because of the Israeli restrictions on Palestinian movement. As Bourdain did, Fadi brings the politics of Palestine into the process of cooking. Instead of going through episode by episode, I focus on themes which affect quotidian life in Palestine and are part of how Fadi (and other food activists) perceive food politics in Palestine. The themes are: food under occupation, mobility, long-standing Palestinian presence, and the ethics of care.

In the ten episodes of "*teta*'s Kitchen," Fadi presents the "grandmother" (*teta*) as the chef of the episode and presents himself, in this context, as her humble student. The idea of the "grandmother" (*teta*) in this context is similar to the Italian "grandmother" (*nonna*) in contemporary Italian culinary discourse. The term "grandmother" acts as a shorthand for the knowledge of the ascending generation, a stand-in for authentic food know-how, thought to be slipping away in the younger generations, as it is often embodied knowledge, not written recipes. Throughout, Fadi speaks in Arabic with most of the *teta*s, and in English when addressing the online audience. English and Arabic subtitles are supplied, signaling the aim of welcoming both monolingual English and Arabic speakers. The absence of Hebrew subtitles indicates that Israelis are not the imagined audience. The *teta*s are referred to as *Imm* or *Umm* (mother) plus the name of their son or daughter. With Fadi as our guide, we the audience enter virtually into the *teta*s' homes. As we are welcomed into their immaculate kitchens, we also note the presence of pressure cookers and refrigerators, along with wood-fired outdoor ovens and old kitchen implements. Some of the technologies, like an outdoor wood-fired oven, fueled, in part, by pruned olive twigs, evoke past cooking strategies, but there is no attempt to present a timeless Palestinian or homogeneous cuisine. One of the ironies of cooking with Fadi via contemporary media like YouTube or Skype or Zoom is that he is showing us foods unmarked by barcodes, gathered by hand, and sold for cash, in contrast to many of the foods that North Americans regularly consume.

Fadi's overall goal is to provide a venue for the *teta*s to demonstrate their impressive skills. For instance, he drew attention to onion chopping. He points out how a *teta* can cup an onion in her left palm, and quickly dice it with her right hand, without even getting a cut, an embodied skill I view with mystified awe. Fadi throws himself in with most of us who would be likely to lose a finger; gazing at the camera, he confesses that he uses a cutting board. This act of chopping appears in many episodes but has another purpose alongside indicating a Maussian "technique of the *teta*'s body." Fadi uses it strategically to demonstrate that in this particular context, he, the Palestinian man, educated as a chef in France, is deferential student learning a different kind of cooking skill from the *teta*s. In several episodes he notes how the *teta*s "make us proud of Palestinian cuisine." On one occasion he does diverge from the *teta*'s wisdom. Fadi looks at us, the audience watching on our own screens, and tells us that he is finally going to "teach the *teta*s something" as he has been only learning from them so far. He objected to the use of industrial Maggi chicken stock in a cube, saying that it is so much better to make one's stock with the meat bones and freeze it. Here appealing to the pious frugality of the *teta*s, he noted it was less wasteful and joked: "That is the Palestinian economy! Don't waste!" In another episode, Fadi adds more olive oil than the *teta* suggests, telling us he loves it so much he could drink it, and when the *teta*s use spoons to stir, he tells us he prefers to use his hands.

Mobility

However much Fadi does not want the Israeli narrative to dominate his show, the occupation is always present in each episode of "*teta*'s Kitchen": many Palestinian contemporary food practices are inevitably affected by the occupation's disruption of circulations of people, food commodities, and culinary knowledge around and through Palestinian communities. In the recipes and narratives about them, one hears about the transformations in movement or the possibilities of movement. These changing mobility patterns, many of them initiated by their occupiers rather than by Palestinians themselves, feature in many episodes. For instance, in Episode 9 on Yaffa, Fadi talks of the days when there was regular movement between Bethlehem and Yaffa, but now travel between these relatively close cities is difficult.[13] Although they managed to send him a fish from Yaffa to cook for the show, the fresh fish that used to flow from Gaza and Yaffa to Bethlehem with ease has now stopped due to Israel's regimes of control, making fish scarce on Bethlehem's menus. This episode opens with some sweeping views of Yaffa, including mosques and churches before we are introduced to *teta* Nadia; a theme of this episode was the ethnic cleansing of Yaffa and the continuing erasure of Palestinian presence. Fadi notes that it is quite painful "as a Palestinian" to see how Yaffa has changed, especially as his family's orange groves in Yaffa had been confiscated decades ago.

Often the cameraperson takes the viewer out of the kitchen. In some episodes, the cameraperson films Fadi as he travels to other Palestinian towns, to illustrate their distinctive food products. The time-consuming process of moving around as a Palestinian under occupation appears in several episodes, capturing one of the first shocking impressions one has when touring around the West Bank: how long it takes to move around a small place. In Episode 3, he notes it takes twice as long as did in the past to travel from Bethlehem to Sebastia because of the checkpoints. In Episode 5, "Makluba in Nablus," Fadi complains about the length of the voyage, but notes that the smells of the food cooking in the Nabulsi suq are "worth the three-hour drive." The first Palestinian microbrewery, Taybeh Beer, exports its beer, and more recently, a cabernet sauvignon wine called Nadim, which Fadi tastes in Episode 4. It is not only the mobility of Palestinian people but also their products which are stymied by the occupation. Madees Khoury of Taybeh Beer talks about the time-consuming process of getting consumable products out of Palestine, what with the bureaucracy of export permits and the difficulty of finding a driver who can and is willing to transport their products to Israeli ports. I first heard of these incredibly byzantine processes from olive oil producers who want to export;[14] since the borders and ports are controlled by the Israelis, there is no option but to go through the bureaucracy (and expense) to launch one's food products to foreign markets. Madees notes that exporting Palestinian consumable commodities abroad is so difficult that "if you can succeed in this country, you can make it anywhere."

Fadi notes that he comes from a long line of businesspeople and entrepreneurs who traveled widely; his father's family lived in India and Japan for a time, and his mother's family has Italian and French influences on their cuisine through marital ties, yet they have maintained their family home in Bethlehem since 1838. Fadi often notes in *teta*'s Kitchen that the transregional movement of people through Bethlehem started before the forcible displacement of the Nakba in 1948 as Bethlehem has for centuries been a site of pilgrimage. He notes the cosmopolitan nature of Palestinians, many of whom traveled widely, while highlighting the difference between voluntary movement through trade and involuntary movement through the forced expulsions from the continuing expansion of illegal Israeli settlements in the West Bank. Fadi notes that Bethlehem dishes have been preserved among the Bethlehemites in Chile, even though the language was lost.[15] Another point Fadi makes is that the people of Palestine share a love of travel to other parts of their country, difficult as that movement can be, but also abroad. Early in Episode 7 when Fadi introduces us to Imm Eyad, the camera rests on the refrigerator in her kitchen, which is adorned by fridge magnets and photos from many parts of the world. She describes herself as "Bint Battuta," making reference to one of the most famous travelers in the Muslim world of the fourteenth century, Ibn Battuta, who memorably narrated his travels from Tangier to the Arabian Peninsula, East Africa, and Central Asia to China.

Fadi notes that the best way to preserve cuisine is to cook together, but even before the Covid-19 restrictions, it was difficult for West Bank Palestinians to do this. In Episode 9, the audience views *teta* Nadia communicating over Skype, forced to taste their respective versions of the same dish rather than sharing the same dish together. Fadi closes with a statement that he hopes all the checkpoints will be removed in the future so they can have an actual social interaction along with cooking and eating together.

Long-standing Presence in Palestine

Fadi addresses one of the most implausible myths of Zionism: that Palestine was a "land without people for a people without land." Underpinning all episodes is the theme of the long-standing Palestinian presence farming the land, the generations of shop keepers in Palestine's food suqs, and the rich variations in food traditions according to products and preparations that are specific to particular regions of Palestine. Palestinian cuisine is not presented as homogeneous or unchanging.

One of the key themes in Fadi's work is demonstrating the length of time of Palestinian presence. Fadi addresses the camera, noting the length of time these merchants have been present in the food suqs of Palestine's ancient towns. In Episode 7, we are taken to Hebron. He visits a shop where Turkish delight, which he samples with enthusiasm, has been made by the same family for 150–160 years, and 80 years in that particular shop. In Episode 5 as we are being taken through the famous food suq of Nablus, in response to Fadi's question, the owner of a spice shop answers that his family have been in the same shop since 1936.

He notes that Bethlehem butchers who appear in *teta*'s Kitchen have been in Bethlehem for 5 generations, yet the freezer we are shown as the "treasure chest of the chef" indicates the imbrication of the butchers in the modern world, where the capacity to freeze food has been as revolutionary in Palestine as elsewhere. Although he did not mention it specifically, the dependence of freezers on consistent electricity makes them vulnerable to power outages. But all the cooking tactics resonate with older, more established forms of cooking that are deeply connected with the land and preserving its products for functional use.

Ethics of Care

The politics of Covid-19 restrictions appear in *teta*'s Kitchen, but as Fadi notes in Episode 1, most of the time, the Israeli occupation is the reason for Palestinians being locked in, as the Israelis have long imposed curfews and lockdowns for "security" reasons. He opens the episode by cracking a few jokes about the global reaction of those unaccustomed to lockdown was the bread-baking craze of the early phase of the Covid-19 era. Following with the bread theme, he shows us everyday Palestinian breads like *kmaj* (a bread like pita) and *shrak* (thin flatbread). He takes us, the viewers, to visit the Shweiki Bakery in Bethlehem. What we see are not ambitious neophyte home chefs trying out their sour dough, but fourth-generation bakers, baking fresh dough laid out on a rotating disc, covered with stones from the Dead Sea and circulated into the oven.

As I recall from my own in-person tour with Fadi, not only does this bakery smell delicious but it has a small sign that encourages those who cannot afford to pay for bread to help themselves. Fadi noted this sign in his episode, introducing the audience to the everyday standards of decency in Palestine, where those who are experiencing hard times will be treated with dignity and respect instead of shaming. This practice, one might note, is in stark contrast to the way in which foreign aid money is handed out, requiring Palestinians to perform their abjection in order to receive aid. In his episode "Julia's Christmas Cake," Fadi urges the audience to make a few more cakes and hand them out to people who are going through tough times. He highlights an important theme in Palestinian foodways throughout his presentations: the ethical dimension of food and its sharing, and the obligation to be generous.

In one episode, the dish they are preparing is an iftar meal to break the fast in Ramadan. Fadi uses the occasion to talk about how Palestinian Christians and Muslims have lived in Palestine over the centuries by respecting each other's religious customs. As a Christian, he does not fast during Ramadan, but he also does not eat in front of his fasting colleagues. He notes that if one cooks while fasting, one cannot do the intermittent tasting that is part of ordinary cooking, so they tend to go light on the salt, so as not to accidentally make the dish inedible.

Teta Imm Salama teaches us the nuances of *maftoul*, which he notes is *not* the dish which is described often as "Israeli cous cous" but rather a distinct dish made of burghul wheat, rolled by hand; he notes "this [dish] speaks Palestinian." In Episode 5, when viewing the beautiful finished *maklubah*, Fadi says, "I can't say it is better than my mother's" indexing the obligation to love the food of one's mother best, a trope that extends far beyond Palestine. In several episodes, he expounds on those *teta*s who are the most talented at imbuing their *nafas* (spirit) into their food, a notion Reem Kassis also dwells upon.[16] As Fadi says, "It's not about the food, it is about the passion," as it is the passion, spirit, and care of the cook that makes the food delicious. Umm Zuheir sings a song as they cook the *akkub*, the famous wild thistle, which the Israelis forbade Palestinians to forage.[17] The song was about selling one's dowry gold to buy *akkub*—so delicious and desirable is this seasonal food; Fadi explains to the audience that this is a wild thistle, resembling the French chardon. This plant provides the name for Fadi's new restaurant, Akub, in London.

Cooking Online

Fadi plays to the camera and he becomes our taster. Online and television cooking focus on the visual and to some extend on the auditory, sounds of sizzling, for instance. But the audience is deprived of the smells, tastes, and touches of the kitchen. In many episodes, Fadi joins the *teta*s in their own kitchens. In some episodes (Gaza, Jaffa, and Im al Fahm), as it is now difficult for Palestinians from the West Bank to travel to these areas without a permit from the Israelis, Fadi, like the audience, is also forced to cook online. The camera crew in each location film the interaction between the *teta* as she cooks together with Fadi, communicating by Skype on their laptops. We mostly see Fadi talking to the camerapersons although on occasion the camerapersons are filmed, behind their cameras. They are not invisible, presenting us with an immaculately finished piece which erases the process of their work, but they and their cameras are very much part of the event, as we see them interact with Fadi. He notes in one episode that the camera crew is feeling hungry because of the smell of their delicious food. He says to the audience, looking into their cameras: "They starve until we are finish shooting" although occasionally, we see him handing off a sample to the camera crew, as if they are small children waiting for a treat or at least surrogate tasters for the hungry viewers. Sometimes Fadi himself hams it up to the camera, as if he were a small boy himself, sticking a finger into a dish, then into his mouth, then pressing his finger to his lips to caution us not to tell on him, as we are engaged as co-conspirators in his naughtiness.

The final presentation of each episode is curated, but never seamless, as sometimes the soundtrack, featuring local Palestinian musicians, bursts in loudly, lending a hint of music video to the cooking show. This makes the presentation of each episode informal, but that is part of its charm as he manages to convey the fun and camaraderie of collective cooking. When we are taken to Nablus, we are given great slo-mo shots of the famous Nabulsi knafeh being prepped on the distinctive round metal plates, again impressing us with the skill and grace of the workers. Fadi assembles a knafeh sandwich with a pita from the shop next door, consuming it with audible zeal. Fadi's camerapersons have to be credited with their gifts of producing beautiful closeups of the food at the end of each episode. All of the camerapersons, songs, and research consultants are credited at the end of each episode; Fadi does not present himself as the sole chef-creator.

The olfactory sensations produced by cooking Palestinian food, with its particular spices, are enthusiastically communicated by Fadi; as in all televised cooking shows, the actual olfactory and gustatory sensations are left to our imagination, although the medium does allow us to "eat with our eyes." We are welcomed and knowledge is shared, but we are left without anything to taste, unless we choose to cook along ourselves.

Conclusion: Filming in the Kitchen and Tasting Online

The first headline in several episodes is "May Palestine Be Free," indexing the overall politics of this YouTube series. Fadi formally and graciously thanks his *teta* hosts at the end of each episode. When they are forced to cook together on Skype, we see Fadi and the *teta*s doing the hand wave at the end, which again is something that seems particularly associated with the Covid/Zoom era; my students and I found ourselves doing this, although we never wave to each other after in-person classes! For the people in Gaza, and for those who want to share food with them from the West Bank, this condition of communicating and sharing from a distance or a screen or a phone is ongoing, Covid or not, due to Israeli restrictions. Zoom cooking is a challenge, as we, the audience, know from trying to keep up with Fadi, and as he points out, it is heartbreaking to cook together yet not be able to eat together.

Fadi is right, in my opinion, that the media reach of the chef is much greater than the reach of the activists who are involved in faith-based groups, highlighting the injustice of what is done to Palestinians in the birthplace of monotheism. The academics who highlight the ongoing dispossession of Palestinians based on an analysis of the unfolding of the ongoing structure of settler colonialism also have less reach in the mainstream media. In one of our in-person encounters, I made a few jokes about how turgid anthropological prose might restrict its audience; I assume that Fadi's hearty belly laugh implied an agreement with my critique of my own discipline! Palestinian food discourses are also likely to reach more people than the endless NGO reports documenting the dispossession of Palestinians. One hopes that Fadi's tour in the final episode documenting how the Jordan Valley went from being Palestine's food basket to being the food basket of the occupation as Israel expands its settlements and monopolizes the available water might have a greater effect.

Fadi Kattan's series "*teta*'s Kitchen" on his YouTube channel is a platform far more accessible to Palestinians who, even before the pandemic, found it difficult to travel to their homeland or to different parts of it. Fadi also notes that recipes can move when Palestinians cannot, and where they cannot, providing possibilities of connection in their now geographically fragmented society. Throughout his conversations with food producers, chefs, and *teta*s, Fadi demonstrates to his audience the complexity of Palestinian peoples and their cuisine; along the way, we get a sense of remarkable humor and generosity, along with an inspiration to try Palestinian cooking ourselves.

Notes

1. One of the chefs featured in Bourdain's episode was Laila al-Haddad, whose Gaza cookbook was released in 2014 to positive reviews. Bourdain also gave a stellar blurb to Reem Kassis' *The Palestinian Table* (2017). Many of us were pleased to see Kassis' publications in the *New York Times* in 2021 on food and olive oil despite the well-deserved reputation of this publishing powerhouse for prioritizing the Israeli narrative. Sami Tamimi's *Falastin* (2020) was enthusiastically welcomed, especially by those who thought he had received much less attention than Yotam Ottolenghi, the Israeli chef with whom he coauthored the cookbook *Jerusalem* in 2012. Sami Tamimi and Tara Wrigley, *Falastin: A Cookbook* (Toronto: Random House, 2020). Reem Kassis, *The Palestinian Table* (New York: Phaidon, 2019 [2017]).
2. Farrah Abuasad, Lama Bazzari, and Fadi Kattan, eds., *Craving Palestine: Soulful Recipes and Inspiring Stories Celebrating Community and Giving Back* (Santa Barbara, CA: Story Farm, 2020).
3. Noda Tarnopolsky, "A Restaurant in the West Bank Makes Its Mark," *Los Angeles Times*, December 21, 2018, https://www.latimes.com/food/dailydish/la-fo-re-fawda-20181221-story.html
4. Fadi Kattan. Interview with Mikey Muhanna for Matbakh, Afikra. Sumac. (October 13, 2021), https://www.youtube.com/watch?v=iqDzo-TTGxo
5. James Hansen, "A Leader in Modern Palestinian Cuisine Is Opening a Restaurant in Notting Hill," *Eater London*, April 22, 2022, https://london.eater.com/2022/4/22/23035253/akub-restaurant-london-fadi-kattan-fawda-restaurant-palestine
6. Shahin's 2018 documentary, *The Seed Queen of Palestine*, https://www.youtube.com/watch?v=XoexxUOeZak. See also Anne Meneley, "Hope in the Ruins: Seeds, Plants, and Possibilities of Regeneration," *Environment and Planning E: Nature and Space* 4, no. 1 (2021): 158–72.
7. See Al Jazeera's documentary "Saving Palestine's Forgotten Food" (2019), https://www.youtube.com/watch?v=tYD070D7iyE. See also Anne Meneley, "The Companion to Every Bite: Palestinian Olive Oil in the Levant," in *Making Levantine Cuisine: Modern Foodways of the Eastern Mediterranean*, ed. Anny Gaul, Graham Auman Pitts, and Vicki Valosik (Austin: University of Texas Press, 2021), 115–32.
8. As Gupta noted for Bourdain: "But he wasn't holding a Facebook conversation with a few hundred angry know-it-all leftists. Bourdain reached millions." Arun Gupta, "Anthony Bourdain (1956–2018)," *Jacobin*, June 11, 2018, https://jacobin.com/2018/06/anthony-bourdain-parts-unknown-obituary
9. https://www.fadikattan.com/
10. Fadi Kattan, "Cooking Palestinian Food: On Indigenous Herbs, Crafts and Community," *The Funambulist*, August 26, 2020, https://thefunambulist.net/magazine/politics-of-food/cooking-palestinian-food-fadi-kattan
11. Bethan McKernan, "'Hummus is Banned in My Kitchen': Meet the Chef Bring 'the Essence of Palestine' to London," *The Guardian*, November 27, 2022.

12 I was reminded here of Brad Weiss' work on alternative pork production in North Carolina, which stresses the idea of "connection" between producers, chefs, and consumers.
13 The distance between them is 35 miles/57 kilometers.
14 Anne Meneley, "Time in a Bottle: The Uneasy Circulation of Palestinian Olive Oil," *Middle East Research and Information Project* (MERIP) 248 (Fall 2008): 18–23; Anne Meneley, "Blood, Sweat and Tears in a Bottle of Palestinian Olive Oil," *Food, Culture & Society* 14, no. 2 (2011): 275–90.
15 Palestine Children's Relief Fund (PCRF, NYC Chapter) "Cooking Makloubeh" with Chef Fadi Kattan (November 17, 2020): https://www.youtube.com/watch?v=7kuFli8j-fw
16 Reem Kassis, *The Arabesque Table: Contemporary Recipes from the Arab World* (New York: Phaidon, 2021).
17 Jumana Manna, Foragers. Film. Viewed at the Arsenal Gallery, Toronto Biennial of Art, March 26–June 5, 2022.

13

Producing Palestine as Layers of Historical Evidence with Interactive Documentaries

Dale Hudson

Historical documentary is typically understood in terms of films that make use of archival footage and photographs to ask new questions or propose new arguments about past events. Some are critical of the archive's institutional practices and self-reflexive on their own process of using archival material, as in Rona Sela's *Looted and Hidden: Palestinian Archives in Israel* (Israel, 2017), which poses questions about Sela's own accountability to locate looted Palestinian materials, including documentary films and photographs, which have been hidden in Israeli military archives. Rendered in her film, the looted and hidden materials carry the visible mark of being "imprisoned" in the Hebrew text and numbers that mark them parentally like tattoos.

Sela *reproduces* images of Palestine that were *produced* by Palestinians, then looted and hidden to support Zionist mythologies. She performs the "responsibility as citizens" that Ariella Azoulay finds when we abandon our when the archive's power implicates us and we no longer see its power.[1] Other forms of documentary, notably interactive ones that operate on web browsers or mobile apps, also perform this same responsibility. They produce Palestine by designing new modes for audiences to access historical images of Palestine that were produced by Palestinians and foreigners, as well as contemporary images of a Palestine that existed historically. Interactive documentaries offer a means for audiences to produce Palestine by layering historical evidence over maps of occupied Palestine today.

This case examines interactive documentaries that prompt audiences to reflect upon asymmetries in the *power to forget* and the *responsibility to remember* history by mapping Palestinian geographies that have been rendered invisible. Zochrot's iNakba (2014) is a mobile app that layers names, locations, and information related to Palestinian villages razed in 1948 onto digital maps. Subtitled The Invisible Land, the app makes Palestine visible *digitally* on land now considered Israeli, functioning as an interactive documentary that is mobile and immersive for self-guided exploration.[2]

Much of this chapter originally appeared as "Mapping Palestine/Israel through Interactive Documentary," *Journal of Palestine Studies* 50, no. 1 (2021): 51–76.

Similarly, Dorit Naaman's *Jerusalem, We Are Here* layers information about the neighborhood of Qatamon (Katamon), which has been heavily gentrified, onto digital maps.[3] In the same way that Zochrot marks razed villages, Naaman marks original ownership of buildings in Qatamon. In addition, users can access official data from the United Nations Relief and Works Agency for Palestine Refugees in the Near East (UNRWA), as well as other data from personal accounts then layer them over existing maps in acts of critical cartography that "remap" in an effort to counter dominant power and its abuses. Here, digital tools help shape meaning, and users can contribute more than user comments.

Palestine is produced in the gaps between historical and contemporary realities and mythologies. These documentaries are alternatives to those available relatively inexpensively either as DVDs or on streaming platforms, and to those that are accessible only through expensive subscription services available to members of large research universities. They are exhibited online without charge, but they require audiences to do more than click the "play" icon. They are designed for viewers accustomed to searching for information online. Users can use the app on- or offsite. They confront history and complicate what viewers think documentary can do. They produce Palestine on the screens of laptops and mobiles, thus affording an accessibility that is not always possible with films. They allow users to produce images of Palestine from databases of image and text. With the ostensible freedoms to select and recombine data in their own customized documentary experience, audiences are no longer mere media viewers but become software users. They experience a simulation of documentary-making. They become coproducers.

The potentially democratic allure of digital technologies, however, can be manipulated toward antidemocratic ends, as awareness of social media has made abundantly clear over the past few decades. Interactive documentaries can both produce Palestine and erase Palestine because digital tools can be manipulated both to facilitate and to impede accountability. They can distract us with their novelty, but they can also help us notice what we might not have seen—or be able to see—not only due to physical distance that exceeds human eyesight but also due to political conditioning to accept certain perspectives while rejecting others. iNakba and *Jerusalem, We Are Here* are designed for ongoing historicized analysis. They are open to new data. They confront the past rather than report the present. They require users to evaluate potentially conflicting evidence.[4] They communicate across incompatible realities rooted in (mis)understandings of history by leaving it up to viewers to evaluate large quantities of data in relation to other data to which they also have access. Moreover, they do not require high-speed internet or vast bandwidth to work. Their use of inexpensive technologies is an important element of their design.

By providing detailed analyses of examples of interactive documentary, this case models reading strategies (i.e., digital literacy) that help us identify how documentaries address viewers differently: iNakba addresses audiences to elicit accountability; and *Jerusalem, We Are Here* addresses audiences to reclaim historical coexistence between different people as a potential model for the present. Like other forms of cultural production, interactive documentaries are nonviolent "weapons" of resistance against erasure and annihilation.[5] The discussion concludes with questions about the surveillance structured into the digital technologies used in interactive documentaries since they interface—that is, communicate—with the internet and mobile networks tethered to military technologies, such as GIS (global information systems). Hacking these, however, can productively disrupt Israeli state branding that veils colonialism under neoliberalism.

What Are Interactive Documentaries?

Interactive documentaries may seem unfamiliar, but they are easy to use. They render data into information through the use of interactive tools that are designed to be intuitive. They require audiences to abandon relatively passive positions as *media spectators* and inhabit obligatory active positions as *software users*. Running on laptops and mobile phones, they integrate with the digital environment of our daily online lives by connecting to familiar platforms such as Google Maps and YouTube. They involve multiple activities like "reading, watching, commenting, sharing content, talking to others, filling in a quiz, playing, and clicking."[6] To experience the documentary, viewers must instruct software to *perform* certain functions. Clicking on icons makes something happen, such as selecting a media file from a database or adding a layer over a photograph or map. Interactive documentaries cannot function without a user.

Some interactive documentaries engage audiences to become comakers by requiring them to select what data to visualize. Many are designed around databases that are open to new data that users can contribute. Rather than fixed final cuts or timed live streams, interactive documentaries have ever-expanding databases to include new material. By unsettling the line between documentary maker and viewer, insofar as the software makes possible, interactive documentaries engage audiences in complicated processes of knowledge production—using digital tools in documentary making as an act of *performance* (acts of *doing* or *process*) whereby data is made legible as information that offers "a lens and framework for understanding."[7] Layering data becomes another way of understanding *how* history is written. Users activate "if, then" equations when they command software to *perform* (e.g., visualize data or make a calculation) by clicking on icons. Users learn *what* happens to their perceptions *if* they reorganize information. Documentaries that include archival footage or layer atop existing digital maps mobilize tension between past and present. More than just reclaiming the past, they *reactivate* it.

Interactive documentaries can mobilize digital tools to teach users to think about the process of knowledge production. Makers often emphasize both incomplete and subjective qualities of evidence, whether archival images or newly recorded testimony. They emphasize that realities are produced, not simply represented. Documentary practices make knowledge visible, audible, and legible. Because most operate on publicly accessible websites, interactive documentaries are largely free to users, which is partly why they are not widely promoted at film festivals. Links to them circulate through journalism, blogs, and social media. They intervene in a shared digital space, extending documentary practice's history of intervening in physical space. Sandi Hilal and Alessandro Petti's Decolonizing Architecture Art Residency (2008–present) leaves Israeli architecture intact as a reminder of ongoing occupation while also repurposing it, so that, for example, Oush Grab military base becomes a park for Palestinians.[8] Comparably, Emily Jacir's *ex libris* (2012) counters the Palestinian memoricide in Israeli military archives by reclaiming plundered books marked "A.P." (i.e., abandoned property) and stored in the Jewish National Library in West Jerusalem.[9] Such projects document by intervening in physical realities. Interactive documentaries can intervene in digitally mediated realities.

Mapping Territorialized History

If Palestinian geographies have been strategically forgotten, it is largely because they have been systemically erased. Ilan Pappé describes the Jewish National Fund's "official Naming Committee whose job it was to Hebraize Palestine's geography," and its "archaeological zeal to reproduce the map of 'Ancient' Israel [which] was in essence none other than a systematic, scholarly, political and military attempt to de-Arabize the terrain—its names and geography, but above all its history."[10] Such erasures are not limited to the past, as Olga Blázquez Sánchez shows when comparing three digital maps of Jerusalem—the Israeli Ministry of Tourism's Eye on Israel, Google Maps, and OpenStreetMap—to demonstrate how "different spatial representations produce different realities."[11] More substantively, she notes the power asymmetries that render Israel's so-called separation barrier in the West Bank invisible on Google Maps, yet clearly labeled as "Apartheid Wall" on the open-source OpenStreetMap.[12] Critical cartography challenges dominant narratives by introducing additional information or interpretations. It shows that cartographers' maps are not representations of reality but visualizations of politics in the guise of representations of reality.[13] Maps make some histories legible and others illegible. They are always "selective representations of reality" that require *coding* by makers and *decoding* by users.[14]

Like documentaries, maps are never neutral, nor are they unbiased tools.[15] Their origins lie in territorial control. They visualize sovereignty and narrate history.[16] As Edward Said explains, "Facts do not at all speak for themselves, but require a socially acceptable narrative to absorb, sustain and circulate them."[17] Google Maps offer one such socially acceptable narrative—a map that appears neutral and scientific. Controlling about 80 percent of the digital map market and generating $3.6 billion in revenue annually, Google Maps appears as a politically unbiased, universally accepted map, yet it has been documented that Google manipulates borders and replaces names based on the user's IP (internet protocol) address, so that the corporation "routinely takes sides in border disputes."[18] Google unlabels places, raising concerns that it has erased Palestine.[19] Microsoft's Bing, by contrast, labels Palestine as such. Google Maps has actually been central to debates on the digital visibility of Palestine, with one of Israel's foreign ministers, Ze'ev Elkin, declaring in 2013 that its use of the term to designate what was previously marked as Palestinian Territories was "in essence" a recognition of "the existence of a Palestinian state."[20] In reality, it is Israel—and not Palestine—that is labeled on Google's base map (a reference map with basic information), which cannot be altered, although layers can be added to it. Interactive documentaries that use Google Maps activate what Ravi Sundaram terms "pirate modernity," which he describes as a "refusal of the legal regime pushed by globalizing elites" and of market solutions to political problems.[21]

Google Maps allows users to locate themselves and their destinations to plot routes. Its basemap is nonetheless a *political* representation of space that endorses particular interpretations of history. Linda Quiquivix found that Google Earth, a three-dimensional map composed of satellite images, offers "a history that begins the conflict at 1967" and thus contributes to "forgetting the violence of 1948."[22] Google's "cartography from above," she argues, can be subverted with "cartography from below," and she offers the example of Thameen Darby's *Nakba Layer* (2006), which indicates Palestinian villages on Google Earth in an effort "to help dismantle the colonial status quo" endorsed by Israel and the Palestinian Authority (PA).[23] Before Google Earth moved to "the cloud," where it is accessible online, it required users to download the software and user-generated layers onto their hard drive. Darby's layer received so many downloads that it became "available and viewable to all Google Earth users by default," a feat unimaginable today.[24] Google Earth is now available online like Google Maps, but users have to locate and request layers, which means that critical cartography remains important.

iNakba and *Jerusalem, We Are Here* all use Google Maps, but only with the latter two are maps central to how users interact with data. Rather than supplementing video testimonies, the maps become sites for examining what Michel Foucault calls "the archaeology of knowledge," uncovering historical data that has been lost, obscured, or discredited.[25] When rendered legible as layers on maps, Palestinian geographies become digital equivalents to "sites of memory" that connect histories with identities and territories.[26] History and memory accumulate in layers, and interactive documentaries that make use of layers on mapping software function like archaeology or forensics. They mobilize the "spatial testimony" that Hagit Keysar describes in DIY aerial photography of East Jerusalem as a reworking of "the victim-expert relations in the production of human rights testimonies."[27] The DIY qualities of attaching cameras to kites rather than drones or satellites, she finds, allow activists using them to say: "Do not look at me, look at this image that I have created and listen to my story." In other words, the photography articulates a "shifting away from the reifying and fetishizing of Palestinian victimhood by reclaiming witnessing and its embodied forms of mediation."[28]

iNakba and *Jerusalem, We Are Here* both allow facts to be added to Google Maps's socially acceptable narrative. Their educational function counters state and corporate control of maps as visual representations of history by "dismantling the official layers" that appear on Google Maps in acts of countermapping and radical historiography that entail investigation, persistence, and risk-taking.[29] Risk is less dangerous for Israelis than Palestinians. More readily than printed maps, interactive ones allow for competing conceptions of space to coexist in separate layers. Jess Bier describes the "segregated landscapes" of Palestine/Israel in terms of symmetries that are emphatically unequal, with Palestinian perspectives discounted or refuted by Israeli ones.[30] Zochrot and Naaman accept their obligation to shift thinking about Palestine by directly addressing fellow Israelis and their allies.

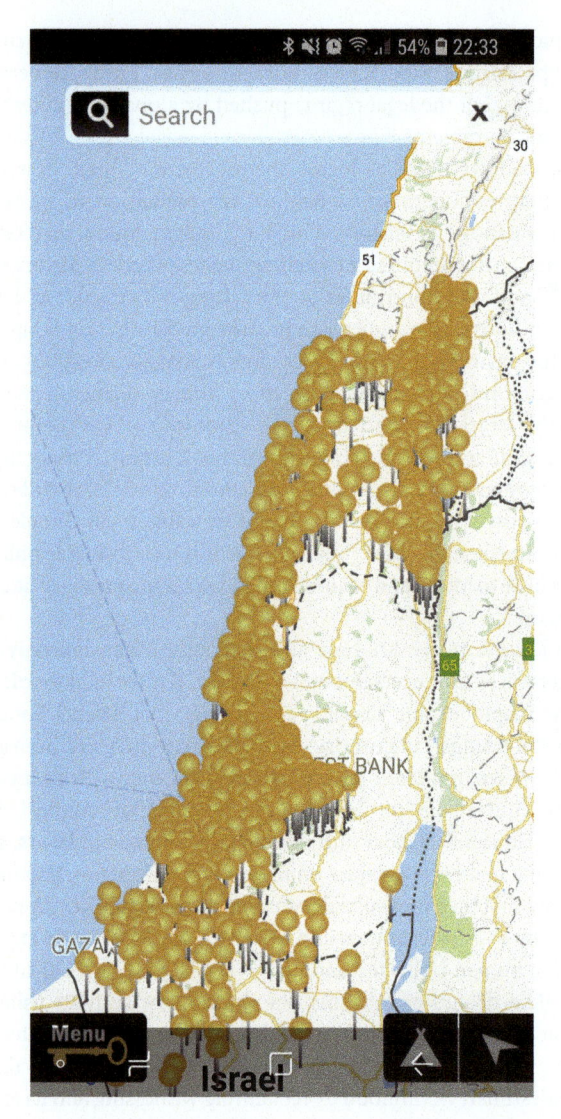

Figure 13.1 A map available through iNakba visualizes Palestinian dispossession. Courtesy of Zochrot.

Immersion in iNakba's History

With iNakba, Zochrot (Hebrew for "remembering" with a feminine, thus nonstandard, ending and the name of the Israeli organization that produced the app) was conscious of how the mere use of the term "Nakba" (catastrophe in Arabic), rather than purportedly neutral terms like "Arab-Israeli war" and "1948 war," did not convey "broad acknowledgement of and accountability for the destruction of hundreds of Palestinian villages" and the creation of hundreds of thousands of Palestinian refugees "largely due to the continued adherence of Jewish Israeli society to colonial concepts and practices."[31] From Zochrot's standpoint, *remembering* is an initial step toward *accountability*. Like B'Tselem—The Israeli Information Center for Human Rights in the Occupied Territories—whose short films that document crimes by the Israeli military are mostly for Israeli audiences, Zochrot focuses on educating fellow Israelis. "Our focus on the Jewish target audience derives from its practical and moral responsibility for Palestinian refugeehood, as well as from its privileged power position under the present regime," the organization states on its website.[32] Zochrot's aim is a "reconceptualization of [the right of] Return as the imperative redress of the Nakba, and a chance for better life for the entire country's inhabitants."[33] Zochrot integrates historical context into the design and architecture of iNakba to debunk Israel's myths, among which the most enduring is that Palestinian lands were unpopulated or uncultivated prior to Zionist immigration. Users see historical data on Palestinian villages and farms clearly mapped. Zochrot believes that "peace will come only after the country has been decolonized, enabling all its inhabitants and refugees to live together without the threat of expulsion or denial of Return."[34] iNakba applies such research to how users interact with the app.

With iNakba, users access files containing historical information, visual images, and videos of Palestine's invisible geographies on Google Maps's familiar interface, which is often assumed credible in representing geographies without bias. iNakba augments perceptions of reality with content and context. Users can see Israel marked in large letters, yet Palestine marked only by dotted lines. Israel, however, is nearly entirely covered in orange and yellow markers, denoting Palestinian towns and villages that no longer exist (see Figure 13.1). Their sheer density makes clear that Palestine was never "a land without a people." When users expand the view, Palestinian localities identified with orange markers cover most of the land of present-day Israel. The interface allows *what has been rendered physically invisible* to be viewable on handheld devices. Names of Palestinian geographies are labeled in white pop-up windows that appear when users scroll over orange markers. Tapping them opens pages with information on the locality, its 1948 population, the date it was occupied, the names of the military operation and the occupying unit, and the locality's history before and during occupation, including depopulation through Israeli settlement. Thus, for Zayta, a tiny village of 380 people, "no traces of houses are left," iNakba informs the user. The image of a flowering cactus (*sabbar* in Arabic), which iNakba also offers, provides another layer of meaning. For Palestinians, it symbolizes patience, generosity, and community.[35] Israelis appropriated the word as *sabra* to designate native-born Jewish Israeli citizens. The late Kamal Boullata, an artist and historian of Palestinian art, has argued that on the one hand, "Israeli Jews raised the indigenous plant to the status of a national symbol; on the other, Palestinians saw in it the very incarnation of their national dispossession."[36] For Boullata, cactus hedges in so many of the earliest photographs of Palestine conveyed how the "thorny and tenacious plant" served to mark borders between farms.[37] The choice of the image of the cactus, then, is important symbolically. Its meaning exceeds what the photo represents

Significantly, iNakba does not layer photographs over live images captured on a mobile phone's built-in camera, as is the case with locative AR (augmented reality) games like *Pokémon Go*. Instead, it presents photos and texts on the screen, prompting users to compare two distinct realities: a physical present with a mediated past. "Amidst tall grasses, wild flowers, and trees covering parts of the site, one can see a well, still in use," reads the app's description of Zayta, but its "surrounding lands are cultivated by Israeli farmers."[38] Many Palestinian villages are now marked by forests planted by Israel to conceal and deny their prior existence.[39] Their size and shape reveal one aspect of what Saree Makdisi calls an "erasure of erasure," processes by which Israel

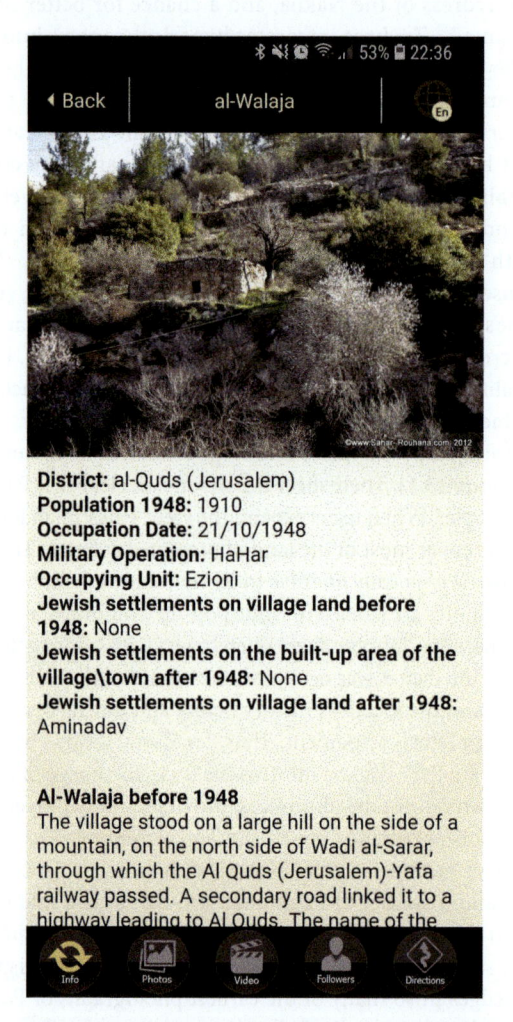

Figure 13.2 A screen from the iNakba app that projects the historic Palestinian village of al-Walaja on top of the present-day Jewish settlement Aminadav, similar to the one of the kibbutz where Zayta once existed. Courtesy of Zochrot.

erases its erasure of occupation to *itself*, if not to the world, by camouflaging walls with attractive vegetation on the Israeli side while leaving concrete bare on the Palestinian side.[40] In the case of Zayta, iNakba provides data on the Jewish National Fund's plans for a kibbutz (see Figure 13.2).

iNakba also maps de-territorialized Palestinians living in refugee camps, including the Neirab camp in Syria, with a current population of some 20,000 inhabitants living in a former barracks in a 0.15-square-kilometer area, whose housing situation UNRWA describes as "deplorable"; or the Shatila camp in Beirut, which, along with the adjacent Sabra camp, was the scene of a notorious massacre in 1982. The information provided by the app includes, for example, UNRWA data on current environmental conditions in Sabra and Shatila, which are described on the app as "extremely bad" with "damp and overcrowded" shelters and a "sewage system [that] needs considerable expansion."[41] Images for the nearby Burj Barajneh camp (population of nearly 18,000) include an informal electrical grid whose dense web of wires covers the street like a canopy. The camp, iNakba tells users, is "overpopulated" with "narrow roads" and "an old sewage system," and it is "regularly flooded in the winter."[42] In Mar Elias Camp, home to 674 refugees from the Galilee, there is a "high incidence of chronic disease."[43] Although improving infrastructure might be interpreted as ruling out a future return, public health issues can also not be ignored. The app documents and maps such complexities.

iNakba's design and architecture allow users to move through the database at their own pace and to contribute images and texts of their own. With the "Contact Us" button, users can send an email or place a phone call. This sort of engagement unsettles conventional distinctions between documentary maker and audience. iNakba becomes a collaborative project. iNakba documents an unresolved history by visualizing historical geographies and historicizing the environmental consequences of "making the desert bloom," notably in Gaza, where water is diverted into Israel causing an ongoing humanitarian crisis. The app is also mobile, allowing users who feel safe traveling to compare historical photographs of sites with their current physical remnants. iNakba promotes Zochrot's larger aims of opening discussion on the right of return by reactivating Palestinian history through a mapping of Palestine's invisible geographies with augmented realities of historical data. Its launch in Israel turned into a breaking news story, exemplifying how documentary can initiate discussion outside the elitist spaces of film festivals.

Jerusalem, We Are Here as Revisiting History

Media maker, scholar, and educator Dorit Naaman's *Jerusalem, We Are Here* is an ongoing interactive documentary to remap the former Palestinian neighborhood of Qatamon, which is now considered a Jewish neighborhood. Naaman says that reading Ghada Karmi's *In Search of Fatima*, she noticed that Karmi's landmarks were "now unmarked," and that the streets now bore "the names of Israeli militaristic landmarks from the 1948 war." While half of the neighborhood is comprised of original Palestinian houses, very few are marked by stone carving inscriptions, so the houses exist, but their Palestinian owners are actively erased and forgotten.[44] "Through this process, I realized that if we—as Israelis—do not face the past and remedy its wrongs," Naaman writes, "we will have no future."[45] Initially Naaman imagined looking for descendants of the dispossessed. Rather than record oral histories that might interest only family and historians, she imagined developing interviews into public art and activism by projecting the interviews onto Qatamon houses because, as she explains, "I am an Israeli and I really wanted to force the Israelis to come to terms with al-Nakba."[46] At the same time, it felt "wrong to ask people to experience their trauma or to tell me their story of loss just in order to educate Israelis," she adds.[47] *Jerusalem, We Are Here*'s Arabic title, *Ya Quds, nahnu huna*, honors the city's Arabic name, al-Quds. The project conveys a reverence for the city by those who know and love it—and acknowledges that it was (and remains) an *Arab city*. Users move virtually through streets, past and present, via mapping software that renders visible the city's invisible geographies where the historical mix of ethnicities, religions, and cultures has been erased or diminished. Naaman's documentary is guided by accountability for past dispossession and by hope in light of historical coexistence. She notes that "1948 is almost 70 years ago, and we need to collect the memories and documents from the people who are still around, who remember. There's a sense of urgency to this."[48] The project is set in West Jerusalem, but some residents of Qatamon found themselves in East Jerusalem, which has been under occupation since 1967 and was annexed by Israel in 1980. Its Palestinian residents are policed by checkpoints and their movements tracked by surveillance cameras, rendering the occupation both physical via infrastructure and digital via surveillance.

The product of a decade's work in building relationships and gaining trust, the documentary opens with a video of Anwar Ben Badis and Mona Halaby—both Palestinian, though only Ben Badis lives in Qatamon. They sit inside Jerusalem's Lev Smadar theater, formerly The Orient, then Regent Cinema. As red curtains open to unveil the silver screen of another era, images appear of theater manager Fernando "Nando" Schtakleff during the 1940s. Nando had a passion for home movies, and Naaman joins Ben Badis and Halaby to watch his images of Jerusalem and family holidays spent in Haifa, Jaffa, and Tel Aviv as violence erupts all around. By the time Nando returns to Jerusalem from his family holiday, his home movies have already become documents of the city prior to destruction and dispossession (see Figure 13.3). "From home movies to citizen journalism, Nando documents his hometown's destruction," the video explains, adding that, "Like most Palestinian Arabs, Armenians, Greeks, and other non-Jewish citizens of Palestine, Nando will eventually be expelled." The video ends with Ben Badis, Halaby, and Naaman exiting the theater and going on to "revisit Katamon to uncover its lost stories" (see Figure 13.4).[49] They thus reactivate history by providing a polyphony of subjective interpretations of space that reject the simplification of complexities in expository "voice of authority" or "fly-on-the-wall" observation, both of which position one perspective as the only one. By offering two different tours by two different guides, the interactive documentary rejects the notion that knowledge can be reduced to a single point of view. Naaman is not, as in an observational documentary, an invisible observer but an on-screen participant, who guides audiences on her tour of the neighborhood but does not privilege it more than the tours by Ban Badis and Halaby. *Jerusalem, We Are Here* is an archeological project that operates with different politics than the kind of Israeli documentaries that attempt to reconstruct "ancient" history. Viewers delve deep into history to explore repressed archaeologies of knowledge. In some regards, the documentary engages in the multilayered forensic analysis that Eyal Weizman identifies as a "politics of verticality" by which occupation occurs at the different levels of surface, subsoil, and airspace.[50] Here, history has been erased at all levels. Prior to 1948, Qatamon was predominantly inhabited by Greek Orthodox Palestinians, along with some Protestant Armenians, mostly professionals, merchants, and educators. Today, it is considered a Jewish neighborhood, but it has been so gentrified that "one is more likely to hear English or French than Hebrew [since] Israelis are simply priced out."[51] Still, its "distinctive Arab architecture" has reduced Palestinians to consumable style rather than historical presence.[52] By digging down through layers of history, the interactive documentary makes present digitally what has been made absent both physically and politically.

Jerusalem, We Are Here is available in Arabic and English, and will eventually also be distributed in Hebrew. Users can select: virtual tours with audio commentary by guides, experts, and witnesses; black-and-white and color photographs; ambient sounds and music; and detailed information about the sites and the people who lived, worked, or entertained in them. They can also select particular points along the tour route to move through mediated representations of urban space. They can watch short videos produced collaboratively that deal with brief or imagined visits to houses now altered beyond recognition. The project mobilizes an interactive map with historical information and images. Layers over the base map are color-coded to indicate buildings constructed before or after the Nakba, as well as ones that have been identified as the houses of specific families, or the buildings of embassies, factories, monasteries, and so forth. Google Maps's base map can be layered with printed maps from 1934 and 1938, or with aerial photographs, or maps from 1918, 1946, and 2016. The information on Smadar Cinema, for example, includes a photograph of the official marker in Hebrew and English. The photo is annotated to indicate that the Palestinian era of the cinema's history has been omitted. The project remaps Qatamon, "not street by street, but house by house," so that it "disrupts distinctions between public and private, inside and outside, past and present" in an interplay between the "materiality of the streets and buildings" and the "evanescence of histories, memories, and stories."[53] Users constantly encounter prompts to read more or contribute to the documentary. Like iNakba, there is no way to consume all of the data at once. It requires revisitings that invariably follow different trajectories through the site's architecture.

Jerusalem, We Are Here rekindles this history, digitally erasing checkpoints, walls, and barriers. It layers the economically and racially segregated Jerusalem of today with its multiethnic and multireligious past. Users can toggle between "Tours," a component of the documentary that adds information to Google Street View panoramas, and "Remapping Jerusalem," another component of the documentary that visualizes physical and political realities at different dates over Google Maps's base map. Some maps are rendered by hand, others, by aerial photography. Street View provides an intimate IP look into communities subjected to erasure and surveillance thanks to policies ranging from security to gentrification. The perspective is at the eye level of a pedestrian. It simulates visual experiences of occupying space with one's body without feeling intimidated, thereby allowing Palestinian users to occupy space digitally without the accompanying fear of occupying it physically.

Figure 13.3 Screen grab of Nando Schtakleff's home movies repurposed as part of *Jerusalem, We Are Here*. Courtesy of Dorit Naaman.

Figure 13.4 A choice of interactive virtual tours within the documentary. Courtesy of Dorit Naaman.

Hacking Surveillance?

iNakba and *Jerusalem, We Are Here* do not escape the complicity that is built into our reliance on mapping technologies designed for military use. Enhanced visibility of Palestinian geographies brings enhanced surveillance by Israel. These interactive documentaries allow users to "visit" Palestine from the relative safety of their homes, but our homes are identifiable on GPS via IP addresses and AGPS (assisted GPS used on mobile devices). The systems that push content to users (click-to-view) also pull (or identify) location to network providers in what has been termed "participatory surveillance."[54] In other words, the very act of participation subjects users to control. Just as closed-circuit video cameras monitor physical space, every movement in cyberspace is tracked. The data is stored on servers where it can be sorted and rendered into information. Mobile phones operate with GPS and SIM (subscriber identity module) cards that facilitate state surveillance. Palestinians are familiar with Israeli police arriving at their doorstep thanks to GPS.[55] Jewish Israelis are also not immune to surveillance: performances such as the *Occupy WiFi* project (2014) by artist-activist Yoav Lifshitz with the Israeli Pirate Party collective bypassed state laws on public protests by operating in the invisible space of free Wi-Fi.[56]

Google's parent company, Alphabet, actually offers credits to nonprofits for using its Google Maps platform, allowing them to harness an "immersive location experience"[57] that "integrates seamlessly with iOS, Android, and desktop applications," luring activist and advocacy groups alike.[58] In so doing, Google collaborates with states to consolidate cartographies of power embedded in corporate security regimes. Google Maps, then, functions like a checkpoint, though not necessarily like the Israeli ones segregating Palestinians in the post-Oslo zones whose boundaries are unmarked on Google Maps. Alternatives exist, such as Creative Commons's cartography and documentation software.[59] Early on, Zochrot used OpenStreetMap, and iNakba does not require GPS (common on apps with wearable displays on hardware, such as headsets or eyeglasses) so that participation is not *locative* and thus averts some of the participation-as-surveillance risks inherent in location-specific software.

iNakba and *Jerusalem, We Are Here* intervene in Israel's self-branding as a digitally innovative state. Adi Kuntsman and Rebecca Stein note that Israel is "what some have called the most important technology incubator next to Silicon Valley," yet few acknowledge that "growth [is] fueled by the sector's close ties to the military industrial complex, with technologies honed in militarized contexts frequently reengineered for civilian ones."[60] Innovation takes the form of "techno-security" that loosens the "distinction between civilian population and combatant population" and erodes the foundations of international law.[61] Installed on mobile phones, GPS reconfigures ideas of mobility and visibility: on the one hand, it enables precision when traveling; on the other, it involves being tracked.

Despite the risks of militarized and monetized surveillance inherent to operating across internet and mobile networks, iNakba and *Jerusalem, We Are Here* promote accountability and capacity to think historically and empathetically. They adopt strategies that reject Israel's militarized counter-resistance, whether monitoring physical and virtual spaces or profiting by selling such technologies to repressive regimes. They engage a "thinking through digital media" that adjusts to situational contingencies and intervenes in localized spaces.[62] They can provide *virtual transportations* for Palestinians, unable to travel due to Israeli restrictions, and *visual translations* for Israelis, unable to recognize what appears invisible to them. They can alter perceptions and build solidarities.

Notes

1 Ariella Azoulay, "Photographic Archives and Archival Entities," in *Image Operations: Visual Media and Political Conflict*, ed. Jens Eder and Charlotte Klonk (Manchester: Manchester University Press, 2016), 157.
2 iNakba mobile app, iPhone ed., v.2.4.8 (Tel Aviv, Israel: Zochrot, 2014), iOS 7.0 or later, https://zochrot.org/en/keyword/45323.
3 *Jerusalem, We Are Here*, directed by Dorit Naaman, with research and tour guiding by Anwar Ben Badis and Mona Halaby (Canada/Jerusalem, 2016), https://jerusalemwearehere.com/#/.
4 Craig Hight, "The Field of Digital Documentary: A Challenge to Documentary Theorists," *Studies in Documentary Film* 2, no. 1 (2008): 3–7; Dale Hudson, "Undisclosed Recipients: Database Documentaries and the Internet," *Studies in Documentary Film* 2, no. 1 (2008): 79–98; Kate Nash, "Modes of Interactivity: Analysing the Webdoc," *Media, Culture and Society* 34, no. 2 (March 2012): 195–210, https://doi.org/10.1177/0163443711430758; Judith Aston, Sandra Gaudenzi, and Mandy Rose, eds., *i-docs: The Evolving Practice of Interactive Documentary* (London: Wallflower, 2017); Patricia R. Zimmermann and Helen De Michiel, *Open Space New Media Documentary: A Toolkit for Theory and Practice* (New York: Routledge, 2018).
5 Joseph Massad, "The Weapon of Culture: Cinema in the Palestinian Liberation Struggle," in *Dreams of a Nation: On Palestinian Cinema*, ed. Hamid Dabashi (London: Verso, 2006), 32.
6 Nash, "Modes of Interactivity," 196.
7 Dale Hudson, "Interactive Documentary at the Intersection of Performance and Mediation: Navigating 'Invisible' Histories and 'Inaudible' Stories in the United States," *Studies in Documentary Film* 14, no. 2 (2020): 128–46. See also, Diana Taylor, *Performance* (Durham, NC: Duke University Press, 2016), 133.
8 Alessandro Petti, Sandi Hilal, and Eyal Weizman, *Architecture after Revolution* (Berlin: Sternberg Press, 2013).
9 Helga Tawil-Souri, "Cinema as the Space to Transgress Palestine's Territorial Trap," *Middle East Journal of Culture and Communication* 7, no. 2 (2014): 169–89, https://doi.org/10.1163/18739865-00702005.
10 Ilan Pappé, *The Ethnic Cleansing of Palestine* (London: Oneworld, 2006), 226.
11 Olga Blázquez Sánchez, "Collaborative Cartographies: Counter-Cartography and Mapping Justice in Palestine," *Journal of Holy Land and Palestine Studies* 17, no. 1 (2018): 81. OpenStreetMap operates under Open Data Commons Open Database License (ODbL), allowing anyone to share, create, and adapt its data so long as they attribute, share-alike, and keep it open. Open Data Commons, "ODC Open Database License (ODbL) Summary," Open Data Commons, https://opendatacommons.org/licenses/odbl/summary/. Accessed November 25, 2013. Data is contributed by individual users as well as national mapping agencies and other organizations.

12 Sánchez, "Collaborative Cartographies," 78. As of October 2020, the wall is no longer labeled on OpenStreetMaps.
13 Arthur Jay Klinghoffer, *The Power of Projections: How Maps Reflect Global Politics and History* (Westport, CT: Praeger, 2006), 6.
14 Jeremy Black, *Maps and Politics* (Chicago, IL: University of Chicago Press, 1997), 11.
15 Google Maps adapts the Eurocentric Mercator projection model, which was developed in the sixteenth century to facilitate maritime navigation and also placed the European subcontinent in the position of mastery at center top of the world.
16 Klinghoffer, *The Power of Projections*, 12.
17 Edward Said, "Permission to Narrate," *Journal of Palestine Studies* 13, no. 3 (Spring 1984): 34, https://doi.org/10.2307/2536688.
18 Greg Bensinger, "Google Redraws the Borders on Maps Depending on Who's Looking," *Washington Post*, February 14, 2020, https://www.washingtonpost.com/technology/2020/02/14/google-maps-political-borders/.
19 Caitlin Dewey, "Google Maps Did Not 'Delete' Palestine—But It Does Impact How You See It," *Washington Post*, April 9, 2016, https://www.washingtonpost.com/news/the-intersect/wp/2016/08/09/google-maps-did-not-delete-palestine-but-it-does-impact-how-you-see-it/.
20 As cited in Helga Tawil-Souri and Miriyam Aouragh, "Intifada 3.0? Cyber Colonialism and Palestinian Resistance," *Arab Studies Journal* 22, no. 1 (2014): 102.
21 Ravi Sundaram, *Pirate Modernity: Delhi's Media Urbanism* (London: Routledge, 2010), 13, 174.
22 Linda Quiquivix, "Art of War, Art of Resistance: Palestinian Counter-Cartography on Google Earth," *Annals of the Association of American Geographers* 104, no. 3 (2014): 445, https://doi.org/10.1080/00045608.2014.892328.
23 Quiquivix, "Art of War," 446, 447.
24 Quiquivix, "Art of War," 451.
25 Michel Foucault, *The Archaeology of Knowledge and the Discourse on Language*, trans. A. M. Sheridan Smith (New York: Pantheon, 1972).
26 Pierre Nora, ed., *Les lieux de mémoire*, new edition (Paris: Éditions Gallimard, 1997).
27 Hagit Keysar, "A Spatial Testimony: The Politics of Do-It-Yourself Aerial Photography in East Jerusalem," *Society and Space* 37, no. 3 (June 2019): 524, https://doi.org/10.1177/0263775818820326.
28 Keysar, "A Spatial Testimony," 536.
29 Stephanie Hankey and Marek Tuszynski, "Exposing the Invisible: Visual Investigation of Conflict," in *Image Operations: Visual Media and Political Conflict*, ed. Jens Eder and Charlotte Klonk (Manchester: Manchester University Press, 2016), 176.
30 Jess Bier, *Mapping Israel, Mapping Palestine: How Occupied Landscapes Shape Scientific Knowledge* (Cambridge, MA: The MIT Press, 2017), 11.
31 Zochrot, "Our Vision," Zochrot, 2014, https://zochrot.org/en/content/17.
32 Zochrot, "Our Vision." Documentaries available at *B'Tselem Shorts: Visual Impact Documenting the Seldom Seen* (Israel: B'Tselem, 2007), DVD.
33 Zochrot, "Our Vision."
34 Zochrot, "Our Vision."
35 Nasser Abufarha, "Land of Symbols: Cactus, Poppies, Orange and Olive Trees in Palestine," *Identities* 15, no. 3 (2008): 365, https://doi.org/10.1080/10702890802073274. It also symbolizes loss, familiar to audiences from flashback scenes in *Al-makhdu'un* [*The Dupes*], directed by Tewfik Saleh (Damascus: National Film Organization, 1973).

36. Kamal Boullata, *Palestinian Art: From 1850 to the Present* (London: Saqi, 2009), 183.
37. Boullata, *Palestinian Art*, 184.
38. iNakba mobile app.
39. Pappé, *Ethnic Cleansing*, 228.
40. Saree Makdisi, "The Architecture of Erasure," *Critical Inquiry* 36, no. 3 (2010): 519–59, https://doi.org/10.1086/653411.
41. iNakba mobile app.
42. Ibid.
43. Ibid.
44. Ghada Karmi, *In Search of Fatima: A Palestinian Story* (London: Verso, 2002); Dorit Naaman, "Lessons for the Future from Jerusalem's Palestinian Past," The Conversation, May 13, 2018, https://theconversation.com/lessons-for-the-future-from-jerusalems-palestinian-past-95768.
45. Naaman, "Lessons for the Future."
46. Dorit Naaman, interviewed by interns, "Interview with Dorit Naaman about 'Jerusalem, We Are Here,'" *Jerusalem Fund*, May 11, 2017, http://www.thejerusalemfund.org/17755/interview-dorit-naaman-jerusalem.
47. Naaman, "Interview."
48. As cited in Mary Pelletier, "Take a Tour of West Jerusalem's Palestinian History," *Al Jazeera*, April 19, 2017, https://www.aljazeera.com/indepth/features/2017/03/jerusalem-170319103904879.html.
49. *Jerusalem*, Naaman.
50. Eyal Weizman, *Hollow Land: Israel's Architecture of Occupation*, new edition (London: Verso, 2017), xvi–xvii.
51. Olga Gershenson, "'We Are Victims of Our Past …': Israel's Dark Past Comes to Light in New Documentaries," *Tikkun* 33, nos. 1–2 (2018): 75, https://doi.org/10.1215/08879982-4354534.
52. Gershenson, "'We Are Victims,'" 75. In Israeli parlance, the term "Arab" undercuts Palestinian existence.
53. Zimmermann and De Michiel, *Open Space New Media Documentary*, 74.
54. Mark Poster, "The Information Empire," *Comparative Literature Studies* 41, no. 3 (2004): 317–34, https://doi:10.1353/cls.2004.0036.
55. Linda Quiquivix, "When the Carob Tree Was the Border: On Autonomy and Palestinian Practices of Figuring It Out," *Capitalism Nature Socialism* 24, no. 3 (2013): 185, https://doi.org/10.1080/10455752.2013.815242.
56. See the website of the *Occupy WiFi* performance piece: Israeli Pirate Party, "Occupy WiFi," 2014, http://occupywifi.org/en/.
57. See "Welcome to Google Maps Platform," Google Cloud, https://cloud.google.com/maps-platform. Accessed October 15, 2020.
58. These features are promoted widely, for example, by Google Cloud partner Sword Connect, "Work Smarter and More Efficiently with Google Cloud Solutions by Sword Connect," Sword Connect home page, https://www.sword-connect.com; and on the website of the app *Iconic Framework*, "Google Maps: A Comprehensive Maps Platform That Drives Real-World Insights and Immersive Location Experiences," *Iconic Framework* (n.d.), https://ionicframework.com/ integrations/google-maps.
59. "Attribution-ShareAlike 2.0 Generic (CC BY-SA 2.0)," Creative Commons, https://creativecommons.org/licenses/by-sa/2.0/. Accessed October 15, 2020.
60. Adi Kuntsman and Rebecca L. Stein, *Digital Militarism: Israel's Occupation in the Social Media Age* (Stanford, CA: Stanford University Press, 2015), 9.

61 Armand Mattelart, *The Globalization of Surveillance*, trans. Susan Taponier and James A. Cohen (London: Polity, 2010), 161.
62 Dale Hudson and Patricia R. Zimmermann, *Thinking through Digital Media: Transnational Environments and Locative Places* (New York, NY: Palgrave Macmillan, 2015).

14

Palestine and the Question of Queer Arab Becoming

Sophie Chamas

If I Fail, If I Die, I'll Come Back Every Time[1]

In their introduction to the special issue "Queering Palestine," Leila Farsakh, Rhoda Kanaaneh, and Sherene Seikaly ask, "can nonqueer Palestinians, and non-Palestinian queers and nonqueers, hear the Palestinian queer anti-colonial critique?" Meaning, can queerness serve as a "decolonial practice that allows Palestinians and *others* to move beyond the reified notions of sovereignty, statehood, and identity that the Oslo process exemplified"?[2] In this case, I attempt to address these questions by thinking through the relationality between queer Arabness and Palestine with a focus on how non-Palestinian queer Arabs cultivate a sense of their queerness, their Arabness, and the dialectical potentiality of their entanglement via an engagement with the Palestinian struggle.

In what follows, I look to how a queer Arab engagement with Palestine not only disrupts Western homonationalism and Arab heteronationalism but enables a reconceptualization of Arabness itself via its dialectical intertwining with a particular understanding of queerness. This episode explores what I argue is not only a material but an ontological and epistemological relationality between queer Arabness and Palestine.

I challenge framings of queer Arabness as a hyphenated identity that assumes the stability of "queer" and "Arab," and think it dialectically, making sense of queer Arabness as a mode of becoming that destabilizes both understandings of queerness and dominant understandings of Arabness. I am interested, in particular, in the role that Palestine and a commitment to Palestine play in defining and distinguishing queer Arab identity. I theorize the transformative effects that engagement with Palestine and imperialism has had and can have on how we understand both queerness *and* Arabness. Rather than seeing queer Arabs as imbibing an LGBTQ+ identity from without, that is "foreign" to the Middle East, I think through how their engagement with Palestine is productive of a distinctive mode of being queer and doing queerness that, in turn, epistemologically and ontologically disrupts hegemonic approaches to knowing and embodying Arabness.

I develop and ground my argument through an engagement with the music video for the Mashrou' Leila song "Cavalry." Mashrou' Leila was, until its dismantlement in 2022, one of the most popular music groups in the Middle East. The indie-rock band was fronted by an openly queer lead singer and notable for its engagement with gender and sexuality through both its music and its public platform. The music video for "Cavalry," directed by Jessy Moussallem, focuses on Palestinian children challenging the Israeli occupation of Palestine, and was inspired by the Palestinian teenager Ahed Tamimi, who was arrested in 2017 for confronting Israeli soldiers outside her home in the West Bank village of Nabi Saleh. The video also depicts the arbitrary and violent Israeli invasions of Palestinian homes and portrays soldiers "searching through children's bedrooms, arresting the young men of the household and cutting off the branches of an olive tree."[3]

The four-person indie rock band has been both celebrated and vilified since its formation in 2008 for its lyrical engagement with a variety of social justice issues, and has found itself banned from performing in several states, including Jordan and Egypt, as well as targeted in its native Lebanon. The band has been singled out, both positively and negatively, for its engagement with gender and sexuality and for having an openly queer front-person and lyricist, and Arab states' responses to the band's output and performances have most often been framed as a reaction to this.

Band members have expressed ambivalent feelings about the fixation on the relationship between queer activism and their work. Balram writes that, when it comes to queer front-person Hamed Sinno, "while LGBTQ+ rights in the Middle East is a cause that" the band is "happy to champion," they are "wary of the entire group being reduced to a 'queer band.'"[4] While recognizing the importance of these articulations and wanting to avoid reproducing a one-dimensional portrait of the band, I engage with its work with a mind to how it has circulated and predominately been received, rather than the multifaceted nature of band members' intentions. My interest in this case is to think with the potentiality of a body of work that, for better or worse, is perceived to be queer or of relevance to queer Arabs by queers in the Middle East, homophobes in the Middle East, and Western observers invested for a plethora of reasons in the politics of gender and sexuality in the region. My interest, then, is in thinking with the potentiality of a song and music video centered on Palestine, produced and disseminated by a band that has been constructed as one of the public-faces of queer identity and representation in the Arab world.

In focusing on the lyrical and visual dimensions of "Cavalry," I also think through cultural production's capacity to disrupt and redirect both epistemologically and ontologically. As the link between Palestine and the Arab imagination is being actively severed by Middle Eastern states eager to normalize relations with Israel, as LGBT activism in the region becomes increasingly NGO-ized and proto-homonationalist in nature,[5] as the West insists that queer Arabs disavow the region and Palestine so that they may be folded into safety, I examine the political potentiality of a queer Arab embrace of a *becoming with* Palestine. Cavalry is a cultural text that presents Palestine as the *stuff* of queer Arabness by layering stories of queer Arab and Palestinian marginalization onto one another, creating a palimpsest of sorts that interrupts and disrupts *multiple* hegemonic understandings of these ways of being, and offers up a template for queer Arabness as a mode of becoming whose capacity for continuous unfolding can be sustained by drawing inspiration from Palestine and Palestinianness.

Palestine as Mirror, Palestine as Map

In June of 2019 Mashrou' Leila released a music video to accompany its single "Cavalry" from its album *The Beirut School*. The clip opens with a young Palestinian girl confronting an Israeli soldier for detaining, we assume, a relative of hers—a teenager who, she screams, had done nothing wrong. She proceeds to confront another soldier, this time one seated in a tank, yelling for him to come up out of the vehicle and face her. She turns, then, marching toward a group of more soldiers. As she moves toward them, her speech fades and Hamed Sinno's singing voice enters the fray (Figure 14.1).[6]

Sinno's lyrics open with a commentary on the arrogance of those in power, those who sit on "thrones," as the camera pans to a young boy pushing a soldier standing in his path. "Tyranny," Sinno sings, "blooms disobedience." The voices of the children intertwine with Sinno's, the young girl we met at the start joins the young boy, whom we learn is her brother, helping him shove the soldier, screaming "my little brother has more dignity than you. He's a 4-year-old kid. Get out of my land." Sinno sings: "If I die a hundred times, I will come back a hundred times with sharpened sword."

The music video is an obvious commentary on and indictment of Israeli settler colonialism and Israel's oppression of the Palestinian people via, among other mechanisms, the routinized violence of the Israeli Defence Forces (IDF), which, more than merely seeking to police and control, also seeks to discipline and to stifle Palestinians' will and ability to resist. The opening scene of the video, as mentioned earlier, is clearly an homage to the bravery of Ahed Tamimi, who went viral when she was filmed slapping an Israeli soldier in 2017. The video, more broadly, celebrates ordinary and vulnerable Palestinians' perseverance in the face of impossible odds, highlighting in particular the courage in defiance of the most vulnerable members of Palestinian society—children who, simultaneously, are presented as those most possessed by and committed to the possibility of Palestinian futurity because of their youth, because time, and more specifically the traumatic nature of Palestinian temporality, has yet to break them down and suffocate their hopefulness.

"If I die a hundred times, I will come back a hundred times," Sinno sings—another homage, this time to the Palestinian's stubborn will to continue existing publicly, loudly, and defiantly in the face of a settler-colonial machine determined to invisibilize, to kill, to relegate to slow death, or to debilitate, physically, affectively, and geographically, the indigenous reminder of the still unfolding crime that enabled its emergence and facilitates its persistence. This insistence on life and perpetuation, this notion that existence is, in itself, resistance, is why some scholars have theorized Palestine and Palestinians as queer.

Scholars like C. Heike Schotten have drawn links between Edward Said's framing of Palestinians as "troublesome" and queer theory's commitment to the anti-normative.[7] If queer theory is about and for those whose being is disruptive to the order of things,

Figure 14.1 Still from "*Cavalry*." A young Palestinian girl confronts an Israeli soldier standing atop a tank. Courtesy of Mashrou' Leila.

to racial capitalist heteronormative patriarchy, and if it aligns itself politically with those who challenge regimes of normalization, then, these scholars argue, Palestine can be conceived of as queer.[8] In particular, the argument that existence is resistance—a sentiment associated with the Palestinian struggle—has been framed as a queer mode of defiance: the Palestinian refusal to "go away," as Said put it.[9]

What are we to make of Palestine and Palestinians being presented as both mirror and map in this music video? More than merely standing with Palestine, the band tells us that it *sees itself* in Palestine—Palestine helps it make sense of its own experiences in the Middle East and is the means through which it chooses to analytically communicate its encounters with marginalization and violence in the region to its audience(s) and its detractors. In the commentary that accompanies the music video, the band writes that "the children in the film reflect Mashrou' Leila's own struggles with political power, having recently been banned from being with their audiences in Jordan and Egypt, and finding themselves at the center of yet another human rights polemic." Palestine, here, emerges as mirror. The music video is also aspirational. It "reminds us," the band writes, "perhaps of the energised idealism we had as youths coming into the world, and believing we could change it, before political fatigue left us jaded and defeated." Palestine, here, emerges as map, as *method*, as guide. In my engagement with "Cavalry," I am attempting to distinguish between a *standing with* Palestine and a *seeing oneself in* Palestine, and to demonstrate the potentiality of the latter ontological orientation.

Becoming with Palestine

As the music video continues, more children gather to defy the soldiers and Sinno sings, "I splinter into an army that looks like me, we'll stick together and resist." The beat and Sinno's singing pick up when a soldier yells at the children to shut up and one responds defiantly, "we will not shut up!" More children gather. As they defy the soldiers, shoving them, screaming at them, asserting their belonging to the land and its belonging to them, Sinno sings: "Your army and his excellency has got nothing on me." In the English version Sinno sings: "You and your cavalry, you got nothing on me." I will return to the distinction between the two versions later in this section.

One could read the video as simply a commentary on the events unfolding on screen and those they are meant to be representative of in Palestine. The video *is* a gesture of solidarity—the band has said as much. But there is also more at play. There are two narratives, two stories being told, through the same lyrics. Two seemingly different and disconnected stories that, through the ability to articulate them using the same set of words, through the lyrical mirroring of two seemingly distinct experiences, reveal an entanglement that might otherwise not be visible.

Sinno's lyrics were penned in the first person. To hear the song without exposure to the music video is to assume we are being sung a story about Sinno and the band's experiences more broadly. "Cavalry" was penned, after all, in the aftermath of what has been called the "Rainbow Flag Incident" in Cairo in 2017, when the Egyptian state engaged in a crackdown on Egypt's LGBTQI+ community after attendees at a Mashrou' Leila concert were photographed raising rainbow flags. Sinno has explained that the track "is basically about embracing defeat and just going for it anyway. It's about not expecting to win, necessarily, but to fight anyway."[10] A solely aural engagement with the song presents us with one story—the story of a band maligned for daring to stand up to power and challenge societal norms, asserting its will to persist. A muted engagement with the music video paints a picture of Palestinian defiance in the face of settler colonial violence, drawing on what can be considered iconic imagery. When the lyrics are married to the visuals, the story expands, travels, weaves, entangles, and stitches together the queer and the Arab, the queer and the Palestinian, the Palestinian and the queer Arab.

Over the last couple of years, Mashrou' Leila found itself occupying a position of "marginalisation and abjection" in the Middle East.[11] Rather than attempting to produce aural and visual art that could encourage the band's assimilation back into the region, with the release of "Cavalry" in the aftermath of the crackdown in Cairo, the band chose to associate and fuse itself with another marginalized and abject figure—that of the Palestinian. This figure, while long demonized and dismissed in the West, has also experienced disenfranchisement and oppression in the Middle East first because of the long-term and ongoing maltreatment of Palestinian refugees living in neighboring Arab countries and more recently as more and more Arab states have embraced normalized relations with Israel.

The band's approach to Palestine on the back of the violent experiences it faced in the region is an important critique and rejection of nationalism that mirrors queer theory and queer activism's framing of it as a "form of institutionalised violence and exclusion."[12] In the Middle East, as elsewhere, state legitimacy and nationalism are deeply intertwined, and in order to service the state, nationalism has depended for its reproduction and weaponization on scapegoats who can inspire a sense of national fragility and authorize a legitimized and legitimizing violence in the face of it—queers, feminists, communists, refugees, migrants, the working classes, and more. Mashrou' Leila, a Lebanese band, in the aftermath of a series of violent incidents that resulted in band members being hounded in their native context and saw some of them choose to propel themselves into exile, releases a song that entangles it with Palestine. Instead of attempting to prove its Lebaneseness and to assert belonging to Lebanon, the band chooses what Stefano Harney and Fred Moten call possession by dispossession by *becoming with* Palestine and Palestinians.[13]

We see here a reconceptualization of Arabness via its queering, beyond the nation-state—an invitation to remake Arabness by seeing oneself in the experiences of those most marginalized in the region and recognizing the links that bind seemingly disparate experiences of rejection and oppression. We are invited to recognize what can happen to our sense of self when we acknowledge that "this shit is killing you too, however much more softly, you stupid motherfucker!"[14] This is an Arabness and a queerness that begins from a place of abjection and marginalization which exists across multiple spatial contexts, from the United States to Palestine to Lebanon, and which commands a reckoning with not only imperialism but postcolonial nationalism. We have here an approach to queer Arabness, to queerness and to Arabness, as a "coalitional" rather than a static or essentialized identity that serves as an invitation into a particular kind of politics and the becoming otherwise that it might enable.[15]

Queer Arabness, then, emerges here not as an identity but as an orientation in the world that derives from a particular kind of engagement with particular kinds of lived experiences understood in relation to others that, on the surface, might appear unconnected but are, in fact, entangled. Cultural productions like Mashrou' Leila's "Cavalry" invite us to do both queerness and Arabness otherwise, and to think about the potential of their coupling when approached as anti-identitarian states of being, thinking, and doing. This music video is an example of how both "dominant Arab" and Western "discourses can be 'unhooked, transformed, or rearticulated.'"[16]

"Cavalry" is a call to "transcend national loyalties and conventional ideas of belonging"[17]—to think through what queerness can become when it is made contingent on a commitment to Palestine without reducing queer commitments to Palestine to a commitment to Palestinian queers, and to contemplate the political potentiality of a coalitional identity premised on recognizing the connections between seemingly disparate experiences of marginalization. What if what it means to be Arab is to stand with Palestine? What if to be queer is to stand with Palestine? What if Palestine is the stuff of queer Arabness? What does that make queer Arabness? Might this be, to borrow and play with Lauren Berlant and Elizabeth Freeman, a simulation of Arab nationalism or pan-Arabism with "a camp inflection"?[18]

Queer Arabness, here, becomes a kind of politics that can inspire new modes of becoming not just for queer Arabs but for queers and Arabs more generally. Queer Arab engagements with Palestine challenge both queer and Arab identity politics. I follow Sarah Hamdan's call to reclaim Arabness "as a politics of location for the subject" in "an attempt to reinvent a collective imaginary in a non-essentialist and non-relativist manner," and to refuse "an essentialist" and "romanticized" approach to Arabness that frames it as a "pre-existing authentic identity," thinking it, instead, "as political subjectivities-in-becoming."[19]

I am invested in approaching queerness as a doing, a queering, which the lens of becoming enables. I follow Scott Lauria Morgensen's call to "learn from subjects in-the-making" as we attempt to navigate the logics (nationalism, settler colonialism, heteronormativity, homonationalism) that underpin and nurture systems of inequality.[20] Beyond trying to locate and describe queer Arab identity, we might think of it as a practice, in some instances, that results in "a certain unsettling" in relation to dominant conceptualizations of both sexual and national identities.[21] Approaching queer Arabness as a becoming, rather than being, allows us to think through the potentiality for queerness to allow Arabness to be conceived not as "a static identity but a generous and active one."[22] A queer engagement with Palestine, I argue, can facilitate this reconceptualization and alternative embodiment.

We might approach the entanglement of Palestine with queer Arabness as inspiring an "ethical position of becoming."[23] Part of what I am attempting to point to is the potentiality of what Rosie Braidotti calls "becoming-imperceptible"—identifications and orientations that emerge from the destabilization rather than reification of identity categories.[24] I am pointing to the political potentiality of queer Arab discourses that refuse queer Arab subjects' invisibilization in *both* the West and the Middle East but also refuse to define and stabilize these identities in ways that can make them recognizable or palatable in either of these contexts, approaching the dialogue between queerness and Arabness in ways that destabilize both of these categories and inspire new modes of being towards an otherwise.[25]

It is worth noting that the song "Cavalry" was released in both English and Arabic, with slightly different lyrics accompanying each version. Overall, the English version does read as a translation of the Arabic, with variations in language attributable to how best to capture meaning rather than the desire to present an alternative message. The Arabic language lends itself much more easily to metaphor and poetics than English, and the Arabic version of the song is less direct and plays more with imagery and symbolism. But there are variations in the English that warrant attention. While in the Arabic version Sinno repeats the refrain, "your army and his excellency, have got nothing on me," in the English version they sings, "you and your cavalry, you got nothing on me." The Arabic version addresses, directly, Arab rulers and the Arab ruling class more broadly through this framing using vernacular Arabic—*ma'aleeh* (his excellency)—while the English version's "you" leaves things more open to interpretation. The "you" and their cavalry could be anyone—Arab states, the United

States, and, when coupled with the music video, Israel. And the "me," when coupled with the music video, becomes less obvious, becomes multiple: Is it Sinno, the band, the children, Palestinians, Palestine, or all of them all at once?

In terms of the rationale behind this being the band's first English-language release, members have said it is a response to the band's growing fanbase in the US context in particular. However, it is worth sitting with the fact that the band's first English-language release was one that made undeniable its commitment to the Palestinian cause and its political investment in the Middle East, intervening in a Western discursive context that has otherwise fetishized and exoticized the band and its members as tokens of Arab queerness, and used their work and the violence they have experienced to further solidify a picture of the region as uncivilized and backwards. With this, the band also refuses to become assimilable within the West.

Palestine and Palestinians are presented in "Cavalry" as *method* and as *map*. The coupling of the lyrics and the visuals tell us that for Sinno and Mashrou' Leila, Palestinians have taught them how to live on and, importantly, fight on. As Sinno sings along to a subversive spectacle of unarmed Palestinian children standing up to Israeli soldiers armed with guns and tanks, we can almost imagine or visualize the children's actions as cartographically guiding the lyrics—leading Sinno toward more and more defiant language, to an embrace of steadfastness and perseverance regardless of the odds, regardless of how cyclical or routine defeat has become. Importantly, the band presents children and young girls more specifically as the embodiment of Palestinian resistance and as those with whom it identifies, intervening in the masculinist logic that predominates within the Palestinian liberation movement and questioning who is, in fact, the model of resistance and heroism that one should aspire to emulate.

As Israeli soldiers cut down an olive tree, an elderly man approaches, yelling, "I raised this tree like my own child. Shoot me but don't cut it." As the tree falls and the man is violently dragged away by Israeli soldiers, his grandchildren descend upon his captors. Women and children gather around a military vehicle filled with detained men, screaming at and physically confronting the soldiers. As the vehicle drives away, the young girl with whom the music video begins chases it, screaming for her sibling: "don't worry brother, prison can't take away your freedom." To return to the olive tree, its destruction juxtaposed with the defiance of the children reminds of Chilean poet Pablo Neruda's famed words: "They can cut all the flowers, but they cannot stop the coming of the spring." Resistance, we are shown, always lives on, will always blossom, so long as its affective infrastructure, its visceral soil, is tended to and nurtured.

Sinno sings, "you've got nothing on my heart. You've got nothing on me. At the bottom of every tower is my soil. I sprout as a polished pen." Mountains began as pebbles, Sinno tells us through poetics and word play—Rome wasn't built in a day. And, where strength depends on generating hopelessness and defeatism, every voice raised in defiance is an attack. I am reminded here of an argument not uncommon within the Palestinian context and scholarship on it, that every violent response to Palestinian resistance bolsters that resistance and inspires more of it, fueling a rage against settler colonialism and a commitment to fighting for Palestinian futurity. This is one of the ways in which scholars and activists have made sense of Israel's commitment to *debilitating* rather than necessarily killing Palestinians—to snuffing out their will and ability to resist; to putting out the torch of their fury and their love by isolating them, by slowing or breaking their bodies, by turning them against one another by forcefully creating collaborators, and a host of other mechanisms.

Sinno has described the message of "Cavalry" as one of resistance "against government oppression" and as a call "to fans to continue supporting resistance,"[26] echoing Schotten's framing of queerness as "a kind of commitment to those forms of being deemed troublesome, unnatural, perverse, or fake, a commitment that resonates with Said's decolonising insistence on Palestinian existence."[27] Through "Cavalry's" visuals and its lyrics, then, we could argue that Palestine is presented as queer. Queer Arabs, in all their troublesome-ness as well, emerge as kindred. The liberation of one is dependent on the liberation of the other, the oppression of one is entangled with that of the other, and their resistances feed into one another, sustain one another, help construct and hold up the affective scaffolding needed to persist against the odds, in spite of defeat, toward impossible futures.

"Cavalry" features an Arabic outro in both versions of the song where Sinno sings: "you have your values, and love is ours. You have your customs; we have our music. You have traditions; *we own the future*." The song and music video reveal the importance of cultural production and the value of discursive interventions more generally that are aimed at cultivating affective attachments—that are aimed at guarding the heart(s) that Sinno sings about. We are shown the value of fighting back regardless of the odds or the outcomes because of what that might mean for others—Palestine as method and map—for, in particular, future generations and for those oppressed in other contexts. Queer Arabness routed through Palestine becomes a decolonial politics and a decolonial practice, and Palestine allows the queer Arab to see that regardless of location, they can still intervene in and reshape home; they can still remake the Arab and remake the queer—they need not settle for one or the other, nor for lesser versions of them.

Conclusion: Producing Palestine, Unbuilding Nations

"Cavalry" can be read as a message aimed at multiple audiences. It announces to the West that queer Arab liberation will not come at the expense of Palestine, even for those queers who are not Palestinian. It announces that queer Arabs will not accept a Western embrace if it is contingent on a betrayal of the Palestinian cause. It also announces to the Arab world that Palestine is a queer issue—that queer Arabs and queer Palestinians have always existed in the region and that Palestine is as much their cause as it is anybody else's. Importantly, it also announces that Palestine is an Arab issue in the face of regional nationalisms that rely on a demonization and abandonment of the Palestinian people, now more than ever. It announces that there can be no Arab pride and there can be no Arab freedom until Palestine is decolonized. It announces to queer Arabs that the nation-state, Western or Middle Eastern, will not liberate them, and that, to paraphrase the Combahee River Collective, *none of us are free until all of us are free*. It is an invitation into queerness and Arabness as and through dispossession—to abandon identity and to become *with* and *in* solidarity—with and through abjection and marginalization. It is a call to not abandon queerness or Arabness, to not be made to choose, but instead to resignify both.

As Palestine is forcefully disappeared from Arab national imaginaries; as the Arab world is produced again, is remade, without Palestine, Mashrou' Leila *produces* Palestine as the stuff of queer Arabness. We see the value of cultural production in *undoing the nation*, in nation *unbuilding*, recalling its role in cultivating the nation and solidifying national sentiment and acknowledging that just as it can ideologically and affectively consolidate, it can also subvert.

Notes

1. The title for this section is borrowed from the English version of the Mashrou' Leila song "Cavalry."
2. Leila Farsakh, Rhoda Kanaaneh, and Seikaly Sherene, "Special Issue: Queering Palestine," *Journal of Palestine Studies* 47, no. 3 (2018): 11.
3. The New Arab, "Lebanese Band Mashrou Leila Releases Anti-Occupation Music Video," *The New Arab*, June 8, 2019, https://english.alaraby.co.uk/news/lebanese-band-mashrou-leila-release-anti-occupation-music-video
4. Dhruva Balram, "A Day with Mashrou' Leila, the New Face of Middle Eastern Pop Music," *Dazed*, May 22, 2019, https://www.dazeddigital.com/music/article/44456/1/mashrou-leila-middle-east-pop-band-interview
5. S. Chamas (2021). Lil Watan: Queer patriotism in chauvinistic Lebanon. *Sexualities*.
6. Both English and Arabic versions of "Cavalry" were released. The same music video was released twice with both versions of the song as an accompaniment. Unless otherwise stated, when I address the song's lyrics I am referencing the Arabic version, with all translations being my own. I do engage the English version later in this case, and touch on the significance of this particular song being the band's first English-language release.
7. C. Heike Schotten, "To Exist Is to Resist: Palestine and the Question of Queer Theory," *Journal of Palestine Studies* 47, no. 3 (2018): 15.
8. Zulfikar Ali Bhutto, "Searching for the Next Intifada: Exercises in Queer Muslim Futurism," *Meridians* 20, no. 2 (2021): 443–65; Walaa Alqaisiya, "Palestine and the Will to Theorise Decolonial Queering," *Middle East Critique* 29, no. 1 (2020): 87–113; Walaa Alqaisiya, "Decolonial Queering: The Politics of Being Queer in Palestine," *Journal of Palestine Studies* 47, no. 3 (2018): 29–44; Leila Farsakh, Rhoda Kanaaneh, and Sherene Seikaly, "Special Issue: Queering Palestine," *Journal of Palestine Studies* 47, no. 3 (2018): 7–12.
9. Schotten, "To Exist," 15.
10. Nadine El-Nabli, "'Lakum 'Adatkum wa-Lana al-Musiqa'A critical engagement with the politics of identity, resistance and affect in MashrouLeila's Music," *British Journal of Middle Eastern Studies* 48, no. 1 (2021): 114–29.
11. Ibid., 119.
12. Nadine Naber, Sa'ed Atshan, Nadia Awad, Maya Mikdashi, Sofian Merabet, Dorgham Abusalem, and Nada Elia, "On Palestinian Studies and Queer Theory," *Journal of Palestine Studies* 47, no. 3 (2018): 70.
13. Stefano Harney and Fred Moten, *The Undercommons; Fugitive Planning and Black Study* (New York, NY: Minor Compositions, 2013).

14 As cited in Suzanne Enzerink, "Arab Archipelagoes: Revolutionary Formations and a Queer Undercommons in Saleem Haddad's *Guapa*," *Feminist Formations* 33, no. 1 (2021): 247.
15 Enzerink, "Arab Archipelagoes."
16 Nadine Naber, *Arab America: Gender, Cultural Politics, and Activism* (New York, NY: New York University Press, 2012): 9.
17 Nadia Atia, "Queering the Arab Spring: Belonging in Saleem Haddad's *Gaupa*," *Wasafiri* 34, no. 2 (2019): 54.
18 Lauren Berlant and Elizabeth Freeman, "Queer Nationality," *Boundary 2* 19, no. 1 (1992): 152.
19 Sarah Hamdan, "Becoming-queer-Arab-activist: The case of Meem," *Kohl: A Journal for Body and Gender Research* 1, no. 2 (2015): 66–82.
20 Scott L. Morgensen, "A Politics Not Yet Known: Imagining Relationality within Solidarity," *American Quarterly* 67, no. 2 (2015): 314.
21 Freccero Carla, "Queer Times," in *After Sex? On Writing since Queer Theory*, ed. Janet Halley and Andrew Parker (Durham, NC: Duke University Press, 2011), 17.
22 Bhutto, "Searching for," 451.
23 Hamdan, "Becoming," 77.
24 Rosie Braidotti, "The Ethics of Becoming Imperceptible," in *Deleuze and Philosophy*, ed. Constantin Boundas (Edinburgh: Edinburgh University Press, 2006), 133–59.
25 José Muñoz, *Cruising Utopia* (New York, NY: New York University Press, 2019).
26 Abeer Almahdi, "Mashrou' Leila Echoes Voices of Arab Resistance at Club Soda," *The McGill Tribune*, October 17, 2019, https://www.mcgilltribune.com/a-e/mashrou-leila-echoes-voices-arab-resistance-club-soda/
27 Schotten, "To Exist," 24.

15

Refractions

Helga Tawil-Souri

In 2012, eleven-year-old Ahed Tamimi was caught on a news camera shaking her fist at an Israeli soldier nearly twice her size after the army arrested her older brother (Figure 15.1). Three years later, she made the news again when tugging at and biting a masked soldier squashing her younger brother sitting on and shoving his knee into the boy's torso (Figure 15.2). By then, in 2014, Ahed had already gained international notoriety and solidly become an icon among Palestinians. As with other symbolic instances, and particularly those involving children, Israeli military forces, politicians, and their supporters rushed to accuse the Tamimi family of "exploiting" their children to purposefully portray a negative image of the Israeli occupation as well as accuse international media of glorifying terrorists (an unarmed little girl standing up to military brutality).

Ahed follows a long line of Palestinian children like Mohamad al-Durra (the terrified little kid screaming and crouching under his father's armpit whose killing in Gaza was caught on film in September 2000), Farish Odeh (the kid defiantly standing in front of an Israeli tank with a stone in his hand, killed by the IDF a few days later for throwing stones), and countless others who, upon being filmed or photographed by news cameras, would become icons of resistance. Just as quickly, the children and their images are also pulled in opposing symbolic directions, accused invariably of being human shields by irresponsible or cruel parents, being the instigators of violence, accused of being shot by Palestinian snipers rather than Israeli soldiers, even of faking their own deaths. Ahed Tamimi didn't die, but the fact that she is fair-skinned, green-eyed, and blonde results in often being accused of not even being Palestinian. In fact, the image of Ahed hoisting her fist up to a soldier would circulate on social media, more than ten years later, as a young Ukrainian girl standing up to Russian soldiers.

Ahed Tamimi is from Nabi Saleh, a tiny village in the West Bank, where starting 2009 in response to lands and a natural spring being confiscated by the military for use by a nearby Israeli settlement, residents began weekly protests. The Friday protests were quickly joined by Palestinian, Israeli, and international activists facing off the Israeli military, and lasted regularly until 2016. Nabi Saleh's population is only a few hundred people and residents are from the larger Tamimi family. One of Ahed's uncles, Mustafa Tamimi, was killed by an Israeli soldier in 2011 when shot in the face at close

Figure 15.1 Ahed Tamimi, age eleven, pointing her fist at an Israeli soldier. Abbas Momani, AFP, November 2, 2012. https://www.alamy.com/stock-photo-nov-2-2012-ramallah-west-bank-palestinian-territory-palestinian-girls-51324683.html?imageid=7B5C08EA-25E8-4162-9F43-10A503444896&p=151045&pn=8&searchId=71a3e8161da8e66ada2972230559f821&searchtype=0

Figure 15.2 Ahed Tamimi, left, age fourteen, biting a masked Israeli soldier who is restraining her twelve-year-old brother. Her mother, Nariman, is on the far right, one of her aunts in the middle. Abbas Momani, AFP, August 28, 2014. https://www.gettyimages.com/detail/news-photo/palestinian-girl-and-women-figth-to-free-a-palestinian-boy-news-photo/485541916?

range with a tear-gas canister. Her father, Bassem, has been imprisoned dozens of times for purportedly sending youths to throw stones and marching without a permit. While Mustafa was in prison, another one of Ahed's uncles was killed. These are just some examples among others. As one journalist writes:

> If the resistance against the occupation was going to produce a symbol for these modern times, it was bound to come from a place steeped in the culture of protest and activism—a place where Palestinian protesters and Israeli military forces, media and activists, would gather week after week. It was also bound to emerge from a family like the Tamimis, whose years-long dedication to organizing and documenting the events in Nabi Saleh have made the village infamous.[1]

In 2017, Ahed made international news headlines yet again. The Israeli military stormed into her house and shot her fifteen-year-old cousin Mohammed in the head at close range with a rubber-coated steel bullet, severely wounding him. Ahed, joined by her aunt and her mother, expressed her anger by slapping and kicking a soldier. The scene was livestreamed[2] by Ahed's mother, Nariman, who would later explain about her Facebook livestreams: "If you take a regular video, people will say it is staged, that it's a lie. But when it happens live it is reality."[3] That the Tamimis are savvy users of media speaks both to many Palestinians' belief that if the world only knew what Palestinians suffer through, world opinion would support their struggle, or, conversely, condemn the accusations against them of exploitation.[4] In both perspectives, the importance of media images—or their prevention—is what's at stake (Figure 15.3).

Figure 15.3 Prints of Ahed and others from the Tamimi family used by activists protesting in London calling for the release by Israeli authorities of Ahed Tamimi, December 2017.

A few nights after this particular slap "went viral," the Israeli military detained Ahed under cover of darkness so as to prevent any media coverage and with the help of night-vision cameras; charged her with assault, incitement, and throwing stones; and held her for three months before her trial. After agreeing to a plea bargain, the seventeen-year-old was sentenced to eight months in prison. Her mother would also serve an eight-month prison sentence.

*　*　*

Around the time of Ahed's scheduled release from prison, in August 2018, Italian graffiti artists Jorit (real name Jorit Cerullo Agoch) and Salvatore Tukios were arrested, given seventy-two hours to leave Israel, and barred from re-entry for ten years after painting a mural of Ahed Tamimi on a section of the Separation/Apartheid Wall in Bethlehem. Upon return to Naples, Jorit explained: "I wanted to bring this girl to the attention of public opinion."[5]

Of course Ahed *already had* the "attention of public opinion" since 2011. After all, Jorit, who hadn't yet been to Palestine, had heard of her. It is curious too that the graffiti artist would deem a mural on a wall keeping Palestinians in and others out, as the medium through which international attention could be garnered—he couldn't have meant *Palestinian* public opinion since Ahed was already well-known by then, nor could he have meant *Israeli* opinion since the mural faced the "Palestinian side."[6] Jorit is a well-known artist, nicknamed by some as the Italian Banksy, and, together with Tukios, he has painted murals all over the world of a cast of characters that includes Jimi Hendrix, George Floyd, Antonio Gramsci, Frida Kahlo, Diego Maradona, Che Guevara, and Yuri Gagarin. Jorit's and Tukios' media presence runs the gamut from official Instagram[7] and TikTok accounts to websites.[8] And while their own official accounts are not the primary way in which their work circulates, it *is* presence on various media—rather than on the Wall itself—that sustains Jorit's claim of his graffito, and perhaps Ahed, garnering international attention.

One can come across the picture of the mural of Ahed in the United States, Italian, or other national and international newspapers, on the Associated Press' Twitter account, and on various TikTok and Facebook posts accompanied by any number of possible hashtags (from the personal #ahedtamimi to the geographic #westbank, from the political #resistance to the mediatic #graffiti). At home in New York City, I first encountered the picture of the mural in the image on an Instagram post of Ahed standing in front of the mural of herself holding up a sign of thanks to Jorit. This particular post was by the Palestinian American spoken-word artist Remi Kanazi, who repost the image from the California-based nonprofit organization the Institute for Middle East Understanding, which itself credits it to a Facebook group of a South African Palestinian solidarity group.

I pick on this example not to further iconicize Ahed Tamimi, nor to celebrate or critique foreign artists' graffiti on the Wall, nor to think about the power of images per se. I use this example instead to unpack the relationship between the real and the virtual, between the territorial and the mediated, to think through how the mediated or the virtual impacts the "real" world. In the following two sections, I break down

Refractions 215

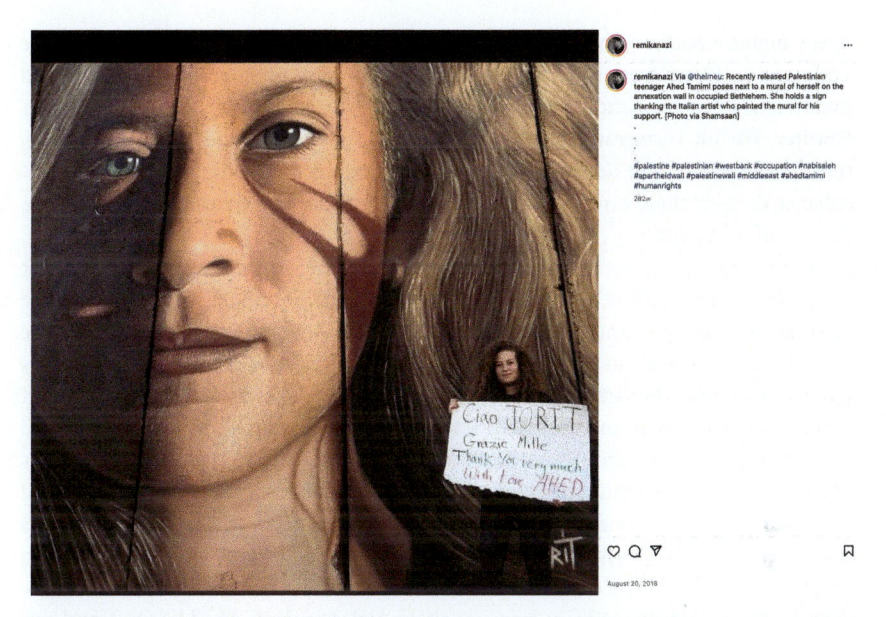

Figure. 15.4 Screenshot of an Instagram page that shows Ahed Tamimi standing in front of the mural of herself on the Wall holding up a sign thanking Jorit, the artist who created the mural. @remikanazi, August 20, 2018.

the image in Figure 15.4 to introduce the notion of a depth of spaces, then address how the grammars of both graffiti and the Wall change once folded into social media and thus create different relations and conceptions of space. The significance of the example is ultimately to demonstrate the transcendence of multiple spaces.

* * *

Figure 15.4 is a screenshot of an Instagram post of a photograph of a girl. She's standing in front of a mural of herself thanking the artist who drew her. The artist painted the mural because the girl already was a symbol of resistance and because he wanted to further her attention. She had become a symbol thanks to news videos and livestream posts of her standing up to Israeli soldiers. In other words, the post includes within it a series of events that led up to its creation: it was determined by a series of events that made the post itself possible.

A quick glance at the post may make one think of a *mise-en-abyme*, a French term denoting the creation of an image within an image that one finds in literature, cinema, photography, or simply by having two mirrors face each other. Translated more literally (*mise* is French for setting up, *abyme* for abyss or depth), *mise-en-abyme* is the action of setting up an image that represents what seems like an immeasurably deep gulf. But the post (and everything that made it possible) is more than that: it is *the setting-up of a seeming depth of spaces*. Like a mirror, the post refracts different and multiple spaces and times: *geographic locations* (Nabi Saleh, the section of the Wall in Bethlehem, Naples, New York City, California, and wherever you dear reader are right now), *physical bodies* (Ahed, her family members, Jorit, Tukios, Israeli soldiers, the Wall, me, and you dear reader), *media artifacts* (graffiti, photographs, recorded and livestreamed videos, hand-written thank-you posters, this book), and *virtual spaces* (Twitter, TikTok, Instagram, Facebook, online newspapers, the document I am typing, the website where you dear reader perhaps purchased this book from). It does not collapse or layer these on top of one another; it includes and transcends them. It is a process of refraction.

Ahed pointing her fist at a soldier on a street in Nabi Saleh in 2011, biting a soldier in an olive grove in 2014, and kicking a soldier outside her house in 2017 were three separate unique space-time events. Ahed standing in front of the mural is also a unique event which took place in a specific location, the same location where Jorit and Tukios painted the mural, the same location where the Israeli military and its contractors built that section of the Wall, and the same location where a Palestinian's home and backyard were confiscated and razed. These events were of course separated by different stretches of time, some of these build directly on each other (the wall is built literally on top of what was someone's home) and some seem more distantly related (the mural is across the street from the Bansky-owned Walled Off Hotel, and thus has little to do with Ahed's notoriety). As the crow flies, Nabi Saleh is 10 miles northwest from where the mural was painted; to get from home to the mural, however, Ahed has to travel five times that distance through circuitous routes and a handful of checkpoints. Jorit and Tukios, living about 1,300 miles further northwest in Naples, likely traveled by plane and car to get from their homes to Bethlehem. While Ahed and Jorit and Tukios had different paths to get to the Wall, it is not difficult to grasp how these were territorial, physical, embodied movements. But the paths that led to their convergence are more complex and dispersed, not only because of the time between them but because of multiple refractions.

A first series of refractions took place in 2011, in 2014, and in 2017[9] when Ahed's territorial, physical, embodied actions were filmed and then circulated across media platforms onto TV, computer, and telephone screens. The real-life events were translated, as it were, into media images that could be consumed in different places and across different times, scenes that traveled beyond Nabi Saleh. Another way to put it is that Ahed's trajectory toward being painted on a mural included having her image circulated, becoming an icon, and being in prison before getting here. Images of Ahed "landed" in Italy where their consumption effected actual, and not simply virtual, change: a decision by a graffitist to travel to Palestine to paint a mural. Another refraction occurred when the face of Ahed was painted, effecting another physical and territorial change, this time on a wall in Bethlehem. The artists documented this part of the process and posted pictures on different media platforms, making what was physical and real (the painting on the wall) travel to virtual space again: other refractions which happen at different moments in time. The changed wall led to other similar productions: for example, passersby and tourists photographed the wall, now with the mural, and post it on Instagram, contributing to the further iconicization and popularization of Ahed as well as the iconization of the wall. The physical effect of the mural on the wall was met with another physical action, that of Ahed standing there. A photo was taken and shared on Twitter and Instagram, creating another refraction when a real event (Ahed standing with the sign) was translated and circulated in virtual space. The original picture was shared and reshared, posted and reposted, refracted again and again, until, in my example, I came across it on my telephone screen thanks to a post by Kanazi. Of course all along these events, other effects and events occur in response to Ahed's videos, Jorit's mural, photographs of the mural, Instagram posts, and so on (see Figure 15.5). The process goes on, in almost infinite possibilities, across physical/territorial and virtual/mediated spaces: each refraction "includes" within it the events that led to its creation, and each subsequently included in whatever next effect it leads to. Each creates a point of departure and the condition for new expression: a seeming depth of spaces.

The social media post that I began with—a photograph of a girl in front of a mural of herself shared on Instagram—is itself an outcome of a series of real and virtual events that were refracted into it, now a media object (an Instagram post) which travels in virtual spaces. But it is misleading to call the post *virtual*.

Had the Israeli military not raided Nabi Saleh, had Ahed never stood up to the soldiers, had videos of Ahed doing so never been filmed and circulated, she wouldn't be standing in front of a mural of herself painted by an Italian holding up a sign thanking him. Had the Wall not been built, had Jorit not gone to Bethlehem to paint the mural,

Figure 15.5 Postcards and magnets made of Jorit's graffiti of Ahed. In one of these you can see Jorit on a ladder in the process of painting. https://www.alamy.com/fridge-magnets-of-16-year-old-palestinian-ached-tamimi-who-gained-world-fame-by-slapping-an-israeli-soldier-and-was-sentenced-to-eight-month-in-jail-in-her-home-in-the-village-nabi-saleh-on-the-west-bank-february-7-2019-foto-eva-tedesjo-dn-tt-kod-3504-image441586955.html?imageid=6E016063-EFFA-40F0-ADC7-2F4540F46C4E&p=1746242&pn=1&searchId=07b34a70b5cf77ee95d568be49f30c26&searchtype=0

had a picture of the mural not been taken and shared on social media, had I not come across Kanazi's post, I would not be writing about this incident. Real-life events led to the creation of the post, just as mediated and virtual objects led to creation of physical, territorial, embodied actions. It is problematic to parse out that some of this process was fully "IRL" (in real life) while other parts where wholly "virtual" since *both* informed the entire process. Refractions are determined by (as in defined by, created as an outcome of) the mix of real events, actual geographies, physical bodies, mediated objects, and circulation in "virtual spaces" that made those refractions possible.

If the separation between the "real" and the "virtual" becomes dubious at best, what then of physical, territorial, and mediated elements? How should we think about something like a wall, or a graffito on a wall?

* * *

The Wall is an infrastructure of violence: a unilaterally imposed artifact by Israel meant to establish facts-on-the-ground following neither accepted borders nor armistice lines and segregating Palestinian communities everywhere it passes. As a physical entity then it can be thought of as already "out of place," in the sense of not belonging where it is. Graffiti[10] by well-known international artists is an objectified and commoditized form of cultural production that often serves the benefit of the artists and those who come to photograph such art rather than Palestinians segregated by the Wall.[11] It should be noted that there has been more than one mural of Ahed on the same wall, and that there are numerous murals of her in various parts of the world, from the Gaza Strip to Uruguay to Australia. She has equally been rendered onto T-shirts, posters, digital art, and many other texts and surfaces (see Figure 15.5). Nevertheless, the Wall itself along with the graffiti painted on it serve as spectacle. As critics rightly claim, such graffiti "presents the overwhelming (ab)use of the wall by international actors to project their own (already amplified) voices."[12] For most Palestinians, any sense of excitement, civil disobedience, or transgression that the act of graffitiing can signify "is completely overshadowed by the monumental vandalism, transgression, and illegality that is the Separation Wall *itself*."[13] In other words, the graffiti on the Wall should not be romanticized, nor should its mocking of the violence of the Wall, as in the case of Banksy's pieces or hotel, be overstated. But they *do* play important spatial roles in understanding the relationship between the real and the virtual. My point is not to suggest that some graffito is going to undo the Wall but rather to "place" the graffito in its location along a series of refractions, without a discrete separation made between "real" and "virtual," and to recognize that the graffito itself is an outcome of different "real" and "virtual" events while also becoming itself included in further "real" and "virtual" actions. I am suggesting that the *very function* of graffiti and the wall change once we consider refraction across multiple spaces.

Graffiti is a form of writing (or drawing) that fills space, consciously created as a claim for visibility. But the visibility is necessarily territorial, situated, and indexed in specific places. As such, graffiti generates territories. Moreover, graffiti, like all art forms and media objects, is open to different interpretations. Graffiti is also ephemeral. The temporal aspect can be understood as paradoxical, since graffiti both preserves a

Figure 15.6 Jorit's completed graffito. Jorit Agoch, CC0 1.0. https://openverse.org/image/b2531e1e-5df3-494f-bcac-41786c10a821?q=ahed%20tamimi

moment but also marks that moment's loss; as one scholar puts it, "the time of erasure or overwriting prefigures all graffiti."[14] Once a surface is graffitied, it often invites others to partake in writing on that same surface. In a sense then, the more a surface is defaced, the more interactive and alive it becomes. Generating territory, being open to interpretation, being both of the moment and ephemeral, and inviting others to participate "in" or interact with it, graffiti offers a different way of relating to a physical/territorial place. The surface may be a specific wall, but in disfiguring the wall, the graffitist reclaims it as a different kind of space (see Figure 15.6). It offers a relation that is open, mobile even.

Once a graffito is photographed it takes on a different and even more mobile grammar. Uploading photos of graffiti to the internet or social media changes the meaning of writing, because it relativizes the spatial and local context, but also the material and physical relationship with the Wall. The circulation of images of the graffiti on the Wall sets the stage for the surface of the Wall to be de-territorialized—to land somewhere else, in a different place and at a different time, no longer tied to itself as a unique time-space. Graffiti circulating "off the wall" is no longer a marker of territory, because the local context loses its importance. The graffito's embeddedness in place is lost. It doesn't mean that the graffito no longer generated that territory, but that it has now been disarticulated from its material context (this in itself is a definition of iconic). The images of the graffito now circulate and land in different places, thus functioning as mobile statements. Territory still plays an important role in another way: included in the graffito are the territorial/physical realities that led to its creation, in this case the series of events when Ahed stood up to soldiers, which themselves were caught on film. The mural wouldn't have happened without those videos, which wouldn't have happened without Ahed's actions. Those embodied, physical, and territorial realities have been subsumed into graffiti now circulating on social media.

The Wall continues to function as a "screen" that eliminates visions, hiding Palestinians behind it. But it now *also* functions as a mediatic screen: attention is paid to its surface, and it portrays and disseminates an image (or a series of images). That surface is itself refracted across other screens: TVs, telephones, computers. As such it is a screen in multiple meanings. It is also a backdrop for the creation of digital content. The graffiti on the Wall is as dependent on social media as it is driven by and responding to social media. Would Jorit (or Banksy for that matter) be graffitiing the Wall if their inscriptions were going to simply stay in place and *not* travel across media? Would their art garner the same kind of popularity? Would they have come to Palestine? Very likely not. Such graffiti is created in great part thanks to technologization, thanks to virtual aspects that not only allow the writing and painting of inscriptions, but their circulation too. When Jorit claims that he wants to bring attention to Ahed, he doesn't mean that the mural *on* the wall will do this, but that the circulation of images of the graffito will. It's not the graffiti nor the Wall that are going to do that work—it is their refractions. If the meaning and the function of the Wall took on a different meaning as a surface for graffiti, it has also now become a character in a social media post.

Instagram, Facebook, Twitter, TikTok, and other social media transform the surface of walls, as well as amplify and accelerate the production of "new" walls. The Separation/Apatheid Wall becomes akin to a mobile or fleeting surface. As one scholar posits with the example of graffiti in Melbourne, Australia: "Instagram also expands the notion of a wall's content, which no longer simply refers to its material structure or visible surface but also its presence within Instagram's 'archive' and as a networked element."[15] Just as graffiti generates territory, now the Wall generates data. It is not simply a wall anymore for it accretes history in a different manner: a surface which grows and changes with each layer of paint added onto it.[16] It becomes a screen that we scroll through, a backdrop for digital content, and a form of digital content itself. The wall becomes transgressive, not in the sense that the physical Wall in a specific location disappears, but in that it challenges static conceptions of space.

Moving graffiti onto the "global window" of the internet and social media builds another a space, a multiplied space. Instagram posts, TikTok videos, websites, YouTube clips, as well as many other examples become the walls of fame that do not erase the Wall but multiply it, increasing its visibility while also disarticulating or dislodging it. They become a force field that animates political energies and sensibilities. The relationship between the real and the virtual, between the territorial and the mediated, between digital technologies and their offline impact, is a set of refractions: an offline event generates an online text which in turn lands into the offline world loaded with the potential gathered from its online and real circulations, which then generates new offline practices and new digital texts, which themselves recirculate anew, and land elsewhere, and on and on. It is a setting up of a space of depth. The power of the image is in the refractions, real and virtual, which it includes and which it enables.

* * *

Notes

1. Yasmeen Serhan, "A Symbol of the Palestinian Resistance for the Internet Age," *The Atlantic*, January 2018. Available at https://www.theatlantic.com/international/archive/2018/01/internet-famous-in-the-west-bank/549557/
2. https://www.facebook.com/nariman.tamimi.1/videos/1941041279245238/
3. https://www.972mag.com/it-is-easy-to-be-a-terrorist-its-much-harder-to-pursue-peace/
4. For a good introduction on the first years of the Tamimi's "homegrown media team," see Ben Ehrenreich, "Is This Where the Third Intifada Will Start?," *The New York Times*, March 15, 2013. Available at https://www.nytimes.com/2013/03/17/magazine/is-this-where-the-third-intifada-will-start.html.
5. https://unita.news/2018/07/30/ahed-tamimi-rilasciata-dopo-8-mesi-di-reclusione-le-donne-sono-una-parte-fondamentale-della-lotta-palestinese-per-la-liberta/
6. Since the Wall is not erected on any official border and serves to separate Palestinian neighborhoods, it is problematic to even suggest that there is such a thing as a "Palestinian side," so I mean this to denote the side from Palestinians are barred from exiting.
7. https://www.instagram.com/jorit/
8. https://www.jorit.it/about
9. Ahed has been filmed more than these three times, but I pick on these as the most well-known and largest-circulating media examples.
10. I am using "graffiti" here to denote a variety of phenomena commonly called tags, graffiti, graffiti art, pieces, murals, stencils, and the like.
11. Julie Peteet, "Wall Talk: Palestinian Graffiti," in *Routledge Handbook of Graffiti and Street Art*, ed. Jeffrey Ian Ross (New York: Routledge, 2016), 338.
12. Ashley Toenjes, "This Wall speaks: Graffiti and Transnational Networks in Palestine," *Jerusalem Quarterly* 61 (2015): 56.
13. Connie Gagliardi, 2020, "Palestine Is Not a Drawing Board: Defacing the Street Art on the Israeli Separation Wall," *Visual Anthropology* 33, no. 5 (2020): 433.
14. David Fieni, "What a Wall Wants, or How Graffiti Thinks: Nomad Grammatology in the French Banlieue," *Diacritics* 40, no. 2 (2021): 75.
15. Lachlan MacDowall, "Walls as Fleeting Surfaces: From Bricks to Pixels, Trains to Instagram," in *Urban Walls: Political and Cultural Meanings of Vertical Structures and Surfaces*, ed. Andrea Mubi Bringheti and Mattias Kärhholm (New York: Routledge, 2019), 237.
16. MacDowall, "Walls as Fleeting Surfaces," 250.

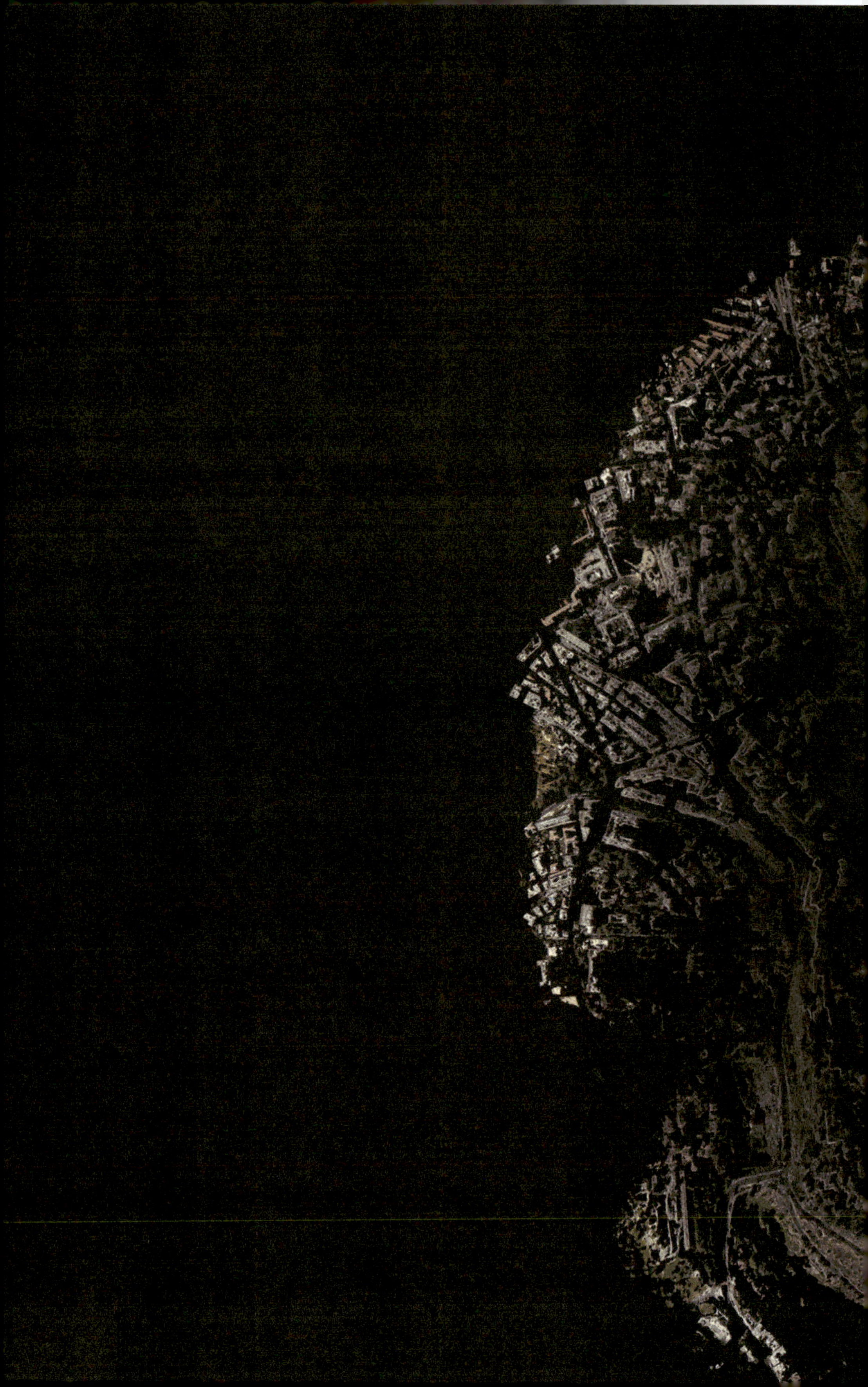

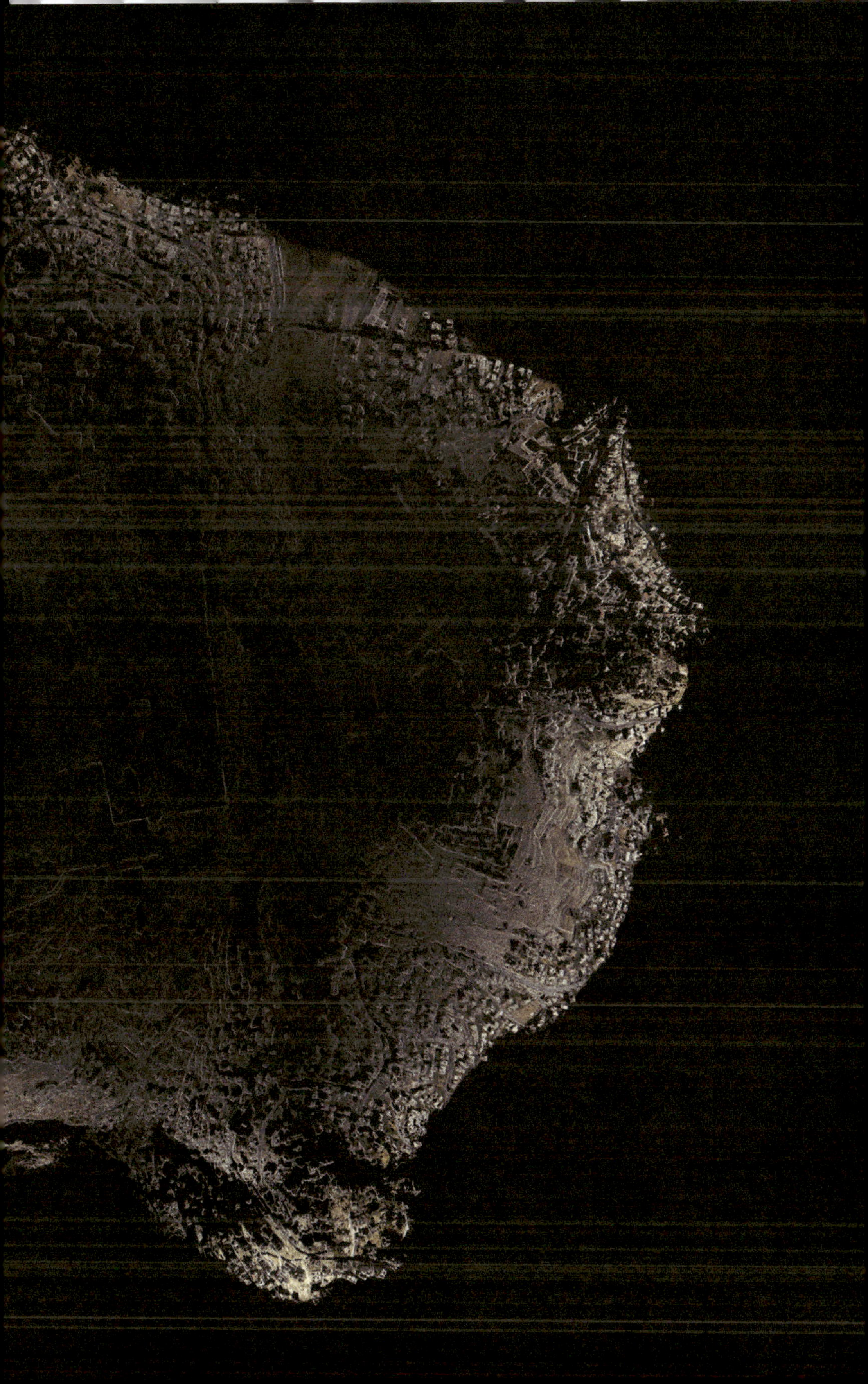

16

Terra ex Machina

Hagit Keysar and Ariel Caine[1]

Jerusalem is a city famous for its walls. The walls of the old city, the infamous separation wall. Yet less known is an invisible wall that encapsulates the old city and its surroundings. Centered on the Haram al-Sharif and spanning approximately 3 kilometers in diameter, this is known as a "geofence," a cylindrical digital barrier from the ground and up into the skies, set to prevent drone flights into or take-offs within the area (Figures 16.2 & 16.5). The volume of this technologically restricted zone follows the geographic coordinates of an already present regulatory no-fly zone (NFZ) that has been enforced by the Israeli security apparatus for more than two decades.

The geofence is a recent technological layer added to the already dense infrastructural sensor stratigraphy of the city. This infrastructure spans wide-ranging volumetric technologies, from underground seismic and waterflow sensors; through heat, sound, and optical street-level surveillance and monitoring systems; to an assemblage of remote-sensing satellite-based mechanisms. However, unlike other layers of surveillance and control, operated locally by state or state-backed actors, the geofence was commissioned by Israel but exclusively controlled and managed remotely by the Chinese drone manufacturer DJI.[2] Its proprietary technology was originally developed in 2015 to help states monitor, regulate, and control the movement of small-scale commercial drones in their sovereign air-space. Yet, sovereignty is a highly contested issue in occupied Eastern Jerusalem, and more so in the holy compound at the heart of this NFZ.[3] In the eyes of the Israeli state, the corporate geofence is a sort of panacea. It attempts to give a definitive, albeit partial, solution to the question of sovereignty in this territory. Its technical invisibility and "remote neutrality" allow it to sink below consciousness. However, as a navigational technology it has real-world effects. It reconstructs space in a machine-readable format, creating a territory that is altered by machines for machines—terra ex machina.

Figure 16.1 Black Hole over NFZ. Point cloud render of Drone flight circumventing the No-Fly-Zone of the Restricted Zone: Temple Mount. 2023.

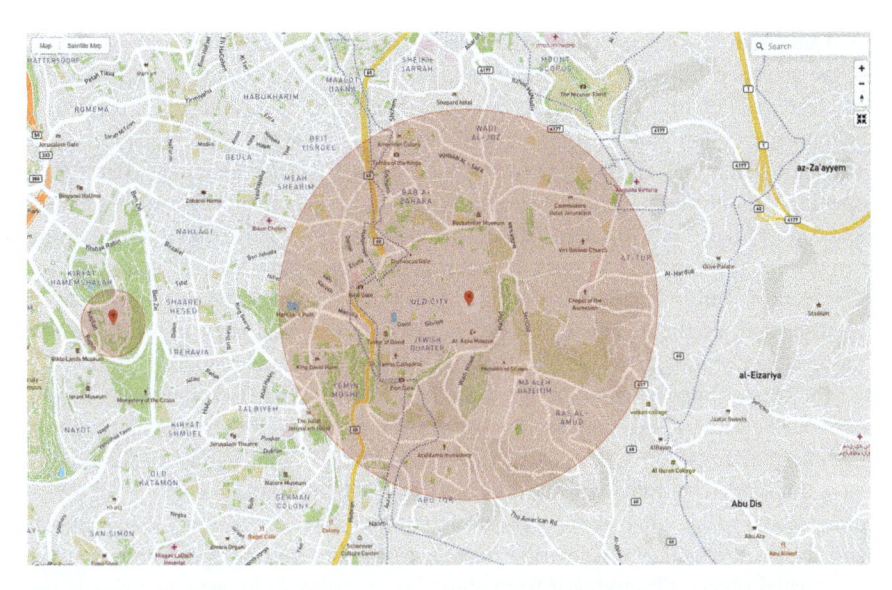

Figure 16.2 The flight restriction zone over the Temple Mount as seen on DJI's website. To its west is the restricted zone above the "Knesset", the Israeli Parliament.

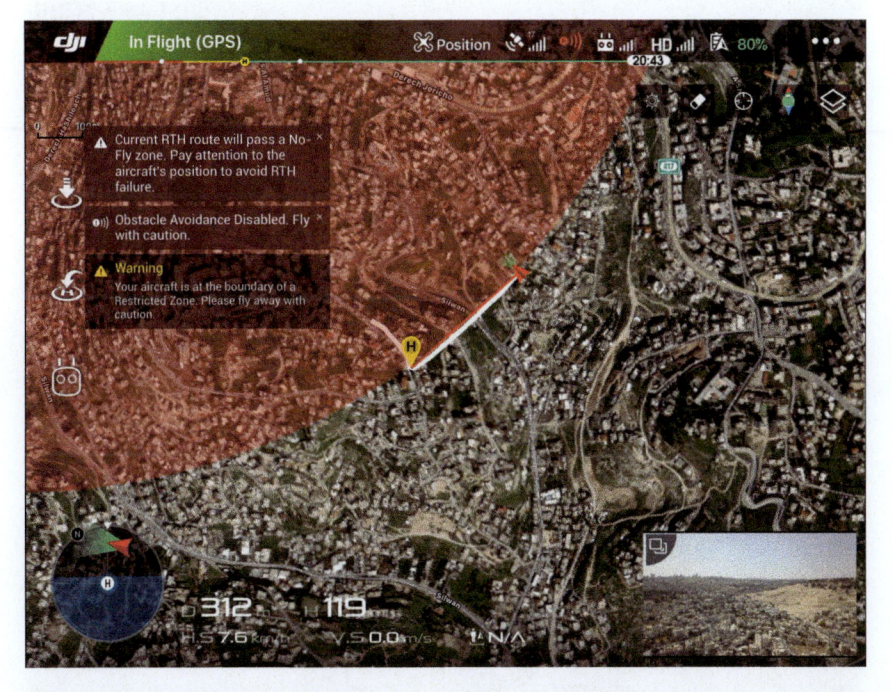

Figure 16.3 Our drone traversing the perimeter of the geofence as seen on the flight's control panel. H signifies "Home", flight starting point, white line is the drone's route, the red triangle is the drone's location, red line is distance from "Home".

This visual chapter looks into the volatile space of Jerusalem through the prism of the geofence. To begin with, we investigate this new invisible technology of aerial and terrestrial control and continue by contrasting it with tactical forms of resistance, balloon/kite photography, that subvert its technological, epistemological, and ontological standing. How can we make visible an invisible barrier and its effects? The opening visualization (Figure 16.1) reflects our experimental endeavor to materialize and conceptualize this invisible barrier. The first stage of our work was to fly a drone toward the geofence and witness the operation of this digital barrier as it suspends the drone in mid-air. After "crashing" against its perimeter, our drone traversed the threshold of the geofence (marked in red); its lens was constantly directed to the epicenter of the restricted zone, the golden dome of Haram al-Sharif.

The three-dimensional point cloud model was computed from the processing of over 10,000 images, taken sequentially along the course of the drone's flight. Using the computational process of "structure from motion", the myriad of viewpoints were transcoded to nodal points, triangulated, and then plotted within virtual three-dimensional space. After weeks of processing thousands of drone images, the material and epistemic effects of this invisible data infrastructure were composed into a visual and spatial object. Observing it from above, as an orthophoto, we could clearly see a circular outer rim of dense visibility, fading gradually toward a sparse, voided center.

Figure 16.4 Screenshots taken from a video documenting lthe drone's flight as it 'crashes against the NFZ.

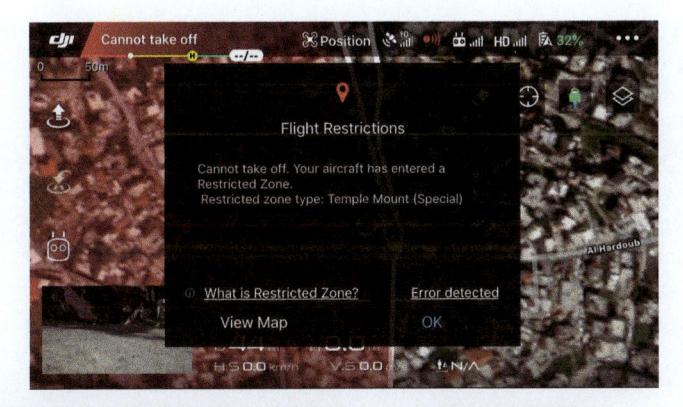

Figure 16.5 "Restricted zone: Temple Mount" is the name of this NFZ in the Israeli civil aviation regulations as well as with the DJI corporation. These images were taken from three different viewpoint: the drones' camera, it's control panel and the radio controller screen.

Because of the geofence's extraordinary size (its perimeter is almost 10 kilometers), in order to circumnavigate it, we had to take off from seven different points along the perimeter. As the drone was in the air, at an altitude of about 100 meters, approaching the restricted zone, we lost sight of it. We could witness it "crash" into the invisible barrier only through the visualization of its movement on the control panel and through the constant voice and text messages warning us from advancing toward a restricted zone (Figure 16.3). At some points in the project, we tested the invisible barrier at street level, only to find the drone hovering in mid-air, disabled (Figures 16.4).

The landscape captured from the drone's line-of-sight is transcoded into discrete spatial coordinate measurement data, positioned within virtual three-dimensional space. In point cloud form, this optical model visually manifests the range of visibility density within the volume of the geofence. It shows the geofence in action, losing accuracy and density of vision toward its center (the Haram al-sharif). When viewing the model from the viewpoint of the drone's lens, it seems complete, showing very little gaps in vision, only a decrease in clarity at the distance (Figures 16.6–16.9). However, once we shift from this prescribed perspective, and freely navigate the model space, we begin to see the voids, gaps, and dissipation of data within this seemingly cohesive optical space. These voids are caused by obstructions to the drones' field of view such as information behind buildings, areas hidden behind hilltops, or within valleys. The voids are a direct result of the distance forced by the geofence itself, amplifying the effect of reduced sharpness, atmospheric haze, and parallax between the drone's images.

228 *Producing Palestine*

Figures 16.6–16.9 Views along the perimeter and toward the center of the geofence, as seen from our 3D model -reflecting the drone's camera gaze and position while flying.

In the first stage of computation,[4] each image within the dataset is scoured by the software in search of high-contrast feature points. Thousands of these feature points are collected per image and are then compared to form a database of shared features between the images. By computing the parallax between these shared features, the photogrammetry software creates the skeletal "sparse cloud," a sparse set of tie-points (green dots in the image 16.10) preserving the basic relations between the original image-set and the 3D environment. It can clearly be seen that the cluster of tie-points which are situated closer to the drone's camera (front of the image) are denser, while those in the background of the image (further away from the drone's camera) are sparser, decreasing in accuracy and density toward the horizon. The 3D model shows the Haram al Sharif as a collection of sparse points (Figure 16.10). Located at the center of the restricted zone, it is also the farthest point from the drone's camera, and therefore, in the point cloud it is visualized nearly as a black hole of sparse data.

The real-world effect of this geofence is a virtual blackout over this part of the city. It means minimizing the multitude of (orchestrated or un-orchestrated) viewpoints that may emerge within this area of protracted conflict at any given time. An image's level of detail is usually determined by parameters of sharpness and resolution. By contrast, point clouds are assessed by their density; their accuracy measured by amount of noise and outlier; the percentage of points which have been erroneously assigned x, y, z position during capture; and their point density. Differing from pixel-based imagery, point density is not a constant parameter but rather it changes throughout the cloud. It is determined by the number of source-images from which computation of the point is derived. The clouds could be likened to a heat-map tracing the intensity of viewpoints as they move and scan the environment. The more the camera moves around an area, examining it from diverse points of view, distances, and heights, the denser and sharper the point cloud will be. The fewer the viewpoints, the sparser and noisier the cloud will be.

Terra ex Machina 231

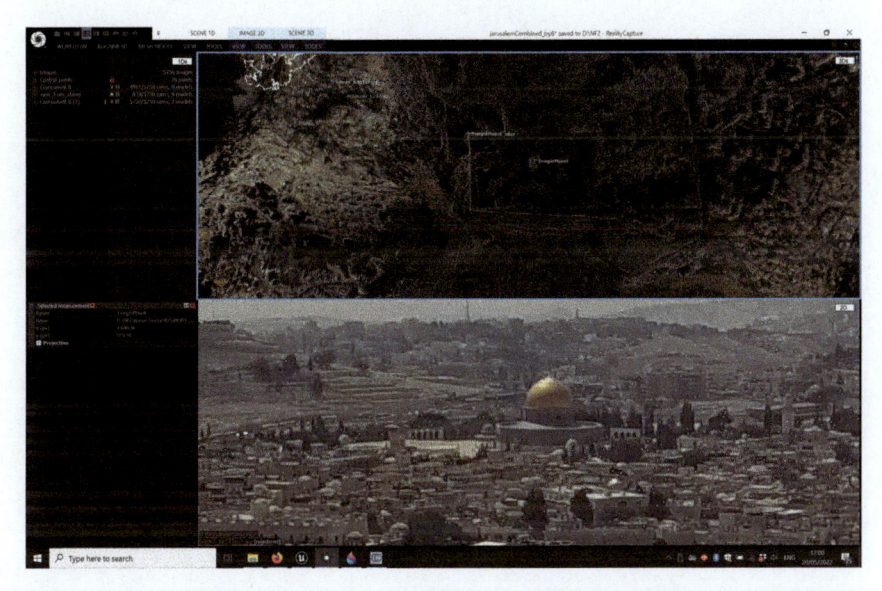

Figure 16.10 Image renders from within our 3D software showing both the sparse pointcloud (top) and identified tie-points on the source images (below).

Figure 16.11 This screenshot shows the list of images (on the left) with three viewpoints of the golden dome along the perimeter of the geofence, and a map of the flight—the route and points along it are marked in light green.

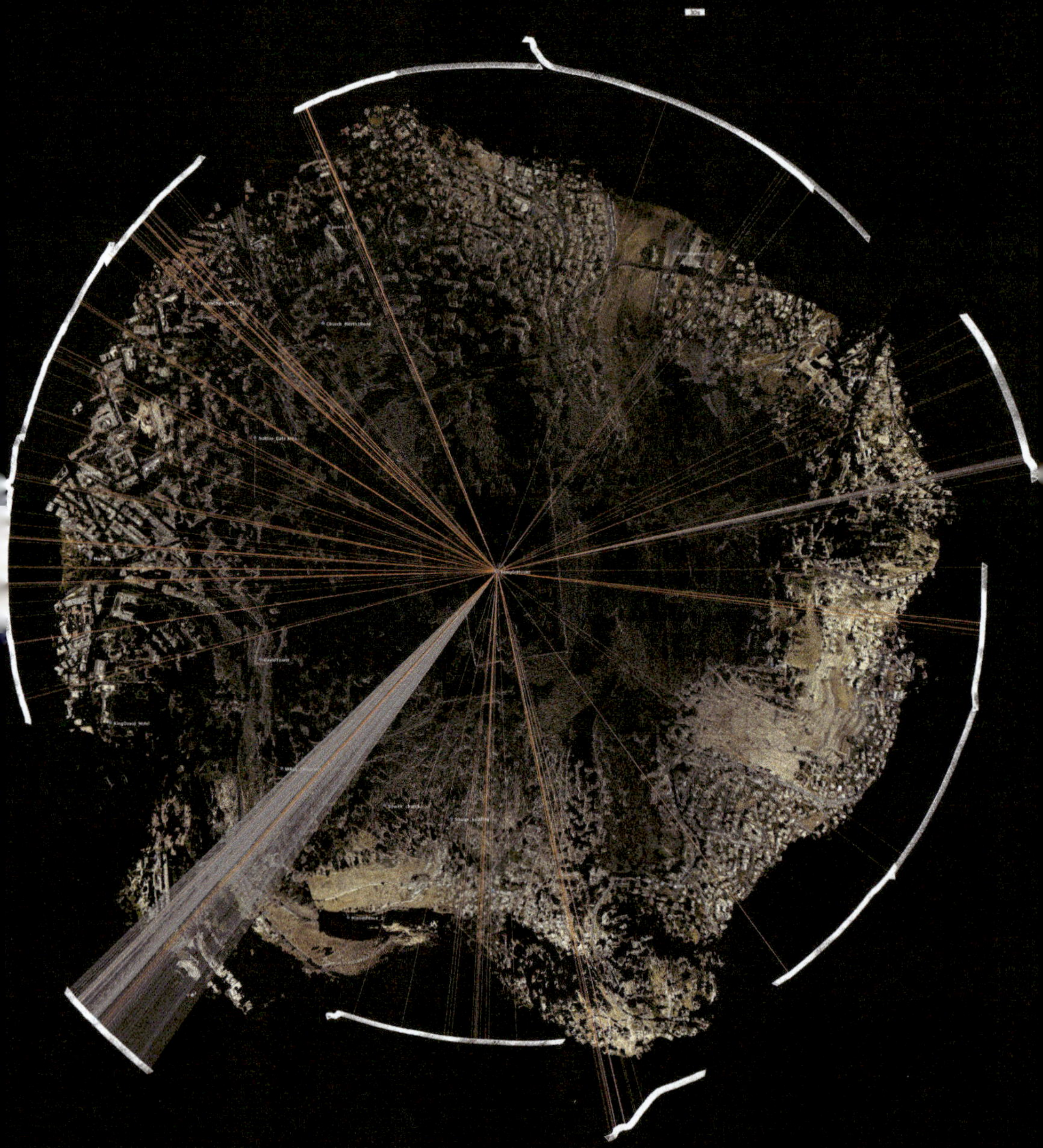

Disrupting the Geofence

The geofence data (geo-coordinates) which are programmed into the drone's GPS system can be hacked in various ways and the ban can be circumvented.[5] It can also be decoded by DJI. Having said that, even if the ban is decoded, flying a drone in eastern Jerusalem is highly restricted and can be risky. Nonetheless, there is no algorithm (yet) that can ban the flight of a camera tethered to a kite or helium balloon.

Between 2011 and 2016 coauthor Hagit Keysar created do-it-yourself aerial photographs with residents, activists, and researchers in Israel/Palestine, using balloons and kites.[6] Each photographic map embeds situated knowledge that defies the myth of turning the aerial view into a gaze from nowhere. We used open hardware and software (developed by publiclab.org) which simulates a pocket camera that is handheld by proxy of a kite. This age-old technique which was reinvented in the 2010's as a tool for civic and community science calls for unlearning some of the invisible barriers that inform and construct our ways of seeing, knowing, and living in the world. Namely, our understanding of expertise, our relations with technological instruments and images, as well as related forms of authority and practices of truthmaking.

In each kite or balloon flight, hundreds of images are created. Only a dozen are chosen for stitching a geo-rectified orthophoto, using an open-source, easy-to-use software.[7] In this project, we returned to DIY aerial images taken during flights in three locations within the NFZ (in Silwan, Jaffa Street and Sheikh Jarah) and reprocessed them into 3D photogrammetric models. (Figures 16.21–16.23). This way, the three pointclouds could be embedded within the 3D model of the geofence (Figure 16.24).

The exact route our drone took in circumnavigating the geofence can be seen in the model through the white markers of triangulated images. The breaks in the route signify the various flights we had to conduct in order to traverse the entire stretch of the geofence. In the images we can see the route of the kite/balloon flight, as it is sent off by people standing on the ground and later retrieved back to their hands (Figures 16.19–16.22).

Data infrastructures are becoming increasingly dominant in managing the various layers of everyday life and rapidly shaping technopolitical futures. The invisible mechanisms and the tacit decisions that structure data make it hard to audit and critique it. This invisibility fertilizers a dominant discourse that treats such technologies as neutral and apolitical solutions to complex problems. For us, the geofence became an instructive case study for critically examining these new digital forms of power. It started with an intuitive question, a curiosity to see how the geofence works in real-time and space, and continued with a few iterations of developing a way of seeing that makes this digital barrier public. The 3D model turned it into a thing that is in the world, visible and legible for humans, that can in turn ask questions about it. Our efforts to make seen an inherently invisible data infrastructure that can only be seen and experienced by a drone system have opened unexpected opportunities for audit, critique, and intervention.

Figure 16.12 A vertical view of the model. It shows all the camera viewpoints manually linked and verified to the Haram al-Sharif 's ground control point (marked in white) calculated along the route of the drone..

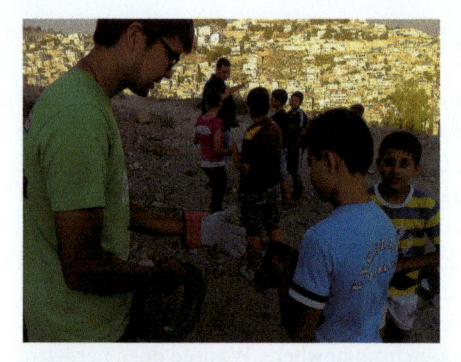

Figure 16.13 Jeffrey Warren, developer of the technique, and children from Silwan creating aerial images using a kite. July 2011. Photo: Shai Efrati.

Figure 16.14 Image taken over Bab a-Zahra, Sheikh Jarah, by a camera tethered to a balloon during a demonstration.

Figure 16.15 Silwan. Kite mappers captured by the camera in flight, July 2011.

Figure 16.16 Silwan kite flying, July 2011.

Figures 16.17 and 16.18 Images taken by a camera tethered to red balloon during a flight from the roof of "Jaffa 23" Gallery, Bezalel. May 2014.

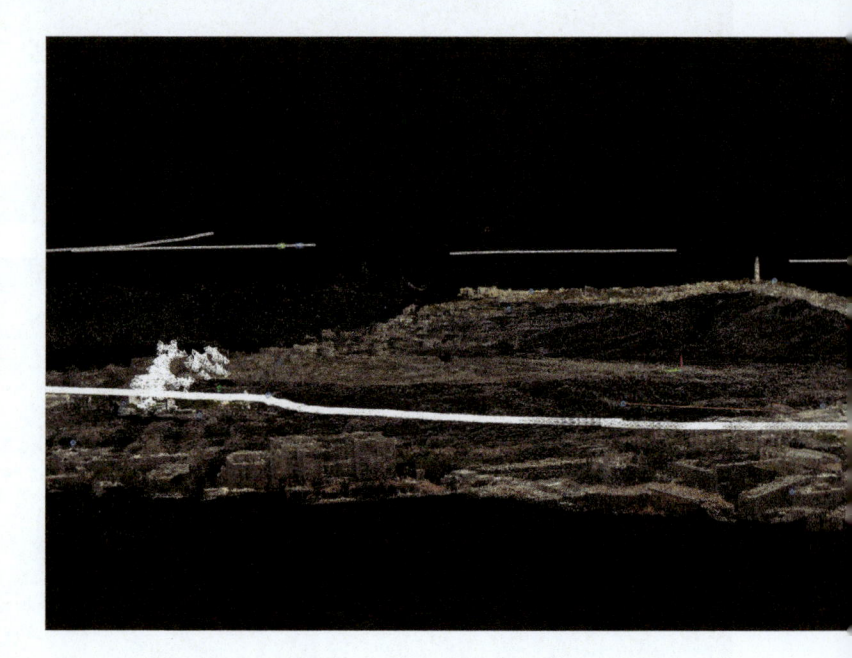

Figure 16.19 Photogrammetry model computed from 358 images from Bab a-Zahra, Sheikh Jarah, Jerusalem. 2011/2023.

Figure 16.20 Photogrammetry model computed from 726 images from flight over the Jaffa Gate area, Jerusalem. 2014/2023.

Terra ex Machina 237

Figure 16.21 Photogrammetry model computed from 859 images from Wadi Rababa, Silwan, Jerusalem.2011/2023.

Figure 16.22 Panoramic render of the photogrammetry model with camera locations combining the NFZ drone flights with the three DIY aerial flights photogrammetry models. 2011/2014/2018/2023.

The drone turned into an indispensable research device, without which the virtual turnstile of the geofence cannot be detected. Indeed, we could visualize the experience of encountering the geofence through system warnings seen in the control panel's annotated satellite imagery. But it wasn't until we reconstructed the restricted space itself through photogrammetry that we were able to make this technopolitical restriction an actual thing, a discrete object rather than distributed and dissociated effects in the world. Like the digital barrier produced by DJI, the reconstructed space we have created is machine-made (photogrammetry) and is based on a non-human data gaze (the drone's GPS-led camera).

However, in contrast to the geofence technology that reconstructs space by machines and for machines, our concluding image turns the data-gaze on its head by reaffirming the irreducible and recalcitrant nature of human agency. Here, the black hole of missing data "blushes" with highly dense visual data retrieved from cameras tethered to balloons and kites, and tightly connected to people on the ground in different places and times. Drawing on Ursula Le Guin's metaphor, we take the "blackout" created by the geofence as a "carrier bag,"[8] which has the capacity to gather and collect that which cannot be reduced into one dominant story. The carrier bag collects, preserves, and maintains the multiplicity of life and experience, its contradictions, and frictions. Terra ex machina is, nonetheless, socially contextualized, situated, and positioned in everyday life.

Notes

1 This project was undertaken in collaboration with Barak Brinker, drone operator and VR specialist.
2 DJI is the largest drone manufacturer globally. It is a leading company in manufacturing civilian drones by capturing over 70 percent of the global drone market (Statista, 2023).
3 Israeli Sovereignty over occupied east Jerusalem and the West Bank was self-declared and instated unilaterally following the 1967 war. Jerusalem's municipal borders were expanded beyond the pre-1967 lines incorporating the entire "holy basin" and extending well into the west bank while sustaining ongoing violations of international human rights and humanitarian law. The postwar status quo stated that the holy compound will be managed by the Islamic Waqf under Israeli supervision. Nonetheless, in recent decades Israeli politicians and right-wing activists have been working toward strengthening Israeli presence and control in the holy compound while weakening the status quo.
4 Photogrammetry is the science of computing spatial and three-dimensional measurements of an object or a scene from sets of two-dimensional perspectival photographs recording it from multiple viewpoints.
5 This includes software hacks that circumvent the electronic restrictions enforced by the ban, or do-it-yourself methods that tinker with the drone's GPS system. One example that demonstrates resistance against this form of spatial control in the old city is a drone flight by an operator in eastern Jerusalem who managed to bypass the ban and raise a Palestinian flag tethered to a drone in protest of the violent Flags March on May 30, 2022, "Jerusalem Day," by religious nationalist Israelis. The drone

was shot by the Israeli authorities and the operator was allegedly arrested. Link to video: https://bit.ly/3T9LZ23
6   Hagit Keysar, "Who Owns the Sky? Aerial Resistance and the State/Corporate No-Fly Zone," *Visual Studies* 35, no. 5 (2020): 465–77.
7   The software developed by public lab, Mapknitter.org, is no longer operational.
8   K. Le Guin Ursula, "The Carrier Bag Theory of Fiction," *Dancing at the Edge of the World: Thoughts on Words, Women, Places* (1989): 149–50.

Figure 16.23 Black Hole over NFZ. Point cloud render of Drone flight circumventing the No-Fly-Zone of the Restricted Zone: Temple Mount. This model includes the clusters of Data formed through use of models from DIY Kite mapping. 2023

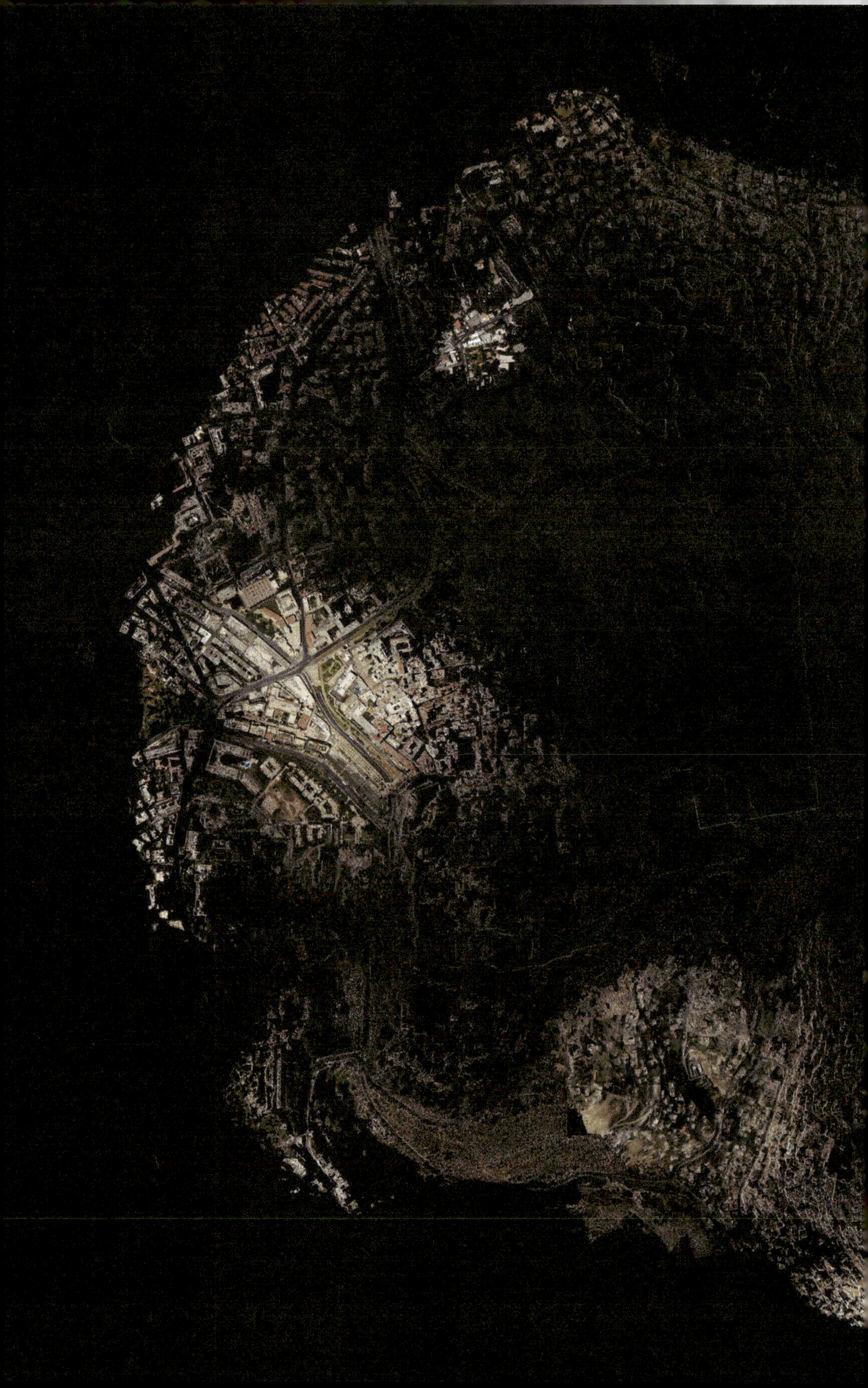

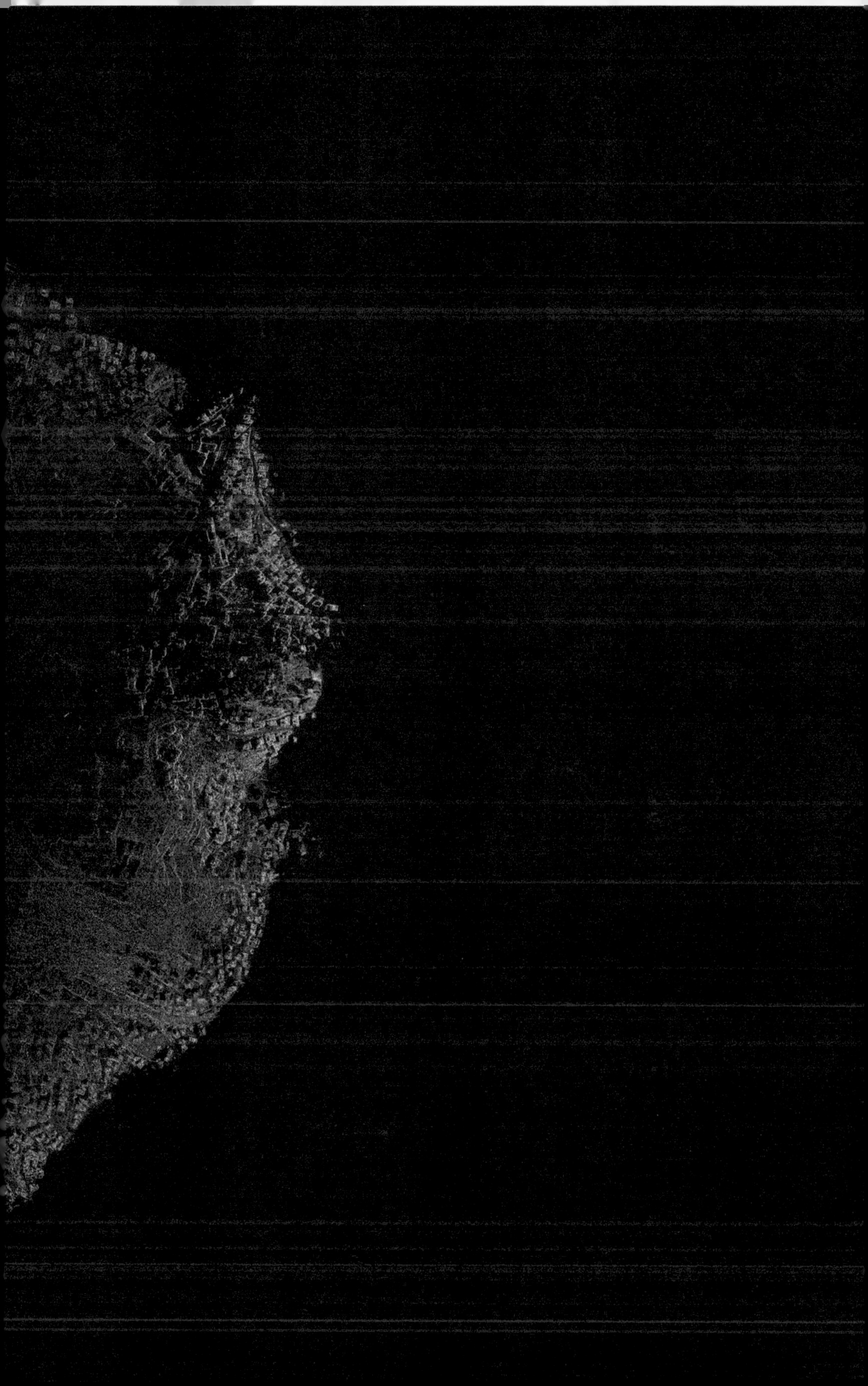

Epilogue

A month into Israel's latest tantrum obliterating the Gaza Strip, we are faced with intensified, horrific violence that is material, affective, discursive, and more. Our bodies, our psyches, our infrastructures, our ways of living, our histories, and our futures are assaulted anew: in Gaza most perniciously, but also elsewhere. Along with those who stand with us, we are also faced with violence that silences, censures, and criminalizes (or certainly attempts to) our voices and our very existence—a violence inexorable to the ongoing Zionist settler-colonial project, buoyed by the West.[1]

While penning this epilogue, this renewed and magnified violence seems to have upended what many of us had hoped we were nearing: a point when Palestinians' existence, aspirations for dignified life, and demand for rights weren't conditional or debatable; a point when Palestinians didn't *still* need to request permission to narrate; a point when Palestinians were not purposefully manufactured out of the frame, let alone through outright disinvitations, omissions, lies, and obfuscations.

We may be in shock, yet we are not entirely surprised. Given the century-long history of dispossession and silencing of Palestinians and destruction of Palestinian life worlds, we know that (self)representation and production were and remain contestable, as so much about Palestine is.

And yet, despite the accumulation of ruination that we carry across generations, despite the renewed carnage of Gaza, despite the libel and censuring, we do stand at a different juncture. A moment different than say, 1984, when Edward Said published "Permission to Narrate"; or even 2009, when Israel went to great lengths to prevent foreign journalists from entering or reporting from Gaza, trying to prevent documentation, while dropping bombs and wreaking lives. These practices—of silencing, stifling, killing—continue today, but they have also been ruptured.

In this moment, Palestinian voices, images, stories, and representations are produced and circulated in ways they previously hadn't. We do not need permission to narrate everywhere: there *are* academic, artistic, popular, and other kinds of spaces where we (and our supporters) perform, express, speak, and are heard, seen, and understood. Documentation of atrocities and of survival in Gaza *do* escape Israel's territorial and mediatic siege: through Palestinians' Instagram accounts, e-sim connections, Hamas' and other movements' Telegram channels, even Israeli soldiers' TikTok posts. Much of the world's population—even if not official representatives—recognizes and supports Palestinian demands for political rights, or, perhaps more simply, demands for life void of constant violence. "Pro-Palestine" demonstrations are widespread across the world. Solidarity networks continue to expand. Social media is awash with Palestinian and supporters' perspectives. Legal cases against those who silence or slaughter us are being filed and considered.

We owe the existence and increase of these actions, or this fissure in hegemonic structures, in part to the response to genocidal threat which the violence from October 2023 onward has made (more) tangible. We also owe some of this to the realization across widening circles that Palestine "occupies a symbolic place as an avatar of rebellion against Western hypocrisy and an unjust postcolonial order"[2]—of course, Palestine is more than symbolic and more than an avatar, but the point remains that Palestine is part of, and increasingly understood as interlinked with, various forms of oppression *and* of struggle. We may equally owe some of this to an increase in academic courses on Palestine, in activist manifestos, identity politics, or the rise of the collective voice of the Global South.

But we also owe this to the continuous production of Palestine.

The urge and the action to document, to record, to describe, to perform, to express, to archive—in short, to *produce*—Palestine is not created only in response to or as a challenge against violence, dehumanization, or silencing; nor does it exigently draw on historical points chosen by Zionism, Israel, or others. We can and do produce without being held in opposition to others' political or institutional objectives, whether material, discursive, psychic, or otherwise. The production of Palestine also traces roots and intertwines with circuits outside hegemonic constraints in all kinds of ways. We use our own slang, we have our own idioms, we connote our own meanings, and we reuse our own materials. What we produce, what we choose to mediatically (re)produce, imbricates our fabrics, herbs, utensils, colors, and fruits. We claim our own ruins, children, and martyrs, and decide which we render into symbols. Palestinians have agency. And production requires agency.

Producing Palestine was conceived with the aim of addressing this discernible increase in the production of Palestine—through ("new") technologies, screens, infrastructures, ways of doing: new permissions if you like. It was also conceived with the hope of accessing, and making accessible, Palestine through the process of its production.

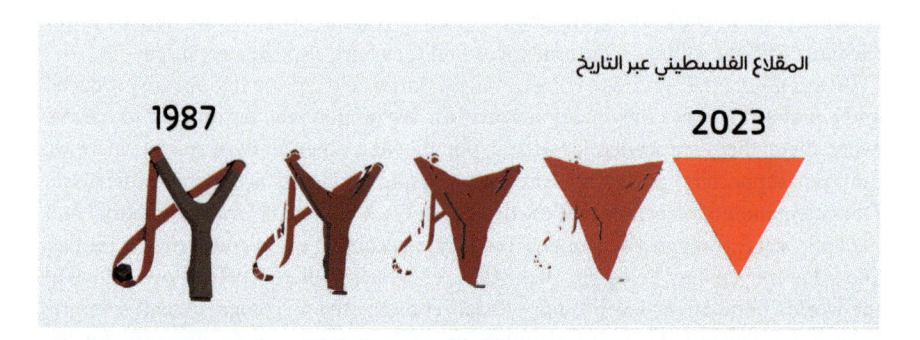

Figure E.1 Palestinian Slingshot, Courtesy of Ahmad N. Shaqour.

Epilogue

The cases in this volume were mostly written between late 2021 and early 2023. Many, now, seem prescient in light of the wars waged on Gaza and on our screens (or might seem like a response to these wars when you are reading this): Abu Obaida, the *keffiyeh*, the image of a paraglider, the importance of food (and starvation), revolutionary posters, digital maps, death and reincarnation, Ahed Tamimi, the transgression of borders, the watermelon, avatars, the accumulation of ruins, questions about exile, return and the day after, and so on. In fact, many of these have taken on renewed forms and meanings since these cases were first conceived and written, and will undoubtedly be disseminated, seized, and appropriated again (and again) in ways unforeseen. They equally already are and will be joined by new "icons"—like the red triangle, evoking, in the sliver of the Palestinian flag, continued struggle, but in shifting forms.

This volume was also conceived to explain, enable, make visible, and activate imaginations of Palestine that are always in conversation with its real and its imagined spatiality and temporality, but that inevitably take place in the present moment.[3] Indeed, it is precisely because of the incessant attempt to obliterate and silence Palestinians that it becomes even more important to document what is produced in the *now*. The volume, as originally intended, is not focused on speculation, or the what if,[4] but on the labor and act of creating, uncovering these acts, and seeing their layers. As Larissa Sansour, the filmmaker, claims: "It is hard to talk about the Palestinian trauma without addressing several tenses, and histories. The Palestinian psyche seems to be planted in the catastrophic events of 1948 and is tied to a constant projection of the future, yet the present is in a constant limbo."[5] It is this constant limbo, this kind of temporal immobility, time on hold, stuckness, that speaks back to Palestinians' spatial immobility and to the inaccessibility of Palestine, that production speaks to.

This volume was further conceived to foreground production as a way of addressing the tension that remains around the question of representation. If the mantra of Palestinian revolutionary cinema in the 1960s was gun in one hand and camera in the other, today it seems more apt to say that with one hand we record and document, and with the other hand, we shoo the recorder and camera away. The question Palestinians seem to still be debating is of what use are (more) images or words when Palestinians are (still) being killed, vilified, and silenced?

There have long been efforts by scholars and non-scholars alike to think through this tension as well as address, and redress, the uneven representations of Palestine and Palestinians. As Ella Shohat explains, "[t]he denial of aesthetic representation to the subaltern has historically formed a corollary to the literal denial of economic, legal, and political representation. The struggle to 'speak for oneself' cannot be separated from a history of being spoken for, from the struggle to speak and be heard."[6] This is in part why we have asked for "permission to narrate." The question of the distribution of visual "rights" (who is visible, who remains invisible, who can see, whose vision is compromised, whose vision is unabated, and so on) has also been, and continues to be, pondered, and critiqued. In the 1970s, we targeted media no differently than the subjects of our wrath, enacting terror to get ourselves heard and seen. In the 1990s, a great deal of mediatic production and self-representation was in the service of bearing witness to our suffering and thus advocating for (human) rights, oriented mostly toward a nebulous "global public opinion."[7] By the 2000s, particularly in curatorial and archival practices, there was growing interest in the aesthetics of the everyday, in centering the quotidian and existential realities of Palestine.[8] These tropes remain, as do questions of representation. Visibility *is* a matter of claiming power. This is in part why we have seen our struggle as related to the representational, the discursive, the mediatic.

Much journalism and mainstream media claims to address the representational, but continues to be plagued by ahistoricity, decontextualization, and bias, *especially* in the context of Palestine. This is not a new claim. In the Palestinian context, the shutdown of communication networks, the prohibiting of foreign journalists, the killing of local journalists, the shadow banning and censuring of social media posts and accounts, all demonstrate the struggle over visibility and the power ascribed to visibility by those attempting to obstruct us from view. At the time of writing, one Palestinian journalist is being killed every twenty hours in Israel's nonstop bombardment of Gaza. But also at the time of writing, the Gazan photojournalist Motaz Aizaza has garnered more followers on Instagram than the president of the United States (and sixteen times more than Israeli prime minister Netanyahu or than the IDF). Even under the most atrocious conditions, Palestinians will still produce, create, post, share, reshare, and be "followed."

If anything has become clear in this moment, it is that a better account is needed for the "representational impasse" (as Roopika Risam calls it) that we find ourselves in. On the one hand, there exists continued misrepresentation, bias, erasure, silencing, and obfuscation, and on the other hand, growing presence, louder voices, global awareness, and solidarity.[9]

The second part of the equation (awareness, presence, solidarity) has a great deal to do with the possibility—or access—that "new" media provides: selfies, blogs, v-logs, self-produced videos shot on phones, live webcam footage, surveillance cameras, camera-mounted consumer drones, GIS mapping, photoshopping, and so on. Today, Palestinians perform Palestinianness through recording videos, photographs, sound bites and text, and uploading and sharing them, in ways that are purposeful and also ad hoc. "New" media offer us a chance to redress misrepresentations, but they also, and arguably more often, offer us a means to participate in forms of production and circulation that have largely been denied to us historically, whether in mainstream media or institutional media (whether Palestinian [PLO, PA], Western [mainstream or not], or otherwise). They allow us to produce.

"Production," as we've intended it in this volume, allows us to reinscribe Palestinians as creators and objects of knowledge—knowledge that is generated, not unearthed or discovered. Producing Palestine is open to the complexity of the social. It allows us to ask not whether media produces the nation, but to suggest that the act of mediation itself *is* the production of the "nation."

The production of Palestine is not a field of detached, marginal, or virtual expressions but a real field of conflict.[10] It is also a field that does not lead us to a conclusion. Producing Palestine is part and parcel of an ongoing process of creation and destruction, representation and erasure. The question is not whether there is an inherent limit in the representational, nor how the representational is connected to the material; the question is what is being produced? For production grounds us in the act of making. Production involves us in and keeps us engaged with the world.

Notes

1. We follow Samera Esmeir's description of "the West" not as a set of states or a geographical place, but a "project that continues to violently universalized itself." Samera Esmeir "To Say and Think a Life beyond What Settler-Colonialism Has Made," *Madamasr*, October 14, 2023 [https://www.madamasr.com/en/2023/10/14/opinion/u/to-say-and-think-a-life-beyond-what-settler-colonialism-has-made/]
2. Tony Karon and Daniel Levy, "Israel Is Losing This War," *The Nation*, December 8, 2023 [https://www.thenation.com/article/world/israel-gaza-war/]
3. See for example Nayrouz Abu Hatoum, "Decolonizing [in the] Future: Scenes of Palestinian Temporality," *Geografiska Annaler: Series B, Human Geography* 103, no. 4 (2021): 397–412.
4. We intend "production" different than Gil Hochberg's "becoming"—the latter geared towards an "ability to imagine otherwise—to take a risk and let go of the investment in predefined collectives configured in familiar political categories (nation-state, ethnicity, nativity, etc.), and in favor of new and still unrecognizable collectives of/for the future" (p. xi). Gil Z. Hochberg, *Becoming Palestine: Toward an Archival Imagination of the Future* (Durham, NC: Duke University Press, 2021). This "becoming" is also echoed in Greg Burris' "radical imagination" in that Palestinians have a right to dream. Greg Burris, *The Palestinian Idea: Film, Media, and the Radical Imagination* (Philadelphia, PA: Temple University Press, 2019).
5. Quoted in Hoda El Shakry, "Palestine and the Aesthetics of the Future Impossible," *Interventions* 23, no. 5 (2021): 669–90, p. 670.
6. Ella Shohat, "The Struggle over Representation: Casting, Coalitions, and the Politics of Identification," in *Late Imperial Culture*, ed. R. De La Campa, E. A. Kaplan, and M. Sprinker (New York, NY: Verso, 1995), 166–78, p. 173.
7. Lori Allen, "Martyr Bodies in the Media: Human Rights, Aesthetics, and the Politics of Immediation in the Palestinian Intifada," *American Ethnologist* 36, no. 1 (2009): 161–80.
8. Hoda El Shakry, "Palestine and the Aesthetics of the Future Impossible."
9. Roopika Risam, "Now You See Them: Self-Representation and the Refugee Selfie," *Popular Communication* 16, no. 1 (2018): 58–71.
10. Echoing Said's "production of knowledge is a real field of conflict." Edward Said, "Zionism from the Standpoint of Its Victims," *Social Text* 1 (1979): 7–58, p. 17.

Bibliography

Abbas, Basel and Ruanne Abou-Rahme. "Being in the Negative," *Cooper Union Talk*, September 21, 2021.

Abbas, Laila, Shahira S. Fahmy, Sherry Ayad, Mirna Ibrahim, and Abdelmoneim Hany Alim. "TikTok Intifada: Analyzing Social Media Activism among Youth," *Online Media and Global Communication*, June 8, 2022.

Abdel Jawad, Saleh. "A Palestinian Sociocide?" Russell Tribunal on Palestine, January 8, 2013. New York, https://youtu.be/fd_tx9-r25s (Retrieved on 5.7.2022).

Abdelal, Wael. *Hamas and the Media: Politics and Strategy*. London: Routledge, 2016.

Abdo, Nahla. *Captive Revolution: Palestinian Women's Anti-Colonial Struggle within the Israeli Prison System*. London: Pluto Press, 2014.

Abdulla, Danah and Pedro Vieira Di Oliviera. "The Case for Minor Gestures," *Diseña* 22 (2023).

Abourahme, Nasser. "Boycott, Decolonization, Return: BDS and the Limits of Political Solidarity," in *Assuming Boycott: Resistance, Agency, and Cultural Production*, ed. Kareem Estefan, Carin Kuoni, and Laura Raicovich. New York and London: OR Books, 2017, epub.

Abourahme, Nasser. "Revolution after Revolution: The Commune as Line of Flight in Palestinian Anticolonialism," *Critical Times* 4, no. 3 (2021).

Abourahme, Nasser and Laura Ribeiro. "Re-weaving Fragmented Space-Time: Notes from a Mapping Project in Palestine," *Lo Squaderno* 15 (2010): 37–43.

Abu Assab, Nour. "Queering Narratives and Narrating Queer: Colonial Queer Subjects in the Arab World," in *Queer in Translation*, ed. B.J. Epstein and Robert Gilett, 33–46. London: Routledge, 2007.

Abu el-haj, Nadia. *Facts on the Ground: Archeological Practice and Territorial Self-Fashioning in Israeli Society*. Chicago: University of Chicago Press, 2001.

Abu Ghoush, Dima. *Emwas: Restoring Memories*, 2016, https://www.youtube.com/watch?v=GaZLp0d6vFA, last accessed January 21, 2023.

Abu Hatoum, Nayrouz. "Decolonizing [in the] Future: Scenes of Palestinian Temporality," *Geografiska Annaler: Series B, Human Geography* (2021).

Abu Hatoum, Nayrouz and Hadeel Assali. "Attending to the Fugitive: Resistance Videos from Gaza," in *Gaza on Screen*, ed. Nadia Yaqub, 136–56. Durham: Duke University Press, 2023.

Abu Khadra, Fahed. *Al-Layl wa-al-Hudud* (The Night and the Borders). Nazareth: Al-Hakim, 1964 [Arabic].

Abu-Sitta, Salman. *The Palestinian Nakba, 1948: The Register of Depopulated Localities in Palestine*. 2000.

Abu-Sitta, Salman. *Mapping My Return: A Palestinian Memoir*. Cairo: The American University in Cairo Press, 2017.

Abuasad, Farrah, Lama Bazzari, and Fadi Kattan, eds. *Craving Palestine: Soulful Recipes and Inspiring Stories Celebrating Community and Giving Back*. Santa Barbara: Story Farm, 2020.

Abufarha, Nasser. "Land of Symbols: Cactus, Poppies, Orange and Olive Trees in Palestine," *Identities* 15, no. 3 (2008): 343–68.

Acosta, Gladys. *Day of World Solidarity with the Struggle of the Palestinian People* poster produced for the Organization of Solidarity with the People of Africa, Asia and Latin America, 1980, https://www.palestineposterproject.org/poster/day-of-world-solidarity.

Ahmed, Sara. *Willful Subjects*. Durham: Duke University Press, 2014.

Ajour, Ashjan. *Reclaiming Humanity in Palestinian Hunger Strikes: Revolutionary Subjectivity and Decolonizing the Body*. London: Palgrave, 2021.

Al Jazeera (communiqué from Anadolu Agency). "iNakba … Tatbeeq el-Ajhaza el-Zakia Yanquluk li-Filasteen qabla el-Tahjeer," *Al Jazeera*, May, 12, 2015, https://tinyurl.com/4sbaduew.

al-Salah, Razan. "Canada Park," Razanalsalah.com.

Al-Samman, Hanadi and El-Ariss Tarek. "Queer Affects: Introduction," *International Journal of Middle East Studies* 45, no. 2 (2013): 205–9.

Al-Shaikh, Abdul-Rahim et al. "Nadwa al-Kharaka al-Filastiniya al-Asira: Al-Jugrafiya al-Sadisa" [Symposium on the Palestinian Prisoner Movement: The Sixth Geography], *Majallat al-Dirasat al-Filastiniyya* 128 (2021): 9–59 [Arabic].

AlBawaba. "Mohammed El-Kurd Backlash Sparks Questions over Palestinian Priorities," *Albawaba*, June 20, 2022, https://www.albawaba.com/node/mohammed-el-kurd-backlash-sparks-questions-over-palestinian-priorities-1481241.

Albrechtslund, Anders and Thomas Ryberg. "Participatory Surveillance in the Intelligent Building," *Design Issues* 27, no. 3 (2011): 35–46.

Allan, Diana. "What Bodies Remember: Sensory Experience as Historical Counterpoint in the Nakba Archive," in *An Oral History of the Palestinian Nakba*, ed. Nahla Abdo and Nur Masalha, 66–87. London: Zed Press, 2019.

Allen, Lori. "Martyr Bodies in the Media: Human Rights, Aesthetics, and the Politics of Immediation in the Palestinian Intifada," *American Ethnologist* 36, no. 1 (2009): 161–80.

Almahdi, Abeer. "Mashrou' Leila Echoes Voices of Arab Resistance at Club Soda," *The McGill Tribune*, October 17, 2019, https://www.mcgilltribune.com/a-e/mashrou-leila-echoes-voices-arab-resistance-club-soda/.

Alqaisiya, Walaa. "Decolonial Queering: The Politics of Being Queer in Palestine," *Journal of Palestine Studies* 47, no. 3 (2018): 29–44.

Alqaisiya, Walaa. "Palestine and the Will to Theorise Decolonial Queering," *Middle East Critique* 29, no. 1 (2020): 87–113.

Amar, Paul. *The Security Archipelago: Human-Security States, Sexuality Politics, and the End of Neoliberalism*. Durham: Duke University Press, 2013.

Amel, Mahdi. "Al Thaqafa Wal Thawra," *Al Hiwar Al Mutamadden, Al Hiwar Al Mutamadden*, May 23, 2016, www.ahewar.org/debat/show.art.asp?aid=518075.

American Colony Photo Dept. The Christmas Story, Y.M.C.A. tableaux. [The Tidings to the Shepherds III] (1934–39), Matson Collection Library of Congress, https://www.loc.gov/pictures/item/2019710696/.

Amrov, Sabrien. "Virtual Reality Encounters at the Israel Museum," *Jerusalem Quarterly* 84 (Winter 2020): 87–104.

Anani, Rana. 2022. "Monther Jawabreh: A Story of an Artist Who Threw Stones in a Shallow Pond," *Palestine Studies. Art and Culture* (blog), July 13, 2022, https://www.palestine-studies.org/ar/node/1652935.

Anderson, Katie Elson "Getting Acquainted with Social Networks and Apps: It Is Time to Talk about TikTok," *Library Hi Tech News* 37, no. 4 (2020): 7–12. https://doi.org/10.1108/LHTN-01-2020-0001.

Anderson, Scott. *Lawrence in Arabia: War Deceit, Imperial Folly and the Making of the Middle East*. New York: Doubleday, 2013.

Arafat, Yasser. "Yasser Arafat's 1974 UN General Assembly Speech," United Nations General Assembly, New York, November 13, 1974.

Aston, Judith, Sandra Gaudenzi, and Mandy Rose, eds. *i-docs: The Evolving Practice of Interactive Documentary*. London: Wallflower, 2017.

Atia, Nadia. "Queering the Arab Spring: Belonging in Saleem Haddad's Gaupa," *Wasafiri* 34, no. 2 (2019): 54–60.

Atshan, Sa'ed. *Queer Palestine and the Empire of Critique*. Stanford: Stanford University Press, 2020.

Awwad, Julian. "The Postcolonial Predicament of Gay Rights in the Queen Boat Affair," *Communication and Critical/Cultural Studies* 7, no. 3 (2010): 318–36.

Azevedo, Mario J. "The Organization of African Unity and Afro-Arab Cooperation," *Africa Today* 35, no. 3/4 (1988): 68–80.

Azoulay, Ariella Aïsha. "Photographic Conditions: Looting, Archives, and the Figure of the Infiltrator," *Jerusalem Quarterly* 61 (2015): 6–22.

Azoulay, Ariella Aïsha. "Photographic Archives and Archival Entities," in *Image Operations: Visual Media and Political Conflict*, ed. Jens Eder and Charlotte Klonk, 151–66. Manchester: Manchester University Press, 2016.

Azoulay, Ariella Aïsha. "The Imperial Condition of Photography in Palestine: Archives, Looting, and the Figure of the Infiltrator," *Visual Anthropology* Review 33, no. 1 (Spring 2017): 5–17.

Babington, Bruce and Peter Evans. *Biblical Epics: Sacred Narrative in the Hollywood Cinema*. Eugene: Wipf and Stock, 2009.

Baconi, Tareq. "Our Lives Are Not Conditional: On Sarah Hegazy and Estrangement," *Mada Masr*, June 24, 2020, https://www.madamasr.com/en/2020/06/23/opinion/u/our-lives-are-not-conditional-on-sarah-hegazy-and-estrangement/.

BADIL. *Papers of Palestinian Youth Conference Right of Return: Towards a Practical Approach*. Palestine: BADIL, 2019, https://www.badil.org/phocadownloadpap/badil-new/publications/research/in-focus/RoR-Conf-Papers-2019-en.pdf.

Bakri, Tariq. "The New Generation: Using Technology to Search for Home," *This Week in Palestine* (2022): 95–6.

Balram, Dhruva. "A Day with Mashrou' Leila, the New Face of Middle Eastern Pop Music," *Dazed*, May 22, 2019, https://www.dazeddigital.com/music/article/44456/1/mashrou-leila-middle-east-pop-band-interview.

Baron, Beth. *Egypt as Woman: Nationalism, Gender, and Politics*. Berkeley: University of California Press, 2007.

Batarseh, Amanda. "Freedom to Imagine: Reflections on the First Palestine Writes Literature Festival," *Jerusalem Quarterly* 87 (2021): 152–9.

Beer, David. "Archive Fever Revisited: Algorithmic Archons and the Ordering of Social Media," in *Routledge Handbook of Digital Media and Communication*, 99–111. London and New York: Routledge, 2020.

Bensinger, Greg. "Google Redraws the Borders on Maps Depending on Who's Looking," *Washington Post*, February 14, 2020, https://www.washingtonpost.com/technology/2020/02/14/google-maps-political-borders/.

Berlant, Lauren. *Cruel Optimism*. Durham, NC: Duke University Press, 2011.

Berlant, Lauren. "The Commons: Infrastructures for Troubling Times," *Society and Space* 34, no. 3 (2016): 393–419.

Berlant, Lauren and Freeman Elizabeth. "Queer Nationality," *Boundary 2* 19, no. 1 (1992): 149–80.

Bernard, Glen. "The Book and the Spade," 1967, https://archive.org/details/upenn-f16-4027_1967_Book_and_the_Spade, last accessed June 30, 2022.

Bhutto, Zulfikar Ali. "Searching for the Next Intifada: Exercises in Queer Muslim Futurism," *Meridians* 20, no. 2 (2021): 443–65.

Bier, Jess. *Mapping Israel, Mapping Palestine: How Occupied Landscapes Shape Scientific Knowledge*. Cambridge, MA: The MIT Press, 2017.

Bishara, Amahl. *Crossing a Line: Laws, Violence, and Roadblocks to Palestinian Political Expression*. Stanford: Stanford University Press, 2022.

Black, Jeremy. *Maps and Politics*. Chicago: University of Chicago Press, 1997.

Blázquez Sánchez, Olga. "Collaborative Cartographies: Counter-Cartography and Mapping Justice in Palestine," *Journal of Holy Land and Palestine Studies* 17, no. 1 (2018): 75–85.

Bollas, Christopher. *The Shadow of the Object: Psychoanalysis of the Unthought Known*. New York: Columbia University Press, 1987.

Boullata, Kamal. *Palestinian Art: From 1850 to the Present*. London: Saqi, 2009.

Braidotti, Rosie. "The Ethics of Becoming Imperceptible," in *Deleuze and Philosophy*, ed. Constantin Boundas, 133–59. Edinburgh: Edinburgh University Press, 2006.

Bromberg, Philip. "Standing in the Spaces: The Multiplicity of Self and the Psychoanalytic Relationship," *Contemporary Psychoanalysis* 32 (1996): 509–35.

Bronstein Aparicio, Eitan. "75% of Visitors to Israel's Canada Park Believe It Is Located inside the Green Line (It's Not)," *Mondoweiss*, June 15, 2014, https://mondoweiss.net/2014/06/visitors-israels-located/, accessed October 29, 2022.

Bronstein Aparicio, Eitan. "Restless Park: On the Latrun villages and Zochrot," trans. Charles Kamen. *Zochrot*, undated, https://www.zochrot.org/publication_articles/view/51029/en?Restless_Park_On_the_Latrun_villages_and_Zochrot.

Brubaker, Roger. "Migration, Membership, and the Modern Nation-State: Internal and External Dimensions of the Politics of Belonging," *Journal of Interdisciplinary History* 41, no. 1 (2010): 61–78.

Burris, Greg. *The Palestinian Idea: Film, Media, and the Radical Imagination*. Philadelphia: Temple University Press, 2019.

Cameron, James (dir.) *True Lies* (1994).

Chamas, Sophie. "Lil Watan: Queer Patriotism in Chauvinistic Lebanon," *Sexualities*, October 9, 2021, https://journals.sagepub.com/doi/full/10.1177/13634607211047523.

Chamas, Sophie and Allouche Sabiha. "Mourning Sarah Hegazi: Grief and the Cultivation of Queer Arabness," *WSQ*, forthcoming.

Chamberlin, Paul Thomas. *The Global Offensive: The United States, the Palestine Liberation Organization and the Making of the Post-Cold War Order*. Oxford: Oxford University Press, 2012.

Cohen, Hillel. *Army of Shadows: Palestinian Collaboration with Zionism, 1917–1948*. Berkeley: University of California Press, 2008.

Contois, Emily and Zenia Kish. *Food Instagram: Identity, Influence & Negotiation*. Urbana, IL: University of Illinois Press, 2022.

Cook, Jonathan. "Canadian Ambassador Honored at Illegal Park," *The National*, June 18, 2009, https://www.thenationalnews.com/world/mena/canadian-ambassador-honoured-at-illegal-park-1.522327, accessed October 29, 2022.

Crawford-Holland, Sasha. "Humanitarian VR Documentary and Its Cinematic Myths," *Synoptique* 7, no. 1 (2018): 19–31.

Creative Commons. "Attribution-ShareAlike 2.0 Generic (CC BY-SA 2.0)," *Creative Commons*, https://creativecommons.org/licenses/by-sa/2.0/, accessed October 15, 2020.

Crehan, Kate. "Gramsci's Folklore Bundle," *Anuac* 11, no. 1 (2022): 55–64.

Cristiano, Fabio and Emilio Distretti. "Along the Lines of the Occupation: Playing at Diminished Reality in East Jerusalem," *Conflict and Society: Advances in Research* 3 (2017): 130–43.
Cyber Definitions. What Does Algospeak Mean? n.d., https://www.cyberdefinitions.com/definitions/ALGOSPEAK.html#:~:text=Algospeak%20is%20a%20combination%20of,as%20TikTok%2C%20Instagram%2C%20Facebook%2C.
Darwich, Lynn and Maikey Haneen. "The Road from Antipinkwashing Activism to the Decolonisation of Palestine," *WSQ* 42, no. 3–4 (2014): 281–5.
Darwish, Mahmoud. "Atfal al-hijarah," Muntada shabab Imiya, Majlis al-hukama', found at https://kalamfikalam.ahlamontada.com/t10600-topic.
Darwīsh, Maḥmūd. *Now, as You Awaken*, trans. Omnia Amin and Rick London. San Francisco: Sardines Press, 2006.
Davis, Uri. *The Golan Heights under Israeli Occupation 1967–1981*. Durham: University of Durham, Center for Middle Eastern and Islamic Studies, 1984.
De Vet, Annelis. *Subjective Atlas of Palestine*. Rotterdam: 010 Publishers, 2007.
Demaio, Matthew. "The Assassination of Basel al-Araj: How the Palestinian Authority Stamps Out Opposition," *Journal of Palestine Studies*, March 16, 2017.
DeMille, Cecil B. (dir.) *10 Commandments* (1956).
DeMille, Cecil B. (dir.) *King of Kings* (1927).
Depth Unknown. "Let the Ground Speak," https://depthunknown.com/depthuknown, last accessed June 30, 2022.
Derbas, Nahed. "Itlaq Tatbeeq 'el-Nakba' li-Ahia el-Quraa el-Filastiniyya 'el-Muhajira,'" *Al-Araby*, May 5, 2014, https://tinyurl.com/8eydr4mt.
Dewey, Caitlin. "Google Maps Did Not 'Delete' Palestine—But It Does Impact How You See It," *Washington Post*, April 9, 2016, https://www.washingtonpost.com/news/the-intersect/wp/2016/08/09/google-maps-did-not-delete-palestine-but-it-does-impact-how-you-see-it/.
DigiView. "All about the Fastest Growing Social Media App—TikTok," 2020, Available at https://digiview.se/articles/everything-you-need-to-know-about-tiktok/.
DJI. "Geo Zone Map—Fly Safe—DJI," 2023, https://www.dji.com/uk/flysafe/geo-map.
Doostdar, Alireza. "Sensing Jinn," *Critical Muslim* 43 (2022): 75–89.
Douglas, Mary. *Implicit Meanings: Selected Essays in Anthropology*. London: Routledge, 1999.
Eco, Umberto. *The Open Work*. Cambridge, MA: Harvard University Press, 1989.
Ehrenreich, Ben. "Is This Where the Third Intifada Will Start?" *The New York Times*, March 15, 2013, https://www.nytimes.com/2013/03/17/magazine/is-this-where-the-third-intifada-will-start.html.
El Shakry, Hoda. "Palestine and the Aesthetics of the Future Impossible," *Interventions* 23, no. 5 (2021): 669–90.
El-Nabli, Nadine. "'Lakum "Adatkum wa-Lana al-Musiqa" A Critical Engagement with the Politics of Identity, Resistance and Affect in Mashrou' Leila's Music," *British Journal of Middle Eastern Studies* 48, no. 1 (2021): 117.
Elia, Nada. "Gay Rights with a Side of Apartheid," *Settler Colonial Studies* 2, no. 2 (2012): 49–68.
Eng, David and Shinhee Han. *Racial Melancholia, Racial Dissociation: On the Social and Psychic Lives of Asian Americans*. Durham: Duke University Press, 2019.
Enzerink, Suzanne. "Arab Archipelagoes: Revolutionary Formations and a Queer Undercommons in Saleem Haddad's Guapa," *Feminist Formations* 33, no. 1 (2021): 245–74.

Erakat, Noura. "The Case for BDS and the Path to Co-Resistance," in *Assuming Boycott: Resistance, Agency, and Cultural Production*, ed. Kareem Estefan, Carin Kuoni, and Laura Raicovich. New York and London: OR Books, 2017, epub.

Escobar, Arturo. *Designs for the Pluriverse: Radical Interdependence, Autonomy, and the Making of Worlds*. Durham, NC: Duke University Press, 2018.

Esmeir, Samera. "To Say and Think a Life beyond What Settler-Colonialism Has Made," *Madamasr*, October 14, 2023, https://www.madamasr.com/en/2023/10/14/opinion/u/to-say-and-think-a-life-beyond-what-settler-colonialism-has-made/.

Ezzedeen Al-Qassam Brigades, https://alqassam.ps.

Fadi Cooks—Julia's Christmas Cake, December 25, 2020, https://www.youtube.com/watch?v=zlG_DFnstYg.

Falah, Ghazi-Walid. "War, Peace, and Land Seizure in Palestine's Border Area," *Third World Quarterly* 25, no. 5 (2004): 955–75.

Faraj, Asra. "Prisoners of the Freedom Tunnel," *al-Mayadeen*, November 8, 2021, https://www.almayadeen.net/news/politics/أسرى-فلسطينيون-من-سجن-جلبوع-الأبطال-من-ألا ضرامكهانرمهمن.

Farouki, Taj and Cheryl Nathan. *My Life Story*, 2001, https://thelibrary.org/lochist/els/farouki.pdf.

Farrell, Henry, Eric Lawrence, and Joh Sides. "Self-Segregation or Deliberation? Blog Readership, Participation and Polarization in American Politics," *Perspectives on Politics* 8, no. 1 (2008), https://doi.org/10.2139/ssrn.1151490.

Farsakh, Leila, Kanaaneh Rhoda, and Seikaly Sherene. "Special Issue: Queering Palestine," *Journal of Palestine Studies* 47, no. 3 (2018): 7–12.

Federici, Silvia. *Revolution at Point Zero: Housework, Reproduction, and Feminist Struggle*. Oakland: PM Press, 2020.

Fieni, David. "What a Wall Wants, or How Graffiti Thinks: Nomad Grammatology in the French Banlieue," *Diacritics* 40, no. 2 (2021): 72–93.

Fineberg, John. *Modern Art at the Border of Mind and Brain*. Lincoln: University of Nebraska Press, 2015.

Forristal, Lauren. "TikTok Was the Top App by Worldwide Downloads in Q1 2022," *TechCrunch+*, 2022, https://techcrunch.com/2022/04/26/tiktok-was-the-top-app-by-worldwide-downloads-in-q1-2022/.

Foucault, Michel. *The Archaeology of Knowledge and the Discourse on Language*, trans. A. M. Sheridan Smith. New York: Pantheon, 1972.

Foucault, Michel. "The Subject and Power," *Critical Inquiry* 8, no. 4 (Summer 1982): 777–95.

Fox, Tessa. "Maamoul: A Sweet Celebration for Christians and Muslims," *World's Table, BBC*, 14 April, 2022, https://www.bbc.com/travel/article/20220413-maamoul-a-sweet-celebration-for-christians-and-muslims.

Freccero, Carla. "Queer Times," in *After Sex? On Writing since Queer Theory*, ed. Janet Halley and Andrew Parker, 17–26. Durham: Duke University Press, 2011.

Fromm, Erich. *Escape from Freedom*. New York: Rinehart & Co, 1941.

Furani, Khaled. *Redeeming Anthropology: A Theological Critique of a Modern Science*. Oxford: Oxford University Press, 2019.

Furani, Khaled and Dan Rabinowitz. "The ethnographic Arriving of Palestine," *Annual Review of Anthropology* 40 (2011): 475–91.

Gagliardi, Connie. "Palestine Is Not a Drawing Board: Defacing the Street Art on the Israeli Separation Wall," *Visual Anthropology* 33, no. 5 (2020): 426–51.

Gershenson, Olga. "'We Are Victims of Our Past …': Israel's Dark Past Comes to Light in New Documentaries," *Tikkun* 33, nos. 1–2 (2018): 73–6.

Gertz, Nurith and George Khleifi. *Palestinian Cinema: Landscape, Trauma and Memory*. Edinburgh: Edinburgh University Press, 2008.

Gibson, Mel (dir.) *The Passion of the Christ* (2004).

Gilmore, Ruth Wilson. *Abolition Geography: Essays towards Liberation*. New York: Verso 2022.

Glissant, Édouard. *Poetics of Relation*. Ann Arbor: University of Michigan Press, 1997.

Google. "Welcome to Google Maps Platform," *Google Cloud*, https://cloud.google.com/maps-platform, accessed October 15, 2020.

Gopinath, Gayatri. *Unruly Visions: The Aesthetic Practices of Queer Diaspora*. Durham: Duke University Press, 2018.

Gramsci, Antonio. *Selections from The Prison Notebooks*, ed and trans. Quintin Hoare and Geoffrey Nowell Smith. New York: International Publishers, 1971.

Gribetz, Jonathan Marc. *Defining Neighbors: Religion, Race, and the Early Zionist-Arab Encounter*. Princeton: Princeton University Press, 2014.

Groys, Boris. "On art activism," *e-flux journal* 56 (2014): 1–14.

Gupta, Arun. "Anthony Bourdain (1956–2018)," *Jacobin*, June 11, 2018, https://jacobin.com/2018/06/anthony-bourdain-parts-unknown-obituary.

Habibi, Emile. *The Secret Life of Saeed the Pessoptimist*. London: Zed Books, 1985.

Haddad-El, Laila and Maggie Schmitt. *The Gaza Kitchen: A Palestinian Culinary Journey*. Charlottesville, VA: Just World Press, 2014.

Hamdan, Sara. "Becoming-Queer-Arab-Activist: The Case of Meem," *Kohl* 1, no. 2 (2015): 66–82.

Hammami, Rema. "Destabilizing Mastery and the Machine Palestinian Agency and Gendered Embodiment at Israeli Military Checkpoints," *Current Anthropology* 60, Supplement 19 (2019): S87–S97.

Hankey, Stephanie and Marek Tuszynski. "Exposing the Invisible: Visual Investigation of Conflict," in *Image Operations: Visual Media and Political Conflict*, ed. Jens Eder and Charlotte Klonk, 169–83. Manchester: Manchester University Press, 2016.

Hansen, James. "A Leader in Modern Palestinian Cuisine Is Opening a Restaurant in Notting Hill," *Eater London*, April 22, 2022, https://london.eater.com/2022/4/22/23035253/akub-restaurant-london-fadi-kattan-fawda-restaurant-palestine.

Harney, Stefano and Moten Fred. *The Undercommons; Fugitive Planning and Black Study*. New York: Minor Compositions, 2013.

Hasso, Frances. *Resistance, Repression, and Gender Politics in Occupied Palestine and Jordan*. Syracuse: Syracuse University Press, 2005.

Heidegger, Martin. *The Question Concerning Technology, and Other Essays*. New York: Harper Collins, 1977.

Hight, Craig. "The Field of Digital Documentary: A Challenge to Documentary Theorists," *Studies in Documentary Film* 2, no. 1 (2008): 3–7.

Hochberg, Gil Z. "Introduction: Israelis, Palestinians, Queers: Points of Departure," *GLQ* 16, no. 4 (2010): 493–516.

Hochberg, Gil Z. *Becoming Palestine: Toward an Archival Imagination of the Future*. Durham: Duke University Press, 2021.

Hudson, Dale. "Undisclosed Recipients: Database Documentaries and the Internet," *Studies in Documentary Film* 2, no. 1 (2008): 79–98.

Hudson, Dale. "Interactive Documentary at the Intersection of Performance and Mediation: Navigating 'Invisible' Histories and 'Inaudible' Stories in the United States," *Studies in Documentary Film* 14, no. 2 (2020): 128–46.

Hudson, Dale. "Mapping Palestine/Israel through Interactive Documentary," *Journal of Palestine Studies* 50, no. 1 (2021): 51–76.

Hudson, Dale and Patricia R. Zimmermann. *Thinking through Digital Media: Transnational Environments and Locative Places*. New York: Palgrave Macmillan, 2015.

Ibraheem, Aamer and Adrien Zakar. "Jawlān," *Middle East Journal of Culture and Communication* 15, no. 4, Special Issue: Keywords in Contemporary Syrian Media, Culture and Politics (2022): 358–66.

Iconic Framework. "Google Maps: A Comprehensive Maps Platform That Drives Real-World Insights and Immersive Location Experiences," *Iconic Framework*, https://ionicframework.com/integrations/google-maps, accessed November 25, 2020.

Ir Amim. "Erosion of the Status Quo on the Temple Mount/Haram al-Sharif—Latest Developments October 2022," https://www.ir-amim.org.il/en/node/2895.

Israeli Knesset. "Basic Laws of the State of Israel: Basic Law: Jerusalem, the Capital of Israel," 1980, https://main.knesset.gov.il:443/EN/activity/pages/basiclaws.aspx.

Jacir, Annemarie. *Milh hadha al-Bahr/The Salt of This Sea*. 2008.

Jacob, Wilson Chacko. *Working Out Egypt: Effendi Masculinity and Subject Formation in Colonial Modernity, 1870–1940*. Durham: Duke University Press, 2011.

Jad, Islah. *Palestinian Women's Activism: Nationalism, Secularism, Islamism*. Syracuse: Syracuse University Press, 2018.

Jameson, Frederic. *Postmodernism, or the Cultural Logic of Late Capitalism*. Madison: University of Wisconsin, 1982.

Jayyussi, Lena. "The Time of Small Returns: Affect and Resistance during the Nakba," in *An Oral History of the Palestinian Nakba*, ed. Nahla Abdo and Nur Masalha. London: Zed Books, 2018.

Kabra, Fawz. "Ruanne Abou-Rahme and Basel Abbas in Conversation with Fawz Kabra," *Ocula*, January 18, 2018, https://ocula.com/magazine/conversations/basel-abbas-and-ruanne-abou-rahme/, accessed November 22, 2021.

Kamil, Meryem. "Postspatial, Postcolonial: Accessing Palestine in the Digital," *Social Text* 144, 38, no. 3 (2020): 55–82.

Kamisher, Eliyahu. *The Fight for a Flower. Roads and Kingdoms*, April 23, 2018, https://roadsandkingdoms.com/2018/the-fight-for-a-flower/.

Kanafani, Ghassan. *Palestine's Children: Returning to Haifa and Other Stories*, trans. Barbara Harlow and Karen E. Riley. London: Lynne Rienner Publishers, 2000.

Karkabi, Nadeem and Aamer Ibraheem. "On Fleeing Colonial Captivity: Fugitive Arts in the Occupied Jawlan," *Identities*, 2020, https://doi.org/10.1080/1070289X.2020.1851006.

Karmi, Ghada. *In Search of Fatima: A Palestinian Story*. London: Verso, 2002.

Karmi, Ghada. *Return: A Palestinian Memoir*. London: Verso, 2015.

Karon, Tony and Daniel Levy. "Israel Is Losing This War," *The Nation*, December 8, 2023, https://www.thenation.com/article/world/israel-gaza-war/.

Kasamanie, Adnan. "Druze Gnosis and the Mystery of Time," in *The Gnostic World*, ed. Garry W. Trompf, Gunner B. Mikkelsen, and Jay Johnston, 349–57. London: Routledge, 2018.

Kassis, Reem. *The Palestinian Table*. New York: Phaidon, 2019 [2017].

Kassis, Reem. *The Arabesque Table: Contemporary Recipes from the Arab World*. New York: Phaidon, 2021.

Kattan, Fadi. "Cooking Palestinian Food: On Indigenous Herbs, Crafts and Community," *The Funambulist*, August 26, 2020, https://thefunambulist.net/magazine/politics-of-food/cooking-palestinian-food-fadi-kattan.

Kattan, Fadi. 2021. "Interview with Mikey Muhanna for Matbakh, Afikra. Sumac," https://www.youtube.com/watch?v=iqDzo-TTGxo.
Kattan, Fadi. "Ma'moul: Toward a Philosophy of Food," *The Markaz Review*, April 15, 2022, https://themarkaz.org/mamoul-toward-a-philosophy-of-food/.
Katz, Cindi and Neil Smith. "An Interview with Edward Said," *Environment and Planning D: Society and Space* 21 (2003): 635–51.
Kawar, Amal. *Daughters of Palestine: Leading Women of the Palestinian National Movement*. Albany: State University of New York Press, 1996.
Keysar, Hagit. "A Spatial Testimony: The Politics of Do-It-Yourself Aerial Photography in East Jerusalem," *Society and Space* 37, no. 3 (2019): 523–41.
Keysar, Hagit. "DIY Drones in Silwan," 2021, https://cargocollective.com/hagitkeysar/DIY-drones-in-Silwan.
Khaled, Leila. *My People Shall Live*, ed. George Hajjar. London: Hodder and Stoughton, 1973.
Khalidi, Rashid. *Palestinian Identity: The Construction of a Modern National Consciousness*. New York: Columbia University Press, 1997.
Khalidi, Rashid. "The Journal of Palestine Studies in the Twenty-First Century: An Editor's Reflections," *Journal of Palestine Studies* 50, no. 3 (2021): 5–17.
Khalidi, Walid. *All That Remains: The Palestinian Villages Occupied and Depopulated by Israel in 1948*. Beirut: IPS, 1992.
Khalili, Laleh. *Heroes and Martyrs of Palestine: The Politics of National Commemoration*. Cambridge: Cambridge University Press, 2007.
Klinghoffer, Arthur Jay. *The Power of Projections: How Maps Reflect Global Politics and History*. Westport: Praeger, 2006.
Kouri-Towe, Natalie. "Textured Activism: Affect Theory and Transformational Politics in Transnational Queer Palestine-Solidarity Activism," *Intimacies/Affect* 37, no. 1 (2015): 23–34.
Kraidy, Marwan. "Revolutionary Creative Labour," in *Precarious Creativity: Global Media, Local Labor*, ed. Martin Curtin and Kevin Sanson, 231–40. Berkeley, CA: University of California Press, 2016.
Kuntsman, Adi and Rebecca L. Stein. *Digital Militarism: Israel's Occupation in the Social Media Age*. Stanford: Stanford University Press, 2015.
Laing, R.D. *The Divided Self*. New York: Pantheon, 1960.
Laing, R.D. *The Politics of Experience*. New York: Pantheon, 1983.
Laing, R.D. *The Bird of Paradise*. New York: Penguin, 1984.
Le Guin, Ursula. *The Carrier Bag Theory of Fiction*. London: Ignota, 2019.
Lean, David (dir.) *Lawrence of Arabia* (1962).
Lefebvre, Henri. *The Production of Space*. Blackwell: Oxford, 1991.
Leibler, Anat and Daniel Breslau. "The Uncounted: Citizenship and Exclusion in the Israeli Census of 1948," *Ethnic and Racial Studies* 28, no. 5 (2005): 880–902.
Lewis, Gail. "Once More with My Sistren: Black Feminism and the Challenge of Object Use," *Feminist Review* 126, no. 1 (2020): 1–18.
Lewis, Tania. *Digital Food: From Paddock to Platform*. New York: Bloomsbury, 2020.
Lionis, Chrisoula. "Peasant, Revolutionary, Celebrity: The Subversion of Popular Iconography in Contemporary Palestinian Art," *Middle East Journal of Culture and Communication* 8, no. 1 (2015): 69–84.
Long, Paul, Sarah Baker, Lauren Istvandity, and Jez Collins. "The Labour of Love: The Affective Archives of Popular Music Culture," *Archives and Records* 38, no. 1 (2017): 61–79.

Lorentzen Sogge, Erling. *The Palestinian National Movement in Lebanon: A Political History of the 'Ayn al-Hilwe Camp*. London: I.B. Tauris, 2021.

Maasri, Zeina. *Cosmopolitan Radicalism: The Visual Politics of Beirut's Global Sixties*. Cambridge: Cambridge University Press, 2020.

MacDowall, Lachlan. "Walls as Fleeting Surfaces: From Bricks to Pixels, Trains to Instagram," in *Urban Walls: Political and Cultural Meanings of Vertical Structures and Surfaces*, ed. Andrea Mubi Bringheti and Mattias Kärhholm, 236–54. New York: Routledge, 2019.

Mahadeen, Ebtihal. "Queer Counterpublics and LGBTQ Pop Activism in Jordan," *British Journal of Middle Eastern Studies* 48, no. 1 (2021): 78–93.

Makdisi, Saree. "The Architecture of Erasure," *Critical Inquiry* 36, no. 3 (2010): 519–59.

Manna', 'Adel. *Nakba and Survival: The Story of the Palestinians Who Remained in Haifa and the Galilee (1948–1956)*. Beirut & Ramallah: Institute for Palestine Studies, 2016 [Arabic].

Manna, Jumana. *Foragers*. Film. Viewed at the Arsenal Gallery, Toronto Biennial of Art, March 26–June 5, 2022.

Mansour, Shadia and DAM. "'They All Have Tanks', Revolutionary Arab Rap: The Index," April 29, 2014, http://revolutionaryarabraptheindex.blogspot.com/2014/04/dam-ft-shadia-mansour-they-all-have.html.

Massad, Joseph A. "Re-Orienting Desire: The Gay International and the Arab World," *Public Culture* 14, no. 2 (2002): 361–85.

Massad, Joseph A. *The Persistence of the Palestinian Question. Essays on Zionism and the Palestinians*. New York: Routledge, 2006.

Massad, Joseph A. "The Weapon of Culture: Cinema in the Palestinian Liberation Struggle," in *Dreams of a Nation: On Palestinian Cinema*, ed. Hamid Dabashi, 32–44. London: Verso, 2006.

Matar, Ahmad. "Palestinians Succeeded to Raise #Palestine Flag with a Drone above Israeli Squatters near AlAmoud Gate in Jerusalem," Twitter, May 29, 2022, https://T.Co/OpBpicfZHf.

Matar, Dina. "PLO Cultural Activism: Mediating Liberation Aesthetics in Revolutionary Contexts," *Comparative Studies of South Asia, Africa and the Middle East* 38, no. 2 (2018): 354–64.

Mattelart, Armand. *The Globalization of Surveillance*, trans. Susan Taponier and James A. Cohen. London: Polity, 2010.

McAlister, Melani. *Epic Encounters: Culture, Media and U.S. Interests in the Middle East, 1945–2000*. Berkeley: University of California Press, 2001.

McCracken, Harry. "Twitter's Big Bet on Topics and Lists Is Just Getting Started," *Fast Company*, 2019, https://www.fastcompany.com/90446827/twitters-big-bet-on-topics-and-lists-is-just-getting-started.

McKernan, Behan. "'Hummus Is Banned in My Kitchen': Meet the Chef Bring 'the Essence of Palestine' to London," *The Guardian*, November 27, 2022.

Meari, Lena. "The Roles of Palestinian Peasant Women: The Case of al-Birweh Village, 1930–1960," in *Displaced at Home: Ethnicity and Gender among Palestinians in Israel*, ed. Rhoda Ann Kannaneh and Isis Nusair, 119–32. Albany: State University of New York Press, 2010.

Meari, Lena. "Sumud: A Palestinian Philosophy of Confrontation in Colonial Prisons," *South Atlantic Quarterly* 113, no. 3 (2014): 547–78.

Meari, Lena, Samera Esmeir, and Ramsey McGlazer. "'You're Not Defeated as Long as You're Resisting': Palestine Hunger Strikes between the Singular and the Collective," *Critical Times*, 2021.

Mecky, Mariam. "State Policing: Moral Panics and Masculinity in Post-2011 Egypt," *Kohl* 4, no. 1 (2018): 94–105.

Meneley, Anne. "Time in a Bottle: The Uneasy Circulation of Palestinian Olive Oil," *Middle East Research and Information Project* 248 (2008): 18–23.

Meneley, Anne. "Blood, Sweat and Tears in a Bottle of Palestinian Olive Oil," *Food, Culture & Society* 14, no. 2 (2011): 275–90.

Meneley, Anne. "Resistance Is Fertile!," *Gastronomica* 14, no. 4 (2014): 70–9.

Meneley, Anne. "The Companion to Every Bite: Palestinian Olive Oil in the Levant," in *Making Levantine Cuisine: Modern Foodways of the Eastern Mediterranean*, ed. Anny Gaul, Graham Auman Pitts, and Vicki Valosik, 115–32. Austin: University of Texas Press, 2021.

Meneley, Anne. "Eating Wild: Hosting the Food Heritage of Palestine," *PoLAR: Political and Legal Anthropology Review* 44, no. 2 (2021): 207–22.

Meneley, Anne. "Hope in the Ruins: Seeds, Plants, and Possibilities of Regeneration," *Environment and Planning E: Nature and Space* 4, no. 1 (2021): 158–72.

Mikdashi, Maya. "Moral Panics, Sex Panics and the Production of a Lebanese Nation," *Jadaliyya*, February 22, 2014, https://www.jadaliyya.com/Details/30261.

Mikdashi, Maya. "Fear and Loathing in Orlando," *Jadaliyya*, June 14, 2016, https://www.jadaliyya.com/Details/33347.

Mitchell, Timothy. "Infrastructures Work on Time," *e-flux architecture*, January 28, 2020, www.e-flux.com/architecture/new-silk-roads/312596/infrastructures-work-on-time/.

Mitchell, W.J.T. "Holy Landscape: Israel, Palestine, and the American Wilderness," *Critical Inquiry* 26, no. 2 (2000): 193–223.

Mohsin, Maryam. "10 TikTok Statistics That You Need to Know in 2022 [Infographic]," 2022, https://www.oberlo.com/blog/tiktok-statistics.

Morgensen, Scott L. "A Politics Not Yet Known: Imagining Relationality within Solidarity," *American Quarterly* 67, no. 2 (2015): 309–215.

Moscrop, John James. *Measuring Jerusalem: The Palestine Exploration Fund and British Interests in the Holy Land*. London: Leicester University Press, 2000.

Moten, Fred. "Blackness and Nothingness (Mysticism in the Flesh)," *South Atlantic Quarterly* 112, no. 4 (2013): 737–80.

Moten, Fred. *Stolen life*. Durham: Duke University Press, 2018.

Musih, Norma and Eran Fisher. "Layers as Epistemic and Political Devices in Mobile Locative Media; The Case of iNakba in Israel/Palestine," *Continuum* 35, no. 1 (2021): 151–69.

Mustafa, Mustafa. "Laila Shawa Draws on Top of a Landmine," *Al Akhbar*, July 12, 2014, https://al-akhbar.com/Literature_Arts/34566.

Naaman, Dorit. "Interview with Dorit Naaman about 'Jerusalem, We Are Here'," *Jerusalem Fund*, May 11, 2017, http://www.thejerusalemfund.org/17755/interview-dorit-naaman-jerusalem.

Naaman, Dorit. "Lessons for the Future from Jerusalem's Palestinian Past," *The Conversation*, May 13, 2018, https://theconversation.com/lessons-for-the-future-from-jerusalems-palestinian-past-95768.

Naber, Nadine. *Arab America: Gender, Cultural Politics, and Activism*. New York: New York University Press, 2012.

Naber, Nadine, Sa'ed Atshan, Nadia Awad, Maya Mikdashi, Sofian Merabet, Dorgham Abusalem, and Nada Elia. "On Palestinian Studies and Queer Theory," *Journal of Palestine Studies* 47, no. 3 (2018): 62–71.

Najmabadi, Afsaneh. *Women with Moustaches and Men without Beards: Gender and Sexual Anxieties of Iranian Modernity*. Berkeley: University of California Press, 2005.

Nash, Kate. "Modes of Interactivity: Analysing the Webdoc," *Media, Culture and Society* 34, no. 2 (2012): 195–210.

Nashef, Nadim. "Palestinian Youth Assert Right of Return with Direct Action," *Electronic Intifada*, September 11, 2013, https://electronicintifada.net/content/palestinian-youth-assert-right-return-direct-action/12760, accessed March 7, 2022.

Nashhef, Khaled. "Tawfik Canaan: His Life and Works," *Jerusalem Quarterly* 16 (2002): 12–26.

Nashif, Esmail. *Palestinian Political Prisoners: Identity and Community*. London: Routledge, 2008.

Nashif, Esmail. *Images of a Palestinian's Death*. Beirut: Arab Center for Research and Policy Studies, 2015.

Nasrallah, Elias. *Shahadat "ala al-Qarn al-Falastini al-"Awal* [Testimonies on the First Century of Palestine]. Beirut: Al-Farabi, 2016 [Arabic].

Nassar, Issam. "'Biblification' in the Service of Colonialism: Jerusalem in Nineteenth-Century Photography," *Third Text* 20, no. 3–4 (2006): 317–26.

Newton, Casey. "Why Vine Died," *The Verge*, 2016, https://www.theverge.com/2016/10/28/13456208/why-vine-died-twitter-shutdown.

Nora, Pierre, ed. *Les lieux de mémoire*, new edition. Paris: Éditions Gallimard, 1997.

Norman, Julie. *The Palestinian Prisoners Movement: Resistance and Disobedience*. London: Routledge, 2021.

Obeid, Anis. *The Druze and Their Faith in Tawhid*. Syracuse: Syracuse University Press, 2006.

Ogden, Thomas. "The Concept of Object Relations," *International Journal of Psychoanalysis* 64 (1983).

Open Data Commons. "ODC Open Database License (ODbL) Summary," Open Data Commons, https://opendatacommons.org/licenses/odbl/summary/, accessed November 25, 2013.

Palestine Children's Relief Fund (PCRF, NYC Chapter). "Cooking Makloubeh" with Chef Fadi Kattan, November 17, 2020, https://www.youtube.com/watch?v=7kuFli8j-fw.

Palestine Open Maps. https://palopenmaps.org/, last accessed June 30, 2022.

Palestine Remembered. "Wadi Hunayn," https://www.palestineremembered.com/al-Ramla/Wadi-Hunayn/index.html, account here referenced 2014, link accessed June 29, 2022.

Palestine Remembered. "Mission Statement," https://www.palestineremembered.com/MissionStatement.htm, last accessed June 30, 2022.

Pappé, Ilan. *The Ethnic Cleansing of Palestine*. London: Oneworld, 2006.

Paulsen, Kris. *Here/There: Telepresence, Art, and Touch at the Interface*. New York: MIT Press, 2017.

Pelletier, Mary. "Take a Tour of West Jerusalem's Palestinian History," *Al Jazeera*, April 19, 2017, https://www.aljazeera.com/indepth/features/2017/03/jerusalem-170319103904879.html.

Peteet, Julie. "Wall Talk: Palestinian Graffiti," in *Routledge Handbook of Graffiti and Street Art*, ed. Jeffrey Ian Ross, 334–44. New York: Routledge, 2016.

Petti, Alessandro, Sandi Hilal, and Eyal Weizman. *Architecture after Revolution*. Berlin: Sternberg Press, 2013.
Political and Armed Struggle, Palestinian National Liberation Movement Beirut, 1969.
Poster, Mark. "The Information Empire," *Comparative Literature Studies* 41, no. 3 (2004): 317–334.
Pratt, Nicola. "The Queen Boat Case in Egypt: Sexuality, National Security and State Sovereignty," *Review of International Studies* 33, no. 1 (2007): 129–44.
Preminger, Otto (dir.) *Exodus* (1960).
Puar, Jasbir. "Citation and Censorship: The Politics of Talking about the Sexual Politics of Israel," *Feminist Legal Studies* 19, no. 133 (2011): 133–142.
Puar, Jasbir K. *The Right to Maim: Debility, Capacity, Disability*. Durham, NC: Duke University Press, 2017.
PublicLab. "MapKnitter," https://publiclab.org/wiki/mapknitter.
Quiquivix, Linda. "When the Carob Tree Was the Border: On Autonomy and Palestinian Practices of Figuring It Out," *Capitalism Nature Socialism* 24, no. 3 (2013): 170–89.
Quiquivix, Linda. "Art of War, Art of Resistance: Palestinian Counter-Cartography on Google Earth," *Annals of the Association of American Geographers* 104, no. 3 (2014): 444–59.
Qutami, Loubna. "Unsettled Debts: 1968 and the Problem of Historical Memory| Reborn as Fida'i: The Palestinian Revolution and the (Re)Making of an Icon," *International Journal of Communication* 16 (2022): 4659–83.
Radio Hara: Episode 1 Shweiki Bakery. 3/26/2020.
Rancière, Jacques. *Dissensus: On Politics and Aesthetics*. London: Bloomsbury, 2010.
Rangan, Pooja. *Immediations: The Humanitarian Impulse in Documentary*. Durham, NC: Duke University Press, 2017.
Revolution until Victory, Palestinian National Liberation Movement. Beirut, 1969.
Rifkin, Mark. *Settler Common Sense: Queerness and Everyday Colonialism in the American Renaissance*. Minnesota: University of Minnesota Press, 2014.
Risam, Roopika. "Now You See Them: Self-Representation and the Refugee Selfie," *Popular Communication* 16, no. 1 (2018): 58–71.
Robinson, Shira. *Citizen Strangers: Palestinians and the Birth of Israel's Liberal Settler State*. Stanford: Stanford University Press, 2013.
Sabah Al-Yasmine podcasts; Reem Kassis (5/12/2020), Sami Tamimi (5/6/2020), Mohamed Hadid, a Palestinian Icon (4/22/2020).
Said, Edward. *Orientalism*. New York: Vintage Books, 1979.
Said, Edward. *The World, the Text, and the Critic*. Cambridge, MA: Harvard University Press, 1983.
Said, Edward. "Permission to Narrate," *Journal of Palestine Studies* 13, no. 3 (1984): 2748.
Said, Edward. *After the Last Sky: Palestinian Lives*. New York: University of Columbia Press, 1988.
Said, Edward. *After the Last Sky: Palestinian Lives* (1999). New York: Columbia University Press, 1999.
Said, Edward W. "Zionism from the Standpoint of Its Victims," *Social Text* 1 (1979): 7–58.
Saifi, Zeena. "'They Were Shooting Directly at the Journalists': New Evidence Suggests Shireen Abu Akleh Was Killed in Targeted Attack by Israeli Forces," *CNN*, May 26, 2022, https://www.cnn.com/2022/05/24/middleeast/shireen-abu-akleh-jenin-killing-investigation-cmd-intl/index.html.
Salaita, Steven. "Architectures of Delusion," *Mondoweiss*, September 13, 2021, https://mondoweiss.net/2021/09/architectures-of-delusion/ (Retrieved on 5.7.2022).

Salamanca, Omar Jabary, Mezna Qato, Kareem Rabie, and Sobhi Samour. "Past Is Present: Settler Colonialism in Palestine," *Settler Colonial Studies* 2, no. 1 (2012): 1–8.
Sandoval, Chela. *Methodology of the Oppressed*. Minneapolis: University of Minnesota Press, 2000.
Sayigh, Rosemary. *The Palestinians: From Peasants to Revolutionaries*. London: Zed, 1979/2007.
Sayigh, Yezid. *Armed Struggle and the Search for State: The Palestinian National Movement*. Oxford: Clarendon Press, 1997.
Schechner, Sam. "You Give Apps Sensitive Personal Information. Then They Tell Facebook," *The Wall Street Journal*, 2019, https://www.wsj.com/articles/you-give-apps-sensitive-personal-information-then-they-tell-facebook-11550851636.
Scholten, Frank. Man on a horse (1921–23), NINO F Scholten 2: 19, Netherlands Institute for the Near East and Leiden University Library, https://digitalcollections.universiteitleiden.nl/view/item/3427811?solr_nav%5Bid%5D=bfe3ecc338f51da01e25&solr_nav%5Bpage%5D=0&solr_nav%5Boffset%5D=13.
Schön, Donald A. *The Reflective Practitioner: How Professionals Think in Action*. London: Routledge, 2017.
Sciullo, Nick J. "Boston King's Fugitive Passing: Fred Moten, Saidiya Hartman, and Tina Campt's Rhetoric of Resistance," *Rhizomes: Cultural Studies in Emerging Knowledge* 35 (2019).
Sender, Hannah. "'Putting Me in Jail Would Be Their Biggest Mistake'—Palestinian Artist Khaled Jarrar Talks to Art Radar," *Art Radar*, July 7, 2013, https://artradarjournal.com/putting-me-in-jail-would-be-their-biggest-mistake-palestinian-artist-khaled-jarrar-talks-to-art-radar/ (Retrieved on 1.7.2022).
Serhan, Yasmeen. "A Symbol of the Palestinian Resistance for the Internet Age," *The Atlantic*, January 2018, https://www.theatlantic.com/international/archive/2018/01/internet-famous-in-the-west-bank/549557/.
Shaheen, Jack. *Reel Bad Arabs: How Hollywood Vilifies a People*. North Hampton, MA: Olive Branch Press, 2001.
Shahin, Mariam. "The Seed Queen of Palestine," *Al Jazeera*, 2018, https://www.youtube.com/watch?v=XoexxUOeZak.
Shalhoub-Kevorkian, Nadera. "Infiltrated Intimacies: The Case of Palestinian Returnees," *Feminist Studies* 42, no. 1 (2016): 166–93.
Shammas, Anton. *Arabesques*. Berkeley: University of California Press, 1988.
Shane, Charlotte "Why Do We Love TikTok Audio Memes? Call It 'Brainfeel.'" *The New York Times*, August 17, 2022, https://www.nytimes.com/interactive/2022/08/17/magazine/tiktok-sounds-memes.html.
Sheehi, Lara and Stephen Sheehi, *Psychoanalysis under Occupation: Practicing Resistance in Palestine*. London: Routledge, 2022.
Shehadah, Firas. "Notes on the Logic of Speed," *Journal of Visual Culture* 20, no. 2 (2022): 236.
Shezaf, Hagar and Jonathan Jacobson. "Revealed: Israel's Cyber-Spy Industry Helps World Dictators Hunt Dissidents and Gays," *Haaretz*, October 19, 2018, https://www.haaretz.com/israel-news/.premium.MAGAZINE-israel-s-cyber-spy-industry-aidsdictators-hunt-dissidents-and-gays.
Shohat, Ella. "The Struggle over Representation: Casting, Coalitions, and the Politics of Identification," in *Late imperial culture*, ed. R. De La Campa, E. A. Kaplan, and M. Sprinker, 166–78. New York: Verso, 1995.

Snaije, Olivia. "Israeli Regulation of Farming and Foraging Can Make Agriculture a Difficult Task for palestinians," *New/Lines Magazine*, February 10, 2022, https://newlinesmag.com/reportage/in-the-west-bank-plants-are-political/.

Sontag, Susan. "Posters: Advertisement. Art, Political Artefact, Commodity," in *The Art of Revolution: 96 Posters from Cuba*, ed. Dugald Stermer, vii–xxiii. London: Pall Mall Press, 1970.

Sorek, Tamir. "'The Only Place Where an Arab Can Hit a Jew and Get a Medal for It': Boxing and Masculine Pride among Arab Citizens of Israel," *Sport in Society* 12, no. 8 (2009): 1065–74.

Srouji, Dima. "Sebastia," 2020, https://vimeo.com/463782519, last accessed June 30, 2022.

Srouji, Dima. "A Century of Subterranean Abuse in Sabastiya: The Archeological Site as a Field of Urban Struggle," *Jerusalem Quarterly* 90 (Summer 2022): 58–74.

Srouji, Dima. "Vignettes of Subterranean Palestine," *The Avery Review* 56 (2022), http://averyreview.com/issues/56/vignettes-of-subterranean-palestine.

Statista. "Global Market Share of Drone Manufacturers 2021," 2023, https://www.statista.com/statistics/1254982/global-market-share-of-drone-manufacturers/.

Stein, Rebecca. *Itineraries in Conflict: Israelis, Palestinians, and the Political Lives of Tourism*. Durham, NC: Duke University Press, 2008.

Stevens, George (dir.) *The Greatest Story Ever Told* (1965).

Steyerl, Hito. "Artifacts: A Conversation between Hito Steyerl and Daniel Rourke," *Rhizome*, March 28, 2013, https://rhizome.org/editorial/2013/mar/28/artifacts/.

Steyerl, Hito. "A Tank on a Pedestal: Museums in an Age of Planetary Civil War," *e-flux*, February 2016, www.e-flux.com/journal/70/60543/a-tank-on-a-pedestal-museums-in-an-age-of-planetary-civil-war/.

Stoler, Ann. "Archiving as Dissensus," *Comparative Studies of South Asia, Africa and the Middle East* 38, no. 1 (2018): 43–56.

Suleiman, Terese. "Barudah wa Kitab," April 15, 2017, https://www.youtube.com/watch?v=3YOIapG5aeo.

Sundaram, Ravi. *Pirate Modernity: Delhi's Media Urbanism*. London: Routledge, 2010.

Swedenburg, Ted. *Memories of Revolt: The 1936–1939 Rebellion and the Palestinian National Past*. Minneapolis: University of Minnesota Press, 1995.

Swidler, Anne. "What Anchors Cultural Practices," in *The Practice Turn in Contemporary Theory*, ed. Theodore R. Schatzki, K. Knorr-Cetina, and Eike von Savigny, 74–92. London: Routledge, 2001.

Sword Connect. "Work Smarter and More Efficiently with Google Cloud Solutions by Sword Connect," Sword Connect home page, https://www.sword-connect.com, accessed November 25, 2020.

Sykes, Christopher Simon. *The Man Who Created the Middle East: A Story of Empire, Conflict and the Sykes-Picot Agreement*. Great Britain: William Collins, 2016.

Tamimi, Sami and Tara Wrigley. *Falastin: A Cookbook*. Toronto: Random House, 2020.

Tarnopolsky, Noda. "A Restaurant in the West Bank makes its Mark," *Los Angeles Times*, December 2018, https://www.latimes.com/food/dailydish/la-fo-re-fawda-20181221-story.html.

Tarrash, Shahira and Craig Brown. "How TikTok Is Exposing Dissent and Repression in Israel-Palestine," *Resistance Studies*, 2021, https://wagingnonviolence.org/rs/2021/06/tiktok-dissent-in-israel-palestine/.

Tawil-Souri, Helga. "Digital Occupation: Gaza's High-Tech Enclosure," *Journal of Palestine Studies* 41, no. 2 (2012): 27–43.

Tawil-Souri, Helga. "It's Still about the Power of Place," *Middle East Journal of Culture and Communication* 5 (2012): 86–95.

Tawil-Souri, Helga. "Cinema as the Space to Transgress Palestine's Territorial Trap," *Middle East Journal of Culture and Communication* 7, no. 2 (2014): 169–89.

Tawil-Souri, Helga and Miriyam Aouragh. "Intifada 3.0? Cyber Colonialism and Palestinian Resistance," *Arab Studies Journal* 22, no. 1 (2014): 102–33.

Taylor, Diana. *Performance*. Durham: Duke University Press, 2016.

Teta's Kitchen: Rabet 2020. Episode 1: Wara' Dawali and Qusa Mahshi. Bethlehem. Teta Laurette Zoughbi. https://www.youtube.com/watch?v=VvnTE6RSuJI.

Teta's Kitchen: Rabet 2020. Episode 2: Mulukhiyah in Jericho. March 12, 2020. Imm Yusuf and Imm Ashraf, https://www.youtube.com/watch?v=bfmjvIffRVQ.

Teta's Kitchen: Rabet 2020. Episode 3: Musakhan in Sebastia. Hajja Fatma and Hajja Samah. Women Restaurant Entrepreneurs and Olive Oil, https://www.youtube.com/watch?v=pNJHMa3a7O.

Teta's Kitchen: Rabet 2020. Episode 4: Maftoul & Beers. Taybeh. Imm Salama, https://www.youtube.com/watch?v=iDu1KJ6YFpM.

Teta's Kitchen. Rabet 2021. Episode 5: Maklubah in Nablus. Imm Zoheir, https://www.youtube.com/watch?v=ik3Em1zurtc&t=734s.

Teta's Kitchen. Rabet 2021. Episode 6: Sumakiyeh in Gaza. Imm Jayab, https://www.youtube.com/watch?v=ZJ3Eeqy5IZ0.

Teta's Kitchen. Rabet 2021. Episode 7: Stuffed Lamb Necks in Hebron. Imm Eyad, https://www.youtube.com/watch?v=W2ocvDn61iM.

Teta's Kitchen. Rabet 2021. Episode 8: Rabi'ieh in Umm al-Fahm. Imm Ala', https://www.youtube.com/watch?v=fnc4GOkW9-Y.

Teta's Kitchen. Rabet 2021. Episode 9: Madfooneh in Yaffa. Teta Nadia, https://www.youtube.com/watch?v=c6XT5fI5rP8.

Teta's Kitchen. Rabet 2021. Episode 10: Mansaf in the Jordan Valley, https://www.youtube.com/watch?v=bLsS5U0e9mA.

The New Arab. "Lebanese Band Mashrou Leila Releases Anti-Occupation Music Video," *The New Arab*, June 8, 2019, https://english.alaraby.co.uk/news/lebanese-band-mashrou-leila-release-anti-occupation-music-video.

The Plate (Hummus with Fadi!). April 7, 2022, https://on.theplate.org/our-creators.

Toenjes, Ashley. "This Wall Speaks: Graffiti and Transnational Networks in Palestine," *Jerusalem Quarterly* 61 (2015): 55–68.

"Tunnel Crossing between Lebanon and Israel Went 22 Story Deep," *Middle East Monitor*, June 3, 2019, https://www.middleeastmonitor.com/20190603-tunnel-crossing-between-lebanon-and-israel-went-22-storeys-deep/.

University College London. "Filming Antiquity: Reels of Lankester Harding," https://www.youtube.com/watch?v=nVkvLiKIvUw, last accessed June 30, 2022.

University of Pennsylvania Museum of Archaeology and Anthropology. "Ancient Earth: Making History Everlasting," 1940, https://archive.org/details/upenn-f16-4015_1940_Ancient_Earth_Making_History, last accessed June 30, 2022.

Vishmidt, Marina. "All Shall Be Unicorns: About Commons, Aesthetics and Time," *Open! Platform for Culture, Art & The Public Domain*, September 3, 2014, www.onlineopen.org/download.php?id=128.

Walsh, Dan. *The Palestine Poster Project Archives: Origins, Evolution, and Potential*. Master's Thesis. Georgetown University, US, 2011.

Watad, Muhammad. "Israeli Court Sentences 5 Years in Jail for the Freedom Tunnel Prisoners," *Al-Jazeera* (Arabic), May 22, 2022, https://www.aljazeera.net/news/humanrights/2022/5/22/ملكمة-إسرائيلية-تفرض-السجن-5-سنوات-على

Weimann, Gabriel and Natalie Masri. "TikTok's Spiral of Antisemitism," 2021, https://doi.org/10.3390/journalmedia2040041.

Weiss, Brad. *Real Pigs: Shifting Values in the Field of Local Pork*. Durham, NC: Duke University Press, 2016.

Weizman, Eyal. *Hollow Land: Israel's Architecture of Occupation*. London: Verso Books, 2007/2017.

Weizman, Eyal. "Introduction: Forensis," in *Forensis: The Architecture of Public Truth*, ed. Forensic Architecture, 9–32. Berlin: Sternberg Press, 2014.

"What Does ALGOSPEAK Mean?" Cyber Definitions: An Academic Look at "Cyber Speak," https://www.cyberdefinitions.com/definitions/ALGOSPEAK.html.

Wiles, Rich. *Behind the Wall*. Sterling, VA: Potomac Books, 2010.

Williams, Raymond. *Marxism and Literature*. Oxford: Oxford University Press, 1977.

Wyler, William (dir.) *Ben-Hur* (1959).

Yazbak, Mahmoud. "The Muslim Festival of Nabi Rubin in Palestine: From Religious Festival to Summer Resort," *Holy Land Studies* 10, no. 2 (2011): 169–98.

Younes, Hamza. *Al-Hurub Min Sijn al-Ramleh* [The Escape from Ramleh Prison]. Self-published, 1999 [Arabic].

Zananiri, Sary. "From Still to Moving Images: Shifting Representation of Jerusalem and Palestinians in the Western Biblical Imaginary," *Jerusalem Quarterly* 67 (2016): 64–81.

Zananiri, Sary. "Imaging and Imagining Palestine: An Introduction," in *Imaging and Imagining Palestine: Photography, Modernity and the Biblical Lens, 1918–1948*, ed. Karène Sanchez Summerer and Sary Zananiri, 1–28. Netherlands: Brill, 2021.

Zananiri, Sary. "Indigeneity Transgression and the Body: Orientalism and Biblification in the Popular Imaging of Palestinians," *Journal of Intercultural Studies* 42, no. 6 (2021): 717–37.

Zananiri, Sary. "Costumes and the Image: Authenticity, Identity and Photography in Palestine," in *The Social and Cultural Histories of Palestine: Essays in Honour of Salim Tamari*, ed. Sarah Irving, 70–101. Edinburgh University Press, 2023.

Zimanyi, Eszter and Emma Ben Ayoun, eds. "In Focus: Humanitarian Immersions," *Journal of Cinema Studies* 61, no. 3 (Spring 2022): 154–94.

Zimmermann, Patricia R. and Helen De Michiel. *Open Space New Media Documentary: A Toolkit for Theory and Practice*. New York: Routledge, 2018.

Ziyadah, Tawfiq. "Here We Remain," *Awad al-Nad: Majallah thaqafiyah fasaliyah*, edited by 'Adali Al-hiwari 74, no. 8 (2021). https://www.oudnad.net/spip.php?article436.

Zochrot. "Our Vision," 2014, https://zochrot.org/en/content/17.

Zochrot. "Procession of Return to the Villages of Latrun," https://www.zochrot.org/activities/activity_details/52157/en?Procession_of_Return_to_the_Villages_of_Latrun.

Zochrot. "Our Newly Designed Application is Coming Soon," https://www.zochrot.org/articles/view/56528/en, last accessed June 30, 2022.

Zochrot. "Return," https://www.zochrot.org/sections/view/19/en?Return_Vision, last accessed June 30, 2022.

Zulkifli, Arief. "TikTok in 2022: Revisiting Data and Privacy," *Computer* 55, no. 6 (2022): 77–80, https://doi.org/10.1109/MC.2022.3164226.

Index

Al Aa'sam, Mu'ain 60
Abbas, Basel 8, 80, 87–9, 92
Abbas, Laila 58
Abdelal, Wael 56
Abou Hatoum, Nayrouz 14, 25
Abourahme, Nasser 73, 163
Abou-Rahme, Ruanne 8, 80, 82, 87–9, 92
Abuaker, Sarona 8
Abu Akleh, Shirine 44, 165
Abuasad, Farah 170
Abu-Assad, Hany 107
Abu el-Haj, Nadia 64
Abu Ghoush, Dima 74–5
Abu Jihad (Khalil Al Wazir) 148, 151
Abu Obaida 51–3, 60, 245
    professionalizing *al-mulatham* 56–7
    speech in Gaza 56
    TikTok clips 57–8
    tweets of 51–2
Abu Zeid, Nazih 95–7, 100, 102, 104
    personal and political life 102
accountability 30, 181–2, 186–7, 190, 193
accumulate/accumulation 99, 150, 185, 243, 245
Acosta, Gladys 141, 143, 145 n.33
Adams, Eddie 144 n.3
aerial ban 10
affiliative association 162
Agamben, Giorgio 147
agency 46, 95, 158, 244
Aizaza, Motaz 246
Akar, Khalid 163
akkub 177
Akub 170, 172, 177
"algospeak" 59
AlJazeera 56
Allan, Diana 105 n.4
Allen, Lori 80
Alphabet 193
Amnesty International 79
Andrés, José 169

anti-Blackness 160
anti-colonial movements 9, 40–1, 44, 80, 158
anti-Semitism 5
Aouragh, Miriyam 76 n.19
app/apps 6, 8–9, 58, 64, 70–3, 79, 181–2, 189. *See also* iNakba
Arab-Israeli war 186
Arab nationalism 125, 205
Arabness 135, 205
    queer 199–201, 204–5, 207–8
    reconceptualization of 199, 204
Arab uprisings 48
Arafat, Yasser 120, 148
    keffiyeh 138–9, 143
al-A'raj, Basel 161
archeology
    and "art of war" 67–8
    verticality and destruction 64
archive/archiving/archival 7–9, 19, 24–5, 34, 41, 46, 51–4, 57, 60, 64–5, 69–70, 73–4, 91, 102, 151–2, 181, 183–4, 220, 244, 246
al-Ardah, Mohammed 156
Arendt, Hannah 48
art 14, 40, 53, 149–50, 187, 190, 203, 218
    forms, classical 40
    poster (*see* posters/poster art)
    of war 67–8
artist 8, 15–16, 41, 43, 45, 53–4, 64, 69, 80, 82–9, 91–2, 94 n.33, 158, 170, 187, 214–16, 218. *See also specific artist*
Associated Press 214
At Those Terrifying Frontiers Where the Existence and Disappearance of People Fade into Each Other 80, 87–91
audience 4, 9–10, 28, 56–7, 70, 81, 173–4, 176–8, 181–3, 187, 189–90, 207
audio 34, 53, 58–9

"Audio Memes" 58
audiovisual tropes 80
augmented reality (AR) 71, 188–9
Azem, Muhammad 66
Azhari, Zaid 66
Azoulay, Ariella Aïsha 87, 93 n.10, 145 n.26, 181

Bab a-Zahra 234, 236
BADIL, "Putting the Right of Return into Practice" 35
Balfour Declaration 144 n.11
Balram, Dhruva 200
Bamieh, Mirna 170
Banksy 172, 218, 220
    Italian 214
Bazzari, Lama 170
Beer, David 52
being-in-the-world 156
The Beirut School 201
Ben Badis, Anwar 79, 190
Ben-Gurion, David 129
    "War on Infiltration" 82
Berger, John 89
Berlant, Lauren 205
Bethlehem 19, 82, 163, 165, 170–2, 174–6, 214, 216
Bible 65–6
biblical anthropology 65
Bier, Jess, segregated landscapes 185
bin Lumah, Mailoud Najah 163
Black feminism 159–60
Black Lives Matter 44
"Black September" events 113
Blázquez Sánchez, Olga 184
Bollas, Christopher 159
border 2, 4, 27, 31, 48, 53, 69, 71, 79, 82, 86, 91, 95, 99, 107–12, 116, 175, 184, 187, 218, 221 n.6, 238 n.3
Boullata, Kamal 187
boundary/boundaries 7, 53, 96–7, 99, 107, 193
Bourdain, Anthony 169, 173, 179 n.1
Boycott, Divest, Sanctions (BDS) 31, 35
Braidotti, Rosie, "becoming-imperceptible" 205
British archeological expedition 65, 67
B'Tselem 187

bureaucracy 31, 174–5
Burj Barajneh camp 189

camera 10, 87–8, 107, 115, 165, 173, 175, 177, 185, 188, 190, 193, 211, 214, 230, 233, 238, 245
Canaan, Tawfik 129
Canada Park 80, 83–7
cases 7–10, 96, 244–5
celebrity chef 169
centering 74, 246
The Chelsea theatre 17
Child, Julia 169
Christianity 137
    in Hollywood biblical epics 121
    proto-Christianity 133
cinema 17, 64, 81, 107, 115, 135, 191, 245
cinéma verité 115
climate emergency 31–2
climate refugees 31, 35
cloud model 226–7
Cold War 69, 133, 137
collective 2–3, 7, 9, 15, 19, 32–3, 52–3, 60, 75, 82, 87, 92, 150–2, 159, 163, 170
    labor 68–73
colonial 4, 8, 41, 46, 63–5, 73, 97, 104, 115, 185, 187
    authorities 66, 107
    roads and settlements 164
    violence 67, 203
colonial destruction 8, 65, 68
commonism 150–1
common sense 97, 99
    form of embodied 104
    theological 99–102, 104
computation 230
conjunctures 4, 39–40, 48, 49 n.2
connections 2, 8, 28, 33–4, 36, 53, 64, 82, 172, 180 n.12, 204
cookbooks 170, 179 n.1
cooking online 171, 177–8
cooking shows and food preparation 9, 178. *See also* food
co-resistance 73–4
counter-forensics 8, 65
counter-terrorism 161
Countless Afghan Futures 29
Countless Arab Futures 29

Countless Lebanese Futures 29
Countless Palestinian Futures (CPF) 8, 28, 36
   gamification and iteration 28–30, 32
   strengths of 36
Covid-19 pandemic 80, 178
   restrictions 170, 175–6
Craving Palestine 170
creative production 2
creativity 41, 172
Cristiano, Fabio 71
Cuba
   poster from 54
   solidarity poster 140–1
cultural production 2, 14, 40–1, 49 n.2

DAM 155–6, 158
   "All of Them Have Tanks" 155
Darby, Thameen
   geo-mapping 69
   "Nakba layer" 69, 185
Darwish, Mahmoud 40, 91, 166
Dayan, Moshe 67
decolonization and decarbonization 31, 81, 156, 199, 207
de-contextualization 66
Democratic Front for the Liberation of Palestine (DFLP) 75
Depth Unknown 65, 74
destruction 1, 5, 8, 31, 64–5, 75, 149, 151, 186–7, 190, 243, 246
diaspora 1–3, 7, 14, 25, 34, 43, 45, 71, 75, 79, 81, 150, 165, 169
digital 4, 10, 39
digital age, poster art in 44–7
digital mapping 64, 70–2, 79, 181–4
digital media 79, 81, 194
digital media tools 80
digital technologies 10, 182–3, 220
discourse 4–6, 32, 65–6, 100, 105, 151, 172–3, 178
disembodiment and re-embodiment 88
dislocation 7, 39
displaced/displacement 5–6, 13, 34, 49 n.2, 66, 69, 72–3, 80, 82, 85–6, 91, 108, 110–11, 115, 170, 175
dissent 45
Distretti, Emilio 71
DJI 224, 233, 238, 238 n.2

flight restriction zone (Temple Mount) 225, 227, 239
documentary 6, 9, 74, 189, 191
   on biblical anthropology 65
   historical 181
   images 66
documentary making
   digital tools in 183
   simulation 182
documentation 9, 28, 68, 114, 127, 159, 193, 243
domination 27, 63
Douglas, Mary 98–9
drone's GPS system 233, 238 n.5
Druze 95–105
al-Durra, Mohamad 44, 211

Eco, Umberto 28
Egypt 98, 112, 200, 202
   authorities in Gaza 112
   LGBTQI+ community 203
Elkin, Ze'ev 184
emancipation 2, 9, 40, 43, 46, 150–1, 159, 163, 165
Emmaus Nicopolis 85
Emwas 74–5
Erakat, Noura 73
erasure 1, 5, 36, 65, 83–4, 171, 174, 182, 184, 188–9, 191, 219, 246
Escobar, Arturo 27
Esmeir, Samera 247 n.1
ethnographic documentation 127
Eurocentric Mercator projection model 195 n.15
everyday life/everday lives 10, 13, 32, 36, 40, 54, 91, 100, 102, 115, 233, 238
exile 2–3, 5, 43, 81–2, 86, 113, 116, 156, 160, 164, 166, 168 n.30, 204, 245
existence 1, 3–5, 35, 65, 72, 84, 91–2, 94 n.33, 98, 114, 184, 188, 201–2, 207, 243–4

Facebook 170, 179 n.8, 213–14
Falsafat al Muwajahah Wara al Qudban/The Philosophy of Confrontation Behind Bars 151
Fanon, Frantz 156–8
Farouki, Taj 20

Farsakh, Leila, "Queering Palestine" 199
Fatah pamphlet 163
Fawda 170–2
filiative association 162
film 6–9, 13, 53, 64–6, 68, 74–5, 81–2, 107–8, 114–15, 125, 133, 135, 137, 141, 143, 181–2, 187, 211. *See also specific films*
Fineberg, Jonathan 46
first intifada (1987–1993) 53, 111, 151
Fisher, Eran 70, 73
food 9, 169, 174–5, 177–8, 179 n.1
   chefs and media 169–71
   politics 171–3
   suqs 175–6
foreign policy 33–5
Foucault, Michel, archaeology of knowledge 185
Freeman, Elizabeth 205
The French Chef 169
French Revolution 149
Fromm, Erich 158
fugitive crossings 107–8, 116
   Gilboa 117
   image and repetition 114–15
   return of refugees (1948 to 1956) 108–11
   Separation Wall 108
fugitivity 9, 108, 114–17
The Funambulist 171–2
Furani, Khaled 4
future/futurity 1, 7–8, 14, 25, 28, 30–1, 33, 35–6, 39, 43, 52–3, 63, 72–3, 82, 108, 117, 149–50, 157, 201, 206, 243, 245

Galilee 82, 97–104, 109–11, 113, 189
gamification and iteration 28–30
gaming/game 8, 28, 30, 35–6, 71–2, 163, 188
Gaza 40, 72, 74, 89, 92, 155, 169
   brutal destruction 5, 24
   cookbook 179 n.1
   Great March of Return 25, 82, 87–8, 94 n.28, 164
   Israeli war against 39, 44–5, 57
   Palestinian diaspora 25
   Strip 39, 45, 51, 88, 111, 218, 243
gentrification 191

patterns 24
Tel Aviv 15
geofence 10, 224, 226
   age-old technique 233
   black hole of missing data 238
   as carrier bag 238
   data (geo-coordinates) 233
   disrupting 233, 238
   extraordinary size 227
   flight's control panel 225
   golden dome 231
   photogrammetry model 236–7
   real-world effect 230
   3D model 229–31, 233
Gheith, Sama 46
Gilboa Prison 108, 116–17, 156
Gilmore, Ruth Wilson 165–6
   infrastructure of feeling 165
Glissant, Édouard 104
   Poetics of Relation 102
global information systems (GIS) 183
Golan 9, 95–6, 101–4
   and Galilee 98–100, 104
   reoriented 96–7
Google Earth 69, 83, 185
Google Maps 84–5, 183–5, 187, 191, 193, 195 n.15
Gopinath, Gayatri, curation 53
graffiti 7, 10, 39, 172, 214–16, 218–20, 221 n.10
Gramsci, Antonio 102
grandmother 14, 173. *See also tetas*
Grassroots Al Quds 80
Great Arab Revolt (1936–9) 131, 139
Great March of Return 25, 27, 82, 87–8, 94 n.28, 164
Groys, Boris 149, 151, 152 n.9
Gulf Crisis (1989–91) 113

Habibi, Emile, *The Secret Life of Saeed: The Pessoptimist* 149–50
Hadid, Bella 170
Hadid, Mohammed 170
Halaby, Mona Hajjar 79, 190
Hall, Stuart 49 n.2
Hamas 30, 35, 51, 53, 56–7, 60, 243
Hamdan, Sarah 205
Haram al-Sharif 224, 226, 230, 233
Harding, Lankester 67

Harney, Stefano 204
    The Undercommons 149
Harvard excavation 66, 68
Al-Hashemi, Faisal 125
Hebron/Khalil 91, 163, 176
Heroes of Spoons 117
Hilal, Sandi 183–4
historicization 66
history/histories 16, 34, 39–40, 43–4, 46, 58, 60, 64–5, 72–3, 79, 88, 96–7, 102, 107, 147, 149, 168 n.30, 181–3, 243
    al-mulatham/a 53–5
    immersion in iNakba's 186–9
    Jerusalem, We Are Here 189–92
    mapping territorialized 184–5
Hochberg, Gil 247 n.4
"Holy Land" 85, 123, 171
Hourani, Khaled
    "The Colours of the Palestinian Flag" 45
    "The Story of the Watermelon" 45
human rights and national sovereignty 44
Human Rights Watch 79

al-ia'lam almuqawim (resistance media) 52, 56
icon 10, 41, 43–6, 48, 85, 161, 182–3, 211, 216, 245
identity/identification 1, 3, 9–10, 31, 39, 43, 46, 48, 52, 88, 91–2, 98, 120, 133, 135, 143, 156–60, 165–6, 185, 204–5
image 1, 8, 35, 43, 44, 46, 59, 60, 64, 66, 84, 123, 187, 189, 215, 220–1, 230–1, 235
    mulatham/a 52
    of Palestinian resistance 54
    and repetition 114–15
    reproduction technologies 9
    re-structuration 64
imagination 3, 7–8, 10, 14, 25, 28, 35–6, 39–40, 43–6, 48, 49 n.2, 96, 116–17, 149, 156, 163–5, 200.
    See also return, imagining
immediation 80, 89
implicit 98–9
iNakba 10, 70–3, 79–80, 85, 181–2, 185, 193

history, immersion in 186–9
Palestinian dispossession 186
infiltrators 82, 93 n.10, 108, 110–11, 114–15
Infiltrators 108, 114–15
infrastructure 2, 25, 51, 64, 72–3, 76 n.19, 79, 97, 99, 148, 150, 155, 165–6, 189–90, 224, 233
Instagram 6, 45, 58, 170, 214–17, 220, 243, 246
interactive 64, 70, 85, 181, 185, 219
interactive documentaries 79, 185
    digital technologies 183
    digital tools 183
    hacking surveillance 193–4
    immersion in iNakba's history 186–9
    Jerusalem, We Are Here as revisiting history 189–92
    knowledge production 183
    mapping territorialized history 184–6
intifadas 40, 44
Intifadat al-Aqsa 156
Iqrit Community Association 82
Iron Dome system 24
The Israel Falafel 17
Israeli Defence Forces (IDF) 201
"Israeli hummus" 172
Israeli Information Center for Human Rights in the Occupied Territories 187
Israeli Occupation Forces 86
Israel/Israelis 24, 31, 160, 163, 185
    "Agreement on Disengagement" 96
    colonial and discriminatory practices 4
    colonization 57, 114
    Declaration of Independence 46
    militarism 166
    as settler-Apartheid state 157
    Sovereignty 71, 238 n.3
    special counter terrorism 161
    and US foreign policy 13–14
    visual translations 194
    war against Gaza 39, 44–5, 57
Italian Banksy 214

Jacir, Annemarie 63, 81
    Milh hadha al-Bahr/The Salt of this Sea 63–4, 73, 81

Jacir, Emily 81
  ex libris 184
Jaffa/Yaffa 7, 14–16, 19, 24, 63, 81–2, 174, 190, 235
Jameson, Fredric 35
Jarrar, Khaled 108, 114–15
al-Jasmine, Sabah 170
Jawabreh, Monther, ما كان يعرف *As Once Was Known* 54–5
Jerusalem/Al-Quds 10, 14, 24, 80, 224, 238 n.3
  geofence (*see* geofence)
  volatile space of 226
Jerusalem, We Are Here 10, 79–80, 182, 185, 189–93
Jewish Israelis 70–1, 73–4, 112, 187, 193
Jewish National Fund (JNF) 46, 75, 83, 184, 189
Jorit 214, 216–17, 220
  graffito 219
  postcards and magnets 217
journalism 190, 246
Jum'at al-kawtshuk 164

Kamamji, Ayham 156–8
Kanaaneh, Rhoda, "Queering Palestine" 199
Kanafani, Ghassan 40, 81
  A'id 'ila Hayfa ("Return to Haifa") 27, 81, 85
Kanazi, Remi 214, 217–18
Karmi, Ghada
  Return 27
  In Search of Fatima 189
Kassis, Reem 177
  The Palestinian Table 179 n.1
Kattan, Fadi 169–70
  cooking online 177–8
  ethics of care 176–7
  food politics 171–2
  on global food issues 172–3
  "Hummus with Fadi" episode 171–2
  "Julia's Christmas Cake" episode 176
  long-standing presence in Palestine 175–6
  mobility 174–5
  Teta's Kitchen 171, 173–6, 178
Kayed, Ahmad 66
Khaled, Laila 120, 144 n.3, 161
Khalidi, Rashid 4, 107

Khouri, Rasha 170
Khoury, Madees 174–5
Klein, Melanie 158
Knesset 96
Kochav, Ran 165
Krausz, Franz 46
kuffiyeh/keffiyehs 6, 9, 54, 57, 119, 245
  Arafat's 138–9, 143
  Bedouin 123, 126–7
  Cuban solidarity 140–1
  disguise 134–5, 141
  fellah 120, 129, 141
  Jesus 136–7
  Lawrence's 124–5
  marking bodies 119–20
  Moses 132–3
  "A Nazarene" 122–3
  Simon the Cyrene 128–9
  terrorist 142–3
  Three Wise Men 130–1
  visual appearances 120
Kuntsman, Adi 193

labor 2–3, 7, 39–41, 43, 45–6, 48, 66, 245
  creative revolutionary 40–3
  layer as collective 68–73
Laing, R. D. 157
Lam w lan nasmah b'al-musawamah 'ala qurana 'Imwas, Yalo, Beit Nouba 84
land 1, 5–6, 8, 14, 22, 25, 31, 34, 63–5, 68, 71, 74, 79–81, 83–4, 96, 107, 109, 111, 114, 117, 123, 157–8, 166, 170, 175–6, 187–8, 203, 211, 219, 220
landscape 4, 9, 11 n.9, 22, 27, 44, 48, 64, 66, 69–70, 73, 75, 85, 95–6, 109, 120, 227
landscape-as-ideology 48
LA Times 170
Lawrence of Arabia 125
Lawrence, T. E. 120, 125
  keffiyeh 124
layers (Nakba) 5, 8, 14
  as collective labor 68–73
  ecology of 73–5
  as forensics 64–8
  vs. maps 63–4
  topography 64
  vertical vision 64, 75

Lebanese Resistance 163
Lebanon 7, 22, 43–4, 109–11, 113–14, 116, 163, 200, 204
Lefebvre, Henri 46
Le Guin, Ursula 239
Lewis, Gail 159–60
LGBT/LGBTQ/queer activism 199–200, 203–4
liberal Zionism 16
liberation 6, 9, 11 n.9, 28, 43–6, 53, 116, 133, 156, 160, 207
  anti-colonial politics 41, 48
  collective resistance after 32
  Palestinian ruling class 30, 35
  of Palestinians 44–5
  queer Arab 207
  techné of 156–7, 159, 162, 164, 166
Liberation Graphics Collection of Palestine Poster 43
Lifshitz, Yoav 193
local 3, 39, 75, 103, 120, 172
Long, Paul, affective archive 52

Maasri, Zeina 41
mainstream media 4, 58, 170, 178, 246
Makdisi, Saree, erasure of erasure process 188
Mansour, Salah 69
Mansour, Shadia 155–6, 158
  "All of Them Have Tanks" 155
Mansour, Suleiman 40
map/mapping 4, 10, 41, 63–5, 69, 72, 75, 79, 103, 113, 165, 183, 191, 193, 206, 233
  apps 8
  digital 64, 70–1, 79, 181–4
  food 170
  Google Maps's base 191
  Palestine as 79, 181, 201–3, 207
  technologies 8
  territorialized history 184–6
March of Return to Latrun 85
Mar Elias Camp 189
"Marmite hummus" 172
Ma'rouf, Abu 110–11
Mashrou' Leila
  "Cavalry" 10, 200–8, 208 n.6
  marginalisation and abjection 203
Massad, Joseph 153 n.13
materiality 27, 32, 64, 67, 163, 165, 191

Mawsim Nabi Rubeen (Prophet Ruben Festival) 127
"May Palestine be Free" episode 178
Mazen Halabi 97–105
McMahon-Hussein Correspondence 144 n.11
meaning-making process 120, 166
media/medium 3–4, 8–10, 36, 39–40, 45, 51, 56, 64, 74, 80, 82, 88, 169, 211, 214, 246. *See also* social media
  affordances 5
  artifacts 216
  chefs and 169–71, 178
  images 170, 213, 216
  interactions 5
  in media res 5–7
  print 41
  production of Palestine 6
  spectators 183
  technologies 4, 79, 81
mediation 6, 67, 80–1, 84, 88–9, 92 n.3, 96–100, 104, 185, 246
memory 5, 14, 41, 52, 64, 70, 72, 75, 97–8, 100–1, 103, 105, 159, 185, 190
Mevo Heron settlement 83
Microsoft's Bing 184
migration problem 11 n.9
Milh hadha al-Bahr/The Salt of this Sea 63–4, 73, 81
mise-en-abyme 215
Mitchell, Timothy 150
Mitchell, WJT 1, 48
mobile apps and documentaries 8–10, 70, 181
modernist museum 147–9, 152 n.9
Mohr, Jean 84 n.35, 88–9, 91
Morgensen, Scott Lauria 205
Moten, Fred 204
  Stolen Life 107
  The Undercommons 149
Moussallem, Jessy 200
Muhanna, Mikey 170
mujassam 75
mujtama'a muqawim (resistance society) 56
al-mulatham/a 8, 51–2, 61 n.1
  history 53–4
  non-containment of 60

Palestinian TikTok 57–60
   professionalizing 56–7
al-mulatham almajhool 57
al-muqawimah 160, 164
museumification 9
museums 9, 64, 66
   archives in resistance 151–2
   asynchronicity 148
   before/after revolution 149
   colonial 66
   commonism 150–1
   fugitive objects 148–9
   object in battle 147–8
music 10, 13, 57–8, 83, 127, 177, 191, 200–4, 206–7
Musih, Norma 70, 73

Naaman, Dorit 10, 79, 182, 185, 189–90. *See also* Jerusalem, We Are Here
Nabi Saleh 200, 211, 213, 216–17
Nablus 59, 161, 164, 176–7
Nafi'at, Munadil 156
Nakba 4, 14, 35, 46, 149–50, 175
Nakbaization 4
"Nando" Schtakleff, Fernando 190
Nashif, Esmail 151
Nasrallah, Elias 109–11
nationalism 2, 131, 161, 168 n.30, 204–5
Neruda, Pablo 206
NESCO, Memory of the World program 43
network/networks 6, 9, 36, 52, 57, 67, 73, 75, 87, 96, 102, 108, 111, 114–16, 123, 163, 183, 193, 244, 246
new media 4, 6, 79, 81, 246
no-fly zone (NFZ) 10, 224, 233
   black hole over 224, 239
   crashes against 226
   photogrammetry model 237
No Man's Land 85

Object Relational school 158
object relations theory 158
objects 2, 9, 48, 64, 66, 85, 147–8, 246
   fugitive 148–9
   revolutionary (*see* revolutionary objects, forging)

occupation 5, 25, 45, 60, 64, 74, 79, 84, 86, 91, 95, 112, 155, 160–1, 163–5, 176, 184, 187, 189–91, 200, 211, 213
   Fadi's food politics 171–2, 174
   Golan 95
Occupied Palestine 157, 160, 163, 172, 181
   hang-gliders 162–3
   security zone 163
Occupied Palestinian Territories 40, 44
Occupy WiFi project 193
Odeh, Faris 211
Omar 107, 116
Open Data Commons Open Database License (ODbL) 194 n.11
OpenStreetMap 184, 193, 194 n.11
Oslo Accords 91, 114
Oslo agreement (1993) 44
Oush Grab military base 184

Palestine 1, 13, 25, 28, 151, 182, 185, 244
   and Arab imagination 200
   becoming with 203–7
   historical images of 181
   Israeli occupation of 200
   as mirror/map 201–3
   multiple imaginations and contra-imaginations of 10
   "New Vision" of 120
   Palestinians and 1, 3–4, 10, 39, 48, 202, 204, 245
   porous 102–5
   producing 2–3, 169, 246
      expressions and imaginaries 7
      global concern 3–5
      unbuilding nations 207–8
   queer Arabness and 199, 201, 204–5, 207
   sixth geography 111
   and Syria 96
   and transnational Palestine 160
Palestine Children's Relief Fund (PCRF) 170
Palestine-Israel 35
Palestine Liberation Organization (PLO) 34, 44, 51, 113–14
   All For the Resistance 42
   military action 141
   Nous Vaincrons (We Will Win) 42

poster artwork 41
revolutionary creative labor 40–1, 43
Palestine Open Maps 69, 79, 85
Palestine Poster Project Archives 41, 43
Palestine Remembered 19–20, 69–70, 72–3
  estate at Wadi Hunayn 20–1, 24
Palestinian(s) 11 n.9, 89, 117, 169, 181, 243
  constellations of objects 161
  dissociate and disassociate 157
  fugitive crossings 107–8
  identity 135, 157, 160
  illegal infiltrators 107, 109, 111
  liberation movement 206
  modernity 139
  nationalist movement 160, 168 n.30
  Palestine and 1, 3–4, 10, 39, 48
  permeant identification 160
  resistance 51–4, 155, 158, 160
  revolutionary cinema 245
  revolutionary period 39
  selfhood, good objects 165
  strategy of liberation 11 n.9
  "Summer of Return" 82
  sumud and resistance 92
  sympathy-deserving suffering human 80
  virtual transportations for 80, 194
Palestinian Authority (PA) 30, 33, 35, 51, 185
Palestinian-centric revolutionary aesthetic 41
Palestinian Fedayeen 53
Palestinian National Council 91
Palestinian-ness 119–20
Palestinian refugees 43, 69, 72–3, 82, 89, 108, 111, 187
  maltreatment of 203
  return of 9, 13, 64, 69–70, 81, 86, 111
Palestinian Revolution 149, 158–60, 163
Palestinian Slingshot 244
Palestinian Youth Movement 45
pan-Arabism 205
Pappé, Ilan 184
participatory surveillance 193
Parts Unknown 169
past/pastness 2–7, 9, 28, 48, 53, 64, 71–2, 75, 83, 97–104, 117, 147, 181, 183, 191

People's War 160, 164
Petti, Alessandro 184
Philosophy of the Confrontation Behind Bars 152
photogrammetry 230, 233, 236–8, 238 n.4
photograph/photographs/photography 7, 24, 68, 83–5, 91, 94 n.35, 123, 148–9, 181, 185, 187, 189, 191, 215, 217–18, 226, 233
physical bodies 216
pirate modernity 185
The Plate 171
Pokémon GO 71, 188
political space of appearance 48
popular culture 4, 7, 9, 40–1, 43, 119, 151, 160
Popular Front for the Liberation of Palestine—General Command (PFLP-GC) 163
popular resistance (*al-muqawimah al-sh'abiyah*) 9, 39, 156, 159
  low-tech tactics 164
  techné 160
postcolonial colony 153 n.13
posters/poster art 8, 39–40, 48, 149
  in digital age 44–7
  fedayee 43–4
  icons of revolution and symbols of Palestine 43–4
  "Palestine Uprising Hues" 46–7
  PLO's revolutionary creative labor 40–3
  "Visit Palestine" poster 46
power 6–7, 35–6, 48, 67, 85, 149, 181
  digital forms of 233
  of images 214–15
present 2, 31, 35, 48, 72, 75, 82, 87, 100, 103, 105, 147, 149–51, 157, 182–3, 190–1
prison 9, 57, 60, 103, 108, 111–13, 116–17, 151, 156, 158, 160–1, 213–14, 216
production 1–2, 4, 8, 10, 39–40, 44–5, 247 n.4
  creative 2
  cultural 1, 14, 40–1, 49 n.2, 81, 155, 182, 200, 204, 207–8, 218
  media 6
  of Palestine 1, 3, 7, 244, 246
"pro-Palestine" 243–4

Qadri, Yaqoub 156–8
Qassam/Qassam Brigades 51, 54, 56–7, 59–60
queer/queerness 10, 199–200, 204, 207
   Arabness/Arab identity 199–201, 204–5, 207–8
   and nonqueers 199
   theory 201, 204
Quiquivix, Linda 69, 185

Rabinowtiz, Dan 4
Rabin, Yitzhak 83
racial dissociation 157
"Rainbow Flag Incident," Cairo 203
Ramallah 14, 19, 81, 83, 88, 114, 148, 171
Rancière, Jacques 43
reflection 24, 28, 53, 88, 170
refractions 10, 216–21
refugees 3, 9, 13, 31–2, 35, 43, 64, 69–70, 72–3, 81–4, 86, 108–11, 187, 189, 203
reincarnation 5, 98
   Golan 96–7
   porous Palestine 102–5
   and question of mediation 98–9
   temporality of 103
   theological common sense 99–102, 104
remote neutrality 224
remote-sensing satellite-based mechanisms 224
representation 3, 6, 10, 41, 43, 63–4, 69, 71, 81, 91, 114–15, 121, 147, 169, 184–5, 191, 245–6
re-territorializations 6–7
return 7, 13–14, 25, 36, 69, 72–3, 80–2
   affective ecology 25
   imagining 27–8, 85
      Apartheid Wall 34–5
      decolonization and decarbonization 31–2
      foreign policy 33–4
      radically transformative policies and ideas 30–1, 35
      resistance 32–3
      ruling class 30
   physical and affective reorientation 25
   of refugees (1948 to 1956) 108–11
   rehearsing 81–2, 92
revolution 8, 39–41, 147, 163
   culture of popular 158–60
   icons of 43–4
   museum before/after 149
   revolutionary consciousness 163–4, 166
   revolutionary creative labor 39–40
      PLO 40–1, 43
   revolutionary imagination 163
   revolutionary objects, forging
      bullet and gun 161–3
      culture of popular revolution 158–60
      good objects/attachments 157–8
      spoon 156–7
Rifkin, Mark 100
roadblock cinema 115
Robinson, Shira 82

Safadi, Jowan 117
Said, Edward 3, 116, 184, 201
   After the Last Sky: Palestinian Lives 88–9, 91, 94 n.33
   "Permission to Narrate" 243
   production of knowledge 247 n.10
Al-Salah, Razan 8, 80, 83–6. *See also Canada Park*
Sansour, Larissa 245
Sansour, Vivien 170
Sayigh, Rosemary 160, 163
Sayigh, Yezid 163
Schotten, C. Heike 201, 207
screens 48, 89, 104, 114, 174, 188, 220
Sebastia 64–5, 70, 74
   archeology and art of war 67–8
   collective labor 68–73
   colonial museums 66–7
   colonial violence 67
   Harvard excavation 68
   Roman forum 65–8, 75
second intifada (2000–2004) 53, 111, 115, 156
security 21–4, 114–16, 176, 191, 224
Seikaly, Sherene, "Queering Palestine" 199
Sela, Rona, *Looted and Hidden: Palestinian Archives in Israel* 181
sentipensar 28
Separation/Apartheid Wall 9–10, 107, 114, 172, 184, 214, 218
   graffiti on 218–20
settler-colonial/settler-colonialism 1, 9, 25, 46, 80, 86, 98, 116, 148–50, 156, 158, 166, 170, 178, 201, 206

Shammout, Ismail 41
Shatila camp, Beirut 189
Shawa, Leila, *Fashionista Terrorista* 54–5
Shefa'amr 109–11
Shohat, Ella 245
Silwan, kite flying 234
Simon the Cyrene, costume keffiyeh 128–9
Sinno, Hamed 200–1, 203, 205–7
sites of memory 185
Six Day War 74, 137
social media 7–8, 10, 36, 45, 51–4, 57–60, 160, 182, 211, 215, 217–20, 244, 246
sociocide 115
software users 182–3
solidarity 5, 35, 41, 48, 72–4, 82, 89, 92, 140–1, 157, 162, 194, 203, 207, 244
Sontag, Susan 40
space 1, 3, 5–10, 27, 32–3, 35, 39, 41, 45–6, 48, 49 n.2, 86, 151–2, 215, 219–20, 233
spatial testimony 185
spectator 80, 88–9, 183
Srouji, Dima 64, 67, 71, 74
Stein, Rebecca 193
Steyerl, Hito, "A Tank on a Pedestal: Museums in an Age of Planetary Civil War" 147
structure from motion process 226
struggle 3, 6, 8–9, 11 n.9, 19, 25, 33, 41, 45, 48, 54, 72, 89, 148, 150–1, 157, 164, 199, 202, 245
struggle-identity 160–1, 166, 168 n.30
Suleiman, Terese 161
Sundaram, Ravi 185
Sykes-Picot Agreement 125, 144 n.11
symbol 7–8, 41, 43–6, 54, 160, 215
    al-mulatham/a 60
    watermelon as 45–6, 48
Syria 9
    "Agreement on Disengagement" 96
    authentication process 99
    authoritarianism 97
    Neirab camp 189
    secret intelligence services 103
    Separation of Forces Agreement 95
Syrian Druze 95–6, 104
    teachings and cosmologies 98
Al-Syrian, Hosh 170

Tamimi, Ahed 10, 200–1, 211–14, 221 n.9, 245
    attention of public opinion 214
    Instagram post 215–16
    refractions 216–18
Tamimi, Sami
    Falastin 179 n.1
    Jerusalem 179 n.1
Tawil-Souri, Helga 6, 10, 48, 76 n.19, 115, 169
techné of liberation 156–7, 159, 162, 164, 166
technology 1, 4, 7–10, 31, 39, 64, 69–70, 79, 81, 83, 92 n.3, 156–7, 169, 173, 182–3, 193, 220, 224, 226, 238, 244
Tel Aviv 14–15, 23, 113, 172, 190
telepresence 81
"Temple Mount" 10, 225, 227
temporality 2–3, 8, 40, 43, 46, 64, 73, 97, 99, 101, 103, 201, 245
terra ex machina case 10, 224, 238
territory 2–3, 7, 13, 27, 63–4, 71, 86, 96, 101, 112, 163, 185, 218–20, 224
tetas 173–4, 177–8. *See also* grandmother
Teta's Kitchen 171, 173–6, 178
text 4, 10, 17, 52–3, 58, 88–9, 96, 109, 181–2, 188–9, 200, 218, 220–1, 227
theory of "object use" 159
3D 35, 65, 68, 229–31, 233
TikTok 8, 52–3, 57, 214, 220, 243
    Palestinian 53, 57–60
time 9, 39, 49 n.2, 86, 89, 149–52
time-consuming process 174
tourism 15, 19, 34, 85
traditional *fellahin* aesthetics 139
transformational infrastructure 165
Tukios, Salvatore 214, 216
Twitter 51, 214, 216

Udna (Baladna) 35, 82
the United Nations 28, 94 n.35
United Nations Relief and Works Agency for Palestine Refugees in the Near East (UNRWA) 182, 189
United States (US) 7, 13–14, 160, 204, 214
Unity Intifada 57
University of Pennsylvania Museum of Archeology and Anthropology 66
US-Israeli relations 133

video 5, 8, 10, 27, 53, 56, 58, 60, 65, 73, 80–1, 84–6, 89, 170–2, 177, 190, 200–4, 206–7, 208 n.6. *See also specific video*
virtual 6–8, 10, 59–60, 80, 214, 246
    layer 70–3, 76 n.19
    post 217
    real and 218, 220–1
    representations 6
    spaces and speculative abstractions 8, 69, 79, 193, 216–18
virtual reality (VR) 79, 92 n.3
virtual returns 8, 72
    Canada Park 83–7
    humanitarianism and empathy 80
    opaque portals 87–92
    rehearsing 81–2
    virtual possibilities and limits 79–81
Vishmidt, Marina, *All Shall be Unicorns* 150–1
vision 7, 10, 15, 25, 82, 169–70
    neutral technology of 83
    vertical 64, 73, 75
visual aesthetics 53
visuality 6, 41, 85
Visualizing Palestine 69
visual thinking 46
volume/volumetric 74, 120, 224, 227, 245–6

Wadi Hunayn 7, 14, 19–21, 24–5
wall 1, 9–10, 34–5, 43, 83–4, 107–8, 114–15, 117, 172, 184, 214–20, 221 n.6, 224. *See also* Separation/Apartheid Wall
Wallish, Otte 46
Walsh, Dan 43
war (1948) 69, 186, 189
"War on Return" 82
Warren, Jeffrey 234
Waze navigation app 70, 73

Weizman, Eyal 66
    politics of verticality 191
West Bank 14, 16, 19, 39, 41, 45, 57, 60, 64, 72, 74, 84, 88–9, 91–2, 107, 111, 116, 161, 169, 177–8, 184, 211, 238 n.3
    illegal Israeli settlements 175
    separation barrier 184
When I Saw You 81
Where We Come From 81
white supremacy 160
Winnicott, Donald, theory of "object use" 159
worldliness, Palestinians' 4

Yaffa. *See* Jaffa/Yaffa
Yafo Creative House, AirBnB 15–16
Ya Quds, nahnu huna 190
The Yasser Arafat Museum, Ramallah 148–9
Younis, Hamza 108
    breaking out of Israeli captivity 111–14
Your Father Was Born 100 Years Old, and So Was the Nakba 85, 87
YouTube 9, 59–60, 171–3, 178, 183, 220

Zagha, Oudai 59–60
Zayta 187–9
zionist/zionism 4, 16, 43, 46, 91, 109, 129, 135, 153 n.13, 155, 175, 187, 244
    logic of land claim 65
    settler-colonial project 243
Ziyadah, Tawfiq 158
    "Here We Remain" 155–7
Zochrot 10, 70, 72–4, 79, 83–4, 181–2, 185–7, 189, 193
Zoom cooking 178
Zubaidi, Zakaria 156